To Clyde R—
friend of Jo—

Warren K. Urbom
March 2013

Enjoy. God bless.
John Clinton
3/22/13

BISON BOOKS

LAW IN THE AMERICAN WEST

Series Editor

John R. Wunder, University of Nebraska–Lincoln

To Joyce Crawford Urbom
—wife, mother, grandmother, great-grandmother,
sister, aunt, cousin, niece, friend—
who made living a pure joy.
1929–2010

Called to Justice

The Life of a Federal Trial Judge

WARREN K. URBOM

Foreword by William Jay Riley

University of Nebraska Press | Lincoln and London

Manufactured in the United States of America

∞

Library of Congress Cataloging-in-Publication Data

Urbom, Warren K.
Called to justice: the life of a federal trial judge / Warren K. Urbom.
p. cm.
Includes bibliographical references.
ISBN 978-0-8032-3983-8 (cloth: alk. paper)
1. Urbom, Warren K. 2. Judges—Nebraska—Biography. I. Title.
KF373.U73A3 2012
347.73'2234092—dc23
[B]
2012014821

Set in Arno Pro by Kim Essman.
Designed by Ashley Muehlbauer.

1. (*opposite*) Joyce Urbom, emcee of Lincoln chapter of Sweet Adelines, about 1983. Photograph in author's possession.

Contents

Illustrations

Foreword

Tribute to a Federal Trial Judge

This memoir recounts the life of an extraordinary federal trial judge and a most remarkable human being. Judge Warren Urbom weaves a rich tapestry on life, lawyering, and judging, covering subjects common and not so common. We learn about Warren Urbom's humble, rural upbringing in western Kansas and southwest Nebraska, the loss of one of his eyes at the hands of his older brother, and young Warren's path to a Methodist ministry detoured to a professional life in the ministry of justice. We then witness Warren Urbom emerge as an exemplary trial lawyer and jurist. Judge Urbom also shares his personal recollections on the emotional trauma of his involvement in a fatal car accident and the later loss of his beloved wife, Joyce, to cancer.

As a trial lawyer and judge, Warren Urbom encountered the challenges and surprises arising from the drama of human affairs presented in an American federal courtroom. As a judge, he applied the law when required and common sense when discretion was appropriate. His judicial career addressed issues both great and small. Judge Urbom applied his wisdom and creativity in important cases involving civil rights, women's equality, freedom of religion versus government regulation, criminal sentencing, RICO, and life-and-death issues, including the death penalty and abortion. And he applied the law with the same dedication, fairness, and respect in cases involving long hair and potato chips as he did in the nationally famous Wounded Knee trials.

It is during the historic Wounded Knee litigation when one of Urbom's hallmarks was on display: his judicial temperament. Judge Urbom will tell you that, in presiding over his first trial, three years before the Wounded Knee trials, he used a sharp tone with a lawyer who interrupted him. At that time Judge Urbom resolved to forever maintain his patience and respectfulness, which he recognizes as one of the basic virtues of a judge. This commitment served him well throughout his career, but perhaps had the greatest challenge during the Wounded Knee cases. In managing cases against more than 130 defendants arising from the 1973 standoff between the American Indian Movement and the U.S. government, Judge Urbom eventually earned and received the Indians' respect and trust through his fair and impartial rulings.

Judge Urbom asked the "whys" of judicial practices and traditions and thereby tested and adapted innovative concepts in witness oaths, juror note taking, jurors questioning witnesses, lawyers questioning jurors, opening the court session, ponderous trials, and jurors resting or sleeping at trial. This memoir presents a rare insight into the busy life of a federal trial judge; for example, in 1984 Judge Urbom was trying two, and at one time three, jury trials simultaneously, including a seven-month civil jury trial.

Judge Urbom inquires, "What makes a first-rate trial judge?" and then succinctly captures the essence of an ideal trial judge and, at the same time, in my view, describes the author. Warren Urbom weighed competing interests fairly and wisely, just as a judge must.

I know Judge Urbom from his stellar reputation, from experiencing his judicial skills in 1976, when I was a young trial lawyer and appeared before him for a week-long trial (*Securities and Exchange Commission v. American Beef Packers,* No. CV-76-O-68), and now having the privilege to review his work as I sit on the Eighth Circuit Court of Appeals. Judge Urbom's January 9, 1984, trial notes declared in frustration, "The 8th Circuit has so little confidence in district judges." The Eighth Circuit has outstanding district judges in whom the Eighth Circuit has great confidence. Among these distinguished judges, none is more outstanding than Warren Urbom. He is held in the highest regard throughout our circuit and in the federal judiciary nationwide.

Urbom's memoir is written for the benefit of the public and lawyers alike. He informs and teaches with clarity and the practiced skill of a wordsmith. Quotable views on judging, the rule of law, lawyers, and life in general abound in this text. In April 2002 Judge Urbom mentored the law students and lawyers in the Robert Van Pelt American Inn of Court, and me too, saying:

> Respect the law.
> Honor the law.
> But never worship the law.
> The law does not represent our highest standards.
> The law is the lowest common denominator, that is, a set of rules of minimum acceptable behavior, and you can do better than that.

Judge Urbom has done better than that.

In this memoir you will encounter the work of an accomplished author; every story is compellingly told and every paragraph beautifully written. Each story paints a vivid portrait of the human affairs, good and not so good, happy and sad, confronting a life so well lived. You will also witness what drives one of the legendary trial judges of his generation. His remarkable story is told here.

I thoroughly enjoyed reading Warren Urbom's memoir, and so will you. Judge Urbom, thank you for your life's commitment and service to the ministry of justice.

William Jay Riley, Chief Judge,
Eighth Circuit Court of Appeals

Acknowledgments

I owe much to many for this book's life. My wife, Joyce, was the instigator of the idea, and pushed me mercilessly to get going on it. Although she lived to read most of it, I delayed too long, and she died in 2010 without knowing of its completion. She was a realistic and loving critic.

Top laurels for manuscript work go easily to Ellen Lefler, my extraordinarily gifted judicial assistant for over twenty-five years. Her suggesting cases and experiences that deserved development, relentlessly fingering through hundreds of legal files and other records, putting the thousands of words of the manuscript on a computer flash drive in proper format and style, questioning my unclear sentences, searching for countless people who could verify the sources of photographs to clear copyright requirements, proofreading the manuscript and communicating with the editor were all priceless steps in the book's progress.

Law clerks, past and present, provided information for accuracy of the appendix that summarizes their lives after their clerkships with me. Marc Pearce, who has worked with me as my law clerk since 2000, has made certain the citations of legal cases and other works are accurate and appropriate, and has made my writing life easier by doing matchless legal work.

I am grateful to my editor, Matthew Bokovoy of the University of Nebraska Press, as well as readers Harvey Perlman and Dr. John Wunder, chancellor and professor of history and journalism at the University of Nebraska–Lincoln, respectively, and Dr. Darrel Berg for their thoughtful suggestions for refinement of the manuscript. U.S. District Judge Richard G. Kopf was the first to read the manuscript at my request, and pronounced it "perfect." I reacted by saying I wanted ideas for improvement, but he stood his ground. That has energized me to retrace the manuscript to make it as near to his hypothetical standard as I am capable of making it. I am appreciative of the generous foreword by the respected chief judge William Jay Riley of the Eighth Circuit Court of Appeals.

The deputy-in-charge of the clerk's office, District of Nebraska in Lincoln, Pat Merritt, and her deputies, as well as the clerks responsible for the archives of the Eighth Circuit Court of Appeals in Kansas City, Missouri, have been diligent in obtaining court files from those archives.

Thanks to the countless people, mostly nameless, who have spent much time trying to find pictures of people I wanted to include in the book: Karen Keehr, Linda Hein, and Paul Eisloeffel at the Nebraska Historical Society; Tammi Peterman at the *Lincoln Journal Star*; Ryan Thompson and Jeremy Schultz, deputy U.S. marshals of Lincoln, Nebraska; Richard Brown from the Office of the Clerk of the Nebraska Legislature; Ernie Chambers; Millie Adams and Frenchette Prince, circuit executive and assistant circuit executive, respectively, Eighth Circuit Court of Appeals; Joe Haas and Tim Thomas of the office of the clerk of the U.S. District Court of South Dakota; Reverend Everett Sileven, now known as Dr. Everett Ramsey, going to another city for a copy of a video; Duane "Whitey" Nelson, digging through his "stuff"; Alan Kirshen, going into his attic; the Baylor law firm in the persons of Walter E. Zink II, John Baylor Jr., and Susan Baylor, combing their storage areas; John Thorne's widow; Albert and Irene Krieger; the Florida State Bar Association and the National Association of Criminal Defense Lawyers. Others include Ruthie Klein, Elkhorn Valley Museum and Research Facility; the Norfolk Chamber of Commerce, Norfolk, Nebraska; Jessica Waite, curator at the Stuhr Museum, Grand Island, Nebraska; Mr. and Mrs. Kenneth Shriver, Norfolk; Ringer Partners Management, manager of the Prospect Hill Cemetery; the Madison County clerk of court, Madison, Nebraska; Norwalk County Recorder's Office, Los Angeles; Forest Lawn Cemetery, Los Angeles; the Superior Court of California County, Los Angeles; Tamiment Institute Library, New York University; Cass County District Court, Plattsmouth, Nebraska; Richard H. Blomgren; Ann Nicholson, Washington University College of Law; Daniel Aaron Weir, National Association of Criminal Defense Lawyers; Olan Mills photographers; Harry Weddington, U.S. Army Corps of Engineers; Nikki Credic, U.S. Department of Justice; Pam Sweeny, Lifetouch Church Directories and Portraits; KMTV; Vic Richards, WOWT; Parul Shah, Administrative Office of the United States Courts, Washington DC; Krista Popp, Melanie Falk, P. J. Rabel, Natalie Cummings, Peggy Hayne, and President Frederik Ohles, Nebraska Wesleyan University; Brad Clark, Townsend Studio; Doris Vieregg; Roger Elrod, Anderson Studio; Deb Border, dean of students, BryanLGH College of Health Sciences; Joanne Lepore of the Professional Photographers of America; Ward Urbom; Karen Koch and Betty Carr of Sweet Adelines; Jeff Carney, *Omaha World Herald*; Dan Bliss of Universal Information Services; Our Savior Lutheran Church, Lincoln; Ray Gartner; Roxanne Dunbar-Ortiz; Melina Rorick; David Turk, U.S. Marshal Service; Patti Jo Peterson, *The Journal*, Plattsmouth, Nebraska; Maxine Maul, formerly with the *Louisville Messenger*; Penny Berger, attorney; Luta Pleiss; Craig Arent; and Robert and Pam McCurry.

The manuscript has been a six-year project. I was interrupted by two shivering events: my accident of 2008 and Joyce's death in 2010, each sucking my energy to write for nearly six months. My friends have been peerless through all the years. Thanks to everybody.

Called to Justice

Prologue

Invitation to Resign

> The Moving Finger writes; and, having writ,
> Moves on: nor all your Piety nor Wit
> Shall lure it back to cancel half a Line,
> Nor all your Tears wash out a Word of it.
>
> —*THE RUBAIYAT OF OMAR KHAYYAM*, STANZA 71

It is January 2, 1975. Two years ago two hundred American Indians invaded the village of Wounded Knee on the Pine Ridge Reservation in western South Dakota. Armed, they held off federal law enforcement officers for seventy-one days, until a peace of sorts was agreed upon. Most of the invaders were arrested and charged in federal court with an assortment of crimes. I am one of the federal judges assigned to try those cases.

For the past eleven days I've listened to the testimony of traditional Indians, historians, and archaeologists in support of and opposition to the Indians' prime defense. The defense asserts that this court has no jurisdiction; that is, a treaty forged in 1868 between the Sioux Indians and the United States means that this court has no power to decide whether any Indian is guilty of any crime committed on the reservation. If I say the treaty means that, the Sioux will have shown that they compose a sovereign nation independent of the United States, all the charges will be dropped, and the Indian defendants will go free.

John Thorne, an impassioned cause lawyer from San Jose, California, is making his closing argument on the motion to dismiss the charges. He tells me, "[I am out to] get into your guts." He drills me with reminders of two hundred years of broken promises, lies, and deceptions by the United States to the Indians. I am bound, he insists, by moral law; it is immoral to allow the law to be built on the false and arrogant assertion that the Indians are ignorant savages. He knows, he says, that I'm a religious man. "And I am certain in my mind you are suffering with this decision, that it's hurting, because I think it's getting right down into your guts and you are feeling it. That's what you get for taking the job. But you are big enough for it."

When I say to him that the law as interpreted by the Supreme Court of the United States is against him and ultimately it is *that* court who has to say it has been wrong, he shoots back:

> No, . . . I disagree completely. . . . All you have to do is grant the defendants' motion and dismiss the cases. It will never get to the Supreme Court, unless the government makes an appeal, because I guarantee we [defendants] won't. There's no need to. Justice [will have] been done [if you dismiss these cases], and a great, great moral suasion will spread across this land. I don't care about the Supreme Court. . . . You have seen the people . . . and know what they are like. . . . To say no, let the Supreme Court do it, . . . that's the real buck passing that I don't think we need.

I ask, "What shall I do with my oath to uphold the law when the United States Supreme Court has declared what the law is? Do I just say . . . I don't like that law so I'm going to change it? Is that what I do?"

Thorne says, "What would you do, Judge, if the Congress passed a law and said every third child born to a family shall be put to death, if the issue came before you?"

"I might resign, Mr. Thorne. That's different from saying I will not obey what the United States Supreme Court has said is the law."

Thorne: *"As you put the question, Judge, in this case, your duty is to resign if you honestly do not think the defendants' position is legally sound, when you know what the facts are."*[1]

The hearing is over. Each side has said its piece.

I rise slowly from my swivel chair, find my way through the huge doorway behind the bench, walk through the library of my chambers and into the reception room, where I meet the lawyers, learn their addresses for mailing their copies of the opinion I must prepare, thank them for their work, and make my way to the main office of the chambers. I slump into the large brown leather chair that sits in its familiar spot behind my desk. He's right, of course, I think to myself. The law of this case *is* built on an arrogant assumption of the ignorance and savagery of Indians. The long hearing was convincing that the Indians were not and are not of that ilk. If I can do nothing about that, the invitation to resign has a point, but the thought is chilling.

Now I'm exhausted. My mind sighs, "It's okay. Maybe he's right. Maybe it's time to step down. Maybe you've had enough of judging."

And every single day of the past four and a half years I have thought this was the dream job of all jobs.

1

The Rocky Road to a Judgeship

Every federal judge has a story. Not just a story, but a *story*. It's an account of his or her becoming a federal judge. It's about as true as modesty requires and as restrained as the ego allows. The outcome is always sweet, but the process is nerve-wracking.

In a way my story begins in the summer of 1939, in Minden, Nebraska, with my uncle and aunt, Elmer and Dora Leaf. Their daughter Marjorie, my age, had died of pneumonia, and I had the impression I was to be a temporary distraction from their grief. I remember four things about that visit. First, I was embarrassed that my sole pair of socks had holes in the heels. Second, the Leafs had ginger ale in their icebox every day, and I thought if I ever grew up and could afford it, I would have ginger ale in my icebox all the time. Third, I saw the scariest move ever, *Night Must Fall,* starring Robert Montgomery and Rosalind Russell. Fourth, Uncle Elmer took me to visit a newly elected member of Congress, a young lawyer with a practice in Minden, Carl T. Curtis. Mr. Curtis's office was cluttered with cardboard boxes being packed with books to be sent to Washington DC. I had never met such an important person, so I was quiet except for exchanging hellos with him. He and Uncle Elmer visited about the impending move, and that was that. I didn't realize, of course, that Carl Curtis would become an important factor in my future life, but I doubt I'd have done or said anything different if I had. I did not see Curtis again or have any communication with him that I can recall for the next thirty years—that is, until 1969. I knew *of* him in 1969, of course, because of his political celebrity and the fact that in the 1960s we both served on the

2. Warren Urbom on taking the oath of office of a U.S. district judge, May 4, 1970. Photograph by Edholm & Blomgren, Lincoln, Nebraska.

governing board of Nebraska Wesleyan University, although we had no interaction that I know of.

On September 17, 1969, at 11:20 in the morning, a secretary left a note on my desk at the Baylor law firm in Lincoln, Nebraska, where I'd practiced law for sixteen years. The note asked that I return a telephone call from Judge Robert Van Pelt.[1] When I called, I was asked a single question: Are you a Republican? I said I was a registered Republican, and the conversation ended.

I had no suspicion of what that was about.

A dozen days later, on September 29, I learned what it was about. That day Richard "Dick" Smith, an attorney whom I knew principally through our mutual attachment as alumni and members of the governing board of Nebraska Wesleyan University, called and asked me to meet him in the

Tepee Room of the Cornhusker Hotel that evening after the Lincoln Bar Association meeting. I wondered whether it was about some emergency at Nebraska Wesleyan I hadn't heard about, or perhaps some case he'd like me to take a look at, or some nonlegal undertaking he wanted to invite me to help on. It was none of those.

At the Cornhusker Hotel that evening Dick Smith explained that the judgeship to be vacated by U.S. District Judge Van Pelt was his if he chose to take it and that he had not yet made up his mind.[2] Again, there was a question: If he chose not to take the position, would I be available to take it?

The idea was a teeth-rattling clap of thunder. Racing through my mind were thoughts like *Is he really saying what I think he's saying? Does he mean me? I've been a trial lawyer seventeen years. I love oral combat in the courtroom. I'd have to give that up.* And *Could I be objective? I mean, really objective? What would it do to my family, the change of lifestyle? I haven't thought this through.*

It is true that I had given a wisp of thought to standing for appointment to the state trial bench or perhaps even to the state supreme court, but I had taken no step toward either, nor had I ever mentioned it aloud, not even to Joyce, my wife. More than that—much more than that—I stood in awe of the federal trial court and the judges I knew who occupied it during my professional life. These men (no woman had yet reached the position in the District of Nebraska) were giants, and their place was exalted. I was no giant. I was also thinking, *I know that the president of the United States appoints federal district judges, and President Nixon doesn't know me or anything about me. And I know the Constitution requires that he make the appointment with "the advice and consent of the Senate," and I have no contact with our Senators. So who's kidding me?*

In the twenty seconds (or was it five or thirty?) I looked at Dick Smith and let my mind twirl. I settled into a mode of rationalizing: perhaps it would be permissible to say yes because I have no expectation of ascending to the exalted place.

I said yes.

That same evening I wrote to my brother Ward:

> Without relating the details—of which there aren't many—I want you to know that there is some possibility of my being named U.S.

> District Judge to fill the spot being left by Judge Van Pelt's retirement. I consider it still quite remote and am doing nothing to bring it about. But should the unlikely occur I want you not to be utterly unprepared. Dick Smith has the nomination if he wants it but is not yet able to decide. Even if he decides he cannot take it, there are other formidable candidates—like Bob Denney and Hale McCown. My lack of active participation in Republican party affairs must stand as a distinct weakness to my possibilities. Anyway, it's an enormous honor to be even in the wings, even if the stage itself never opens. I'm not rearranging my life on the strength of what's happened to now, I assure you. This is all in confidence, of course.

But I did begin to discuss the situation with Joyce and our four children. Allison, who was eight, reacted this way: "Why would anybody want to be a federal judge? All you do is sit there and say, 'Motion sustained, Mr. Mason!'"

How could I explain to an eight-year-old that I was as uncomprehending as she was, but for a different reason? She couldn't understand why *anyone* would want to be a federal judge. I couldn't understand why anyone would think *I* should be a federal judge.

A few days later, on October 5, the *Lincoln Journal* newspaper carried under the title "One Paragrapher" merely, "Speculation over possible successors for retiring U.S. District Judge Robert Van Pelt should not exclude Warren Urbom, highly respected Lincoln attorney."

That morning, a Sunday, U.S. Senator Carl Curtis telephoned me at home, saying that if I was interested in the federal judgeship, he would like me to fly to Washington to talk with him. I did that on Wednesday, October 8.

Carl Curtis was perhaps five feet eight inches tall (my height), portly, quick of speech, bespectacled, and virtually bald. He gave me a noodle-like handshake and an amiable smile. We visited about the practice of law. About one of his trials when he practiced in Minden, Nebraska, that he was particularly proud of. About my meeting him when I was thirteen (he didn't recall that, but recalled Uncle Elmer and Aunt Dora) and of our devotion to Nebraska Wesleyan University. We talked for perhaps half an hour in his office and then walked to the office building of Nebraska's other U.S. senator, Roman Hruska. On that walk Senator Curtis asked me the only question he ever asked me, then or since, about how I felt about the law.

“It’s the job of a judge to follow the law, isn’t it?” he asked. I said, “Yes, it is.” I suppose if I had been more experienced I might have given a more sophisticated answer, but I was satisfied with it then and still am. It was an honest answer, suitable for a short walk.

I met Senator Hruska for the first time at his office. He was a well-built man, nearly six feet tall, with graying black hair, dark eyebrows, and a forceful, slightly accented voice, suggesting his Czech heritage. He was known as an avid citizen of Omaha and was the ranking Republican on the Senate Judiciary Committee. My conversation with him was abbreviated because he was readying himself for hearings by that committee on the fitness of Judge Clement Haynsworth of South Carolina to be the successor to Supreme Court Justice Abe Fortas, who had resigned.

On my return to Lincoln I wrote to my mother-in-law and father-in-law, Mr. and Mrs. Charles Crawford, of my feelings, of the visit to Washington, and of my gratitude for being in their family. Joyce, I assured them, was an ideal partner for me, and I continued to be thankful for her support, her character, and her love. About the possible appointment I told them that Senator Curtis was solidly behind me and that Senator Hruska, although “terribly preoccupied with the Haynsworth hearings,” was gracious and had given me an “optimistic impression” as to an appointment. I said, “I still find the whole thing incredible.”

But within days matters took a turn. Entirely unexpectedly, Senator Hruska walked into my office in Lincoln, saying that Chief Judge Richard Robinson (he and Judge Van Pelt were the only two federal district judges in Nebraska) would be required by law to step down as chief judge in four years upon his reaching the age of seventy, even if he opted to continue as an active judge, and that whoever was selected to fill Judge Van Pelt’s vacancy would then become chief judge. He said the chief judge should reside and be stationed in Omaha, where the bulk of the federal chief judge’s work needed to be conducted. Then came the question: Would I be willing to move to Omaha if I were appointed?

The question was another surprise. I hadn’t thought about the chief judgeship. But I *had* thought about the pleasant fact that I had no strings attached to me, no pledges I’d made, no wrinkled baggage to drag beside me. I wanted to keep it that way.

After a moment, I responded that I felt I had to become a federal judge, if at all, without any commitment of any kind, except to honor my oath of office. I said if I found that justice could best be dispensed from Omaha or any other place, I would move to that place at once, but I had no basis for making that decision in advance of assuming the bench. Hruska left.

I felt good. I had turned the corner. I wanted the appointment, but maybe even more I wanted to feel free, and I did feel free.

There was a further complication. Earlier that year the Senate had before it a bill to create several dozen judicial positions, including another district judgeship for Nebraska. The *Lincoln Journal* on October 19 reported, "Political sources say Hruska very much wants to have Republican National Committeeman Donald R. Ross of Omaha filling that new bench slot."

I could see dark clouds gathering.

Senator Curtis called me on Friday, October 17, asking that I meet with him at his room at the Cornhusker Hotel at nine that evening. At the hotel he invited me to a seat, then seated himself and told me there had been a report from someone in my church that I had been involved on behalf of John F. Kennedy, a Democrat, in his campaign against Richard Nixon for the presidency in 1960—indeed that I had been Nebraska's *principal financial supporter* of Kennedy in that campaign. I assured the senator that there was no grain of truth in such a report.

He also said that from an article in the *Omaha World-Herald* he deduced that Senator Hruska was being pressured by his political organization to delay my appointment until a third judgeship was authorized by Congress, then to have Donald Ross appointed to fill it so that Ross would have seniority over me and would become chief judge (the judge with the most seniority in the district would automatically become the chief judge of the district), and I could be appointed after Ross to fill the Van Pelt vacancy. Senator Curtis said he thought Senator Hruska had no part in such a plan. I said that a *World-Herald* reporter had told me the day before that the third-judgeship bill had passed the House committee and that passage by the whole Senate was expected within two weeks. Curtis acknowledged that Hruska was dragging his feet, but not because of opposition to me. That was reassuring, but Curtis's view that passage of the bill authorizing a third judgeship for Nebraska would not come about for "several months" and that my appointment could not be delayed that long seemed a bit too optimistic.

My assessment was that the reporter was right, the article was right, and if passage of the bill was imminent, my appointment would be delayed until after a third judgeship could be authorized. My gloomier side was showing.

Two obstacles now appeared: Who would be chief judge? Must the nominee live in Omaha? Donald R. Ross was a principal in both questions. Some headlines began to appear:

Patronage Squabble Looming? Hruska, Curtis May Not Agree on Van Pelt Job

LINCOLN JOURNAL, OCTOBER 19, 1969

U.S. Judge Vacancy Is Touchy

OMAHA WORLD-HERALD, OCTOBER 28, 1969

The gathering of dark clouds continued when Senator Curtis gave me a copy of three letters dated October 29 and addressed to President Richard M. Nixon. One was signed by Senators Hruska and Curtis: "We respectfully submit the name of Mr. Warren K. Urbom of Lincoln, Nebraska, for United States District Judge for the vacancy brought about by the retirement of Judge Robert Van Pelt." Another was signed by Hruska alone. It made clear his position that the chief judge should reside in the Omaha area and that three options existed: (1) the nominee could establish residence in that area; (2) he could declare that he would forgo service as chief judge if and when the contingency occurred; or (3) the nomination and confirmation of a nominee to fill the vacancy could be delayed until a nominee could be selected and qualified who would reside in the Omaha area.

The Hruska letter further pointed out that the Senate had already passed a bill that would give the District of Nebraska a third judgeship and that the House of Representatives was then holding hearings on a similar bill. He proposed a "reasonable delay" to await approval of the legislation before making a judicial appointment to succeed Van Pelt and suggested the wisdom of having "a conference with the Attorney General or other appropriate persons."

Hruska was urging that Donald R. Ross of Omaha be appointed to the new position, and then perhaps I could be appointed to the Van Pelt spot. Such a delay was of no great importance, except that by then I had learned that delay in federal appointments can be disastrous to an expectant appointee. Coupling that with the rumor of my support of John F. Kennedy, weird as it was, the dark clouds grew darker.

Sen. Hruska Backs Urbom, Hedges Time

OMAHA WORLD-HERALD, OCTOBER 29, 1969

On with the Appointment

LINCOLN JOURNAL, OCTOBER 29, 1969

The third letter was signed by Senator Curtis only. It said he would give a complete answer to the Hruska letter later but added, "I . . . wish to notify you [at this time] that I totally disagree with [Senator Hruska] both as to facts and conclusion."

Soon thereafter Senator Curtis made it known publicly that he thought residence in Omaha or Lincoln made no difference in the responsibilities of the chief judge.

Weeks went by without resolution of the impasse.

Curtis Disagrees on Judge Premise

LINCOLN JOURNAL, OCTOBER 30, 1969

Hruska Takes Judge Issue to Nixon

OMAHA WORLD-HERALD, NOVEMBER 1, 1969

Curtis: Confirm Nominee

LINCOLN JOURNAL, NOVEMBER 10, 1969

Why the Delay?

LINCOLN STAR, NOVEMBER 22, 1969

Frivolous Delay on Judge

LINCOLN JOURNAL, NOVEMBER 22, 1969

Judgeship Creating Curtis, Hruska Split

OMAHA WORLD-HERALD, NOVEMBER 25, 1969

Senator Curtis was a stalwart in support of me, and I was grateful. He brought me whatever could be considered good news, and the bad as well. Most of the bad came to him from some person never identified for me, nor did I ever ask. Besides the claim that I had been a huge contributor to Kennedy was another, that I had been seen marching with rebellious university students down 15th Street from the State Historical Society to the State Capitol Building in Lincoln in opposition to the ongoing Vietnam War. That too was wholly untrue but nevertheless disheartening and draining.

One story that *was* true, however, related to my noninvolvement in politics. In a column by Darwin Olofson of the Washington Bureau of the *Omaha World-Herald* on November 25, 1969, under the headline, "Judgeship Creating Curtis, Hruska Split," Olofson observed that when Senator Curtis turned to me after Dick Smith withdrew as a candidate, "it raised some Republican eyebrows in the state." Nonetheless, the article continued, "there has been no suggestion from either senator that party activity, or the lack of it enters into their disagreement on the timing of the Urbom appointment."

In December Donald Ross took a job with Nebraska Consolidated Mills and withdrew from judicial consideration. That, as matters developed, changed virtually nothing.

On December 9, 1969, a note from my secretary, Marlene McGuire, said that Judge Van Pelt had telephoned, saying he had a call from Mr. Kyle of the American Bar Association to report the Association's preliminary assessment of my qualifications to be appointed to the federal trial bench. The report was a thumbs-up. The note also said that Van Pelt had some things to talk about, including a committee to which he had been appointed, regarding extracurricular activities of judges.

In a journal I had been keeping I wrote on January 22, 1970:

> Van Pelt just returned from Wash. Sen. Curtis says that Hruska is irritable about the matter, so Curtis will go to the Justice Dept. Says FBI noted rumor of [my supposedly participating in a moratorium march

3. Donald R. Ross prior to his becoming a federal judge. Photograph by *Lincoln Journal Star*.

4. U.S. District Judge Robert Van Pelt, Judge Urbom's immediate predecessor in office. Photograph by Townsend Studio, Lincoln.

> in opposition to the Vietnam War] but Van Pelt thinks that's of no great importance, except to give Hruska something to fuss about.
>
> As a result, I've come to suppose it may be July 1 before the log jam is broken.

I had no basis for any prediction; I was just trying to keep my hopes alive.

On January 26, 1970, I hired Rodney Johnson to be a law clerk if I should be appointed; in the meantime he was to work part time with Judge Van Pelt and part time with the Nebraska Crime Commission. I had been in the line of officers of the Grand Lodge of Ancient Free and Accepted Masons of Nebraska since 1966, a process that would ordinarily lead to the office of grand master in 1971–1972. I put before an ethics committee of the judiciary the question of whether I should continue in the line and take the grand master's role if elected or abandon my Masonic membership altogether. I noted that the lodge's failure to elect blacks to membership was a concern,

5. Senator Roman L. Hruska. Photograph courtesy of the clerk of the U.S. District Court for the District of Nebraska.

6. Senator Carl T. Curtis. Photograph in author's possession.

as was the fact that litigation regarding state-church relationships, an area of interest to Masonry, might come before me as a federal judge.

Adding to that the considerable time the position of grand master would take, I had asked for the committee's recommendation for accepting such a position or not. I had heard nothing from the committee, but now understood the reference to a "committee regarding extrajudicial activities of judges" mentioned by Marlene McGuire in her note of December 9. My journal entry of January 27, 1970, said, "Van Pelt called to say that [the] ethics committee met in Wash. & decided it would not write opinions on inquiries by non-judges [meaning me] but its thinking is that I should not accept grand mastership of [the Masonic Lodge of Nebraska] because of time, school-church litigation, lack of Negroes. But wants not to have to decide whether [I] should remain a Mason." (My interpretation: Don't renew the request when I become a judge, because the question is applicable to many judges.)

On March 11, 1970, President Nixon nominated me for appointment to the federal district court, sending my name to the Senate for such advice and consent as it wished to offer, as required by the Constitution. That was in no way a defiance of Senator Hruska's reluctance. It was a foregone understanding that my nomination would never go forward through the Senate without approval of both Nebraska senators. Senator Hruska continued to delay, the press indicated, in order to "check out" some things, hoping the third judgeship for Nebraska (and coincidentally, I suspected, a chief judgeship for Donald Ross) might still be worked out.

I was still predicting July 1.

The press had been carrying news of the nomination of Judge G. Harrold Carswell of Florida as successor to Supreme Court Justice Abe Fortas since the nomination of Judge Haynsworth was rejected. The word was that Senator Hruska was serving as floor manager in the Senate to press forward the approval of Judge Carswell, but some complaints about Carswell had been raised, including concern about racism on his part and assertions that in his judicial role he was "mediocre." My journal entry for March 17 says, "Today Hruska told a news commentator on a national TV hookup that even if Judge Carswell were mediocre, as is being charged by some, 'the mediocre "judges, people and lawyers" are entitled to representation on the Supreme Court.'"

Whew! I thought, nobody ever said being a U.S. senator was easy!

On the morning of March 18 Cella Heitman, a *Lincoln Journal* reporter, called me, saying that she had looked over clips of the newspaper and found that Senator Hruska had early suggested that a solution to my problem could be had by my moving to Omaha. She asked if I had considered doing that. I said I had, and if I became a federal judge and if the business of the court could best be handled from Omaha, I would have no reluctance to move. I said I wouldn't know what would be best for the court until I became more familiar with it, and I would make no pre-appointment commitment about it.

My journal entry of Wednesday, March 18, reported, "By mid-afternoon Sen. Curtis called, saying that Sen. Hruska had rousted him out of the gymnasium (I think he said the steam bath) with the report that I had agreed to move to Omaha. I gave him the account as it occurred & agreed to learn from the newspaper the exact story as it appeared."

Actually, the story hadn't yet appeared, but Cella Heitman read the proposed story to me. Senator Curtis was concerned that the story—especially the lead sentence—gave the impression that I had "caved in" to Senator Hruska by making a concession in order to move the confirmation along. He asked that I discuss it with Judge Van Pelt, which I did. When he said the story sounded all right, the senator still wasn't satisfied, so I talked personally with Judge Van Pelt and then Cella Heitman. I explained the problem to her and suggested that any implication of a concession be removed. She agreed, saying she would rewrite the last sentence and emphasize that I said I had made and would make no commitment. Senator Curtis had said he was also concerned that the story looked like he had joined in the concession, so Cella agreed to separate any reference to him from the lead sentence. Senator Curtis and I agreed that he might appropriately call Jack Hart, the managing editor of the *Lincoln Journal*.

Both Senator Curtis and Cella Heitman suggested that Senator Hruska apparently was looking for a way to retreat gracefully and might use this incident to do so.

Early the next morning, March 19, Senator Curtis called, saying that he was reporting back to Senator Hruska that I had said to the reporter that no commitment would be made and that if and when I became a judge and the business of the courts was of first importance, I would consider where the court administration could best be handled. Curtis said that he had talked with Jack Hart, the managing editor of the *Lincoln Journal*, as we had agreed would be appropriate. I was grateful for Senator Curtis's sensitivity to appearances, and told him so.

That morning's *Lincoln Star* reported that the House of Representatives had passed the omnibus judgeship bill with Nebraska's hoped-for third judgeship deleted. That meant the matter would go to conferees of the two houses for some kind of compromise.

By 8:45 a.m. Cella Heitman had called again. Senator Hruska had issued a statement that morning that the getting of a third judgeship by means of the conferees, if at all, would take several weeks or even months, and he was not willing to postpone my confirmation that long. Cella said she was killing the story about my moving to Omaha. (In fact it wasn't killed, but was at the bottom of an eighteen-inch-long article.)

Great news arrived just after noon from Senator Curtis: not only had Senator Hruska returned his "blue card," signifying his assent to my confirmation, but he had arranged a hearing before the subcommittee of the Judiciary Committee for March 26 at 10:30 a.m. The purpose was to question me regarding my fitness for the judicial position. The panel would be Senators James O. Eastland, chairman of the Judiciary Committee; Roman Hruska of Nebraska; and Quentin Burdick of North Dakota. Senator Curtis said he would send some statements made to the subcommittee by previous nominees for use as a guide if I wanted to use them. All of that was quieting news.

John Duffner of the attorney general's office called in midafternoon and briefed me on procedure before the subcommittee:

> No witnesses, please, except your senators and members of Congress, i.e., members of the House of Representatives. It's traditional that the senators come, optional as to representatives. Questions will be few and will not require preparation. . . . Give a short statement of appreciation, and write a note sometime to the president. Lyndon Johnson was miffed by a couple of judges who didn't. . . . Timing of confirmation and issuance of the commission are uncertain because of the interstice between the subcommittee's hearing and full Committee's approval. . . . The Committee is so occupied with the Carswell nomination . . . that the Committee has no regular schedule for this or similar matters. . . . Within a month you should be on the bench.

Whoa! Only two days earlier, on March 21, I was predicting an answer by July 1. On March 23 Senator Hruska called to invite Joyce and me to breakfast on the morning of the Senate subcommittee hearing. He was friendly and gently apologetic for "having been abrasive at times." He hadn't been, and I told him so. (I thought it impolitic to remind him that the day following his defense of mediocrity in judges he decided to endorse me!)

Senator Curtis called a few minutes later, saying that having breakfast with Hruska was a good idea. Earlier he had asked me to meet him at his office before the hearing and had said we would have lunch following

7. (*Left to right*): U.S. Senator Roman Hruska, Lois Curtis, Congressman Robert Denney, Warren Urbom, John Duffner of the Justice Department, Joyce Urbom, and Senator Carl T. Curtis, immediately after the hearing before the Senate Judiciary Committee, April 26, 1970. Photograph in author's possession.

the hearing, but acknowledged that breakfast as guests of Senator Hruska would be even better. He was sure that Hruska's friendliness was sincere.

In the mail came an invitation to become a member of the American College of Trial Lawyers.[3]

It had been a good week.

Breakfast on March 26 was in the main Senate dining room, with Senator Hruska, Senator Curtis and his wife, Mr. Duffner of the Justice Department, and Congressman Robert Denney of Nebraska. Then we moved to the hearing in Room 2228 of the New Senate Office Building. Senators Eastman and Burdick couldn't make it, so Senator Hruska presided and alone held the hearing. Curtis and Denney spoke complimentarily; I spoke barely; Hruska questioned perfunctorily. It took half an hour and was altogether pleasant. A photographer took pictures at the rear door of the Capitol.

Judge Van Pelt phoned on April 7, saying that he had just had an extended telephone conversation with Senator Curtis, who reported on the Carswell situation. He said that on April 6 the Senate rejected a motion 52–44 to recommit the Carswell nomination to the Judiciary Committee and would vote on confirmation of that nomination on April 8. That action had divided the Judiciary Committee into three factions—Republican, Democrat, and civil rights—resulting in taut feelings and declination to approve district or any other judges or other matters by the "round robin" method, by which approval could be given by telephone without a meeting. Instead a committee meeting would be necessary for approval of my nomination. A lag of two or three days before confirmation by the full Senate must be expected; in the normal course of things the president would sign the commission in one day, and it would go to the Justice Department for engraving; a day or two later it would be mailed to me. I could plan an induction ceremony for perhaps April 27 and almost certainly for May 1. At 10:15 a.m. on April 21 Senator Curtis phoned to say that the full Judiciary Committee had just approved my nomination. That was three days earlier than I had expected. He said that Senator Hruska was then still in the committee meeting, but had sent word out to get to me. He understood that the nomination would get to the full Senate Thursday, the 23rd, lay over twenty-four hours, and be voted on the 24th. But that was a Friday and such matters are usually not taken up on Fridays, so Monday would probably be the day.

Confirmation by the full Senate came on April 23. Senator Curtis notified me at 12:20 p.m. During the afternoon I talked with Senator Curtis, Senator Hruska, and Congressman Denney; none would be able to come to my oaths-taking ceremony on May 5 because that was a Tuesday, and they had to be in Washington for congressional duties. I could have scheduled the ceremony for Monday, when I later learned they could have come, but other scheduling events made that a poor choice. Monday, April 4, was our oldest daughter's sixteenth birthday, and she wanted to be at the county courthouse for her first driver's license test that morning. A former chief justice of the Supreme Court of Nebraska, Robert G. Simmons, would be memorialized that morning too.[4] I was sorry about having no congressional members at my oath-taking, but I decided I'd live with it rather than rob Kim of her long-awaited driver's license at the earliest possible time.

8. The Urbom family moves items into the Federal Building in Lincoln, May 2, 1970. (*Left to right*): Randy, Allison, Joy, Kim, Joyce, and Warren Urbom. Photograph by *Lincoln Journal Star*.

Lloyd McDowell's story in the *Journal* that evening said I was a leader in Senator Curtis's previous campaign for reelection. I called Lloyd to tell him I wasn't. He said that was a part of the wire story from Washington, but he would put a note on the city editor's desk about it. I said that all I wanted was for him to know so it wouldn't be reported by default, because a gratifying feature of my nomination was the complete lack of political motivation, except the bare fact of my registration as a Republican. This story is the only taint on that.

I did write the president, thanking him for the appointment, as I'd been advised to do.

Duffner called on April 25 to say the president had signed the commission on the 24th. On Monday, the 27th, Joyce found a yellow slip in the mailbox at home notifying us that an attempt had been made to deliver a package, which could be picked up at the post office before 5:00. She didn't make it by then, but found a friendly employee who got the package for her. I went home and found family, friends, and neighbors waiting. The grand opening of the commission was duly held.

The oaths-taking day was May 5. The *Journal* said two hundred people were there, and I think that's about right. They were standing in the hallway and along the sides of the courtroom inside. The ceremony was perfect. Judge Van Pelt administered the oaths, my dad helped me don my new robe, nice speeches were made, I responded, and then I greeted people in the reception room of the judge's chambers. We retired to the University Club for lunch with the participants, relatives, Dr. Darrel and Ruth Berg,[5] and Dr. Vance and Barbara Rogers.

The move of my office into the third story of the four-story limestone building was during the weekend, before the taking of the oath of office. The judge's chambers were immediately to the south of the courtroom and consisted of a reception room, two adjoining rooms accommodating two law clerks, the judge's office, and a library running parallel to the judge's office and between the office and the courtroom. All rooms of the chambers were ample in size, all lined with plaster and bordered by oak frames and doors.

But for me the attraction of the chambers was the antique furniture.[6] The massive oak desk of the judge was constructed the same on both the front and the back, apparently to accommodate two persons—practicing lawyers or other coworkers—sitting across from and facing each other. The secretary's desk matched the judge's, but was somewhat smaller. Oak chairs with leather seats were plentiful in all the rooms. A stately six-by-six breakfront with two vertical glass doors outlined with oak strips stood against one wall of the judge's office. Oak chairs with leather seat coverings were at an oak conference table in the middle of the judge's office and conveniently placed elsewhere about the rooms. A leather-covered lounge invited visitors to remain in the reception room, and three- and four-shelved oak bookcases with horizontal drop-down glass doors and a circular bookcase supplied places for all the books a federal judge should need close at hand. The chambers were nice, commodious, comfortable, and well-kept, but they showed their age, probably having been in place since 1906, when the first phase of the building was completed.

9. Courtroom No. 1 in the Federal Building at 9th and P Streets, Lincoln, where Judge Urbom took the oaths of office and presided over trials during 1970–1975. Photograph by Bob Gorham, May 3, 1972, *Lincoln Journal Star*.

The courtroom—Courtroom No. 1—was "the sublime" of the building. It extended from the third to the fourth floors, was "adorned in heavy, dark oak," and according to the Lincoln historian Jim McKee, as quoted in the *Lincoln Journal-Star*, was "the building's most interesting feature."[7] The courtroom had a special dignity and a proud elegance, highlighted by walls covered with carved plaster figures and leather-covered doors. The bench, elevated three steps above the floor, its writing surface slanted slightly downward toward the judge, was next to the witness seat, which was next to the jury box. Acoustics were excellent, even without sound-enhancing devices. I used that courtroom almost every day for the first five years of my tenure, and I loved it.

At about 3:00 p.m. on May 5 Attorney Herb Friedman called for an appointment about getting a temporary restraining order. I saw him at 3:30 and told him to file his motion, but that I would not rule on it until notice was given to the opposing counsel, and I would then set a time for a hearing. Friedman got an oral agreement from opposing counsel, and I set the hearing for the next day at 10:00. It was a Civil Rights Act case arising from a boy's alleged suspension from sixth grade because he wore blue jeans, cut off and frayed above the knees, contrary to school policy. So that night Rodney Johnson and I researched the law until 11:00.

The next day, Wednesday, I sat alone—one *is* alone up there—at the bench and entered an order against the Lincoln Public Schools. The schools didn't resist, saying the boy, Eric Barnaul, never was suspended as far as they could tell. The school welcomed him back but put on no evidence because the principal was out of town. I relied on the affidavits presented by the boy's counsel. Signing of the order was at 10:40, exactly twenty-four hours after my taking the oath of office.

On Thursday I had only two criminal arraignments and one appointment of counsel to represent an indigent criminal defendant. On Friday I had an oral argument on a motion to dismiss a class action. That was the day, in late afternoon, I began to feel confident that I could do this job.

So I was ready to move on. I remembered that the word around town was that the appointment was for life. My commission says I stay only "during good behavior."[8]

POSTSCRIPT TO MY *STORY*

Carl Curtis was in the Congress, the House and the Senate, for forty years. The title of his book is *Forty Years against the Tide*.[9] He retired from the Senate in 1979 and died on January 24, 2000. He lived in Lincoln after he retired, and I saw him and his second wife, Mildred, quite often. His first wife, Ruth, died before he retired.

Roman Hruska lived with his "mediocre" statement until he died in 1999. He served in the House and Senate for twenty-three years, retiring in 1976. The new federal courthouse in Omaha bears his name.

Within a year after I took the oath of office, Congress awarded Nebraska a third district judgeship, and Robert Denney was appointed to fill it in early 1971. His name graces the federal courthouse, completed in 1975, in Lincoln.

Seven months after I was sworn in, Don Ross ascended to the Eighth Circuit Court of Appeals, succeeding Harry Blackmun, who became a justice

10. Judge Richard G. Kopf, Judge Urbom's successor.
Photograph by Harry Weddington.

of the Supreme Court of the United States in June 1970, succeeding Justice Abe Fortas. Ross soon came to me, saying, "I want to be your friend." He *has* been my friend, as well as an outstanding circuit court judge.

My dad, age seventy-six, robed me at my swearing-in ceremony. He died in 1987.

Judge Richard Robinson chose to take senior status and to step aside from the chief judgeship in 1971. I then moved into the chief judgeship, where I remained for fourteen years (at that time there was no law requiring relinquishment of the title, except upon reaching the age of seventy, which for me would have been in 1995), then withdrew from that position in 1985 to make sure Judge Lyle Strom could serve as chief judge before his age would prevent it. He did so serve and did it well. I found that the duties of the chief judge could be appropriately fulfilled from Lincoln, so didn't move away. Judge Richard Kopf, my successor as federal district judge, served as chief judge while living in Lincoln. Other than Senator

Hruska in 1969–70, to my knowledge nobody has said that the chief judge should reside in Omaha.

Richard Dier of Holdrege, Nebraska, was appointed to fill the vacancy left by Judge Robinson's taking senior status in 1971. Dier served one year, dying in Little Rock, Arkansas, while in an evening recess from a trial. He was succeeded by Albert Schatz of Omaha in 1973.

Dick Smith practiced law with Woods Aitken in Lincoln until a few years before his death in 2004.

Warren Burger succeeded Earl Warren as chief justice of the Supreme Court from 1969 until his retirement in 1986.

One mystery remains. If I wasn't close to any senator, if I wasn't active in politics, if I never mentioned to anyone any interest in judicial office, who would pass a word compelling enough to result in the unremitting efforts of Senator Curtis to make a judgeship real?

C. M. "Barney" Pierson might have had something to do with it. He was a real estate lawyer in Lincoln and very knowledgeable about Republican politics. He didn't do trial work and sometimes asked me to try a case of his, and a time or two he sat through such a trial with me. I would refer to him the reading of abstracts of title that needed to be examined. That's a slim reed for gauging the strength of a political connection. And I'm not sure he had the ear of Senator Curtis.

Dick Smith was another possibility. He was close to and had influence with Senator Curtis. He knew me only from afar, except that we both sat on the Nebraska Wesleyan University governing board. I doubt that he was sure that I had the temperament and legal ability to be a good prospect for the federal trial bench. Even so, he was the one sent to feel me out about interest in the position.

I count out Jim Ackerman, an attorney about whom it was said that nothing happened in Nebraska Republican politics without his approval. If he had had a part in my selection, he would have discussed my prospects with Vance Rogers, then president of Nebraska Wesleyan University. But Rogers was not even aware that I was in the picture for a judgeship until after I had traveled to Washington to meet with Senators Curtis and Hruska, so Ackerman probably had little or nothing to do with my journey to the bench, as was true of Rogers.[10]

Robert Van Pelt can't be counted out. He knew me as a lawyer and, more particularly, how I conducted myself in a federal courtroom. He was the first to inquire about my political affiliation—"Are you a Republican?"—before speculation about his replacement became serious. After I had been publicly revealed as a bona fide candidate for the position, Judge Van Pelt called me often, carrying messages from Senator Curtis about how the appointment process was going, bringing me word from the Administrative Office of the Courts, or slipping me advice about what I would need—one or more law clerks, a bailiff, a robe, choices of books for a chambers' library, an installation ceremony, ideas of who might appropriately fit the protocol for a particular act of ceremonial preparation, a reminder to thank the president for the appointment, if it were to come to that.

I never asked any of them—not Pierson, not Smith, not Ackerman, Van Pelt, or anybody else—who it was who called the play in the huddle or centered the ball to me or ran as the pulling guard with Carl Curtis. No one mentioned the subject, and by now all the suspects have died. I don't know, and I'm not likely to find out. That's all right. I don't need to know. But if I were a gambling man, my money would be on Van Pelt.

If it was Judge Van Pelt alone or in collaboration with another, he seemingly was doing acts quite similar to those Justice Abe Fortas suffered from immediately before I went through the selection process. While Fortas was on the Supreme Court, he continuously gave consultative assistance to President Lyndon Johnson, including suggestions of who should be appointed federal district judges. A claim made against Justice Fortas was that these acts were in violation of the constitutional doctrine of separation of powers, inasmuch as the president was in the executive branch of government and Fortas was in the judicial branch. If that claim were valid, a similar claim could be made that a district judge in the judicial branch in interacting with a senator of the legislative branch regarding a power assigned to senators violates the doctrine of separation of powers. I offer no answer. I only make the observation and say I am constantly thankful for Judge Van Pelt's kindly and constant service on my behalf. It has altered my life, all for the better.

The truth is I had a life before the judgeship. A good life, I could always have gone back to it.

2

Growing Up

My first memory is one I would rather be forgotten, but it is not likely to be. My brother Ward and I were out shooting sparrows with Ward's BB gun. I was three; Ward was seven. After a while he looked at me, aimed the gun at me, smiled, and pulled the trigger. My left eye seemed to explode. I remember nothing of the next many months except throwing myself off my mother's lap and pounding my head on the floor for relief from the pain. Nothing helped.

The doctors were precise: I would never see from my left eye again. Now, seventy-seven years later, my family members were with me to celebrate my eightieth birthday. They—Joyce's and my four children, their spouses, and eleven of twelve grandchildren (ranging in age from twenty-five to two)—had come from elsewhere in Nebraska and from Arizona, Texas, Missouri, and South Carolina. Scheduling choices hadn't accommodated our gathering on December 17, the real anniversary date, so four days at Lake Okoboji in Iowa and December 26 and 27 at our home in Lincoln were substituted. These days were rollicking, sharing, laughing, happy times, filling my cup to overflowing.

There was one hitch. On the day everyone left our house, I noticed it. A cloud had entered the center of my right eye, leaving a hazy, sometimes empty space where the letter of a word I was trying to read was supposed to be. A round, black or red or blue spot the size of a grapefruit blotted every wall, floor, refrigerator, wastebasket, or other sizable object in my line of vision. When I watched television, the moving lips of any close-up speaker were distorted into a twisted, inverted V.

The three specialists in Lincoln and Omaha who examined me in the next few days reached no diagnosis. One spoke of a possible cyst behind the macula; the others suspected a hole in the macula, though pictures revealed none and none could be seen. Two types of treatment were described if the condition proved to be macular degeneration: surgery at the back of the eye, with four to six weeks of disability, the first two of which would have had me lying face down in bed, and medication by injection deep into the eyeball. Neither assured success, and neither sounded inviting.

What I know is that I have only one seeing eye. It has served me all my life. It took over for both eyes after the BB accident and let me see everything I saw. It let me read millions of words, drive thousands of miles, avoid countless mistakes, and admire and befriend men and women. With its help I've delved into the acts and motives of young and old, defended guilty and innocent, and judged both the humble and the haughty. And now, since 2005, this eye, my beloved companion, is failing. What it sees is distorted by an uneven, restless rippling.

December 17, 1925, is the date of my birth. Atlanta, Nebraska, is my town of birth. It was and is a tiny town, with maybe a hundred residents. (My next-door neighbor, Bob Zimmerman, says he was born *in* Atlanta. He says to be born *in* Atlanta you have to have your knees bent. I don't believe that.) My parents, Clarence and Myrl Urbom, my brother Ward, and I lived a mile south of town on a farm. We moved to a farm near McDonald, Kansas, when I was about two, so I'm told.

The day of the BB accident was a cool day, November 8, 1929. That's when Ward and I were playing in a granary at our rented farm we knew as the Hastings Place in northwest Kansas. The house was a two-story, white, wooden structure a couple of hundred feet from the granary. I think Mother was in the house. Dad was in the east field. The setting was natural, the activities usual.

I now know that after I was shot my parents and Ward took me to a doctor in, I believe, Atwood, Kansas, and a few weeks later to Dr. Sunbury in Holdrege, Nebraska, and Dr. Wilcox in Kearney, Nebraska. Dr. Wilcox recommended that there be no removal of the natural eye until the bone structure had developed fully. That surgery was done years later, when I

11. Ward Urbom, age seven, and Warren Urbom, age three, November 1929. Photograph in author's possession.

was seventeen, in the summer of 1943. For years, until I had the natural eye removed and replaced with an artificial eye, colds settled in the blind eye, giving me throbbing headaches. But I learned to live with it pretty well, I think. Half-blind was better than all-blind.

Probably the hardest part was that the natural eye—the blinded one—was ugly and got uglier as time went by. The iris was greenish yellow and splattered enough that the eye didn't really look in any particular direction, ever. It was just ugly. People were gracious about it generally, and I tried not to put my eye on display or take steps to hide it, except that I didn't object when a photographer would touch up a picture to make the eye look somewhat natural.

The family version of the air rifle event has been that the BB glanced off a nail in the granary wall into my eye. I don't think so. I've always had a memory of Ward's raising the gun and firing it right at me. What's more, there was no wall in a location to cause a bounce in my direction. It doesn't matter. I know Ward didn't mean to blind me or even to hurt me. We've remained fast friends, and I've never blamed him for any part of the incident.

That granary on the Hastings Place provided a place for fun of many kinds. Ward and I once decided to build an elevator that would take us to the rafters above the driveway that comprised the floor of the granary. We rigged up a flat, heavy piece of platform from a combine, hooked a rope to it—no block and tackle—and tossed the rope over the rafter. I was given the go-ahead to hoist Ward upward. Of course, I couldn't. Nor could he lift me or himself. So much for creativity.

Remembrances of the hayloft in the barn are all good. Ward and I visited the Hastings Place in 1995 and relived tumbling down the hay chutes that led to the mangers, racing our little wagons around the hayloft, and climbing the ladder that allowed us to ascend to the horizontal braces along the walls and inch our way around the perimeter of the loft six feet off the floor. We saw the big door at the east end, where hay could be lifted into the loft. The barn made the whole trip worthwhile.

We also recalled the windmill that stood just west of the barn. We loved to climb to the top and sit on the platform and chew sweet cane. And if our folks weren't watching we could grasp the two-by-fours that enclosed the opening to the platform and then swing our bodies to and fro fifteen feet above the ground. Life was good, blind eye and all.

Every boy needs a big brother. Someone to talk with sometimes, walk with sometimes, to learn from. How to smoke corn silks or grapevines, how to make a corncob pipe, how to swim in a forbidden river or rescue a sled that has fallen through the ice, what is a "homo," how to talk to a girl, how to shave—these are all too private to discuss with just anybody, especially parents. Big brothers know things like that. How they find out, nobody knows.

Ward and I went to the Busy Bee School, a one-room schoolhouse maybe half a mile from our house on the Hastings Place. Miss Alice Chance taught the eight or so students, two of whom were in my grade and a similar number in Ward's. No kindergarten was offered. The first two grades sort of melded together, and by the end of the first year I was in the third grade. Ward too took two grades in one year or skipped one and was in the seventh grade by the time we moved to the next school. About all I recall of the year at the Busy Bee School is learning to read by use of flash cards that phonetically guided us through the sounds of letters.

My third and part of my fourth grades were at Little Beaver School, another one-room country school, about three miles south of McDonald and a couple of miles southeast of the Schurock Place, which my parents rented. Ward and I rode Beauty, our Shetland pony, to school in all seasons, but walked when Beauty shied and left us without a seat.

Of course, my memory is better about Little Beaver School and the year and a half of my third and fourth grades. I remember fighting mock battles with Ward on the way to school, using wild sunflower stalks for clubs, banging them together till they were broken, seeing who wielded the toughest stalk.

I remember too a man coming to the schoolhouse and asking Milla Fuller, our teacher, who I was and asking me what made my hair so curly. I didn't know, but told him I thought it was the rain. He laughed and seemed to think it was an odd answer. I didn't tell him I thought he had asked an odd question.

I don't know why we moved to Kansas in the 1920s. It wasn't because the lap of luxury awaited us. Our first house (I have only the dimmest recollection of it, but the memory is verified, if not created, by a snapshot we have) was an unpainted, wooden, tiny, two-story, ramshackle place. I suppose Mom and Dad chose the McDonald area because Dad's Uncle John Urbom's sons, Ed, Frank, and Oscar, lived there. The Hastings Place, a considerable improvement, followed that first one, and the Schurock Place was better yet, though none of them had electricity, running water, or an indoor toilet.

Our sister Beverly was born June 15, 1930, in St. Francis, Kansas, the only one of us to be born in a hospital. In those days most babies were born at home.

The schools' report cards from those years reported more than grades. They were from the Lincoln School Supply Co. in Nebraska and carried such nifties as "What is worth doing at all is worth doing well," "Obedience to law is an essential element in patriotism," and "A pupil who smokes cigarettes need not worry about his future for he has none." Maybe that explains why Ward and I developed such pure characters.

The 1930s were tough for farmers. Not only was the national economy in a depression, but the Great Plains, including Kansas and Nebraska, were further crippled by a drought. High temperatures, hot winds, and lack of rain left the land parched. That "the Dust Bowl" was an appellation often given the Great Plains is an indicator that I didn't invent the name.

More than once, when we lived on the Schurock place, we were blanketed to a scary degree by dust storms. On one of these occasions Ward and I were in a metal grain bin southwest of the house at midafternoon. Though there were no clouds as such, the wind began to roar and the sky suddenly turned pitch black. We held hands and ran to the house, though we could see nothing, not even the house. Dad was working in a field just to the north of the house and made his way home by following the barbed wire fence that defined the field. Mother put a lamp in the north window, but Dad wasn't able to see it. When he got home, his clothes, thighs, and hands were badly ripped from the barbed wire. Our hayrack was blown half a block to the east; we figured it had blown over our heads as Ward and I made our way to the house from the grain bin.

By the time the storm was over, the sky was a brilliant red, spawning rumors that the world was coming to an end. Eerie as the color was, a more believable explanation was that the wind had blown red dirt from Oklahoma into adjacent Kansas.

By mid-spring of 1932 our family had moved back to Nebraska, this time to Arapahoe in Furnas County, about twenty miles west of Atlanta. Our parents rented a farm a few miles south of Arapahoe, a farm I remember primarily for its flies. The summer was hot and dry. To try for some semblance of coolness, Mother had Ward and me help her wet sheets and hang them on outside doors and windows—wherever and whenever a slight but always hot breeze lazed its way toward the house.

In the 1930s the whole middle of the country, at least, was subjected to hot winds, grasshoppers, flies, and a lack of rain. In short, the weather and its consequences made life anywhere, and certainly on a farm, hard to enjoy. It was in those years that I became firm in my conviction not to grow up to be a farmer.

The fourth grade was tougher because of the midterm move to Arapahoe, but I made good friends and had fun. That's when I met Edgar Reed. He was the tallest and gangliest and slowest boy in our fourth grade class. Katherine Kuska and Allie Findley were the two teachers of the fourth, fifth, and sixth grades. Their procedure for giving math quizzes was to have us do the problems at our desks, and as soon as one of us finished, he or she was to go to the blackboard and write his or her name. The result was that Edgar would almost always be confronted with a sea of names on the board by the time he got there. He'd pick up a little piece of chalk, squeeze it between the thumb and forefinger of his hand, and, no matter how many names were there or how close to the top of the board the top name was, he would stretch up and slip in just above that top name the words "Ed Reed." Some of us would giggle or sniff because he did that. Now I think it was his way of saying he wanted to feel he was special, at the top of the heap, in *some* way.

I didn't see much of Edgar over the next few years, not until we were pin setters at the duck-pin alley in Arapahoe.

A perpetually prominent feature of Arapahoe is the river that runs by it. The Republican River has its origin in eastern Colorado, enters Nebraska at the state's southwest corner, wanders eastward near Nebraska's southern border, eases northward along a line of small towns, including Cambridge, Arapahoe, Edison, and Oxford, for some two hundred miles, and at about Superior dips into Kansas to stay. At Arapahoe low to moderate bluffs provide the boundaries of a valley rich in black dirt that would yield abundant crops of wheat, corn, alfalfa, and soybeans when it received a decent share of rain or when irrigation made its way to Nebraska. The population was 1,017 when we arrived and has maintained a commendable stability ever since, unlike many small towns of the region.

The flood struck on the evening of Friday, May 31, 1935, gathering its volume and force from the river's tributaries in eastern Colorado and western

Nebraska, including the Arikara, Frenchman, Stinking Water, Red Willow, Medicine, Muddy, and Turkey Creeks. Before sundown Arapahoe was isolated; the roads south, west, and east of town were closed. By Sunday devastation was widespread up and down the river, west and east, but Arapahoe proper was left intact. Elsewhere houses, animals, railroad tracks, farm implements—anything in the way—were overwhelmed. Headlines declared:

**Flood Sweeps Valley; Six Perish in Water—
Mill Employees Spend Two Days without Food or
Water as River Roars—Communications Cut Off
and Homes Swept Away amid Terrific Damage.**[1]

A long-lasting effect of the flood was the creation of a series of dams, lakes, and reservoirs promoted by the ardent efforts of Congressman Carl T. Curtis, beginning with the Harlan County Dam and followed by six dams along the river in southwestern Nebraska.[2]

Arapahoe got its name from a small band of Indians who wintered in the valley in 1871.[3] I've learned that the Arapaho tribe is generally pictured as having been prominent in the area of my hometown, though I never saw any Indians in or around Arapahoe. The Pawnee, I understand, were east of the town, the Cheyenne were to the north, the Ute to the west, and the Kiowa to the south. A monument marks the spot of a battle between the Pawnee and the Sioux, known as the 1873 Battle of Massacre Canyon, near Trenton, Nebraska,[4] some sixty-four miles west of Arapahoe. Neither did I ever see any buffalo in or around Arapahoe or in Nebraska, though buffalo were said to have roamed the region before the turn of the twentieth century.

When I joined the series of trials arising from the Wounded Knee takeover of 1973, I had no inkling that I had American Indian blood. During those trials, which lasted a year, I saw and heard many American Indians testify. At one point fourteen chiefs and headmen were seated in the jury box awaiting their turn to testify about the 1868 treaty between the Sioux and the United States. Someone asked if a photograph could be taken of that scene. I said yes, and the photograph appears now on the back of a book about the hearing.[5] Years later, probably in the mid-1980s, my brother Ward sent me newspaper clippings and bits of documents suggesting that our mother's father was the son of a full-blooded Choctaw woman named Naomi Leach. My mother's father was Absalom Vallandingham (known as A. V.) Irelan (who spelled his last name without an ending "d," although my mother always added it). As I study that photograph now I can see that Granddad Irelan could fit neatly into the jury-box picture. His face was deeply lined and dark-skinned. His nose was somewhat beaklike and ample. His hair was thin and gray. His voice was deep, supporting his strong and commanding appearance. He was probably not over five-feet-ten and maybe 180 pounds when I knew him.

Granddad Irelan grew up in Ohio, where he worked in coal mines, belonged at one time to the Ku Klux Klan, later moved to Nebraska, settled near Atlanta until he moved to Arapahoe, and was a rancher or farmer. I think he had a reputation of being something of a scalawag, probably no worse. He went broke raising cattle and farming, and came to live with us when I was in high school. His bedroom was fashioned from our front porch, where he spent most of his time. He read a good deal, went to church rarely, laughed heartily, smoked a stinkpot of a pipe, and often played cards at the local tavern and croquet on a sand lot adjacent to the tavern.

By the time he lived with us Granddad Irelan had an old car that no longer would turn to the left. He drove it every weekday morning to the post office downtown to pick up his mail. He would steer the car to the right, round and round, block after block, until he could right-turn it into a diagonal parking slot in front of the post office. Then he'd get his mail (what little there was of it), back out, and right-turn the car back home. As far as I know he never had a wreck, probably because the drivers in Arapahoe knew that at 9 a.m. A. V. Irelan was on the road, and they gave him his space.

Granddad Irelan's sense of humor can be illustrated by one of his occasional questions to me when I would come home from church. He might ask, "Did the preacher talk about me today?" I'd say, "No, he didn't," and Granddad would say, "He should have. Preachers are supposed to talk about sinners!" I liked Granddad Irelan.

Recently, I happened upon a scrapbook I've kept. Among other things, it holds my elementary school report cards. In glancing through the grades

12. Absalom Vallandingham Irelan, also known as A. V. Irelan, Warren Urbom's grandfather. Photograph in author's possession.

I felt good about what I saw until my eyes stuck on a line in my fourth grade report card: a D in Penmanship. I confess I can't remember all that happened when I took that report card home, but my recreated memory has it about like this: My mother asked, "What's this?"

I answered, "I think it's a D."

"I know, but why?"

"I guess my teachers don't think much of how I write."

"Miss Findley and Miss Kuska?"

"I guess so."

"What do *you* think about your writing?"

"I don't think much of it, either."

"Maybe your dad could help you." So, my father and I had a sit-down. He asked me to write my name. I did.

He asked, "Do you like your name?"

"It's okay."

"Mother and I like it too. If we all think it's nice, don't you think maybe it deserves to look nice?"

"I don't know how to do that."

"Let's see if I can help. Try this: stretch out your fingers all the way. Don't scrunch them up. Then hold the pencil just tight enough so it doesn't slip. And don't move your fingers or your wrist. Move your whole arm. That way you can get full ovals and curves and letters and words."

"If I do that, will Miss Findley and Miss Kuska notice?"

"I don't know. Just try it anyway."

When I think about it now, I am kind of amazed. Here was Dad with his eighth grade education and his big, dirt-farmer hands, a quiet man, telling me about the beauty of words and how to make them look beautiful.

Many years later I was curious about what had happened after our sit-down, so I looked up the report cards again. For the first semester of fifth grade, I got a C in Penmanship; for the second semester I got a B. For the first semester of sixth grade, I got a B; for the second semester I got an A. Miss Findley and Miss Kuska *had* noticed. And just at the end of the line with the A, where a parent had to sign, was "Clarence Urbom" in handsome script.

Recesses at school were taken up with several different activities. Marbles was one. I had so little money I didn't have many good marbles, so I tried to make up for it by beating boys I played with. We played mostly box marbles, I think it was called. A square about a foot on each side was marked out by lines on the ground; marbles were placed inside the square on tiny peaks of dirt, and a player earned the marbles he knocked out of the square without the shooter staying in the square. I was pretty good at it, even against players like Phil Benjamin and Bill and Hugh Harrington, though I lost my fair share too.

Mumble peg was another. We used a jackknife with one blade open and the point of the blade pinned alternately against the hand, wrist, shoulder, and other parts of the body, flipped from a standing position and with varying grips. When the blade stuck into the ground, the player could move on to the next release point. Points were scored by getting the blade stuck in the ground from each designated position in turn. Sometimes the rule was that the losing player had to pull a peg from the ground with his teeth. The winner got three whacks of the knife to drive the peg into the ground. The goal often was to drive the peg deep enough into the ground so that the loser couldn't pull it out with his teeth without getting a taste of dirt. We spent hours on the game.

In sixth grade I began to blossom in spelling. By seventh grade I was chosen, along with Drexel Maaske, to represent Arapahoe in a countywide spelling contest. Drexel had always been a star speller and was surprised when I was selected to join him. We studied hard, or, as we might say because we could spell it, assiduously. Neither of us won the contest, but I at least felt good about being there. I felt sheepish about losing a round on the simple word "status," especially when I had breezed through "sovereign."

On moving into Arapahoe proper our family lived for a short time in a brick house south of the Burlington Railroad tracks. The house was owned by Granddad Irelan. It had the first sidewalk of any house we ever lived in, and it was on that sidewalk that Ward, Bev, and I learned to roller-skate.

On a nameless place just north of the brick house was a giant tree, a cottonwood, that provided a great place for a swing. It also is remembered as the spot where Ward and I had a favorite trick we played on Bev, four years younger than me. Ward or I would convince her that we could show her how to nail a glass of water to the tree trunk. As he or I would hold the nail against the glass, the nail would fall to the ground, and he or I would ask Bev to pick up the nail while he or I continued to hold the glass against the tree. Of course, when she stooped to pick up the nail, the glass would tip and the water would pour out on her neck or back.

Never much of an athlete and shorter and skinnier than all the others, I didn't go out for any organized sports. I played with pick-up teams of softball and football, and was what then was called a halfback in football. I was quick enough and fast enough to run around the line or even through it sometimes, but the likes of burly Jack Slife were something to avoid. I can see him yet, barreling straight at me. I can hear the grunt when he slammed into me. In softball I was a mediocre first baseman, lucky to get chosen at all.

By ninth grade I was into the political whirl. To my surprise I was elected president of the class. The same thing happened in tenth grade, and in eleventh! I didn't really campaign; modesty seemed to suggest not to. The class deserted me on the vote for the twelfth grade class presidency, and Darrell Brown beat me. I confess I wanted *that* presidency even more than the others, though I don't know why. Just the honor, I guess.

I worried quite a bit. Polio was on everybody's mind, and mastoid infection or mastoiditis (I'm not sure which it was, or if there was a difference) hovered like a deadly snake, ready to snap us. I feared every tiny ache in my stomach was appendicitis. None of these struck me, but enough did to kids I knew to keep me worried.

One thing we boys liked to do was watch other kids fight. Sometimes boys more aggressive than I would egg other boys into fighting, even making up stories—lies—to make them mad enough to fight. One Saturday night a bunch of us did that to Max "Gunner" Girch and a boy whose last name I can't remember but whose first name, I think, was Vince. I don't remember the story that we made up, but Gunner finally got to Vince on the sidewalk beside Williams Department Store and swore at him, prompting Vince to go into a crouch and rush Gunner with a rapid set of hooks to the body that were interrupted by one Gunner uppercut to the nose. That ended the fight. A bloody nose was all that resulted, but it seemed to satisfy our curious fascination with the manly art. I never fought—and was very quiet around a set-up fight—for the same reason I didn't date girls in high school: I was too little and too scared.

Money wasn't easy to come by, so I took whatever job I could find. The first was working in a print shop that published a weekly newspaper, the *Public Mirror*. I poured lead, swept the floor, ran errands, and found a better-paying job setting duck pins at the duck-pin alley. I don't remember for sure, but

I think I got about two cents a line for lifting my body with my arms so my feet wouldn't be struck by the flying pins and oncoming pin balls, picking up the pins a bowler had knocked down, putting the pins back on the designated spots, rolling the balls back to the front holder, and repeating the process. It was fun. I worked lots of hours, learned to bowl (duck-pin balls and duck pins are smaller than regular bowling balls and pins), and I made what seemed to a high school boy like pretty good money.

Edgar Reed was a pin setter too, for a while, doing the same things I did. He was a good pin setter. We tried, of course, to outdo each other in resetting the pins in the least amount of time. He was a pretty good duck-pin bowler too, and, because pin setters were allowed to bowl free when we weren't busy, we got to play quite a lot. He called me "War'n," and I called him "Ed." We were friends of a sort, the kind you see accidentally, unless you work together. By then he had dropped out of high school. Eventually, it was said, he was sent to the reform school in Kearney, Nebraska. I never learned why. I never knew anybody else who actually went to reform school. Maybe that's part of why I mention him. But it's also because he seemed to be more determined than most to play the cards he was dealt, shabby and unskilled as they seemed to be. Being around him made me remember the biblical saying, "Every one to whom much is given, of him will much be required."[6] Maybe it worked the other way too.

I got a paper route when I was about fourteen, delivering the *Omaha World-Herald*. I generally carried the papers in a bag on the handlebars of my bike, but in case of bad weather Mother would take me around in our car. During one contest I won enough points to get taken by train to Lincoln to see the University of Nebraska play the University of Pittsburgh in football. "Mailman" Jones was Pittsburgh's star runner, and Nebraska couldn't stop him often enough to keep from getting beaten. That was my first experience with Nebraska football, and I was stuck.

The last job I had while still in high school was at Williams Bros. General Store, run by Bede and Speck Williams. Bob Snyder and I tested cream, candled eggs, cut meat, and sometimes stayed until midnight to carry people's groceries to their cars.

To take the place of sports in high school I did a lot of activities, such as being editor in chief of the *Tomahawk*, our class's contribution to the *Public Mirror*; editor in chief of our senior yearbook, called *Iagoo*; president of the band; member of the boy's glee club and the mixed chorus; and more. I kept busy, and I loved it all, except the music.

From fourth grade on I took music lessons. For a while I took violin. We didn't have the money to buy a nice violin, but my parents found an old one somewhere for, I think, ten dollars, and bought it for Ward. Ward used it a year or so and passed it on to me. I struggled with the violin for three or four years. Harvey Corn and Harry Geiger, the school's music teachers, were very patient with me. I felt sorry for them, but at least they got paid for what they did. As far as I could tell, I didn't get a thing but squawks. Gwen Stevens, our cousin, tired of her alto saxophone, so I was the lucky one to get it. I played it—I played *at* it—in my high school years in marching band and the school orchestra. I'm sorry to say I was the happiest kid in town when I finally finished high school so I didn't have to try to make music anymore. Persistence may be wonderful, but it wasn't enough when the talent was weak.

One lucky thing came out of my saxophone experience, though. In my junior year I was selected to participate in a music clinic in Norton, Kansas, with kids from Arapahoe and other nearby towns. Arrangements were made for us to stay the night at selected houses of resident volunteers. I was dropped off at the house designated for me, met my house mother, put my suitcase and saxophone in the bedroom, and decided to see the downtown of Norton. An hour or so later I had seen the stores and other places of interest and walked back toward the designated house, but soon realized I didn't know the address, the location, the name of the family who lived there, or anything else about the place. By then darkness was coming on.

I had had nothing to do with making trip arrangements. I had no idea where the other students from Arapahoe were staying, where our music teacher was staying, who from Norton was in charge, *or anything*! I wandered around for a while more, trying to think of something worthwhile to do. I could think of nothing. The sidewalks were dark, and I was very lonely. I decided I had to walk up to a house, any house, and beg for help. Maybe somebody there knew something about this music clinic and could help me by some magic to get connected. I memorized the little speech I would give to whoever came to the door, then walked to the porch of a house, climbed the steps, and knocked on the door.

A lady opened the door, looked at me, and said, "Oh, you don't need to knock. Just come on in. Your things are in the bedroom there where you left them." I couldn't believe it. It was a miracle. Small, maybe, but a sure miracle.

Sometime around junior high school I found that words were a special attraction. I loved to read the dictionary. Almost any word would lead to the need to explore another, and then another, and so on. Ada Morris was one of the encouragers of such behavior, and she expanded the appeal of words to speaking and writing.

The writing came first. For an English assignment in my sophomore year I wrote a little story called "Everlasting Life." I think it was about death, and I think it had to do with a young man who waded into the ocean, probably to take his own life. Miss Morris asked me to read it to the class. I did, and her response was quiet and confident and so moving I can't describe it. But I haven't forgotten her saying something like, "When I am an old lady, sitting on my porch, rocking, I'll be reading a novel. I'll take off my glasses, close the book, and say to myself, 'I remember this author. I knew him when he first read to us one of his short stories.' And I'll smile."

I was embarrassed, a little. But I was thrilled too, right down the middle of my back.

Miss Morris touted public speaking too, and theater. The towns around Arapahoe had declamatory contests that included readings (speeches) and one-act plays. In my sophomore, junior, and senior years I gave a reading (humorous or oratorical) and acted in a play. I did well enough each year that I got a superior rating for the reading and a best actor award for the play. We also had a class play in our junior and senior years. I had a lead in the junior class play but was not chosen for any part in the senior class play. I never felt the call to a lifetime of the theater, thank goodness. Public speaking, though, was irresistible.

Graduation came in May 1942. I was salutatorian (second scholastically) at our graduation ceremony, Ara Jane Hill having bested me in the grade race.

World War II had begun the previous December with the bombing of Pearl Harbor. The next morning our high school assembly listened by radio to President Franklin D. Roosevelt's request to Congress to declare a state of war. Our patriotism went sky high. For example, we forewent our senior class's Sneak Day because it typically entailed a secretly planned automobile trip, most commonly to Beaver City, some fifteen miles away. Gasoline was on the list of things to conserve, so we did.

Our graduating high school class had seventeen boys and seventeen girls. When we gathered for our fiftieth reunion in 1992, seventeen remained—three boys and fourteen girls. Thirteen of the boys (maybe fourteen, but I have no word of one, Paul Pilkington) had served in the military during World War II, two of whom, my cousin Ernest Irelan and Jerry Hill, were killed in the line of duty.

Upon finishing high school I was sixteen, working at Williams Store, not old enough to be drafted, not affluent enough to enroll in a college, and not satisfied enough to stay in Arapahoe. Paul Pilkington, a friend and high school classmate, and I planned to go to Denver to begin our independent lives. My parents didn't balk, except at our plan to leave in early December. My mother particularly wondered why we would go just prior to my birthday and Christmas. We didn't have a good reason, except that we were eager to feel free. "Pilk" decided within a few days of our planned leaving not to go. I was disappointed and frightened without his company, but I was hot to trot, so my parents took me to Oxford, fourteen miles to the east, where I kissed my parents good-bye and spent a nervous but exciting and determined night on the uncomfortable seat of a Burlington Railroad car. Arrival in Denver was, as I remember, at about 9 a.m. on a dry, cool day.

From a *Rocky Mountain News* "Rooms for Rent" column I spotted an ad for a room on Washington Street at about East 15th. On asking I learned the location was only about twenty blocks away, and, not knowing anything about the streetcar system or routes, I walked, carrying my one small suitcase. Mrs. Harrington, I think her name was, was the lady of the house and showed me a comfortable basement room. I settled in and started looking for a job.

After being unsuccessful for two or three days by studying the want ads, I inquired at an employment agency. The only skills I could report were A's in typing (eighty-seven words a minute), shorthand, and a business law course, all at Arapahoe High School. The interviewer phoned Mr. A. J. Frejeau of Weicker Transfer and Storage Company on Wynkoop Street, told him of me, described me as "bright as a new penny," and set an appointment for as soon as I could get to the Weicker office. Mr. Frejeau, the general manager, greeted me. He said he had nearly given up on me (I'd walked the fifteen blocks), hired me for the OS&D (Overage, Shortage, and Damage) Department, and taught me to figure out the streetcar routes and schedules. I was grateful.

The work at Weicker was good for me. One older man, twenty-nine-year-old Harland Krapp, formerly of Grand Island, Nebraska, and the son of Grand Island's chief of police, and I *were* the OS&D Department. We were to field reports of incorrect shipments of goods carried by truck around the Rocky Mountain area, resulting in overages, shortages, or damaged goods. I liked the work and the people I worked with and those in the nearby Claim Department. I felt lucky. I was especially proud that I could afford to buy and send to my parents a chime clock for a Christmas present. I have kept it since my parents' deaths. It chimes in the main office of my chambers.

On the day before Christmas I didn't have to work, so in the afternoon I enjoyed my favorite pastime—going to a movie. On leaving the theater I bought a tamale from a street vendor, and by the time I got to my room (by then I had moved into the Page Hotel, closer to work) I was sick to my stomach. I went to bed and slept the night.

The next day I received a telephone call from my mother. Long-distance telephone calls were a rarity, perhaps because of the cost, perhaps because, for whatever reason, they were generally used only for emergencies. My mother explained that she had tried to reach me earlier in the day, but the lady who answered the call at the hotel said that I wasn't in, that I had come in the night before, was drunk, had paid my bill, and had left with some friends. My mother said she hadn't mentioned this to my father, but she suspected he and she would decide that I should come home to stay for a time.

My mother was mortified, as I was. As insistently as I could, I told her of my having eaten a bad tamale that made me sick, that when I came in I did not pay my bill, that I was not drunk, that indeed I never in my life had had as much as a swallow of beer or liquor, that upon getting to the hotel I went directly to my room and slept all night, sick to my stomach. Such a story sounds suspicious, but it's all I had. And it was true.

As soon as we quit talking on the telephone, I went to the manager's office and told the manager my story. She listened but said only, "I don't know anything about it. I didn't say anything to anybody about you, and I don't know whether you were drunk or not." I begged her to call my mother and tell her that, but she said she wouldn't. My distress brought no help from her.

Mother and I talked a few more times, and I wrote her, imploring her to believe me. I think she did. She let me stay!

In August 1943 it was obvious that my bone structure had reached maturity, and Dr. Wilcox recommended replacement of my blind eye with an artificial one. He performed the surgery, removing the eyeball. I was sedated, but I don't know with what. I felt no pain but could hear the sucking sound when the eyeball was lifted from its socket.

The eye socket healed quickly, and I went to Denver Optic Company for the artificial eye. The selection process of these ready-made eyes was to pick out one from a drawer of dozens, trying to match the color, size, and shape of the good eye. The first few I got were glass and very fragile. They cost five dollars apiece. Precautions I took included wearing eyeglasses to protect against the glass eye's breaking while in the socket and to keep the natural eye from being injured by bumps or flying objects.

As soon as I reached eighteen, in December 1943, I registered for military service. But my half-blindness was an obstacle. I had heard that one-eyed people couldn't enlist; I didn't try to enlist, so I'm not sure. Nor do I remember my classification by the draft board leading up to and during World War II, except that it left me eligible, at most, for "limited" service, whatever that would entail. On a couple of occasions after registering, I was called upon to report in the early morning, and on each occasion my eyesight was checked and I was released to return to work at Weicker.

By now I had gotten a promotion to Weicker's Claim Department, where the same sort of work was done, except it involved claims filed after OS&D had made an investigation and had tried to correct erroneous delivery or damaged goods. The pay was okay. I lived pretty simply, worked a lot, studied a fair amount, and enrolled in a night course in accounting at Barnes

School of Business. My closest friend was Harland Krapp. I didn't date; I didn't know anybody to date, but I was looking.

On March 11, 1944, I was again to appear for word about draft possibilities. I arrived at about 8 a.m., was herded without explanation with half a dozen other young men into an army van, and was whisked off to Fort Logan, just west of Denver, where I was inducted into the army.

I was stunned. Among other concerns, I knew that my employer expected me to be at the office that morning. As soon as I had my hair buzzed short and was dressed in my newly issued uniform, I made a telephone call to Mr. Frejeau, giving him my sad tale of being called into service and leaving Weicker shorthanded. I apologized. He was, again, gracious and wished me well. Such occurrences were not unusual, he let me know, because young men were often drafted from their jobs. I hoped it was not often with as little advance notice as I had received. I didn't fault the army for my experience; I thought I probably was careless in my attention to its notices to appear at the draft board's office.

Besides calling Mr. Frejeau, I called Harland Krapp. I asked him to go to my room at 736 Corona Street, pack my belongings into my suitcase, and ship it to my parents in Arapahoe. He said he would, and he did. I told him there was about eighty dollars in the drawer in my nightstand and asked him to send that to me. I have not seen him or the eighty dollars since. Nor have I heard from or of him. So be it.

I did go as soon as possible to see Mr. Frejeau, as well as my coworkers Howard Hicks, Bill Nystrom, and Ed Risley, after I had been restricted to the base for the regulation three weeks. This time I noticed that the workforce at the Weicker office was entirely composed of men older than thirty-nine, the top of the draft-eligible age at the time.

Life as a private in the army wasn't so bad, really. I got twenty-one dollars a month, reasonable food, a bunk to sleep on, basic training, whatever exercise I chose to get, a bundle of assignments I liked, and the climate of the Colorado Rockies. My best friend in those early days was Bob Peck from Riverton, Wyoming, who faked his ability to see well so he could be sent abroad. After his service abroad, he returned to Wyoming and became a newspaper editor and publisher.

I was stationed at Fort Logan, Colorado, all the time I was in the service, except for the month of February 1945, when I was on temporary duty at the Adjutant General's School at Fort Sam Houston in San Antonio, Texas, for study in business administration. Chuck Morrison and I were the two from our unit who attended. The purpose was to learn more about the army's way of administering a reception station and a separation center. I took it seriously and was rewarded by getting the highest cumulative grade of the class.

For nearly two years I was assigned to an office in the Reception Station in Fort Logan, recording in service records information about the inductees. The last two or three months were spent at the Separation Center at Fort Logan, helping prepare the papers for discharge of those who were finishing their service.

I rose in rank at a good pace, moving from private to private first class, to corporal, sergeant, staff sergeant, and technical sergeant in the two-plus years I was in the army. My Separation Qualification Record shows that I was discharged on "17 Apr 1946"; it lists my title as "administrative noncommissioned officer" and describes my duties: "Supervised the activities of 25 enlisted men and 25 civilian employees in the administration of personnel records, correspondence and the preparation of periodic informational surveys for the Adjutant General's Office. Prepared financial statements and paid bills from the unit fund."

That's a pretty good description of what I did. It was office work. I wasn't eligible for overseas service or Officer's Candidate School because of my blind eye. My Honorable Discharge shows my army serial number as 37361504. At separation I was 5' 8" tall and weighed 150 pounds. That represented a growth of two or three inches in height and several pounds added after high school.

One of my broadening experiences at Fort Logan was becoming acquainted with Tom Nakamura, a Japanese American from California. His parents were interned at a relocation center throughout World War II, in keeping with congressional legislation that was enacted over fear of possible disloyalty of Japanese residents, particularly those living on the West Coast. I thought I could understand the fear, but felt sorrow for Tom's family. Tom was a splendid young man who enlisted in the army and spent several months with my outfit. We were in the same barracks, often ate together, and had great fun playing outdoor basketball one-on-one and indoor Ping-Pong. I particularly remember his breezy disposition and smashing forehand. Whether he was ever allowed to go overseas, I don't know.

Another character in my military life was Joe McGrew, by then a thirty-eight-year-old who wanted me to know the ins and outs of life without being tangled up by them. He taught me how to drink beer and cautioned me against smoking too much. He was the first person I knew, aside from myself, who had an artificial eye. He wrote a column called "Sergeant X" for our Fort Logan newspaper and, when he was discharged from the service, handed the job over to me. The weekly column featured the scuttlebutt of the camp and hovered behind the secrecy of its writer's identity. I enjoyed writing it but wasn't good at finding all the juiciest news.

Once I wrote critically of an officer's treatment of an enlisted man, and in retort—so the rumor went—I was threatened with court-martial if I didn't write a retraction. I didn't write a retraction. Whether the threat was real or imagined I never knew, but I felt a real tug toward supporting fairness for somebody in a scrap with an authority figure.

Watching Joe McGrew handle the fact of his artificial eye may have played a part in my efforts to control my head and eye movements to try to have both eyes looking in the same direction at the same time. Others who had artificial eyes, like Bill Redfern, I noticed, did try to do that. Joe's good eye flitted from side to side incessantly, with the artificial eye standing virtually still, making a dizzying effect for others looking at him. I vowed to emulate Bill Redfern, but never mentioned the subject to Joe. In all other ways, though, Joe McGrew was a big brother to me.

Artificial eyes began being made of plastic instead of glass while I was in the army. Word came that a dentist had found that plastic eyes were much sturdier than glass eyes and just as easy to mold. I got my first plastic eye at Fitzsimmons General Hospital in Denver at army expense shortly after induction in 1944.

Artificial eyes, at least those made as long ago as the 1940s, and even when plastic improved their toughness and longevity, remained about motionless. By 2000 techniques had changed; now a ball is implanted into the eye socket and a peg is fastened into both the implant and the artificial eye. The muscles surrounding the implant apparently (I've never had an inserted peg because my implant is of the earlier model) are able to provide considerably more control over the eye movement. The earlier model, on the other hand, features an implanted ball, but nothing fastens the ball to the artificial eye. So the sole possibility for eye movement comes from surface muscles of the socket. Those muscles allow slight turning of the artificial eye toward the inside—that is, toward the nose—and virtually none toward the outside. Exacting shape and lightness of weight seem to permit some added movement, but not a lot. Keeping your head straight when looking at people avoids the need for much eye movement. That's what I learned from watching McGrew and Redfern.

Joe McGrew's four rules for drinking beer were:

1. Sip it, don't guzzle it.
2. Drink only enough for a light buzz.
3. Don't mix it with any other intoxicant.
4. Don't go to sleep until the buzz is gone.

Bowling became a feature of my military life at Fort Logan. I wasn't an outstanding bowler, but I was avid and steady enough to hold my own in competitions with both civilian and military teams in the vicinity. For example, an order was entered on March 2, 1946, that sent our team—Ed Hart, Art Hemmy, Bill Gressinger, and me—on temporary duty: "WP o/a 3 Mar 46, Ft Francis E Warren, Wyo, by Govt MT on TTDY for the purpose of participating in bowling match thereat. Upon compl of this TDY (approx 1 day) will ret proper sta, Ft Logan, Colo." We went, we bowled, and we returned, on and from other trips too, but none as distant, I think, as Fort Francis E. Warren in Wyoming.

Bowling wasn't my only sporting recreation in the service. Just before I was separated from the army, word came to us at Fort Logan that skis from Fort Carson, near Colorado Springs, were available for our free use, so some buddies and I checked some out and made our way to Berthoud Pass for our first skiing adventure. When I was checking my pair out, I asked, "What if I break them?" The reply was, "They'll break you before you break them."

Not so. At the end of a beginner's struggling day I took a turn at a leap

13. Warren Urbom in uniform, probably in early 1944. Photograph in author's possession.

over a tiny mound and went spinning out of control, landing in a heap, with the front half of my right ski perpendicular to the back half. I was okay. I limped down the rest of the slope as well as I could with my left ski on and my ski-less right foot and leg sinking into the snow knee-deep with every step. That was the extent of my untrained skiing pleasure during my military life.

I dated some in the army. Joe Booher and I double-dated a few times, he dating Pat Burns, I going sometimes with a girl named Lucile something, and sometimes with Bugsy something. Dorothy Ammons was the classiest girl I dated, but I lost track of her when I was discharged from the army.

I served two years, one month, and seven days—from March 11, 1944, to April 17, 1946—in the 1770th Service Command Unit. My only medals were the American Service Medal, World War II Victory Medal, and the Good Conduct Medal.

My brother had enlisted in the Army of the United States Air Corps in January 1943.[7] After completing most of his training in the United States, he was commissioned a second lieutenant and given his wings as a bombardier. He and the other members of his crew were transported by the *Queen Elizabeth*, a "large, fast boat" that zigzagged across the Atlantic without escort, and in six days landed in Scotland. They soon were flown to Bungay, England, where his crew were assigned to the 446th Bomb Group and the 707th Squadron. The plane of which he was the bombardier was a B-24 they named *Tail Wind*. The squadron flew thirty bombing missions over France and Germany.

The first mission was on July 5, 1944, and required aiming at a munitions dump near Paris through a cloud cover so dense the target could not be seen. The results were unknown. The second mission was on July 6, when they hit railroad bridge near Sully, Sur Loire, France.

The only casualty to a crew member happened on July 11, the third mission. Their bombing run had just been completed. Ward, as usual, called for a radio check. All crew members answered, but soon someone called out "Help." It took a few minutes to learn that it was a call from the tail gunner, Sgt. Michael P. Blair. Ward ordered the two waist gunners to pull Blair out of the tail turret, and Ward and the waist gunners gave him artificial respiration for four hours, but without success. Death came from total deprivation of oxygen. The scheduling of a mission the next day was apparently a surprise, but Ward says it was "probably the best thing that could have happened."

Those three missions, and the next three, were significant, but it seems to me that probably the sixth, on July 18, most clearly connected Ward's squadron to the Normandy Invasion, which began on June 6, 1944, the "greatest amphibious landing in history."[8] Ward says that on July 18 his squadron "bombed near Caen in support of ground troops." Another source explains that by July 18 the ground troops had been bogged down partly because of hedgerows and trees three to six feet tall and wide, growing atop dirt terraces and preventing tanks from moving over them, thereby stymieing

14. Ward Urbom, Warren Urbom's brother, in about 1943. Photograph in author's possession.

forward movement by the Allied troops.[9] When the tanks approached the hedgerows, the terraces caused them to "belly up." The Germans from the other side of the hedgerows expected to shoot the tanks' undersides, where there was no metal protection.[10] That hedgerow obstruction was solved by about July 26 during what is known as the "Normandy Breakout."[11]

The last twenty of the crew's missions were flown with Ward's as lead crew, which meant that *Tail Wind* was the first plane into the targeted area and the giver of the clue to the rest of the squadron (squadrons were usually ten planes, and sometimes twelve) as to when all the bombs would be dropped simultaneously.

Ward's crew also had at least one disastrously close call. Before the flight of August 24, 1944, he could not get his plane's bomb sight to operate properly, so his lead plane traded places with the deputy lead plane. The deputy lead plane led the flight, but just as the bombs were dropped, the deputy lead plane took a direct hit. Another source suggests that a plane named

Pistol Packin' Bomma II (US-51278) "received a direct flak hit shortly after dropping its bombs; nine crewmen were killed and 2 were taken prisoner."[12] Whether *Pistol Packin' Bomma II* was the plane that took the hit instead of *Tail Wind* we do not know, but the evidence points that way.

Upon completion of their thirty missions and as a lead crew, *Tail Wind*'s crew was eligible to return to the United States, and Ward chose that option. By then he had been promoted to first lieutenant and twice had been awarded a Distinguished Flying Cross. In November 1944 he was transported by ship to the United States. He was assigned to the base at Midland, Texas, where he trained instructors in navigational and bombardier work.

World War II ended with the surrender of Japan on August 14, 1945, and Ward was discharged four days later. Driving in from the east, he deemed Arapahoe to be "one of the most beautiful sights" he had ever seen. He stayed there, fell in love with Darien Hermes—a high school classmate of mine—married her, earned his baccalaureate and law degrees from the University of Nebraska, and has practiced law in Arapahoe to this day, content in every way. Ward is my family hero.

When I returned to Arapahoe to get on with being a civilian, I had a clear sense that I would find my way back to Colorado, and specifically Denver. I liked the city and the mountains and felt comfortable there. One morning as we sat at breakfast my mother said Dad wanted me to go with him to his work. I asked, "Why?" She said it was so I would see what he did for a living. It still seemed mysterious, but I felt some obligation to be aware, at least, of where the money came from that had supported the family for so many years. I rode with him, finding interesting his newly acquired machinery for moving dirt—two graders, as I thought of them, or motor patrols, as he called them. The experience was new to me.

My father was raised on a farm and farming was natural to him. During the 1930s and early 1940s he found it nearly impossible to fight the combination of drought and economic depression, so we moved to the outskirts of Arapahoe in about 1936 to try some other undertaking. He went on WPA (Works Progress Administration) for a short time, worked for the Burlington Railroad on a gang of laborers, and then at the behest of Merle Adams, a county commissioner, built and graded Furnas County roads.

15. (*Clockwise, from top left*): Ward Urbom, brother; Warren Urbom; Anna Myrl Urbom, mother; Beverly Urbom, sister; Clarence A. Urbom, father. January 1944, after Ward had been commissioned and Warren was soon to enter the army. Photograph in author's possession.

Merle Adams developed his own dirt-moving business and hired my dad to run some of his machinery. By the time I left the army, Dad had graduated to being a dirt-moving equipment owner, starting in debt, I'm sure, but was elated at being not only the owner of machinery, but an employer as well.

He now proposed that I work for him, operating one of the motor patrols, to earn the cost of attending college. He had had but three months of college when he was a young man, had dropped out for want of money, and was eager for his children not to be similarly handicapped. With the GI Bill of Rights providing me three years of stipends at sixty-five dollars a month and what I could earn moving dirt, I might make enough to see me through college. I could see no down side to that.

For the next six summers I learned the fine art of moving dirt: building terraces for farmers, leveling land, building dirt dams, grading and creating roads, bulldozing rocks and trees, and doing whatever was needed to let water be irrigation for parched land. Motor patrols, crawler tractors, front-loading scoops, forks, bulldozers—all played a part in my education, a part I learned to like, hard as it was.

I worked long hours, usually from 6 a.m. to 6:30 p.m., with a half-hour off for lunch. At twelve hours a day, six days a week when the weather didn't prevent it, I could accumulate seventy-two hours in a week's time. The rate of pay was $1.15 or $1.50 an hour, depending on which machine I drove that day, motor grader or crawler-type tractor and scoop. The rates were at least as good as anything else I could have done. I earned enough, supplemented with the GI Bill, to get through all seven of my higher education years without being employed during the school terms. (Well, I did work for a philosophy professor grading test papers one semester, but it hardly counts because, though I did get paid, that wasn't a factor in why I worked—I just enjoyed the job.) From the cessation of classes in the spring to the start of classes in the fall I worked for Dad; the rest of the year was devoted to college.

I sometimes wondered whether Dad expected me to take on his dirt-moving business when I finished the formal education I wanted, but we never talked about it. The job had been a sensible and loving gift from my parents. It let me learn to soar where I chose. I think my parents saw that and felt deeply good about it. I shall forever be grateful for their insight.

3

Looking for Answers and Finding Them

My long hours on dirt-moving equipment the first summer after military service offered time for reflection on the past and thoughtfulness on the future. One day in midsummer I had a religious experience, which I interpreted as a call to the Christian ministry. That led me to Nebraska Wesleyan University in Lincoln. I had received a small scholarship—some $37.50 each year for a maximum of four years—from the Nebraska Association of Church Colleges when I graduated from high school. With that, my eligibility for the GI Bill, and the money I was earning from working for Dad, I felt comfortable planning entry at college.

At Nebraska Wesleyan I learned to think more than I thought I could, to care more than I thought I should, and to give more than I knew I had. Four years of competitive debate—where I had to be prepared to build a case for and a case against each side of the topic at hand—strongly pointed to the keystone of debate: the strengths and weaknesses of all sides of any issue must be fully and fairly examined, evaluated, and applied. I have strived to make that the keystone of my judicial arch.

Extracurricular activities were good and plentiful at Nebraska Wesleyan. I was elected president of the Student Senate for my junior and senior years and was active in other leadership groups, including Phi Kappa Phi, Blue Key, and Pi Kappa Delta.

In the early fall of 1948, when classes resumed after the summer recess, I was approached by Sara Jean Hoffman, education director for First Methodist Church, which was just across the street from Nebraska Wesleyan. As a result of that brief, twenty-second conversation, my whole life whirled in new directions. My journal reported the sendoff on October 9, 1948: "Tomorrow Joyce Crawford and I are to lead a discussion on 'How to Get Along with the Opposite Sex' for a group of youngsters." The next day's journal entry announced the successful discussion with the youth and picked up the subtle nudging of destiny's onslaught: "Pleased, relieved and suddenly famished, Joyce and I made our way to the Mayfair for dinner. Maybe the shrimp was poor, but the conversation was sparkling and the girl effervescent. When I suggested . . . a show . . . she . . . consented, and we viewed *The Search* with Montgomery Clift. Great it was." The entry continued, "I suppose there are more natural, clever, sincere, considerate, and sparkling girls, but I don't know where."

The months hurried by, and Joyce and I wasted no time. Within five months I, at least, was in a quandary. I felt we needed to be apart for a time to analyze our feelings and recognize reality. I was twenty-three, with another four years to go before I would finish undergraduate and graduate schools. I knew I was in love with Joyce, but couldn't afford a wife. She agreed that we needed time apart, and had been prepared to suggest it if I didn't. So we stopped dating.

It wasn't easy or fun. We both tried dating others, but nothing much came of that. Fall came and we returned to Nebraska Wesleyan for my senior year and her junior year. Dean Lanning, my roommate at Lillian and Bill Williams's home, was a friend of Joyce's too. He asked me whether I intended to date Joyce again. My response was that I thought I shouldn't unless I decided to ask her to marry me. He said he doubted that was necessary, but I thought it probably was at least fair.

One morning I saw her walking from the Willard Sorority house, where she lived, to Old Main, and her very visage sent me over the edge. I think I decided in that moment that I wanted to be with her the rest of my life. It wasn't that we hadn't been around each other. We were both on the Student Senate, and we had been in the same meetings, but I guess we made a point of being careful not to interact much. But on that particular morning at that particular place her simple walking along the sidewalk made me wilt. So I called her for a date, and she accepted. We gradually resumed regular dating and before long were again into deep breathing and hot panting. On January 19, 1949, I told her I was in love with her. She deferred, saying she wanted to think about how she felt. A month or two later—we think on the 19th of the month, probably March—she said she loved me too. I asked her then to marry me, but she wouldn't make a commitment just yet. In mid-April she accepted my proposal, and we announced our engagement on May 19 at a Willard Sorority banquet.

Wedding plans were made for August a year later (on the 19th, naturally) to allow time for her to finish Nebraska Wesleyan and for me to get through the first year of seminary. By then I had enrolled in Garrett Theological Seminary at Northwestern University in Evanston, Illinois, intending to begin classes in the fall of 1950, having shifted again from law.

I wasn't the smartest student in undergraduate school, but I worked hard. My grades for the four years were at the top of the heap, high enough to try for graduating with honors. That required special written and oral examinations. The written part went all right, so I took the oral examination before a panel of professors of, I believe, a major and a minor. For purposes of the honors examination, I chose philosophy and religion, one of my two majors, and speech, one of my minors.[1] Dr. Charles Patterson, head of the Philosophy Department of the University of Nebraska, and Dr. John Rosentrater, head of the Department of Philosophy and Religion at Nebraska Wesleyan, as well as Dr. Enid Miller Hoffman, head of the Department of Speech at Nebraska Wesleyan, and perhaps others that I do not now recall, were on the panel.

The questions and answers seemed to go pretty well, except for two things. First, at one point Doc Miller asked me what the purpose of speech is. I recalled her teaching us in my freshman year that the purpose of speech is "to get from the audience what you want." At the honors examination, I was skittish about answering differently from her teaching, but I thought for a moment or two and then said, "The purpose of speech is to get from the audience what you want," and then I added, "and to give to the audience what you have to give." I wasn't sure I should say that, but I did. In a flash, Doc Miller slapped my knee and said, "Attaboy, Bommy!"[2] A ton of relief came from that response. The experience seems like a trifle now, but it felt big at the time.

The second moment of anguish came when Professor Patterson asked me for my opinion of personalism. The truth was I knew virtually nothing of it. I said so and explained that I was still in the stage of trying to understand many of the philosophical varieties, rather than to evaluate them, so I had developed no opinion of personalism and would need to later. I didn't feel comfortable with that answer and said so to Dr. Rosentrater the next day. He said the panel had discussed the incident and had agreed that the examination was finished before the subject of personalism came up, and it was not treated as a part of my evaluation. Again, relief! Over fifty years later, I have now been told by a former student of Dr. Patterson's that personalism was Dr. Patterson's philosophical specialty. I hadn't known that, but I could not have answered the question any other way.

I learned a few days later that I would graduate with an AB degree "with highest distinction," the first student in eight years to do so, and would receive the Phi Kappa Phi award for ranking first in the class for the four-year record. It felt very, very good.

During the spring of my senior year, Doc Miller queried me about entering an oratorical contest, but I wasn't attracted to it until she said there was money to be earned by winning. With an engagement ring in the offing, I entered, and Doc was my shepherd.

The subject was James Madison, the sponsor was Hearst Newspapers, the date of the Chicago area tournament was April 12, 1950, the place Orchestra Hall in Chicago, and the possible reward a $1,000 bond for national winners. I thought it was worth a shot.

My theme, as reported by the *Chicago Herald-American*, was "unity within diversity" and "the balance between majority rule and minority rights."[3] The newspaper went on to report, "Urbom accompanied by the instructor, Dr. Enid Miller, head of the college's speech department, arrived in Chicago under dramatic circumstances. . . . When their plane from Omaha was delayed by engine trouble and bad weather, airport officials told the pilot a large audience was waiting in Orchestra Hall to hear Urbom speak.

. . . The prize-winning young orator was then rushed by special car, with Dr. Miller, to the auditorium, where he gave his address 10 minutes later."

I won the college division in Chicago, receiving a $250 savings bond, and went on to Detroit a week later for the Midwest Zone finals at the Detroit Institute of Arts. I lost the Detroit contest but received a $50 savings bond for the effort.

I was elated overall. I had earned $300 in savings bonds, enough to buy Joyce an engagement ring but probably not a cent to spare, even at 1950 prices.[4]

My Nebraska Wesleyan experience ended with two majors: one in philosophy and religion, the other in history. I struggled about my career choices: the Christian ministry? journalism? law? I vacillated, even after finishing at Nebraska Wesleyan. I spent one summer at Iliff School of Theology in Denver instead of working for my father. That summer in seminary convinced me that the Christian ministry was not for me. I applied to three law schools for admission. The University of Nebraska accepted me. The University of Michigan accepted me. Harvard University ignored me. Once I enrolled at the University of Michigan, I vacillated no more, and have never regretted the finality of the decision.

I am not sure what combination of events caused law to be my final choice of professions. The two months in seminary afforded time to ponder, and I made use of it. I reflected that *words* are an undeniable feature of my makeup. Ada Morris and Allegra Morrison had inspired me by reminding me of that. *Speaking* energizes me. Four years of college forensics had proved that. *Competition* is strongly inbred in me. Like Edgar Reed, I play the cards I've been dealt. I have a passion for theology, but the emphasis at Iliff at that time was pastoral counseling, and by the end of the summer I was sure that pastoral counseling was not for me. I love to come to *endings*, and I felt counselors never came to endings. Lawyers, on the other hand, bring conflicts to an end. Maybe that was the defining certainty for me. God couldn't have been serious about wanting someone with my conclusional temperament to suffer a lifetime of inconclusive programs.

That was perfectly clear to me, and I felt no guilt or misgivings, but I hesitated because Joyce and her parents—especially her parents—were

16. Charles C. Crawford, Joyce Urbom's father. Photograph by Kline Studio, Norfolk, Nebraska, in author's possession.

17. Florence Burtis Crawford, Joyce Urbom's mother. Photograph by Kline Studio, Norfolk, Nebraska, in author's possession.

under the assumption I'd be a pastor, and Charles and Florence Crawford had had good experiences with pastors and only bad ones with lawyers. Nonetheless Joyce was accepting of my explanation, and her parents were kind in their willingness to give me the benefit of the doubt for the rest of their lives.

Joyce capped her senior year at Nebraska Wesleyan by being elected Ideal Plainswoman of 1951, signifying that she was the ideal woman to be on the campus. She was everything any college campus could want: beautiful, intelligent, exuberant, a leader.

My first year in law school was challenging and disappointing at the same time. Not only was Joyce's cheerfulness missing, but my mind was not connecting with the legal concepts being presented. Moreover my right eye, the good one, was affected by some malady. I don't know what it was, but

18. Warren Urbom and Joyce Crawford, married August 19, 1951, in Grand Island, Nebraska. Photograph by Vieregg Studio, Grand Island, Nebraska.

it manifested itself in a painful irritation, like sand in the eye. The Student Health Center treated me weekly with Aureomycin but to no apparent effect. Sunlight virtually blinded me; I wore dark glasses but still bent my head downward constantly to avoid light. The thought passed my mind that I was being punished for deserting the ministry, but I fought the idea as preposterous and un-Godlike. Then, in March, seven months after arriving at the first class at the law school, the fog of my mind, the infection of my eye, and the blockage to understanding the legal concepts dissipated. The world turned but no longer whirled. Fortunately no grades were assessed for any class given the first year until the final examination at the end of the second semester. I recovered, received satisfactory grades, and was assured entry into second-year classes in the fall.

During the summer of 1951, following the end of my first year of law school, I worked for Dad, building dams and terraces, and Joyce worked as a counselor at Camp Merri-Mac at Black Mountain in North Carolina. The wedding invitations were mailed from the camp site, and most of the wedding arrangements were made by her sister Phyllis Schmidt in Grand Island, Nebraska. The wedding was in Trinity Methodist Church in Grand Island, presided over by Dr. Alva Clark, who had been pastor at the church in Beatrice, Nebraska, where Joyce lived in her Wesleyan years. Arrangements were perfect, execution was nearly perfect, the bride was radiant (sobbing throughout the ceremony, so she could barely say the vows loud enough to be heard), and we sped away in our 1942 Chevrolet, affectionately known as the Bronze Chariot, with wheel caps clattering from rocks supplied by Kenneth Schmidt and other sly and unrevealed groomsmen. We spent our first night together in a motel in Lincoln, slightly dismayed that we were unable to lose our virginities. The car carried us on to Evanston, Illinois, the next day to the Orrington Hotel. I had a bad cold that compelled me to ask Joyce to drive through Chicago to Evanston. She was reluctant because, having been licensed only a few weeks, she had almost no driving experience and had never driven with a stick shift. But, true to her adventurous disposition, she took the wheel and drove faultlessly for miles through the heavy Lakeshore Drive traffic.

We had planned to spend time at Niagara Falls, but were so anxious to get to the apartment I had chosen in Ann Arbor that we decided to forgo Niagara for a year. The apartment was not a hit. It had been a two-car garage, rearranged to include a living-dining room, a bedroom, a tiny and narrow kitchen, and a bit of a bathroom. It was instantly obvious to Joyce that the apartment would not do, so a month later we moved to 514 Sixth Street, where we stayed for the next two years, though invaded soon by fleas from a previous tenant's dog. Fumigation solved the problem.

My second year in law school was better, much better than the first. I loved having Joyce there, studied hard (she says she saw only the back of my head the whole year), and flourished. Joyce was hired to teach girls' physical education at Walled Lake High School, a consolidated system of 3,200 students.

During the first year I had participated in Case Clubs, in which we presented appellate arguments before student judges. In the second year I was a presiding judge of one of the clubs, Christiancy Case Club. Second- and third-year students could qualify to write for the *Michigan Law Review,* published quarterly, and I did.[5] Senior editors were chosen for the third year, and I served in that capacity in 1952–53.

Socially Joyce and I had a group of law school friends and their wives.[6] I was also invited to join Barristers, a club with little or no purpose except to have fun, and Joyce and I had an occasional party with the members. Bridge was a popular game for us, but the new object of our fascination was television. One of our couple friends, Al and Ellie Feldman, had the first television set we had ever watched, and we watched it some with them. We bought our first TV set shortly before the end of our law school experience.

Women at the University of Michigan were not welcome to enter the Michigan Union by the front door; only the side doors were open to them. We thought the treatment foolish, but gave no serious thought to challenging the legality of it.

One of the early truisms given us by one of the professors in law school was that in the end C students would probably become practicing attorneys, B students would become judges, and A students would become professors. In my case this proved to be accurate. I was a B student, good enough under the Michigan University grading system to allow me to graduate with honors, reflected by a JD degree with distinction instead of an LLB, but not high enough to be ushered into the Order of Coif.

As the end of the three years of law school drew near, Joyce and I pondered where to go. Until then we had figured it would be Colorado, because I had enjoyed living there before and during my army days. Cal Hudson was a good friend and had asked me to join him in setting up a practice in Royal Oak, Michigan, his hometown, near Detroit. That was enticing. Colorado had little to draw us there except the mountains. Nebraska offered the appropriate distance to both sets of parents—mine in Arapahoe, 180 miles west of Lincoln, and Joyce's in Norfolk, 100 miles north of Lincoln.

When we applied a mathematical formula to the issues, Lincoln won by a landslide. It offered everything but a job.

So I applied for a job with law firms in several places in Colorado and Nebraska. I took the offer of Baylor, Evnen and Baylor in Lincoln, not only because it was an offer, but also because it included what I strongly wanted: a chance to learn trial technique from an expert.

4

Practicing Law

F. B. Baylor, the senior partner of Baylor, Evnen and Baylor and looking to retire from trial work, had the reputation of being a master litigator. Another factor in our deciding to accept his offer was the metropolitan lifestyle of Michigan. Lincoln was slower, not really leisurely, but tamer, less ruthless. If I decided to try politics, Nebraska, I thought, would be compatible. I had been a registered Independent, but my friend John Wolfe led me to be enamored of Adlai Stevenson. Neither of us worked for Stevenson, but Joyce and I switched our registrations in Michigan to Democrat so we could vote for him in the primary as well as the general election. Nebraska's political edge was clearly Republican; Michigan's was Democratic. The political climate of prospective places wasn't a factor we dropped into our mathematical system, and I don't think it was a factor in our decision. But we bared the Republican cheek and stayed with it through the ensuing years when we moved to Lincoln, though we voted as often, probably, for Democratic as for Republican candidates.

It was May 4, 1953, before I went to Lincoln at the Baylor firm's invitation for a final interview, which secured the job. Classes, as I remember, were about to be over. Joyce and I didn't wait for the grades or for the commencement ceremony. We loaded everything we owned into our new 1951 Ford, including our very first TV set (which occupied the right front seat of the five-passenger car), and set sail for Lincoln.

Three partners comprised the firm of Baylor, Evnen and Baylor, known around town as the Baylor Firm. F. B. (Bill) Baylor dominated; he owned all the books, furniture, machines, and other property. He was of spindly build and medium height with grayish wispy hair and a commanding presence brought on by a deep voice and assertive manner. After receiving his law degree from the University of Michigan in 1910, he established a practice in Lincoln, gradually building its base on a clientele of casualty insurance companies. He never had more than one partner until Hyman Evnen and F. B.'s son John joined him in 1940 and 1948, respectively.

F. B.'s experiences with partners had not always been pleasant. Guy TouVelle was killed in an automobile accident on May 20, 1940. A few years later George Healey left the partnership and took with him some of the insurers whom the firm had depended on as clients. That betrayal, so the word went, led to F. B.'s insisting that thereafter letters emanating from anyone in the firm be signed with the firm's name only, Baylor, Evnen and Baylor. This irritated other lawyers, strangers, and clients alike, but the practice wasn't abandoned until some ten years after I came aboard. He thought identifying the writer made it easier for him or her to steal clients from the firm. So only the Arabic numeral (mine was 92) assigned to each member of the firm was permitted to appear adjacent to the secretary's initials.

The firm's financial books were also arranged in a peculiar manner. The credits were itemized on the left side and debits on the right. Why? So casual peepers or sneak thieves wouldn't understand what they were seeing. That too changed, but not for a long time.

F. B. Baylor, whom I always called "Mr. Baylor," was not really strange, just different. He was kind, thoughtful, absolutely honest, highly principled, tight with his and our money, outstanding in the courtroom, meticulous in crafting the words of his writings, and a devoted Democrat.

The firm's way of dividing the profits—F. B. Baylor's way, really—was to have each of us draw a small, predetermined monthly amount (mine was $200); after the close of the year, all of us met and talked about how the profits should be shared. I liked this method because it kept us frugal and it was realistic, dealing in the main with what the profits actually were rather than what they might become. The first year or two were killers for Joyce and me, because we were expected to live on the $200 a month until profit-sharing time. Joyce immediately got a job teaching women's physical education at Nebraska Wesleyan University, and we were comfortable in our little two-bedroom house at 336 North 32 that we financed on a

19. F. B. Baylor, founder of the Baylor law firm, in 1910. Photograph courtesy of the Baylor law firm.

shoestring. Unlike many of today's college graduates, particularly those with professional degrees, Joyce and I had no student loans or debts. But neither did we have more than diddly in savings. All in all, we felt lucky.

Joyce made it through that year teaching at Nebraska Wesleyan, finishing just in time to give birth to our first child, Kim Marie, on May 4, 1954, when our neighborhood was awash with lilacs.

Mr. Baylor admirably taught us of the firm how to retire. He did it almost imperceptibly. Other than letting us know one day that he would welcome our investing in the firm by buying shares in the firm's property, he eased out of control by taking fewer cases, taking less money, making fewer decisions, and depending on us to use our own judgment. Then one day we found ourselves in control, almost by surprise.

Hyman Evnen was a gentleman—sweet-natured, funny, friendly, smart. He combed his thick gray hair in a pompadour, rarely wore an overcoat, saw to it that his tie ended well below his belt, and was loved by everybody who knew him. He practiced law out of his head, researched very little, and was an expert in worker's compensation law. He was a Republican. He married Annabelle, and the two of them vowed to have no children. She was a Methodist, he a Jew. He sometimes shared with me his version of

20. Hyman Evnen, partner in the Baylor law firm, upon Warren Urbom's arrival in 1953. Photograph courtesy of the Baylor law firm.

21. John R. Baylor, partner in the Baylor law firm, upon Warren Urbom's arrival in 1953. Photograph courtesy of John R. Baylor Jr.

Judaism. His casket, he said, should be wooden without nails, in case he was expected to "rise to glory." Once I admired his beautiful new Oldsmobile and expressed some envy about it. He said he'd give all the cars he'd ever had for one child like any of mine. I was silenced by that, and I could relate to it. During those years I was learning the art of trying cases in court, Joyce and I were blessed with four children, all wonderful in every way. I thought trying cases was about the most awesome thing on the face of the earth, but it couldn't compare with the excitement of having kids. After Kim in 1954 we had Randy in 1955, Allison in 1961, and Joy in 1963.

John R. Baylor, F. B.'s son, graduated from Harvard Law School and joined the firm in 1948. He had tried to enlist in the military during World War II but was rejected. He then made his way to Canada and served an enlistment in the British army with the American Field Service. His British army unit liberated the Bergen-Belsen concentration camp in Germany in

1945. He was an accomplished chef, raconteur, singer of merry tunes, and a devoted Democrat.

John was brilliant, eccentric, tireless in research, and unsurpassed in creative thinking in legal theory. His obituary in 2006 declared that he would be remembered "for his old-fashioned charm and hospitality." He wore a hat with a turned-up brim, smoked a pipe, and walked at a jaunty pace with one arm crooked from an accident. He remembered everything. He once danced with Jacquelyn Kennedy when her husband was campaigning in Lincoln for the presidency. His acceptance into Harvard Law School came by a simple dialing of the telephone for Harvard Law and asking for the dean, who then was the celebrated Roscoe Pound, lately dean of the University of Nebraska College of Law. If that be unorthodox, John was unorthodox.

I was the associate and partner of those three for seventeen years. From the time I passed Nebraska's bar examination and began practicing with the Baylor firm, it was understood that my primary interest was trial work. The firm accommodated me by assigning most of the municipal court cases to me. Ones I couldn't settle were tried. The "muni" court cases, of course, were small, most of them resulting from automobile accidents involving small amounts of money, but of much importance to me. They were a valuable source of learning. Nearly everything I would experience later was first encountered in muni court, except the presence of a jury and of serious personal injuries. Gradually working my way out of muni court and county court cases and into district court trials with and without juries, I learned to feel comfortable with the surprising behavior of clients, witnesses, and judges.

My very first trial in Municipal Court of Lincoln in 1953 taught me a lesson I was not to forget: Take virtually nothing for granted, not from a witness, a condition, or even a client. Muesborn, my client and the sole defendant in *City of Lincoln v. Muesborn*, was charged with driving while intoxicated. His defense was that he may have been intoxicated but wasn't driving. This was his story: he and his friend had been drinking liquor at home and decided to take a drive; his friend drove a while but then said his "foot was tired," so my client was in the process of trading seats with his friend in a stopped car, but was arrested by a police officer before the vehicle moved an inch. The officer testified to the contrary, and the judge found my client guilty. We filed an appeal to the District Court of Lancaster County, but in light of my client's assurance to me that he had an unblemished criminal record, we decided the best thing to do was to plead guilty and seek a lesser punishment than the municipal judge had dealt out, which was loss of his driving privileges for six months. After I made an argument for a lower sentence, the district court judge, Harry Ankeny, pulled out a rap sheet that recounted a list of my client's half-dozen prior convictions for minor offenses and at least two prior drunk driving convictions. To that my client whispered to me simply, "A pack of lies!" Judge Ankeny sentenced Muesborn to thirty days in jail, a $100 fine, and thirty days' loss of driving privileges. I hadn't taken the precaution of checking my client's past history, to my regret and to my client's.

To my pleasure, a steady stream of assignments of trials in municipal court and county court came my way, and occasionally one in the state district court, gradually increasing in size and seriousness. I tried eight cases in the four months of September through December of my first year with the Baylor firm. I couldn't have been happier.

As cases assigned to me were getting more complex, the firm kept the same philosophy: A person learns to try cases by trying cases. At times a partner would accompany me as the "second chair." That way he (there were no women in the firm then; there are now) could keep careful track of me, watch me, offer tips. In the course of time I was usually on my own, unless the sheer number of witnesses to be kept on the ready or the volume of exhibits called for a helping hand. The final effect of all this is that in the seventeen years I was a member of the firm, I tried an average of almost exactly one trial a month, 209 trials in 204 months. The highest number I tried in a year was twenty-four, coming in 1957 and 1958 each. The lowest was six, in 1958, 1960, and 1963 each. I think all were trials to the end; settled cases didn't count as trials.

Many of my cases were personal injury cases, gradually involving fewer automobile accident cases than other causes of personal injury. For instance, *Jewett v. Jeffrey* was a case in which a four-year-old child, represented by our firm at the request of Lloyd Bevins, a Waverly, Nebraska, attorney, sued his grandfather for loss of a leg from a farm auger accident.

Louis Jeffrey constructed a cattle-feeding mechanism on his farm containing an auger system by which silage and milo fodder were fed from a silo and a bin into the auger, to be carried into a feed bunk. To be able to dump fodder from an outdoor pile into the auger Jeffrey left a ten-foot span of the auger open at ground level, where it crossed the driveway between the silo and the feed bunk. It was an eight-inch auger that turned at a rapid speed and had no cover or protective device over or around it. Jeffrey and Harold Jewett, his son-in-law, farmed together and designed the cattle-feeding mechanism. Harold's four-year-old son, Jeff, frequently wanted to accompany the men while the feeding was going on, and they often took him. On November 3, 1964, while Jeffrey, the grandfather, was in Oklahoma on vacation, Jeff and his father were at the auger and the father was hauling fodder with a front-loader, when Jeff got his left leg caught in the auger. Jewett had placed his son on two planks immediately to the west end of the open part of the auger and then stood about 100 feet away, having just finished hauling the last load.

Three doctors were unable to save the leg from gangrene that developed, and on the fifth day amputation was necessary. A three-inch stub of the left femur remained. Thereafter Jeff's use of his artificial device was remarkable, and by the time of the trial in January and February of 1967 he could do about everything except run.

At the trial demonstrative evidence was the order of the day. We had transparencies displayed by an overhead projector, an artist's conceptions of mechanical prostheses, drawings by the physical therapists, and home movies of Jeff, showing his stub, artificial device, and the manner in which he was able to perform his usual activities.

The claim against the grandfather was that he had not used reasonable care in designing the device to protect the boy from the known danger of operating the auger in the presence of the child. During the presentation of the grandfather's case, an expert testified on the grandfather's behalf that the auger had been correctly and carefully built and positioned. On cross-examination I put to the expert witness a question I had thought through thoroughly before the trial began. I asked him, "Was there any way in your opinion that that auger could have been built or positioned to be any more dangerous than it was?" The expert was noticeably surprised by the question. He paused several moments, then asked, "Any *less* dangerous?" "No," I said, "any *more* dangerous." Again a pause. Then the answer I wanted to hear: "Just by having it extend farther into the cattle pen." I asked, "And thereby be more dangerous to the cattle?" "Yes" was the answer. "But no more dangerous to a child?" "No, not to a child." I was delighted to have the only more-dangerous condition he could think of be directed to the safety of the cattle and not to the safety of a grandchild. Our claim was not about care for cattle. It was about care for a child.

We got our verdict. It was for less money—$36,000—than we had hoped for but within an acceptable range.[1] We didn't want it to be huge because the maximum insurance coverage was not huge, and neither the boy nor his parents wanted the grandfather to be liable for a verdict beyond the coverage. There was no appeal. Jim Bruckner was defense counsel. As always, he was a tiger, protecting his client in every laudable way, a sterling trial lawyer.

Early in my trial career, including the municipal and county courts, where juries were nonexistent or rare, and district courts, where juries were usually the fact finders, I saw the advantage of using demonstrative evidence. It was especially useful in jury cases, but judges accepted and relied on it too. An example was the use of small magnetized model automobiles made to scale that could be moved about on a metallic blackboard to illustrate with reasonable precision distances between automobiles at particular times, as testified to by witnesses. One insurer praised my "alertness" in using such techniques, which were well-known to plaintiffs' attorneys but typically not used by defendants' (meaning insureds') lawyers.[2] Use of such a technique was of value, I'm sure, even though we were not yet into the days of computers and their alluring ways of drawing a viewer's attention.

Perhaps the technique I used that was most often commented on by lawyers and persons who had been jurors was that of memory. In jury trials, especially when I was defense counsel (the defense performs last in each stage of the trial, thus has more time to do the memorizing), I memorized the prospective jurors' names as they were being seated in the jury box and questioned them without notes. And, as often as I could, I questioned witnesses without resort to notes. I thought the technique gave me a bit more believability when I argued that such- and-such was true or that a certain witness had testified to so-and-so.

I learned to use the no-notes technique at the urging of F. B. Baylor. I had to be persuaded that I could do the memory work. He persisted, and I did it. I didn't then and don't now have anything like total memory recall or any more than a fairly good memory, but I studied several memory experts' systems, found the ones I liked, and used them, not only in trials but elsewhere. At one point I memorized the telephone numbers of over a hundred law offices. I memorized a year's calendar and could tell on what day of the week any date of any month that year would fall. I memorized lists of members, grocery lists, things to do, events, outlines of speeches I'd give, anything. It was fun, useful, and, once developed, not difficult. All that helped keep my memory sharp for use in trials.

Ager v. Carper was one trial that helped me later as a judge to be cautious in ruling on motions that can end a trial.[3] My client had been sued by another woman for alienation of affection. My client had admitted in a deposition taken before the trial that she had once committed an indiscretion with the plaintiff's husband, but I had been successful in getting from the trial judge, William Hastings, an order that evidence of that night's activities was not admissible and that the subject was not to be brought up at the trial. On the third day of the trial Max Kier, an able trial lawyer but a loose cannon, began to ask my client on cross-examination the forbidden question, "Did you once spend a night in an Omaha hotel with . . ." I jumped to my feet and interrupted, "Objection, Your Honor. Mr. Kier has been specifically ordered not to ask a question on that subject. I therefore ask for a mistrial." I knew my statement should not have been made within the hearing of the jury, but I wanted the jury to hear it. The judge, who was extraordinarily able and later became chief justice of the Supreme Court of Nebraska, did not admonish me for saying it. Instead he declared a recess and asked both counsels to meet with him in his chambers. There the judge allowed the lawyers to speak briefly, then said he would grant a mistrial if I wanted it. I said I wanted to confer with my client before I gave a final answer. I explained to her that a mistrial, which the judge would grant if she wanted it, would mean that the trial would stop now and we could retry it from the beginning with a new jury a few weeks later. She knew at once that she did not want to do that. She said she was drained from the tenseness of the trial and loathed the thought of going through another one. I asked her if she was sure. She said, "Yes, I'm sure, win or lose." To strengthen her confidence I wrote a note to her and touched her hand. She read the note. It said, "We're going to win this case." I reported to the judge that my client asked that the motion for a mistrial be withdrawn, and she wanted to proceed.

We did win the case. When I talked to some of the jurors after their verdict, one of them said, "Mr. Kier had no business raising that matter he asked about." I admit that by then I was glad he had.

Perhaps the most punishing trial for me as a trial lawyer was a divorce case tried in York, Nebraska, *Norval v. Norval.* Only rarely did I take divorce cases. This one was a favor to a lawyer friend of mine, Byron Norval, the brother of my client.

Harry Norval Jr. sued his wife for a divorce and custody of their four-year-old child, Mark. Our position was that the mother was not competent to have custody of the child, yet was competent enough to be sued for divorce. It was a fine line to walk. The wife had been adopted in Iowa, and only with much effort were we able get her family history of mental disease that could have been inherited. The case took a nasty turn when the wife asserted that her husband was a homosexual and guilty of sexually abusing their son. The apex of the trial came when I called the child as a witness, and the judge, Joseph Ach, over my protest, allowed five-year-old Mark to be cross-examined *by the wife's psychiatrist,* a most unusual procedure. The cross-examination was a vicious display by the psychiatrist, but the child responded with maturity far beyond his age, insisting that his father had never abused him. Judge Ach granted my client a divorce, but granted custody of the child to my client's brother, Byron, and Byron's wife, Kathy.

That state of affairs lasted a few months, until my client asked that I move for a change of custody to my client, the father. One difficulty was that under Nebraska law I had to show a change of circumstances to get a change of custody. Judge Ach had explained in his decree of divorce and custody of the child to Harry's brother that Harry "[did] not have a suitable home of his own . . . or proper facilities to properly supervise and take care of the child . . . and . . . was virtually unemployed and uncertain as to his plans for the future." We hoped we had enough evidence to show there had been a substantial change of circumstances, making Harry capable of providing secure care for Mark.

A problem was that, if these new circumstances were adequate to show an improvement in Harry's ability to care for the child, we had to show that these constituted a change from *the time of the decree* of a few months earlier. Ordinarily that would be easy, because the full record of the evidence would be in the written trial record. Here there was no written trial record, because the court reporter, Art Bass, had died after the trial without reducing his shorthand to writing, and no other reporter could be found who could translate the notes.

In addition, Mary Ann, the mother of Mark, had also filed an application for the modification of the decree regarding custody. She again charged that Harry was not fit or suitable to have custody of Mark, so we had to defend against that charge. We also had evidence that Mary Ann had continued after the decree to try to alienate Mark from Harry. The result was that, in essence, we had to retry the case by calling most of the witnesses who had testified at the original trial.

That was done, despite how time-consuming, expensive, and miserable for the witnesses and parties it was. It was especially cruel to the child, by then age six, to go through the examination and cross-examination a second time. But he did it, with a stoicism equal to that of the previous trial experience. I cannot recall any similarly stellar set of performances by a witness, child or adult, in my professional life.

Whereas at the time of the trial my client, the father, was not employed and had to be considered without a wife because his divorce was granted by Judge Ach, by the time of the second trial (the change-of-custody hearing) he had found a new wife, Brunhilde, had a job with the Department of Welfare of Lancaster County, and had established a home in Lincoln. This change of circumstances, we believed, was sufficient to be grounds for his having full custody of the child. Judge Ach agreed and awarded Harry Norval Jr. full custody of Mark and allowed visitation by Mary Ann one weekend a month. The judge found no material change respecting Mary Ann. Her mental condition, he said, was in a period of remission, but its duration was "unforeseeable and unpredictable." Further, he found that her charges of physical abuse of Mark by Harry were "wholly without factual support."

A feature that helped us most during the entire trial and motions for a change of custody was Mary Ann's contrived and exaggerated claims of misconduct by several persons, not Harry alone. She switched counsel twice, charged that Judge Ach was "biased and prejudiced against her," sought his recusal,[4] and moved unsuccessfully for a change of the trial's location on the ground that she could not get a fair trial in York County. The judge also found that Mary Ann Norval, during visitations between April 21, 1965, and February 11, 1966, "made statements to Mark Norval calculated to poison the mind of said minor child against the plaintiff (Harry Norval Jr.) and the Norval family."

Having listened to testimony of witnesses, including Mary Ann Norval, on at least fifteen days between March 13, 1964, and February 11, 1966, Judge Ach ruled:

> The defendant's objections to the custody by the plaintiff are based on a claim of abuse of the child by the plaintiff and sexual perversion on the part of the plaintiff, but the court finds that such claim is wholly without factual support. Despite testimony by the defendant (Mary Ann Norval) to the contrary, the Court specifically finds that when Mark Andre Norval testified on January 10, 1966, he came with the plaintiff's counsel past the defendant and immediately to the hearing room where this judge was sitting and at that time Mark Andre Norval was not crying, showed no evidence of having been crying, his clothes were neat and orderly, and he gave no appearance of having been mishandled or ill-treated.

I often wondered what happened to the boy, and recently I found out from Harry. Mark lived through his high school years with his father and his father's second wife, although he tried living with his mother for a short time but didn't like it. He died at age twenty-five of a brain tumor. Harry thinks Mary Ann died in about 2000 of colon cancer.

In 1962 I was pleased that F. B. Baylor, my senior partner and mentor of all things pertaining to trials, asked me to try his own case, arising from being struck by an automobile. He had been walking west in a crosswalk across 27th Street immediately north of Van Dorn Street in Lincoln, when he was struck at 7:40 a.m. by the defendant's car, which was proceeding east on Van Dorn Street and turning north onto 27th Street. The testimony was that Mr. Tyrrell, the defendant, did not see Mr. Baylor because he was blinded by the sun until Mr. Baylor was an arm's length away. Mr. Baylor did not see the defendant's car, or he had no recollection of it, until it was two or three feet away. He suffered a fractured left hip, a possible fracture of his right clavicle, and bruises about the face and knees. Dr. Fred Webster testified to 25 percent permanent disability of the left leg; Dr. Mitchell for the defendant testified to 20 percent permanent disability of the leg. There was permanent injury, Dr. Webster testified, from anxiety arising from the doctor's telling Mr. Baylor that the operation of pinning his hip with a ken nail might be unsuccessful in that aseptic necrosis might develop anytime up to three years from the date of the accident. By the time of the trial some symptoms of this condition had already begun.

The highest offer prior to trial was $9,700, raised during the trial to $11,700. The lowest demand by F. B. Baylor was "We will shave $15,000." Mr. Baylor told me he was willing to accept $12,500, if offered. The verdict was for the plaintiff after four hours of deliberation in the amount of $14,200. Harvey Goth, assisted by George Healey (the latter being unable to speak because of loss of his larynx), defended. The defense appealed, and the Supreme Court of Nebraska affirmed, *Baylor v. Tyrrell.*[5]

Mr. Baylor's ability to read the jury in estimating what the ultimate damage award would be, if any, was uncanny. His personal case was a good example of that. Not always—but nearly always—did his long experience and wisdom give him that insight.

The case also made new law in Nebraska: the state supreme court held, in short, that (1) use of a mathematical formula for a lawyer's suggesting to the jury an amount of damages for pain and suffering is acceptable, if each time segment of pain and suffering claimed is supported by evidence of the degree of suffering experienced during each time segment. The criticism of using a mathematical formula, the court reasoned, is directed at the use of an arbitrary money figure over a time segment of pain and then mathematically multiplying it over the life expectancy period, irrespective of whether any evidence supports the same amount of pain during the expectancy period. (2) The damage element of anxiety or mental suffering is properly submitted to the jury where the plaintiff testifies he or she suffered anxiety and mental suffering from the doctor's telling him or her of the possibility that the condition of the injured hip might deteriorate or become worse following an operation and the possibility of another operation being necessary.

The irony is that two weeks after the Supreme Court of Nebraska affirmed our verdict in the *Baylor* case, Fritz Wagener, as plaintiff's counsel, used the *Baylor* holdings against me to the hilt in *Coleman v. Hudson*.[6] I found that the one trouble with my causing new law to be made is that I had to live with it. So did my other clients.

All the foregoing cases were typical in the 1950s and 1960s. The amounts of money that changed hands were not large by today's standards, but they were in amounts that were crucial to the parties.

My experience as a trial lawyer was wonderfully satisfying. After fifteen years I enjoyed the court clashes and I had an honorable reputation. I was asked by another law firm to consider joining it to fill a gap in its ranks. More money was offered than I made as a partner of the Baylor firm, as well as the expectation of at least as much significant trial work. The lawyers I would work with were friends and reputable attorneys. By that offer I was drawn into a careful review of my life status. I was slightly past forty, had four children, and fit my profession. There were options other than joining another firm: moving into politics was one; seeking a judgeship was another. The barrier to politics was Joyce's discomfort. Although she was always an avid people person who loved participating in social events, was protective of confidential information, and lighted up any conversation with her presence, she had no appetite for controversy. When we talked of politics before our marriage she let me know that she doubted that she could be comfortable in political settings. I respected her feelings and stayed clear of all participation in the political world.

But there was more than that. To be honest about it, I think Joyce's reluctance pressed me into a proper decision in my early forties. By then I realized that neither my temperament nor my natural skills were geared to practical politics. I am more shy than is good and only nominally aggressive. Given choices, politics is better left to others.

By the 1960s I was billing more fees than John Baylor, and I became convinced that I should be paid more than he. Hy Evnen said he agreed with me, and we went together to discuss the matter with F. B. Baylor. He quickly told me that my success had gone to my head and to forget comparisons with John. Neither Hy nor I could offer a convincing rebuttal.

In considering the offer from the other firm, the conversation with Mr. Baylor had to be taken into account. On the other hand, I knew that the Baylor firm fit me well. We had taken in three splendid new partners, Art Curtiss, Bob Grimit, and Don Witt. Doug Deitchler, whose interest was estate planning, was about to be discharged from military service and taken into the firm. The money was a living wage, even if not divided equitably, the work was enjoyable, income probably would increase, and I had free rein to enter into other activities as I chose. For example, I had been active in the Toastmasters Club, Nebraska Wesleyan University's Board of Trustees and Board of Governors, the Masonic Lodge, the National Association of Insurance Counsel, and the church on local, state, and national levels, was president of the Lincoln Bar Association and chairman of one or more committees of the Nebraska State Bar Association. I made speeches a lot—to college groups, service clubs, gatherings of all kinds. There was little if anything I wanted to do that I didn't already do or hadn't done.

So, weighing all things, I decided to stay at the Baylor firm, and was quite content. A judgeship? I thought about it but did nothing about getting one.

5

Church and Family

Church has been a part of my life all my life. According to an original certificate, I was enrolled as a member of the Cradle Roll Department of the United Brethren School of Mayflower under the name Warren Keith Urbum on June 3, 1928, when I was two and a half years old. Another certificate says I was "promoted from the Cradle Roll Department to the Beginners Department" of the same school of the same church (in or near McDonald, Kansas) on January 5, 1930, under the same misspelled name.[1]

Sometime after we moved to Nebraska in 1932, we began attending the First Methodist Church in Arapahoe. At least we children did. I was confirmed when I was twelve or so; my only memory of the ceremony is my giggling as a friend and I knelt at the altar. I don't know what we were so tickled about, and I don't even know who the friend was.

Many years later, in 2003, I gave what was reported as a "testimony" at a celebration of 120 years of existence of that First United Methodist Church. This is part of what I said:

> I feel at home here!
>
> My connection with this church began before my birth. My grandfather and grandmother Irelan attended here, not in this building, of course, because it hadn't been built, but in this church. My parents were scheduled to be married here, but a blizzard interfered, so the ceremony took place in my grandparents' home about a half mile east of here. It was here in this building that I first experienced Sunday School and Epworth League.
>
> Teachers such as Mrs. Short, Mrs. Richards, Mrs. Elwell, and

Sonny Moore gave kids like me guidance. They didn't always give me straight A's for deportment. I drove some of them to distraction. It was Mrs. Richards, I think, who taught our class in the lower level of this building.

On one occasion, as I remember it, after I had pushed her to the limit of her patience and into pure exasperation, she pointed her finger right at me and said in a voice that could be heard by all the class, "I doubt that you'll ever amount to anything!" I admit that I had my doubts about it too.

But the teachers persevered, and by and by in what I believe was about 1937 I was confirmed as a member of the church. . . . It was Reverend E. L. Peterson who invited me to give my very first sermon from this pulpit. That was a watershed event for me.

When I was graduated from high school and had finished my military service in World War II, I came back to work for my father, driving heavy dirt-moving machinery. Driving machinery 12 hours a day, 6 days a week, with nobody around, provided an invitation to contemplate my life. Sensing it was decision time, I felt a powerful urge to go into the ministry.

One morning toward the end of that summer in 1946 when it was too rainy to work moving dirt, I went to the barber shop of Andy Koelmel for a haircut. Andy Koelmel's wife, Allegra Morrison, was there. She had been the kindergarten teacher in Arapahoe. I had never had her as a teacher, but she was a member of this church and for a time had lived just across the street from us, so I knew her.

She greeted me as her husband snipped at my hair and she asked, "Now that you are out of the Army, what are you going to do with your life?" I said, "Well, I think I should go into the ministry and I think that means I'll go to Nebraska Wesleyan University." Her response was immediate: "Oh, that's wonderful! You'll go to Wesleyan, and you'll study hard, and you'll go out for debate (I'd never thought of that), and you'll go to seminary, and one day you'll be a bishop!" (I'd never thought of that either.)

She was wrong about the bishop part. But that's not important. What is important is that she said it. She gave me permission to think thoughts I'd never dared to think, and I've never forgotten what she said. . . .

> I did go to Wesleyan. I did study hard. I did go out for debate. I did go to seminary—for one summer—and I loved studying at Iliff School of Theology, but there became convinced that I was not being called to the ministry of the church. So I asked the Law School of the University of Michigan to let me in, and it did. Three years later—50 years ago this year—I earned my law degree and committed my professional life to the ministry of justice, vowing that I would search for, discover, and further justice for every person whom I could touch. I have loved it . . . and I love it still! . . . I feel a direct line from this church to my ministry. So you can see why I say I feel at home here.

Joyce grew up a Methodist, our first close association was at a Methodist church, we were married in a Methodist church, and it was automatic that we would become members of a Methodist church wherever we were. During law school, we belonged to First Methodist Church in Ann Arbor and on our return to Lincoln resumed attendance at First Methodist Church across the street from Wesleyan. We moved into a one-bedroom apartment on P Street and began shopping for a church more centrally located than First Church. Trinity Methodist Church was one of the first we visited, and the next morning the pastor, Vance Rogers, visited Joyce at her office in Nebraska Wesleyan, where she taught physical education, and visited her and me at our apartment, telling us, "You need Trinity and Trinity needs you!" We were hooked and have been members of Trinity ever since.

All four of our children were baptized and confirmed at Trinity. Joyce and I sponsored a youth group named Teens and Twenties there for two or three years, and we have actively led an adult Sunday School class, the Questers, since about 1956. Willard Cook asked me to be the teacher of the class at its beginning, and I did so as the lone teacher for fifteen years. Thereafter I have shared the teaching load with others and taken the role of "administrator," for want of a better title for one who is responsible for continuously seeing to the organizing of things. Joyce has been particularly active in supporting Questers, leading United Methodist Women, and serving on nominating and evangelism committees of the church. From time to time I also served on various committees of the local church and the Nebraska Annual Conference.

Beginning in 1972 I attended the General Conference (worldwide) of the United Methodist Church as a delegate elected by the Nebraska Annual Conference.[2] The General Conference gathers every four years, consists of about a thousand members, and sets the policies of the entire United Methodist Church. I attended six such conferences, participating variously in committees or commissions on global ministries, local churches, conferences, and judicial matters. Probably the most significant act I helped with was writing for the 2000 General Conference a complete revision of the Church's judicial procedure, most of which was adopted after largely combining it with a similar effort made by an attorney from Ohio. The completed version appearing in the 2000 *Book of Discipline* changes the previous version in at least these ways: more mandatory due process, more sharing of information with parties and counselors, more guidance of the presiding officer, more authority to the presiding officer, and more inclusion of usual procedures of civil courts.

In the Nebraska Conference I was a member of the Committee on Clergy Sexual Ethics for at least a dozen years, tending mostly to educate the clergy (and sometimes the laity) about the prevention of clergy's abuse of women and children; my part was an emphasis on the possible legal liability of churches at every level. The committee made and distributed throughout the state a videotape and for several years gave annual workshops on the subject of sexual abuse of women, including the legal ramifications, my bailiwick.

Leading and helping to lead Questers have been very satisfying for me. In the early days—the 1950s and early 1960s—the group was primarily focused on specific biblical topics. We have gradually shifted to other emphases, looking at trends in religious thought and controversies in various fields containing religious overtones, such as abortion, separation of church and state, physician-assisted suicide, evolution (now at war with intelligent design), hate groups, tolerance of other religions (especially since 9/11), the religious thoughts of C. S. Lewis, and books such as *If Grace Is True* and *If Love Is True*, both by Phillip Gulley and James Mulholland. The class typically has about thirty couples and singles as members, with attendance averaging around twenty-five to thirty persons. Some are fairly conservative, arising out of their early upbringing, probably, regarding biblical authority; the rest range from casual to committed liberality. The class is an interesting mix of people who have grown old in Trinity and people who have moved into the stream at various ages, lured by the class's word-of-mouth reputation. Eight retired clergy are members and decently regular attendees. Questers celebrated its fiftieth year in 2007 and is going strong.

When I was trying a case in Kansas City, I stayed with Scott and Patsy Moore for about six months because I got tired of staying in motels. The Moores have been Joyce's and my close friends since college days. By the time of my stay with them Patsy was caught up in the women's movement. I have seen that as my good fortune. It has helped me build my own solid respect for equal justice for the sexes.

My own theological journey has been a continuous movement. For me the doctrinal path has been from a semistrict conservatism bearing commitments learned by my father from his Swedish Lutheran parents,[3] to a liberalism coaxed by the gentle John Rosentrater and the more direct but still cautious Ed Mattingly at Nebraska Wesleyan, to an insistent John B. Cobb Jr., to the assertive Bishop John Shelby Spong and Marcus Borg, and to the sweeping grace and love of Phillip Gulley and James Mulholland. Thus it has been and is; where next is unknown.

The nature of God is not the same for me now as it was earlier. I can best visualize God as being pure spirit, as intimate with me as my breath, urging, calming, inspiring. My role is to be alert, aware, patient, receptive, in tune with the universe, confident, peaceful, and grateful. My prayers are mainly thoughts of expectations of all I need when I need it for whatever I choose that is in tune with the holy spirit of the universe, the unending creativity always simmering, rolling, healing, quieting.

Our four children were born in Lincoln, at Bryan Memorial Hospital, now renamed Bryan LGH Medical Center East. Our first child is Kim Marie. Her health was Joyce's and my first serious challenge. She was born with a herniated diaphragm, which manifested itself by projectile vomiting. Two surgeries followed, one during the first week of her life and another three months later, both of them to stretch her esophagus to enable it to be more fully attached to her stomach. The second one was successful. There has been no complication or problem since.

In conversation Kim pleasantly invites details of others' experiences, fun and sad, pleasant and woeful, good and bad. She is curious, probing the depths and counseling gently.

Kim was educated at Southeast High School in Lincoln, Colorado State University in Fort Collins, and Southern Methodist University in Dallas, with a major in religion and a baccalaureate degree. Flowers are her passion and the object of her skill. While living in South Sioux City, Nebraska, she designed and developed floral placements in homes, businesses, parks, and memorials at the request of owners, tenants, and cities. Her own yard was a spectacular display of the beauty that can be invited by thoughtful and loving placement and care. She and her husband, Scott Rager, an attorney and now president of a group of fifteen insurance companies of Old Republic Insurance Company, live in Oak Brook, a suburb of Chicago. They have four children: Aaron has a master's degree in sports management from Texas A&M; Nicole, a graduate of Nebraska Wesleyan with a double major of biopsychology and Spanish, has pondered on the beaches of South Carolina and now is busily establishing there a business of her own; Christopher, an avid devotee of the golfing world, now a graduate of Morningside College in Sioux City, Iowa, is getting a foothold in the transportation field and dreaming of professional golf; and Joy, a recent graduate of the University of Nebraska at Lincoln, majored in forensic science.

Randall Crawford, our second child and only son, is an excellent tennis player, a patient father, and supportive of his two sons' efforts. Randy is a fine lawyer, even if a reluctant one, who, after a law practice in firms, has been in the forefront of a band of lawyers who bravely and successfully practice alone, by computer, largely at home.

Randy attended Southeast High School in Lincoln, spent a year in Germany as an exchange student, from which he tested out for sixteen hours of credit in German, got his baccalaureate degree at Nebraska Wesleyan with a major in German, served as president of the Student Affairs Senate of Nebraska Wesleyan, and earned his law degree from the University of Nebraska at Lincoln. He has practiced law in Kearney and Lincoln, Nebraska, and in Phoenix and Scottsdale, Arizona. He is now divorced from

22. Judge Urbom's daughter Kim Marie Rager, flower designer. Photograph in author's possession.

23. Judge Urbom's son, Randall Crawford Urbom, lawyer. Photograph in author's possession.

24. Judge Urbom's daughter Allison Lee Raich, nurse. Photograph by Anderson Studio, Lincoln.

Kelli, an art teacher. Their children are Grant, still looking for a future, and Alex, determined to have a professional career in theater, preferably as an actor, who is now a graduate of the University of California at Los Angeles with a major in theater arts.

Allison Lee, our third child, from the beginning has been spirited, unfailingly cheerful (much like her mother), frugal, and practical. After graduating from Southeast High School and attending two rollicking years at Iowa State University, she looked one evening at the "jobs" classified ads and announced, "What this world needs is nurses." She promptly enrolled in nurses' training and received her nursing diploma at Bryan Memorial Hospital in Lincoln. She graduated from University of Texas–Arlington with a baccalaureate degree in nursing and received her master's degree from Texas Wesleyan University. I once preached a sermon in our church titled "Blessed Are the Salty." The biblical reference was to "the salt of the earth"[4];

25. Judge Urbom's daughter Joy Renee Taylor, lawyer.
Photograph by Grad Images© and Marathon Foto™.

the personal face was Allison's, who can put in a single word or phrase—"There you have it!" or "It's a shut case!"—the zesty essence of a situation.

Allison has been a nurse anesthetist, a cardiac intensive care nurse, and a psychiatric nurse at hospitals in the Dallas area. She is divorced from Jeffrey Raich, an insurance executive. They are parents of three children: Joseph (1993), Samantha (1996), and Jacob (2000). They all live in McKinney, Texas.

Our youngest is Joy Renee. As a child she was quiet, observant, shyly assertive with her wants, and carefully meticulous with her words. Maturity sees her the same, but less quiet and less shy. Now she leads more, takes more, and gives more.

Joy disliked (or "hated," as she says) law school, but has loved her twenty years of spirited practice of law, including a fearless eagerness in the federal courtroom, which her partners were wont to avoid. Now she is retiring to a full-time commitment to a rousing family. She is married to George Anthony (Tony) Taylor, whom she met at Washington University College of Law in St. Louis, where they were judging client counseling by students at the law school. She first graduated from Nebraska Wesleyan University and since finishing law school has practiced law with firms in St. Louis. Tony practiced general law for several years and was with the legal department of Anheuser-Busch. He is now general counsel and chief legal officer of Sea World Parks and Entertainment in Orlando, Florida. Joy and Tony are parents of two daughters, Georgi, born in 2000, and Tommie, born in 2001, and a son, Joseph Patrick (Joe Pat), born in 2003. They live in Orlando, having moved there just recently from the St. Louis area. Joy runs a smooth household that enjoys great fun. She titles her homebound self "director of homeland activity, secretary of transportation, and chief relocation officer."

6

A Federal Trial Judge Gives Answers

Great historical events during my own lifetime could have been the cause of the jittery tenseness that seemed to enshroud America in the 1970s. The Great Depression, the drought of the 1930s, World War II, the dread of Communism, the Korean War, and the launch of *Sputnik* into space had passed by the time I joined the judiciary in 1970. During the 1960s President John F. Kennedy, Martin Luther King Jr., and Robert Kennedy had been assassinated. We had endured five years of controversies over the Vietnam War. Television was new but everywhere, the Beatles were at the top of the music charts, the first heart transplant had been performed, and Neil Armstrong had walked on the moon. Our remembered past had been an ocean of rises and falls in our lifetime. The 1960s were behind us, but their incongruity still appeared to be the norm as we peeked into the 1970s.

The 1970s have been called the "Me Decade" because of people's lack of concern for others, their attention on themselves. The mantras and songs of the day were "Take care of No. 1," "I'll do it my way," "I gotta be me!" I remember all that well. While I didn't consider myself either a product of or a castoff from the 1960s, neither did I feel in tune with the mantras of either the 1960s or the 1970s. I took the federal trial bench feeling like an extraordinarily lucky, incredibly happy, middle-of-the road person, quite willing to allow and even to participate in change.

One of the splendid programs developed by the Federal Judicial Center is the set of seminars held at least yearly for newly appointed federal judges and fondly known as the Baby Judges School. The Federal Judicial Center was created by Congress in 1968 to serve federal judges in the realms of education and research. The seminars are geared especially for federal trial (district) judges, though appellate (circuit) judges are welcomed. The primary seminar is a week of intensive instruction on judging in the federal system. Professors and experienced judges suggest to the new judges the usual problem areas and various ways of responding to them. My turn as a student came in late February and March 1971, so I had been on the bench for some nine months before my training week occurred.

The most expansive word I heard at the seminar was "Why?" For me that word came to mean "Why am I doing what I'm doing the way I'm doing it?" Taking the question seriously provoked endless subsequent questions. Why do I wear a robe? Why does the prisoner wear prison-orange suits to court? Why does the bailiff bang a gavel at the opening and closing of court? Why does the judge sit higher than the rest? Why is the judge addressed as "Your Honor"? Why are jurors not allowed to take notes? Why do the lawyers stand when they address the judge and jury? And so on and so on. Not that those questions were raised at the seminar; they weren't. But encouragement to think rationally about what we did as judges was in the air, and it was enlivening.

Answers rested in a variety of sources. Some of them came from Congress as laws that mandated judges to act exactly as stated. Others were the product of written opinions by the Supreme Court of the United States and other courts of appeals in specific cases to be applied in similar cases by trial judges. Areas of discretion remained, even within the strictures of the law. Looking for reasonable answers for the areas of discretion was a challenge.

As a trial lawyer I had seen what many state and federal judges did in many of the areas of discretion. My tentative guess was that there probably were good reasons for their actions in their day, but I thought some of the practices might be like ruts in an ungraded road. If they seemed to remain from neglect, I was willing to try to find better ways.

It was when I read Carl Sandburg's poem *The People, Yes* that I gave thought to the form of oath I required witnesses to take.

> "Do you solemnly swear before the ever-
> living God that the testimony you
> are about to give in this case

shall be the truth, the whole truth,
and nothing but the truth?"
"No, I don't. I can tell you what I saw
and what I heard and I'll swear to
that by the everliving God but the
more I study about it the more sure
I am that nobody but the everliving
God knows the whole truth and if
you summoned Christ as a witness in
this case, what He would tell you
would burn your insides with the
pity and the mystery of it."[1]

It is probably true, as Sandburg says, that no witness knows the whole truth about anything. And it is probably true that lawyers won't ask questions that call for the witness to tell all the truth he or she *does* know. And even if the lawyers should happen to ask for all the witness knows, the judge is almost certain not to let him or her answer some of the questions. I could see no fairness in making a witness *swear* to tell the *whole* truth. So the oath I then started using doesn't require the witness to swear to tell the *whole* truth—just "the truth and nothing but the truth." That will do. I don't know whether the witnesses notice—or the lawyers, for that matter—but I'm satisfied.

As my first criminal jury trial began in 1970, I was sure that neither the jurors nor I could remember the details of the complicated testimony about oil securities unless we had the opportunity to take notes. No trial I had ever had as a trial lawyer permitted note taking by jurors, but the lawyers and judges always took notes. Why not jurors? So I talked with the lawyers in this criminal case and received their assent to allow the jurors to take notes as they listened to the testimony of the witnesses. After the trial was over I asked the jurors what they thought of it. They were enthusiastic. Since then I have routinely instructed the jurors at the outset of a trial that they may take notes if they want to, and I have note pads and pencils handed to them. They dispose of their notes at the end of the trial as they deem fit.

It was later—five years later—that I had a trial at which a friend of Joyce's and mine, Doris Cook, served as a juror. After the verdict she said to me that she had some questions she would have asked of some of the witnesses if she thought she could, and asked me why she couldn't. I hadn't given that any thought and never had experienced such a practice, but when I did come to think of it after that, I decided to try it. It was such a success that I have used it automatically for over thirty years, unless the lawyers from both sides object to it. I have suffered no uncomfortable moment from that decision.

My reasoning for allowing questions by jurors rests on the proposition that each juror, as a critical cog in the wheel of justice, needs as clear an understanding of the evidence as can be offered within the rules of evidence. No rule of evidence or procedure prohibits or discourages questions by jurors. When a juror is uncertain of the meaning, wording, or scope of an answer, it seems to me better to let the uncertainty be known and dealt with instead of being ignored. The procedure I have developed does not allow jurors to ask their questions directly of the witness. The questions are directed to me, either orally or in writing, as the juror chooses, and I then decide whether the question meets the legal rules; if it does, I ask the question of the witness, although the question may be in a somewhat different form and may be preceded by one or more foundational inquiries to make sure the witness has some personal and relevant knowledge of the subject.

In the event the question is not put to the witness, I often give an explanation of why not. If I am unsure about whether the question should be put to the witness, I call the attorneys to the bench and confer with them on the record. If the question is asked and answered, counsel have the opportunity to inquire further about the subject of the question on direct or cross-examination or both. In my experience the jurors do not ask many questions, but those they do ask are usually good, often seeking clarification of some point. I wrote about this in 1982.[2] My view remains the same today.

Giving written jury instructions to each juror to read along as I read them aloud is another practice I began following after leaving the seminar for new judges. I thought then and think now that it must be easier for jurors to argue the fine points of law when each has a written copy of the applicable law to follow.

As to jury selection, my own practice is to ask the attorneys' preferences.

If they prefer that all the questioning of prospective jurors be by the judge, I do it. If they prefer that the lawyers ask all the questions, I allow it, but with time limits decided by me after hearing the lawyers' requests and their rationales. If they prefer some questioning by the judge and some by the attorneys, I allow that, their time limits to be set by me after hearing their requests and rationales. Time limits adroitly and fairly applied have made a difference, I think, particularly when there were signs that the trial would be long or complex, but letting counsel offer their preferences for the manner of proceeding has been preferable to making decisions without their input.

The Baby Judges School also led me to look at how court was opened. It was a tradition that at the opening of every day's trial, at least, the banging of a gavel would invite a solemn declaration of intention. The declaration varied from court to court, I'm sure, but I learned from listening that the one used in the federal courts in my early years was as follows, made by the bailiff as the presiding judge walked up to the bench:

> All rise! The United States District Judge for the District of Nebraska.
>
> Hear ye, hear ye, hear ye! The United States District Court for the District of Nebraska is now open, pursuant to adjournment. God save the United States and this honorable court.

I admit I liked that. It had the ring of antiquity about it. It emphasized the stateliness of the court as an institution. It let all who were present know the court was in business.

Then I began to think about what was actually being said. First, it introduced a judge, not by name, but by saying that somebody there was a judge. Even without the words, it must have been apparent that the person facing the other people, wearing a black robe, and standing on a raised dais was probably the judge. There was nothing wrong with that, but the words added little if any meaningful or unknown information.

Next, the "Hear ye, hear ye, hear ye," were strange, age-old words, but seemed to be saying in modern terms "Listen up! Something important is about to be said." What was the important thing about to be said? That the court was open "pursuant to adjournment." "Pursuant" could mean either of two things: "because of" or "in pursuit of." "Adjournment" means "closing," so "open pursuant to adjournment" could mean either "The court is open because it was closed" or "The court is open so it can be closed." Surely the court was here for a better reason than either of those.

The heart of the matter to me was that the words said nothing about why the people—the parties and the attorneys and the witnesses—were there. Conceivably they came because this day in court could be the most critical day of their lives, but that was not even being acknowledged by the court's opening declaration. Could not a better goal be expressed?

"God save the United States and this honorable court" asked an earnest favor of protection. What I found lacking was any sign of interest by the court in anything but the safety of itself and the United States.

So I wanted an alternative. I wanted it to be short. I wanted it to be literally and unmistakably true. And I wanted it to address the purpose of the gathering in a forthright way. Thus when our court opens the bailiff calls out, "The United States District Court for the District of Nebraska is now in session. May all who come find justice in this place."

The Civil Rights Act case Herb Friedman brought to me the first day I was a judge was settled without a hearing, and the boy, allegedly suspended from sixth grade for wearing short, frayed blue jeans contrary to the dress code, returned to school. That case was a portent of things to come during the early 1970s. A spate of other cases claiming lack of due process of law or denial of equal protection of the law rose up around the country, including in Nebraska. Indeed a similar case was waiting behind Friedman's and went through a full trial for resolution.

Christopher Black, a thirteen-year-old seventh-grade student, was denied continued attendance at Aurora Junior High School because he failed to have his hair cut by a barber in accordance with the school's grooming code. The school board and administrators argued that the case was "frivolous" or "petty" and didn't deserve to be in a federal court. I didn't accept the assertion. The people of Aurora seemed to think the *Black* case *was* important. They demonstrated it by publishing in the Aurora newspaper a full page of support of the school board's action, distributing petitions, taking a poll on the students' views of the school's grooming code, and attending the trial in unusually large numbers. I said in a written opinion, "Under these circumstances, it is obvious that if the court were to treat the matter as being frivolous or petty, it would stand alone."[3]

Before I was appointed to the bench, Judge Van Pelt had issued a restraining order in the *Black* case, halting for the time being the school authorities' suspension of Christopher Black. Earlier, in a different case, Judge Van Pelt had said in an unpublished opinion that the state of the law was fairly summarized in *Breen v. Kahl* as follows: "The right to wear one's hair at any length or in any desired manner is an ingredient of personal freedom protected by the United States Constitution. . . . To limit or curtail this or any other fundamental right, the state has a substantial burden of justification."[4] I chose not to revisit the standard contained in that statement, but rather to determine whether the school authorities responsible for Aurora Junior High School had met that "substantial burden" in the case of Christopher Black. I concluded that they had not.

There were conflicting interests involved, as is inherent in all disputes. The student had a legitimate interest in freedom to develop and express his personality by his hairstyle; the school had a legitimate interest in maintaining an orderly system of excellent education. When these interests collided, it became the court's task to resolve the conflict.

The school authorities made three arguments: (1) the regulation against excessively long hair was directly tied to disciplinary problems; (2) the school wanted to give students who didn't get enough discipline and training at home a chance to become better citizens; and (3) Christopher Black permitted his hair to be dirty, unkempt, and uncombed and emitted a body order offensive to other students. But none of these arguments was proved at the trial. As to (1), no evidence showed that enforcing the code about "excessively" long hair had ever resulted or would ever result in lowering problems of discipline. As to (2), no evidence was shown one way or the other that Black's parents did or didn't give their son sufficient discipline or training. As to (3), the refusal to let Black attend school was based solely on his failure to get his hair cut the way the principal thought it should be, not because he didn't wash his hair or body, and no connection was shown between any offensive odor and his failure to get his hair cut.

Christopher Black's hair was "long, but did not cover the eyes, ears, or shirt collar and lay fairly flat on the head. At the forehead the hair was cut

off [to be] almost square. The hair obviously was cut by an unskilled hand."[5] After a nonjury trial, I granted him a permanent injunction, allowing him to return to school and to have the record of the incident removed from the school records.

This was one of the early recognitions of our time of a constitutional right to express oneself by hairstyle. The hairstyles for the rest of the 1970s and through at least the 1980s reflected substantial differences in the way people, particularly boys and men, wanted to present themselves. Mustaches, beards, sideburns, and long hair, alone or together, were fashionable.

There were limits, though, to how hair could be worn. In *Stoppkotte v. Grand Island Northwest High School,* decided in 1991, I held that a high school could reasonably prohibit a student from wearing his hair below his shirt collar or earlobes during concert choir competitions, where the entire choir might be rated down because one boy wore long hair. "Personal freedoms are not absolute; they must yield when they intrude upon the freedom of others," I said.[6] The school could also ban the wearing of bandanas during school events in light of evidence that some years earlier an unruly youth gang used the bandana as a symbol of the gang. As in Christopher Black's case, I required the school to carry the burden of showing by evidence "a rational and justifiable reason" for banning bandanas. It did.

For a variety of reasons public schools provided the settings for numerous cases in those early years of my judgeship. In the arena of school sports *Reed v. Nebraska School Activities Association* was one.[7] Norfolk High School had no girls' golfing program, and the Nebraska School Activities Association's rules would not allow girls to participate on a boys' team.[8] Debbie Reed, through her parents, asked the court to order the Association to stop prohibiting her from participating on the boys' team. The Association argued that playing golf was not a right, but only a privilege. I held that, even if it was only a privilege, girls and boys must have the same opportunity to participate. The issue, I said, was not whether Debbie Reed had a "right" to play golf; her right was a right to be treated equally to boys by the state agency, Nebraska School Activities Association, unless the Association showed that the different treatment was rationally related to some legitimate objective of the state. None was shown.

The Association also argued that Debbie Reed was free to play golf even if she wasn't a member of a team. I reasoned that the school and the Association afforded interschool competition at some effort and expense simply for the reason that interschool competition was of some benefit to the students. It seemed to me that if the program was of value to boys, it surely would be of value to girls, in the absence of evidence to the contrary.

The Fourteenth Amendment to the Constitution of the United States forbids a state to "deny any person within its jurisdiction the equal protection of the laws." On the basis of the Fourteenth Amendment and the Civil Rights Act, 42 U.S.C. 1983, I issued a preliminary injunction in favor of Debbie Reed, permitting her to play with the boys' team until further order of the court. Six months later her parents asked that the case be dismissed, and I did dismiss it. I remember from press accounts that she did play with the boys' team. I surmise that the parents, Debbie, the Association, and the school board reached an agreement that she could play and that no further action by the court would be necessary. How long she played I do not know.

Equality—or something approaching equality—has been a goal our country has worked to achieve, and has found it not easy to achieve. *Ahern v. Board of Education of School District of Grand Island* raised the issue of whether the discharge of a public school teacher was constitutional.[9] Several similar lawsuits were pending in courts in Nebraska, as well as across the country, claiming lack of due process or equal protection on the part of a state or the federal government or their agencies.

"Due process" means "fairness." Of course there are special requirements in particular situations, but due process is usually viewed as having two parts: procedural due process and substantive due process. In the *Ahern* case, procedural due process had to do with fairness in the process used by the school in reaching the decision to take a job or any other thing of value from a teacher, student, or other person over whom the school had some authority. Generally three features make up fair procedural due process: (1) giving clear notice of what the school wants to take and why, (2) setting a reasonable place and time for the person to prepare for and make a response as to why the thing of value shouldn't be taken, and (3) furnishing an unbiased person or group to make a decision as to the propriety of the proposed taking.

Substantive due process has to do with (1) the school's showing a rational connection between the reason for the taking and a rightful interest of the school, (2) a basis in fact (evidence of what happened) for the taking, and (3) a reason for the taking that is not the exercise of a constitutional right (such as free speech) of the person from whom the taking is proposed to be made. In the *Ahern* case the issue was one of substantive due process. As I analyzed the facts, it seemed to me clear that the reason for the discharge was insubordination in defying the school principal's order to teach economics (and not political action) in an economics class and refusing orders from the school principal not to discuss the slapping of a student by a substitute teacher. The rightful interests of the school were to foster harmony among the faculty members, students, and administrators, and to have economics taught in a class on economics. There was a rational connection between the school's interests and the reason for the discharge: the discharge was because the school's interests (having harmony and having economics taught in an economics class) were not being cared for as Ahern had contracted to do. There was a basis in fact for the discharge, because the evidence was undisputed that Ahern did refuse the principal's order to teach economics and not to discuss the slapping incident. At the time of discussing the slapping incident Ahern, I found as a matter of fact, was not asserting her constitutional right of free speech. She had the right to speak on subjects of public concern, as the slapping incident was, but not at a time and in a place where she had been directed by a superior to do what she had contracted with the school to do.

I made several speeches, some at the request of school boards, about equal protection of the laws and due process of law, illustrating with cases, including the *Reed* and *Ahern* cases. Whether I made any improvement in the understanding of school boards and their employees, I don't know. What I do know is that, after the school authorities across the state, from whatever the sources, understood the elements of due process and equal protection, the incidents and the lawsuits about terminations of teachers in public schools abated to a large extent.

Before I took the bench for my first jury trial, Judge Van Pelt advised me to pick out a simple automobile accident case, because that was what I was most experienced in. That didn't happen. My first jury trial was *United States v. Sheets*, a criminal case charging the defendant Sheets with fourteen counts of securities fraud and the codefendant Osterloh with eleven similar counts.[10] The trial lasted three weeks. As a practicing attorney, I had never tried a case that lasted more than four or five days or one that involved more than one criminal defendant. Despite that, things went well in my first adventure as a judge with a jury, except two poor performances by me.

For one, I was sharp-toned with one defendant's counsel when he interrupted me. I felt bad about it at once and vowed to remind myself as often as necessary that the two primary virtues of any judge are patience and respect. I failed both in one moment. My other faux pas was denying the request of the other defendant's counsel to delay his opening statement to the jury until after the prosecution's case-in-chief was concluded. In the few criminal trials I'd been in or observed, whether state or federal court, no counsel had asked for such a delayed opening statement, so my sense was to adopt the practice I had experienced. I wasn't yet into experimenting with new ideas in the world of trials. I have admonished myself about denying the request because quickly I learned some defense lawyers have a legitimate reason for wanting to wait until the prosecution's case-in-chief is finished before making the defense's opening statement: it allows the defense counsel to talk to the jury about the actual evidence the government *has* put forward rather than what the prosecutor says *will be* the evidence put forward.

On May 4, 1970, the day before I took the oath of office, four students were killed and eight wounded when National Guardsmen fired into a crowd of Kent State University student protestors. The next day, on the campus of the University of Nebraska at Lincoln, the students rallied to protest the widening of the Vietnam War by the incursion into Cambodia and the killings and woundings at Kent State. One effect of the demonstration at the University of Nebraska was soon to be in my hands.

Dr. Stephen L. Rozman, hired as an assistant professor without tenure by the University of Nebraska, was cited in a report of a commission created by directive of the Board of Regents as having done acts during the demonstration "highly inappropriate for a teacher." Whether to renew Rozman's contract in light of his acts was the issue before the Board of

Regents. The decision of the board was not to renew, Rozman filed suit in federal court, and the case was mine to decide. A nonjury trial ensued, and I explained in a written opinion my view of the respective roles of people involved, as follows:

> The competing interests in the dispute are that of freedom of expression, assembly and petition on the one hand and freedom to employ or not to employ on the other. Neither set of interests is absolute. Identifying the finely honed edge which cuts between the sets of interests is the labor of the court. . . . I conclude that the plaintiff professor passed beyond the perimeters of protected freedom of expression, assembly and petition and, therefore, that the non-renewal of the contract was permissible by the university. I offer no view as to the wisdom of the university's action. . . . In no sense am I guided by the rights of private employers to hire or not to hire whom they choose. Private employers are not limited by the Fourteenth Amendment of the Constitution, but public employers are. That amendment prohibits a university, as an arm of the state, from depriving a citizen of life, liberty, or property without due process of law, which means that the university cannot fail to reappoint a non-tenured faculty member arbitrarily or capriciously or for constitutionally impermissible reasons, such as race, religion, or the exercise of rights protected by the Constitution. *Freeman v. Gould Special School District of Lincoln County, Ark.*, 405 F. 2d 1153 (8th Cir. 1969).[11]

On that afternoon, May 5, 1970, a group of students, soon joined by Dr. Rozman, first went to a draft board, where Dr. Rozman urged the closing of the draft board's office for the rest of the afternoon in protest of the Cambodian incursion. No closing occurred. Some students remained, were arrested, and Dr. Rozman spent time helping get the arrested students released to an attorney.

Dr. Rozman again joined students, this time at the Military and Naval Science Building on the University's campus. People gathered during the afternoon and evening, and by midnight several hundred occupied "the pit," an indoor gathering place for students. At about 10:00 the next morning the students drew up a set of demands and a negotiating period developed by early afternoon, involving three members of the administration of the University; namely, President Soshnik; Vice Chancellor and Dean of Student Affairs G. Robert Ross; Dean of Faculties C. Peter Magrath; and several student spokespersons. Notice was read to the students that directed them to vacate the pit within 15 minutes and that continued occupancy would interfere with the holding of an ROTC class in a room nearby. Some of the students and Dr. Rozman sat in the building, after the statement and notice were read, with linked arms "in a mutual declaration of solidarity."[12] Evacuation of about 100 students and Dr. Rozman happened about 10:55 a.m. on May 5.

I found that Dr. Rozman had gone beyond the protection of his constitutionally protected freedom of speech in two respects: by intruding into the work of the administrators in attempting to negotiate a departure of the building and by staying in the building and linking his arms with the students, thereby contributing to the cancellation of a scheduled class session.

> Professor Rozman had a right to present his views by voice and physical presence about the Cambodian incursion and the Kent State tragedy. A time came in the negotiating room, however, when he abandoned temporarily the process of communicating about those subjects and assumed without invitation the role of attempting to break what he viewed to be an impasse. . . . At that point Dr. Rozman was not merely expressing a view as to the rightness or wrongness of the merits of the controversy, but was clothing himself with a procedural function belonging to the administrators. . . .
>
> . . . .
>
> In the present case there were threats of violence and threats of interference with the work of the school and of the rights of other students [to go to class]. The school authorities reasonably could and did conclude that wisdom dictated the cancellation of the class. . . . When the group chooses not to communicate with a united voice, it must bear the consequences of splintered voices. One of the consequences in the present case was that the normal work of the university in hold-

ing an ROTC class and the rights of other students to attend that class were impeded.[13]

A decision not to renew Dr. Rozman's contract was permissible. He had no right to be rehired.

When Charles McClelland and Curtis Rowland filed suit against Maurice Sigler, warden of the Nebraska State Penitentiary, on March 31, 1971, they joined the stream of a civil rights movement carried by the epochal ruling of the Supreme Court of the United States in *Brown v. Board of Education of Topeka*.[14] That holding of seventeen years earlier was pressing society to loosen the bonds of segregation by race. Finding the scope of that loosening was a part of the role of *McClelland v. Sigler*.[15]

The broad facts were undisputed: The East Cell House of the penitentiary was segregated by race. Only white inmates who refused to be housed with blacks were assigned to the East Cell House. The rest of the inmates—of all races—were assigned to the West Cell House. The defense of that official policy was that security of other inmates, as well as prison staff, required the segregation, because the fifty or so whites populating the East Cell House were of such a racist mind that no solution but segregation would provide security for all. Racial incidents had occurred at the penitentiary, some involving violence, including a 1966 assault on a guard and a sexual assault of a white man by three black men.

More than that, my predecessor, Judge Robert Van Pelt, had held just four years earlier in *Moss v. Sigler* that the steps taken by the warden in retaining segregated housing were not unreasonable and the East Cell House did not need to be integrated.[16] That conclusion was supported by a finding of the State Advisory Committee to Institutions and Welfare in 1966 that the East Cell Block should not be integrated because of possible danger to occupants of the penitentiary.

On considering the evidence and the law, I faced the prospect of drawing a different conclusion in the *McClelland* case than my predecessor and mentor had reached in the *Moss* case. In explaining my decision I pointed to three differences between this case and the case before Judge Van Pelt in 1967. First, in the 1967 case no claim was made that the accommodations in the East Cell House were better than the other areas where black inmates were housed. In the *McClelland* case, on the other hand, the inmates claimed and the evidence showed that the East Cell House afforded a more favorable environment. The warden himself testified that the West Cell House was "bad, real bad," because it was ninety-four or ninety-six years old and was more dilapidated than the East Cell House.

Second, at the time of the 1967 holding by Judge Van Pelt the Eighth Circuit Court of Appeals had not yet held unconstitutional an Arkansas statute that racially segregated places of confinement in a boys' reform school. The Eighth Circuit's holding came down later in the year in *Board of Managers of Arkansas Training School for Boys v. George*.[17] That holding was binding precedent on federal district courts in the Eighth Circuit, including those of Nebraska.

Third, for four years since the 1967 case there had been no perceptible change toward integration of the East Cell House, even though the law and society had continued their insistence upon advancement toward complete desegregation of public institutions.

The evidence at the trial of the *McClelland* case persuaded me that, although the personal inclinations of the warden and other officials were toward integration of races generally, and although violence was certainly possible without segregation of the East Cell House, failure to integrate was not justified. I was not convinced that yielding to the whites' demands and giving those most prone to violence the better accommodations of the East Cell House had done or would do anything toward ending segregation by race, but had merely reinforced the prejudice. I wrote, "Threats of recalcitrant prisoners whose racial prejudices are erected to defy the constitutional rights of black prisoners need to be quashed. The prisoners who threaten violence, rather than those who seek their right to nondiscriminatory treatment, should be the ones to feel the weight of the consequences of their overt bigotry. An image of the whole penal system of Nebraska being held at bay by fifty men is unacceptable."[18] An order was entered making the suit a class action, affecting all prisoners of the penitentiary, then and in the future. The judgment as I wrote it insisted upon integration.

In late March the *Lincoln Journal* printed an article under the byline of Harold Simmons, citing Warden Maurice Sigler as saying that he would move black inmates into the East Cell Block "only if I'm ordered to. And when they start carrying them (injured and dead) out, I'll only be able to sit back and say it's not my fault." Appeal to the Eighth Circuit Court of Appeals was filed promptly by Harold Mosher of the Nebraska attorney general's office, representing Warden Sigler.

Editorial opinion offered some skepticism. The *Lincoln Star*, in an editorial on April 30, 1971, wrote, "Judge Urbom is dealing here with a . . . unique situation" because many of the men felt they had nothing to lose. "If already in the pen, just how weighty can the law become for a man? In the case of murder, it could be death, but we are not so sure that this, even, will prove to be the deterrent it might seem to be."

Ten months later the Eighth Circuit Court of Appeals heard arguments and announced immediately from the bench that the judgment requiring desegregation would be affirmed.

In the meantime Warden Sigler had resigned to join the staff of the Federal Board of Parole. His replacement was Charles Wolff Jr. The day after the affirmation by the appellate court was announced the new warden called my office for an appointment to discuss the method of integration. He, Assistant Attorney General Harold Mosher, Counsel Richard Schmeling for the plaintiffs, and I met two days later and had what I called in my journal a "refreshing" conversation. Warden Wolff said he was confident he could complete integration of the East Cell House without trouble if it could be done gradually. He asked for sixty days for making the transition. I told him I was prepared to give him six months. A hearing on a plan submitted by the warden was held a week later. I approved the plan and provided for a progress report in sixty days and a final report in six months.

Integration was made peacefully on Monday, May 8, 1972, some thirty days after the conference with the new warden. I did not know the details of this remarkable accomplishment until I talked with Charles Wolff Jr. thirty-four years later. After a long career in corrections, including as warden of the Nebraska State Penitentiary, deputy director and then director of corrections of Virginia, director of corrections of Nevada, director of work programs, industries and operations in Washington State, and warden of the Nevada State Penitentiary, he retired and returned to Lincoln, where he lives with his wife, Fern. He gave me the following account.

Before the trial that ended in an order to integrate, Wolff, then associate warden, had several conversations with Warden Sigler about integration of the Nebraska State Penitentiary. Wolff encouraged such an integration, because "it was the right thing to do." But Sigler was adamant, Wolff said, becoming irritated with the conversation, and finally telling Wolff, "If you want to desegregate that East Cell House, go ahead and do it, but not till I'm gone, because I'm not going to do it!"

When Wolff became warden and the order from the court came out, he was ready. He talked to many of the inmates about it, saying that desegregation was going to happen and telling the objecting whites, "If you want to spend the rest of your life in this institution without seeing the sun, you can do that. I'll make a place for you—in isolation." He asked for volunteers from among the black inmates to be the first group of twenty-seven to move into the East Cell House. He talked to one of the volunteers—the one he figured was the meanest black man in the pen—saying, "Do you want to go down there? Do you have the balls to do it?" The man answered, "If I don't by now, I won't have time to grow them. I'll go."

Wolff was confident that his plan would work because he had built a reservoir of mutual trust with both the inmates and the staff. Each volunteer among the blacks was interviewed by the Classification Committee in the associate warden's office, and the ones fitting the criterion of compatibility were assigned to the East Cell House. The first twenty-seven were chosen. On Monday morning, May 8, the twenty-seven were assembled at 10 a.m. and sent to the East Cell House. By then the regular residents of the East Cell House were away at work, and when they returned to their cells at noon, their new cell mates were there to greet them. It worked.

All cells in the East Cell House could house four men, but the usual practice was to assign only three to a cell. At first, according to plan, three blacks would be placed together in each of the cells. It was done without incident. Shortly afterward a mixture of races within a cell began. Gradually additional reassignments were similarly made, all without incident.

Warden Wolff's praise for the smooth transition went to others. The press reported on May 9, 1972, that Wolff credited the men's "mature manner in handling themselves" and added, "Both black and white inmates are to be commended on their attitude and conduct in complying with the recent court order." By December 1972 Charles McClelland, the white inmate who with Curtis Rowland, the black inmate, had filed the lawsuit, reported by affidavit in connection with a closing of the case, "Warden Wolff has to the best of my knowledge fulfilled all terms of the court order and integration is now a part of the regular prison policy."

I had finished a pair of hearings one day in August 1973. To Dick Herman, who regularly wrote, among other things, a column called "Statehouse Letter" for the *Lincoln Journal*, the hearings seemed related in a way. One of the hearings was in a suit asking that an injunction be issued halting a federally ordered price freeze on beef and veal.[19] Herman wrote that if I were to order the Cost of Living Council to lift its freeze on beef prices, there would be "headlines from Bar Harbor and Homestead to Juneau and Honolulu." The other case challenged the firing of a state employee.

Having been in the courtroom that day with two other newspapermen—the only spectators—Herman wrote:

> In the richly wooden and dignified, but empty, courtroom, the potential enormity of the situation was too great to truly seize. Imagine: Serious, quiet, courteous Warren Urbom . . . not so long ago an industrious attorney in Lincoln, Neb., able to order and expect obedience from the most powerful mortal currently on this planet, the President of the United States. . . . The trio of reporters was completely without comprehension that minutes later . . . an Urbom order would legally bop two of Nebraska's three state government branches, the executive and the judicial. That involved reversing State Engineer Tom Doyle's 1972 firing of Richard Kiernan, one of Doyle's employees. Kiernan's summary dismissal was previously upheld by the Nebraska Supreme Court.[20]

My reaction? Just doin' my job, sir.

Once in a while a case comes along that is fun because it seems obvious but isn't. Like the haircut case, it may seem trivial, but isn't. So it was with *Potato Chip Institute v. General Mills, Inc.*[21]

General Mills, Inc. made a product it called Chipos. The Potato Chip Institute, a nonprofit corporation getting much of its income from makers of potato chips, sued General Mills on the claim that it shouldn't be labeling and selling Chipos as "potato chips." The potato chip industry insisted that a potato chip is a thin slice of *raw* potato deep-fried in deep fat until crisp, whereas Chipos are thin slices of *dehydrated* potatoes deep-fried. Labeling them as potato chips is misleading, said the potato chip industry. General Mills denied it.

I heard five days of testimony and arguments about the subject, all very interesting. Then I read briefs of the parties, all tightly and briskly drawn. As in every trial, I learned a lot about a subject new to me. I wrote an eight-page opinion that promoting Chipos as potato chips tends to mislead the public because of the past experience of consumers with "a raw potato overlay," but there would be no misleading if the promotion were accompanied by a prominent declaration, such as "fashioned from dried potato granules."

Hence an injunction was issued, allowing Chipos to be advertised and sold as potato chips if accompanied by the appropriate prominent declaration. The Eighth Circuit Court of Appeals affirmed my decision.[22]

In the early morning of August 17, 1970, an emergency telephone call was received by the Omaha Police Department, reporting that a woman or girl was screaming for help from a vacant house at 2867 Ohio Street. Several police cars were dispatched to the vacant house, including one occupied by Officer Larry D. Minard Sr. A suitcase was lying on its side at the doorway. Several officers entered the house, avoiding the suitcase, but the suitcase exploded as Officer Minard was standing near it and apparently inspecting it. He was killed instantly.

Investigation revealed that the suitcase had been rigged to explode on movement. Evidence led to the conclusion that fifteen-year-old Duane Peak was a prime suspect. He was a known member of the National Committee to Combat Fascism (NCCF). Ed Poindexter, also a member of NCCF, was capable of rigging a booby trap bomb. Warrants were issued for the arrest of both Peak and Poindexter. The police made a search of the headquarters of the NCCF pursuant to the warrants. Neither Peak nor Poindexter was found there, but Poindexter was arrested shortly after the search. Before the death of Minard a tip had been received by the police that dynamite might be found in the house of David Rice, also a member of NCCF. A search of Rice's house was conducted pursuant to a search warrant issued by a municipal court judge and an arrest warrant for Peak. Items found in the Rice house included dynamite, blasting caps with wire, dynamite wrapper, orange grip pliers, and a battery. Rice turned himself in when he learned that an arrest warrant was out for him.

After Rice turned himself in and Poindexter had been arrested, clothing of each of them was taken and submitted for examination by the crime laboratory of the Alcohol, Tobacco and Firearms Division of the Treasury Department in Washington. The examinations revealed traces of dynamite. Rice and Poindexter were charged with first-degree murder. At the trial Peak testified that he was present when Rice and Poindexter assembled the booby trap bomb, and that he took the bomb to the vacant house, placed it at the doorway, and called 911 to report screaming from the vacant house. Parts of the dynamite and other items found in the police search of the Rice house were received in evidence over the objection of the defendants. The jury convicted both defendants and fixed their sentences at life in prison.

David Rice and Ed Poindexter appealed their convictions to the Nebraska Supreme Court, partly on the ground that the evidence found in the search of Rice's house by the police officers should not have been received in evidence at the trial because it was found in a police search that was illegal under the Fourth Amendment of the Constitution of the United States. In an opinion written by Judge Clinton, concurred in by Judges Smith and McCown, the court held that the affidavit given the municipal judge in support of the search warrant was "sufficient basis for a finding of probable cause" by the municipal judge from "the following additional allegations based upon the personal knowledge of the Omaha police department and the affiants: (1) David L. Rice is the Minister of Information, National Committee to Combat Fascism; (2) he is a known member of the organization 'which advocates the violent killing of Police Officers'; and (3) the death of a police officer by violence (by means of an explosive booby trap—a fact so notorious at the time in Omaha that even the public had knowledge of it as a fact)."[23] The Supreme Court of Nebraska affirmed the convictions of Rice and Poindexter.

Rice then turned to the federal court, filing a petition for writ of habeas corpus, seeking his release from prison, asserting that neither the search warrant nor the search itself was supported as required by the Fourth Amendment. If so, then under the exclusionary rule, evidence found pursuant to the warrant should not have been allowed to be considered by the jury at Rice's trial.

Many criminal cases are brought to the U.S. district courts from state courts when constitutional issues are presented. The task of the federal court is not to decide the guilt or innocence of the defendant, but to decide whether a conviction was free of any violation of some provision of the Constitution of the United States. Sometimes the claim arises from the Fourth Amendment, which declares, "The right of the people to be secure in their persons, houses, papers, and effects, against unreasonable searches and seizures, shall not be violated and no Warrants shall issue, but upon probable cause, supported by Oath or affirmation, and particularly describing the place to be searched, and the persons or things to be seized."

The exclusionary rule was a creation of the Supreme Court of the United States in 1914 in *Weeks v. United States*.[24] Its main goal has been to provide police officers an incentive to protect carefully the privacy rights of the Fourteenth Amendment. The exclusionary rule says in essence that evidence cannot be used against a house owner, for example, if the evidence was discovered in the house when there was no reasonable cause known to the police to believe there was that sort of evidence in that house. That rule was controversial from its beginning, and walked on wobbly legs until this *Rice* case made its way to the Supreme Court. Simply put, many state court judges and prosecutors were offended by the fact that after two tiers of state courts—the state trial court and at least one appellate court (in Rice's case, that meant the trial judge and the state's supreme court, a total of eight judges)—had held that the dynamite could be considered by the jury in deciding the guilt or innocence of Rice, that the holding could be overturned by a single federal judge, including me.

I can understand the feelings of state judges and prosecutors. I can also understand my obligation to follow the law, hurt feelings or not. My decision was made on the basis of the law as it existed when the case was before me. And I am comfortable in my ruling that the dynamite and its accoutrements were discovered in an illegal search and should not have been received in evidence at the trial.

The Eighth Circuit Court of Appeals affirmed my decision. In doing so Senior Circuit Judge Charles Matthes wrote for a unanimous three-judge court:

> In concluding this lengthy opinion, we are mindful that a brutal crime was perpetrated in which the life of a police officer was ended without justification. It cannot be gainsaid that Judge Urbom recognized the seriousness of the offense and the general public outrage over the crime. Against this background, Judge Urbom exercised painstaking care in resolving the factual and constitutional issues in this case. Having done so, Judge Urbom conscientiously and courageously concluded and demonstrated in two soundly reasoned opinions that the petitioner had been deprived of a basic constitutional right.[25]

Interestingly the issue that the Supreme Court of the United States chose to use to reverse the circuit court's holding was not one raised by the State of Nebraska prosecutors. It was raised by the Supreme Court of the United States itself by directing counsel after the case was lodged in the Supreme Court as follows: "In addition to those questions presented by the petition, counsel are requested to brief and argue the following question: Whether the constitutional validity of the entry and search of respondent's premises by Omaha police officers under the circumstances of this case is a question properly cognizable under 28 U.S.C. § 2254."[26] Section 2254 is the habeas corpus for cases coming from a state court to a federal court.

I have no unease in general with the decision of the Supreme Court of the United States. It thoroughly reviewed the interests at stake and concluded that the search for justice in the guilt or innocence of a defendant trumps the effort of the exclusionary rule to deter unlawful acts on the part of police. However, I think it unfair to apply the new rule to David Rice's case. The law at the time of his conviction was as the Eighth Circuit and I found it to be, and I stoutly think that the rule in effect when Rice was convicted should have been applied to his case, which would allow him a new trial without the use against him of the dynamite and other evidence

26. David Rice, aka Wopashitwe Mondo Eyen We Langa, petitioner in suit leading to change in the law regarding the exclusionary rule. Photograph by *Lincoln Journal Star*.

found by an illegal search. The new rule could well be applied to all cases arising *after* the *Rice* case was decided by the Supreme Court.

The decision of the Supreme Court did not find that the dynamite and accoutrements were legally found or that the Nebraska state courts had been right in allowing the use of that evidence at trial. It found only that the federal court should not have taken the case—not because that had been the law when Rice had his trial, but because the Supreme Court was now changing the law as to when a federal court should take such a case.

The Supreme Court's decision did not diminish the force of the Fourth Amendment; it held only that the federal courts are not to accept habeas corpus cases pertaining to the Fourth Amendment when the issue in the case has already been submitted to two tiers of a state's judiciary for a full and fair resolution.[27] The rule had been otherwise since 1914, but the change was undoubtedly welcomed heartily by prosecutors, state court judges, police, and the public countrywide. Perhaps even by federal judges.

David L. Rice, who prefers the name Wopashitwe Mondo Eyen We Langa, remains in prison today.[28]

Most people probably don't expect to see religion brought into court, but it is there in surprising amounts. In almost every case the issue of religion arises because a government—federal, state, or local—becomes involved in somebody's religious practices or beliefs. The basis of most of the disputes is the First Amendment to the Constitution of the United States, which says, "Congress shall make no law respecting an establishment of religion or prohibiting the free exercise thereof."

"Congress" can also be read as "a state," because states are forbidden by the Fourteenth Amendment to the same extent that Congress is forbidden by the First Amendment. Agencies of the federal government, agencies of the state governments, and persons who are agents of government are all subject to the restrictions, because they all act on behalf of the federal or state governments. Accordingly public schools, public hospitals, prisons and jails, and a host of other entities operated by governments are prohibited from making a "law respecting an establishment of religion or prohibiting the free exercise thereof."

While not the first case to deal with contentious issues between government on one hand and religious and nonreligious persons on the other, *Engel v. Vitale* reawakened the populace in 1962 to such issues.[29] The Supreme Court held that requiring students of a public school to say a particular prayer at the opening of a school day was unconstitutional because of the First Amendment's establishment of religion clause.

Prayer in the public schools has been a particularly sensitive issue across the country in the several decades that followed the *Engel* case. Some fear that God has been driven out of the schools. Some claim that the courts have become enemies of religion. But I think there is nothing to justify any of that. In fact the contrary is true. By insisting upon assiduous attention to the First Amendment, religion's freedom to continue its vital activity is preserved. The First Amendment is designed to *protect* religious beliefs and actions. It does so by insisting that government stay away from them, except to preserve their independence.

For me a cautioning thought is helpful: when considering the wisdom of a governmental act or rule appearing to *help* a particular religious practice or belief, I think of the "particular religious practice or belief" as if it were a practice *different* from my own. Would I want the government to favor that practice or belief? If the governmental act or rule appears to *hinder* or *control* the particular practice or belief, I think of the "particular religious practice or belief" as if it were a practice the *same* as my own. Would I want the government to control or limit that practice or belief? Confronting such a question helps me avoid the temptation to judge the religious practice or belief actually involved. And I must remember that it is *government* control that is the target of the First Amendment's religion clauses, thus allowing the individual believer to have control of his or her religious faith or, in the case of children, allowing the parent, parents, or other custodian to have the freedom and obligation of watchfulness over the child's religious development.

Beginning in the 1970s my court docket has had at least one "religion" case in every decade. The first several arose from the Nebraska State Penitentiary, where prisoners complained that the prison administration denied them instruments or symbols of their practice of religion.

For example, Curtis Rowland, a black Muslim, wanted to wear a medallion around his neck as a symbol of his faith. Although I considered the claim in his lawsuit an appropriate one, the state's interest in security was a compelling one: a medallion strung on a chain, however small, could be used as a weapon. In a prison a weapon of any sort is a constant danger to other inmates and staff alike. So I held that the state's interest trumped the individual inmate's "free exercise of religion" and denied Rowland's claim. Weighing the competing interests in the particular circumstances is the task of the judge. The ruling was affirmed on appeal in *Rowland v. Sigler*.[30]

Much more complex are cases like *Chambers v. Marsh*.[31] The issues in the *Chambers* case were (1) whether the Nebraska legislature's practice of having a prayer at the opening of each day's session was constitutional, (2) whether paying the chaplain from tax funds to say the prayers was constitutional, and (3) whether using tax funds to pay for the printing and mailing of those prayers to legislators' constituents was constitutional. The complexity is apparent from the outcome: I ruled that (1) *was* constitutional, that (2) was *not* constitutional, and that (3) was *not* constitutional. The circuit court of appeals held that taken as a whole (1), (2), and (3) were *not* constitutional.[32] The Supreme Court of the United States held that taken as a whole (1) and (2) *were* constitutional.[33] It did not rule on

27. Senator Ernest Chambers, plaintiff in *Chambers v. Marsh*.
Photograph courtesy of the clerk of the Nebraska Legislature Office.

(3) because the issue of use of tax funds was no longer being raised by the party appealing to the Supreme Court.

Ernest Chambers was a member of the Nebraska State Legislature. As a non-Christian, he objected to the legislature's rule of having a prayer to open each day's session and objected to the use of tax money to pay the chaplain and to print and send the prayers to the legislators' constituents. He sued Frank Marsh, the state treasurer; Reverend Robert E. Palmer, the chaplain; and members of the Executive Board of the Legislative Council of the Nebraska Unicameral, who had engaged Chaplain Palmer, a Presbyterian minister, for each of the past sixteen years.

What became known as the "*Lemon* test," named for the case from which it arose, for determining whether a government's act is constitutional within the establishment clause of the First Amendment, was expressed in 1971 and again in 1973.[34] Three criteria for constitutionality of a law were described:

(1) it must serve a clearly secular, that is, nonreligious, purpose; (2) it must have a primary effect that neither advances nor inhibits religion; and (3) it must avoid excessive governmental entanglement with religion.

I concluded that the First Amendment did not prohibit the legislature's having prayer daily to open its sessions because what the senators did while the prayer was being recited was not "making a law." I reasoned that when a legislature by majority vote invites a clergyman to give a prayer, neither the voting nor the inviting nor the giving nor the hearing of the prayer is making a law. Nobody there was being told he or she had to be there or not to be there.

On appeal, the three-judge panel of the circuit court did not contradict that rationale, but chose to put all elements of the prayer program together and to assess it as a whole, including the paying of the chaplain and the funding of the printing and mailing of the prayers. Noting that the legislature had by formal rule required the legislative prayer and payments, viewed as a whole, the circuit court said, "such state sanctioned, sponsored and financed prayer activities certainly reflect sufficient 'law making' to present a justiciable claim under the Establishment Clause."

I held that the use of tax funds to pay the chaplain and to publish the chaplain's prayers was a violation of the First Amendment's establishment clause. Under the evidence, I acknowledged, the practice of prayers at the opening of a session did have a secular purpose (in addition to a religious one) of bringing the legislature to order by means of a brief and solemn act in a traditional manner. Nonetheless, directing the treasurer to pay from state funds the chaplain for praying and to pay for the printing and mailing of the prayers constituted "making a law," because it was done by the legislature in its governmental capacity and imposed obligations upon the treasurer to use nonlegislators' money. Moreover the payments were "respecting religion" (i.e., about or regarding religion) because they had a direct and substantial effect in advancing religion. Payments for printing and delivering the printed prayers had no secular purpose, thus being at odds with criterion (2) of the *Lemon* test for constitutionality.

The circuit court chose not to separate the "funding" claims from the "prayer" claims, but held that "as a whole" the practice of employing one minister of one denomination and paying for publication and mailing the prayers amounted to "falling into the quagmire" of excessive entanglement of the government in religious affairs—that is, failing criterion (3) of the *Lemon* test. The case went to the U.S. Supreme Court. By a six-to-three vote the Court reversed the circuit court. Six of the justices held that the challenged practice did not violate the establishment clause. It made no analysis under the *Lemon* test. Rather it applied a new test.

Speaking for the six-person majority, Chief Justice Burger wrote, "From colonial times through the founding of the Republic and ever since, the practice of legislative prayer has coexisted with the principles of disestablishment and religious freedom." The next sentence of the opinion said, "In the very courtrooms in which the United States District Judge and later three Circuit Judges heard and decided this case, the proceedings opened with an announcement that concluded, 'God save the United States and this Honorable Court.'" That statement was dramatic, but insofar as it referred to "the United States District Judge" it was not true. No such imploring of God's favor was used when the district court of Nebraska was opened in this case. I know; I presided over the opening. I do not know how court was opened when the "three Circuit Judges" heard this case on appeal in a different courtroom. But none of the statements of how court was opened made any difference in the outcome. The Supreme Court was declaring a shift in the law to say that a longtime practice of opening legislative sessions with prayer validates the practice. The specific statement in the majority opinion is, "In light of the unambiguous and unbroken history . . . there can be no doubt that the practice of opening legislative sessions with prayer has become a part of the fabric of our society. To invoke Divine guidance on a public body entrusted with making the laws is not, in these circumstances, an 'establishment' of religion or a step toward establishment; it is simply a tolerable acknowledgment of beliefs widely held among the people of this country."[35]

One interesting sentence near the close of the majority opinion is this: "Absent proof that the chaplain's reappointment stemmed from an impermissible motive, we conclude that . . . [Palmer's] long tenure does not in itself conflict with the Establishment Clause."[36] In the course of time we may discover what motives in the legislative setting may be deemed "impermissible."

Justice Brennan, with whom Justice Marshall joined, dissented. Justice Brennan began by saying that some twenty years earlier, he had come "very close to endorsing essentially the result reached by the Court today." But he continued, "I have come to the conclusion that I was wrong then and that the Court is wrong today." The rest of Justice Brennan's dissent centered on his conviction that the facts of this case did not meet the prevailing establishment clause doctrine found in *Lemon v. Kurtzman*. He considered it self-evident that the purpose of legislative prayer "is preeminently religious," and to ascribe a secular purpose to it is "an insult" to the persons who began and continued the practice. Further, the "primary effect" of legislative prayer is "clearly religious." "Finally," he wrote, "[T]here can be no doubt that the practice of legislative prayer leads to excessive 'entanglement' between the State and religion."[37]

Justice Stevens's dissent was direct and short. He summarized, "Regardless of the motivation of the majority that exercises the power to appoint the chaplain, it seems plain to me that the designation of a member of one religious faith to serve as the sole official chaplain of a state legislature for a period of 16 years constitutes the preference of one faith over another in violation of the Establishment Clause of the First Amendment."[38]

So, as time rumbles on, we'll see whether we can live with the concept of the Supreme Court's majority, that longevity validates behavior. Is that true in other settings where religion meets law? Does it apply *only* to the intersection of religion and law?

Another of the cases tackling the issue of church and state that fought its way to the Supreme Court and survived there—in a tie—is *Quaring v. Peterson*.[39] Frances J. Quaring was denied a driver's license because she would not agree to have her photograph taken and placed on a driver's license as required by Nebraska law. She sued the director and deputy director of the Department of Motor Vehicles, asserting that the state was infringing upon her free exercise of religion as guaranteed by the First Amendment of the Constitution of the United States.

I found from the evidence at the trial that Quaring had a sincere religious belief that she should not have "any graven images" in her personal world. Although her particular denomination of Christianity did not interpret the Second Commandment literally, as she did, she had no pictures of her family, her wedding, or of any human, including pictures or drawings on her curtains, walls, or food cans. That, she testified, is what the Second Commandment means when it says in Exodus 20:4 and Deuteronomy 5:8 of the King James Version of the Bible, "Thou shalt not make unto thee any graven image, or any likeness of anything that is in heaven above, or that is in the earth beneath, or that is in the water under the earth."

Therefore, having her photograph on her driver's license would be contrary to her sincere religious belief, and she asked that the government be prevented from causing her to suffer the consequences of having no driver's license or of breaching her attachment to the Bible. I agreed with her and ordered the officials of the State of Nebraska to accommodate her by issuing her a license free of the photograph requirement. My finding was that Quaring had a sincere religious belief about the matter and that requiring her to yield to having the photograph was a burden on her. Helping her husband manage a thousand-acre farming and livestock operation, working as a bookkeeper in a town ten miles from her home, and managing a herd of dairy and beef cattle meant that the ability to drive an automobile on a regular basis was important to her.

The State of Nebraska officials argued that Quaring's interest in exercising her religion must be subordinated to the state's more compelling interest of providing law enforcement officers with a quick and accurate means of identifying drivers of automobiles. I agreed there was a benefit to the state, but felt it shrank in relative importance when testimony showed that the state already routinely exempted from the photograph requirement numerous classes of driver's licenses, learner permits, school permits issued to farmers' children, farm machinery permits, special permits for persons with restricted or minimal driving ability, and temporary licenses for persons outside the state whose old licenses had expired. In addition, motorists from states that do not require photographs on licenses and who passed through Nebraska on occasion were free from Nebraska's requirement. Hence accommodating several classes of persons weakens the argument that the state would be heavily burdened by accommodating one more class. No evidence was submitted that large numbers of people were likely to fit into Quaring's class of persons seeking drivers' licenses. On appeal, the Eighth Circuit Court of Appeals affirmed my decision, though Judge George Fagg dissented.[40]

The Supreme Court, without elaboration, left in place my decision as affirmed by the circuit court, saying only, "The judgment [of the circuit court] is affirmed by an equally divided court. Justice Powell took no part in the decision of this case."[41] Apparently, without Justice Powell's participation, four of the justices said the decision was right; four said it wasn't.

Not all cases of religious subjects are focused on the First Amendment's establishment clause. The free speech clause of the First Amendment may also be a key to the decision. *Brown v. Board of Regents of the University of Nebraska* is an example.[42] Sheldon Film Theater, a state-operated art theater on the campus of the University of Nebraska, scheduled and advertised a movie to be shown to the public, but canceled the showing because of the film's controversial content. Suit was filed by Randal B. Brown and others on the ground that the plaintiffs had a constitutional right to see the film. I agreed and entered an injunction requiring the film to be shown to the public.

The movie was *Hail Mary* by Jean-Luc Godard. It featured in a modern setting the birth of Jesus Christ. George Neubert, director of the Sheldon Memorial Art Gallery, had delegated to Dan Ladely the authority to select films for showing. Ladely chose *Hail Mary* because of the reputation of the director.

In two days of advertising the film, Ladely had received four telephone calls objecting to the showing, including one from Senator Bernice Labedz, a member of the Nebraska State Legislature. Senator Labedz had read about, but had not seen, the movie. She said she wanted the film not to be shown because it blasphemed the Blessed Mary and the birth of Christ, offending the senator's religious precepts. She felt that showing the movie might result in demonstrations by others who did not like the film's religious content. Labedz testified that in a telephone conversation with Ladely she told him:

> [The year before there was a] big controversy on the [floor of the legislature] whether or not the Sheldon Art Gallery should be closed, and I said that I didn't want to see them have that type of trouble; that there would be some very difficult times on the floor and that I myself

> would introduce a resolution then—not waiting for the budget . . . and hoping . . . I would get the support of the senators on the floor . . . showing our objections to the film. And I said . . . I did not want to call President Roskens [of the University of Nebraska], whom I consider a very personal friend of mine or Chancellor Massengale, whom I consider a friend.[43]

Director Neubert directed Ladely to cancel the film because it was "offensive to a segment of society and did not merit the efforts it would take to defend it."

The testimony of Senator Labedz, George Neubert, and Dan Ladely led to my writing the following:

> When the senator demanded the banning of the film, Neubert felt compelled to withdraw from the chilly political winds. The legislature had previously reduced state funding and Neubert, not unreasonably, concluded that further budget cuts might be forthcoming were he to disregard the legislator's wishes.
>
> The constitution interjects safeguards against just this type of governmental influence. The effect of such unauthorized use of political power is obvious and the precedent is untenable.

An injunction was entered. The movie was shown to those who chose to see it. I saw the movie and wrote, in an addendum to my memorandum explaining the injunction, "It [the movie] is what critics have called it. From time to time its parts are dull, beautiful, incomprehensible, brave, shallow, penetrating, vulgar, demeaning and, no doubt, blasphemous for some and inspirational for others."[44] No appeal was filed.

The *Hail Mary* case was one that stirred the public's emotional feelings, but another a few years earlier had been at least as volatile. It was the *McCurry* case. A headline in *Temple Times* of East Point, Georgia, on September 4, 1983, read, "Judge Upholds Police in Dragging Worshipers from Worship Meeting and Padlocking Church Building." It referred to an episode at the Faith Baptist Church of Louisville, Nebraska, on October 18, 1982.

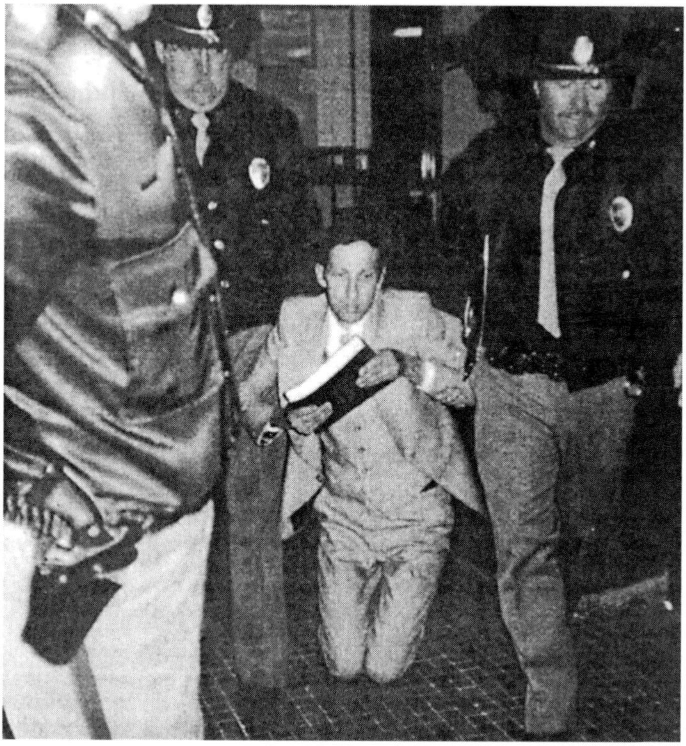

28. Parishioners being removed from the Faith Christian Church school by Cass County sheriff's deputies. Photograph courtesy of Dr. Everett G. Ramsey.

For many years Faith Baptist Church had an ongoing dispute with the State of Nebraska about the church's operating a school without complying with state school laws. The state authorities got an injunction from the state court, affirmed by the Supreme Court of Nebraska, prohibiting the church's operation of the school.[45]

On September 11, 1981, the state district court found that the school was being operated in violation of the injunction issued by Cass County District Judge Raymond Case that directed the sheriff of Cass County to install additional locks on each entrance to the church and school, and being one building, "the building [was] to be unlocked Saturday and Sunday and such other times as the building shall be used for the holding of church services." The court then held the pastor, Reverend Everett Sileven, and Faith Baptist Church in contempt of the court's orders, and insisted that the sheriff "forthwith secure the building by the placing of locks on each of the entrances to the church, the building to be opened on Saturday, Sunday and Wednesday evenings for the singular purpose of religious services."

While an appeal was being taken to the Nebraska Supreme Court by Reverend Sileven and others, the September order was temporarily lifted. Upon dismissal of the appeal for failure to file briefs, the state district court ordered Reverend Sileven jailed for contempt, and on October 14, 1982, ordered the September 11th order to be reinstated and directed the sheriff of Cass County to enforce "the Order of this Court prohibiting the operation of a non-approved school, the first enforcement to be exercised Monday, October 18, 1982; it being the intent of the Court that the parents of children attending thereat shall have advance notice of the action taken by the Court."[46]

It was that Monday morning, October 18, 1982, at about 6 a.m., when the sheriff and ten or twelve of his deputies entered the church and school building. As many—as a hundred people were in the building, and at one time or another during the night the plaintiffs or some of them were there singing, preaching, reading the Bible, and praying. No children were in the building and no classes were being held. When the officers arrived and picked up those in the church who refused to leave and removed them from the building, those persons were praying to protest the jailing of Reverend Sileven and the closing of the school.

A civil suit was brought in the federal court and assigned to me. The plaintiffs were Robert E. McCurry and some sixty-five others from the church, asking for injunctive relief and monetary damages for violation of their First Amendment rights. Violation of both freedom of religion and freedom of assembly were emphasized.

After what I thought was careful research, I dismissed the case, holding that the law enforcement officers were entitled to absolute immunity from both injunctive and monetary impositions. That's saying that officers who are only carrying out orders from a judge cannot be held personally accountable for doing what they are told to do. Robert McCurry, the lead plaintiff, was furious in his expression of condemnation of my action. He wrote in his *Temple Times*, "Religious liberty is dead in America. This fact was confirmed again by Federal Judge Warren Urbom on July 28, 1983, in Lincoln, Nebraska, when he dismissed the sixty-six million dollar civil rights lawsuit brought by sixty-six plaintiffs who were dragged by county and state law enforcement officers from a prayer and worship meeting in a 6:00 a.m. raid at the Faith Baptist Church in Louisville, Nebraska, October 18, 1982."[47]

His fury was understandable. The October 18 scene was not a pretty one. An appeal to a higher court was appropriate. My order did not kill religious liberty in America, but I agree that the three-judge panel of the court of appeals was sensible in seeing that I had stretched the concept of immunity. The appellate panel reversed my decision by a vote of two-to-one (Judge Fagg dissenting) and directed me to apply a different standard—one of *qualified* immunity, rather than *absolute* immunity—and to enter a declaratory judgment in favor of the plaintiffs that the law enforcement officers had violated the plaintiffs' constitutional rights. I was then instructed to determine whether the officers should be liable in money damages, and, if so, how much.

After the remand from the Eighth Circuit Court of Appeals, I held a full-dress evidentiary hearing on the facts, including those relative to the qualified immunity issue. I did as the court of appeals directed me to do: I entered a declaratory judgment for the plaintiffs to the effect that the officers had violated the plaintiffs' constitutional rights, and I applied a standard of *qualified* immunity. In relation to the issue of damages, I found that a reasonable law enforcement officer could have thought that carrying the plaintiffs out of the church was within the scope of the state court's injunction. Therefore, no damages were entered against the officers, except an award of attorney's fees to the plaintiffs in the amount of $34,731.46 and $4,421.27 in court costs.[48]

Both sides appealed. The Eighth Circuit Court of Appeals affirmed my decision. The court said, "The District Court's findings of fact are not clearly erroneous. The most crucial finding of fact was whether the law-enforcement officers actually believed that the court order authorized them to carry praying people out of the church. The state judge who drafted the injunction testified that he did not intend the order to authorize such actions, and plaintiffs argue that the officers should be charged with this knowledge. We hold that, as a factual matter, the District Court did not clearly err in weighing the conflicting evidence and finding as it did."[49] As to the legal issue, the appellate court reasoned:

> The District Court noted that, absent a court order, no reasonable law enforcement officer would think that he could carry praying people out of a church without violating their First Amendment rights. The question becomes, then, whether a reasonable officer could interpret the court order here to authorize such conduct. The state-court injunction stated at some points that the church must be padlocked at all times other than weekends and Wednesday nights, but an earlier order had stated that the building must be locked at all times except Saturday, Sunday, and 'such other times as the building shall be used for the holding of church services.' [Citation omitted.] The officers here carried the plaintiffs out of the church at about 6:00 a.m. on a Monday morning, at a time when a church service was in progress. We agree with the District Court that the injunction was sufficiently ambiguous that a reasonable law-enforcement officer could have interpreted it to authorize what these defendants did.
>
> The question is whether reasonable officers could have resolved the ambiguity the other way. We think they could. Law-enforcement officers should not, on pain of having to pay damages out of their own pockets, be required to anticipate how appellate judges will apply maxims of constitutional adjudication about which even those judges sometimes disagree.[50]

The *McCurry* case was a hard one. Drawing the line between the religious and the governmental interests is not always easy. Respectful allowances of interests on both sides are critical.

7

Wounded Knee and the Fort Laramie Treaty of 1868

Freedom is what,
justice is what,
liberty is what
we want.

—HENRY CROW DOG, FROM
ROXANNE ORTIZ'S *THE GREAT SIOUX NATION*

At the dawn of 1974 my life was about to be absorbed by Native Americans.

I could have avoided it, I suppose, but I didn't see it coming, and when I did see it, I was already deeply involved. I accepted the invitation with the expectation that I'd spend a week trying Native Americans. I stayed a year.

Despite my upbringing in Arapahoe, a town named for an Indian tribe, I saw no American Indians there. The Arapahoe Warriors was the name of our school athletic teams. My first sight of any Indians was as a youngster with my parents at one or more powwows in Trenton, Nebraska, an hour and a half west of Arapahoe and the site of the 1873 Battle of Massacre Canyon. At the powwows our family watched the dances, listened to the drum beats, and marveled at the beaded and feathered clothes. I viewed these as costumes designed in part for tradition and in part for entertainment of the curious whites. In school we read of the fabled Pocahontas, John Alden, Miles Standish, and Massasoit. Movies, by and large, pictured Indians as the constant resister in a by-gone era of America's progress west.

My memory is that Indians were thought of at the time as a subdued, separated, and largely unknown subset of humanity, providing neither danger nor substance to our existence. Experiences in adulthood may have added considerable sociological understanding of American Indians, but it was academic and only mildly personal.

As a judge, I had tried one important case in Omaha that had given me some needed sense of "Indianness." It was *United States v. Stabler*,[1] in which the defendant, Raymond Stabler, was charged with murdering a fellow resident on the Omaha Reservation after an evening of drinking and quarreling. Testimony was largely by American Indians, whose quiet voices, unassuming manner, and unpretentious acceptance of a desolate and pitiable lifestyle told a sordid story of what the jury found to be an intentional but not premeditated killing.

I sentenced the eighteen-year-old defendant to ten years in prison. On appeal, a three-judge panel of circuit judges, with Judge Roy Stephenson dissenting, concluded that a new trial was necessary because I had allowed the jury to consider evidence of footprints in snow and a bloodstained jacket. I have not been able to learn that Raymond Stabler was ever retried. If he was not, it probably was because the appellate court's excluding the footprint and jacket from evidence left the government with what it considered too little evidence to make prosecution well-advised.

Wounded Knee is a spot in the prairie of southwestern South Dakota. It gained an indelible place in the oral history of the Sioux when the Seventh U.S. Cavalry there overtook a struggling band of Sioux men, women, and children led by Bigfoot in December 1890. When a white flag ascended from the wagon of Bigfoot and a disarming of the Indian men was in progress, shooting broke out, killing an estimated three hundred of the Indian men, women, and children and perhaps thirty-one of the cavalry soldiers.[2]

Eighty-three years later, in 1973, Wounded Knee was a tiny village on the Pine Ridge Reservation. On the evening of February 27 some thirty cars approached the village, which consisted of a trading post, a museum, a post office, and a few houses.[3] At least a hundred persons emerged from the cars, shooting and yelling. They reportedly shot out the dawn-to-dusk lights in the vicinity of the trading post, broke into and looted the trading post, carried part of its contents into a nearby church, and held several persons hostage. That much was reported quickly to the Federal Bureau of Investigation, the U.S. Marshals Service (USMS), and the Bureau of Indian Affairs of the Department of Interior (BIA) by Agnes Gildersleeve, keeper of the trading post and witness to the events. That evening the FBI, USMS, and BIA responded by gathering outside the village. Lacking sufficient manpower to enter Wounded Knee to make an investigation and arrests without forcible action, the three agencies surrounded the village by setting up roadblocks at the major points of exit and entry. By the next morning the armed occupiers of the village had set up their own roadblocks between the law enforcement officers and the village to prevent entry by the officers. For seventy-one days the encircling of the village by law officers on the outer perimeter and by the occupiers on the inner perimeter remained constant. By the end of the seventy-one days, negotiations had led to an agreed-upon end to the occupation, and arrests were made.

Although American Indians' dissatisfaction with the United States was of long standing, there were conditions on Pine Ridge Reservation of recent vintage that angered members of the American Indian Movement (AIM). They saw the governing of the affairs of the reservation to be autocratic and corrupt in the person of Dick Wilson, their elected president of the Tribal Council, supported by the police of the BIA. With whatever goal, the AIM members and supporters overtook the village, probably chosen because of the event in 1890, and occupied it with force of arms. During the occupation three Indians were killed, and one U.S. marshal was shot and permanently disabled.[4] Upon the surrender of the occupiers approximately 150 were arrested and charged in federal court in the District of South Dakota with various criminal offenses, ranging from assault of a federal officer, burglary, and cattle rustling to conspiracy to interfere with a federal officer in the performance of duty.

In late 1973 Judge Gerald Heaney of the Eighth Circuit Court of Appeals asked me to be one of several district judges to travel to South Dakota to try cases that had arisen from the incident at Wounded Knee. I said sure. Because a trial of two persons deemed the leaders of the take-over—Russell Means and Dennis Banks—was being had in St. Paul, Minnesota, before

Judge Fred Nichol of the District of South Dakota, the trials we other judges would have would be the "nonleadership" cases.

The plan for proceeding was given me by Judge Heaney, one member of a three-judge panel appointed by Chief Judge Pat Mehaffey of the Eighth Circuit Court of Appeals to oversee the trial proceedings. A series of district judges would try cases simultaneously two at a time, one in Sioux Falls and one in Aberdeen, South Dakota, rotating as needed. I was to talk with Judge Andrew Bogue of the District of South Dakota for further details of the proposed trials. I agreed to be first in line for a trial in early January 1974 in Sioux Falls, and learned from Judge Bogue that it would be a "simple burglary and larceny" case. The lawyers had told him, he said, that it should take about a week to try.

Mindful that we knew only a little about Indian law—that is, law arising from treaties and congressional legislation specifically pertaining to American Indians—my law clerks and I set to work to learn more. Our unfamiliarity with the laws made the process slow but doable.

There was another problem. Security, the U.S. Marshals Service was careful to tell us, had to be tight. The deputy marshals reminded me that members of AIM had participated in at least two affairs of violence in addition to Wounded Knee within the past year. One was in Washington DC, and one in Custer, South Dakota. The marshals urged me to take careful precautions, specifically in selection of rooming accommodations and in the courthouse. The Indians wanted publicity, the marshals said, and could get it only by confrontation.

My staff (law clerks David Pedersen and John Moseman and secretary Marlene McGuire) and I arrived in Sioux Falls on the evening of Sunday, January 13, 1974. Because we had received the dire warnings of possible confrontation, we checked in at the Holiday Inn across the street from the federal courthouse and bedded down for the night with some trepidation.

Entering the courthouse the next morning through the only accessible door proved that security was tight, as we had been told it would be. A magnetometer manned by U.S. deputy marshals blocked entrance. We introduced ourselves to those marshals we didn't know and took an elevator to the judge's chamber and courtroom on the second floor. Marlene busied herself getting her typewriter and accompanying material in place.

The law clerks found the court library, and I looked over the indictment and checked the names of the defendants and the attorneys of record for the parties: *United States of America, Plaintiff, v. Baker and DeCora, Defendants;* Edward Carpenter for the prosecution and John Thorne and Joseph Beeler for the defense.

The telephone rang. I answered it and a deputy marshal asked that I come to the front door of the courthouse: "We have a problem down here." I went to the front door and found a man of perhaps fifty, wearing a full beard, a beaded denim jacket, and a sea captain's cap. He introduced himself as John Thorne from San Jose, California. He explained that the marshals wanted to search his briefcase, but he objected because he represented a defendant in a case that would begin that day. I recognized his name from the case's docket sheet I had seen a few minutes earlier. We talked briefly. He was polite but insistent, and (though I didn't say it) I relied on what I acknowledge now to be nearly unbounded faith in the honesty of trial lawyers. Until one shows he or she is unfaithful, I trust him or her. I told the marshals not to require a search of any attorney who assured them he or she represented a party in the case. I realized somewhat sheepishly that just a few days earlier I had signed an order saying that all bags and packages were to be searched before entrance of the courthouse. I could feel the bristling of the marshals. I understood, but I was the one who had to make the call and be responsible for the consequences.

The first legal matter requiring a hearing was a motion by the defendants to suppress evidence seized at a roadblock halting traffic into Wounded Knee. When court opened I didn't notice that some of the Indians didn't stand when John Moseman, the law clerk who was acting as bailiff, opened court by rapping the gavel and calling out, as usual, "All rise!" as I took the bench and announced the hearing on the motion. When we recessed midmorning, Moseman told me that some of the Indians hadn't stood.

The next morning John Thorne came to my chambers with Madonna Gilbert, who would be a defendant in the second case set for trial. He asked that she be permitted to speak with me. At my invitation they took seats across my desk from me.

She started by saying, "I suppose you have noticed that some of us haven't stood when you have come into the courtroom."

"Yes," I said, "I noticed that."[5]

She continued, "I want you to know we don't mean any disrespect to you or the flag. But we think if we stood it would mean we respect the prosecution, and we don't respect the prosecution."

I responded, "I don't know why we expect people to stand when a judge comes into the courtroom. Nobody has ever explained it to me. Thinking about it now, though, it seems to me that maybe it suggests that we are all in this together, and each one of us wants to get what we can call justice. But if it means to you something else that you don't agree with, then it's all right to just stay seated."

She nodded. "Thank you."

I looked at John Moseman and one of the deputy marshals who was listening and would serve from time to time as bailiff, but whose name I don't remember. I said to them, "From now on just leave out the words, 'All rise' when you open court." The deputy marshal understood, but he wanted to have his say after the two visitors had left the room.

"This isn't the end of that," he said. "If refusing to stand up doesn't do it, they'll do whatever it takes to get attention. They've got a cause and the only way they'll get attention and publicity is by making trouble. Next they'll come into the courtroom without shirts on their backs and with hats on their head. Anything, that's all. Anything."

"We'll see," I said.

"You've got to draw the line sometime. The sooner the better. Right now is the time."

"No, I don't think so."

"Then when *are* you going to draw the line?"

"Whenever what they do keeps us from having a fair trial. Not before. And not standing up isn't keeping us from having a fair trial."

We didn't talk further about it. More challenges seemed likely to come.

The hearing on the motion to suppress took two weeks of evidence and argument. I sustained the motion, meaning the prosecutors could not use the evidence found by the investigators inside the trunk of a car they had stopped at a roadblock. The prosecutors said that without the evidence I had ruled inadmissible they had insufficient evidence to expect to convict the defendants. No trial of that case was necessary. The lawyers then suggested that I stay to hear a similar motion in the next case that involved a different seizure of weapons from an automobile at the same roadblock. I stayed, but asked Judge Paul Benson of the District of North Dakota, who was scheduled to take over from me, to go instead to handle a non–Wounded Knee trial in my assigned courtroom in Lincoln. He agreed.

Monday, March 4, saw development of a major shift in plans. Lawyers from both sides were waiting to talk with me when I arrived at the chambers in Sioux Falls. Albert Krieger of the defense team took the lead in asking that I assume responsibility for all Wounded Knee cases, except those involving charges against the AIM leadership being tried in St. Paul by Judge Fred Nichol. There were about 130 defendants in the category of nonleadership cases. Krieger argued that the five defendants who were next up for trial had agreed to waive a jury because they had confidence in me. The prospect of more defendants agreeing to trial without a jury was good, he said, only if I stayed on. In addition, more defendants than otherwise would be likely to plead guilty or *nolo contendere*, thus avoiding trials. A series of nonjury trials to one judge could save a lot of time. That would be especially true in a series of cases in which the charges were of conspiracy to interfere with a federal officer (FBI or U.S. marshal) in the performance of duty during a "civil commotion." A judge in a nonjury trial could hear the testimony regarding a civil commotion and use it in each nonjury trial thereafter without rehearing it, whereas each jury, which would be a different collection of jurors, would have to hear the evidence anew. Krieger also proposed that if I would stay with the cases, all trials could be completed within nine months to a year; otherwise, if any other judge or judges he thought might be available were to have the trials, completion would require at least three years because every trial would have to have a separate jury. None would be tried to a judge without a jury.

The assembled prosecuting attorneys—the special prosecutors (private practicing attorneys from Rapid City, South Dakota) and Assistant U.S. Attorney Ed Carpenter—assented, but I urged them to think more about it, because I had heard that U.S. Attorney William Clayton of the District of South Dakota was not enthusiastic about the proceedings up to that date. Clayton was involved in the leadership cases in St. Paul, but was keeping in close touch with the Sioux Falls cases also. If Judge Heaney approved, I said I'd stay.

By week's end it was settled. I would take all Wounded Knee cases except those being tried by Judge Nichol in St. Paul.[6] If matters moved more swiftly than we thought they would with multiple judges trying cases by jury, we would continue with me alone. If not, a switch back to the multiple-judge scheme would be made. My law clerks and I would examine files of the remaining cases and receive from the prosecutors a fair description of the available evidence in each of the remaining cases that would likely make trial of that case a genuine goal; if the indication was not strong, I would dismiss the case. Efforts would be made by defense counsel to identify nascent pleas of guilty or *nolo contendere*. That comprised the outline of what became known as "the Plan"—with one addition: I insisted that the trials be moved from Sioux Falls to Lincoln as soon as practicable in deference to my family. Assent was immediate.

Word of approval of "the Plan" came from Judge Heaney on March 7. He was less optimistic than I. My optimism was qualified, I admitted, because so many people were keys to success, and anywhere along the line "the Plan" could be obstructed to its death. I worried that the question was not *if* but *when* that would happen.

The fragility of the operation was easily seen. Few of the more than one hundred defendants at this point even knew of "the Plan." Every defendant had a right to a jury trial, no matter what his or her attorney said. Moreover most of the attorneys who might be involved didn't know of "the Plan." (Indeed during the months I was involved, forty defense lawyers from across the country and a dozen prosecutors from within the seven-state Eighth Circuit were recruited to represent their respective sides at given times.) Despite the agreement of the current lawyers who approved "the Plan," any lawyer or defendant could fire the deadly torpedo of refusing to cooperate.

We moved forward, albeit through hazards, both expected and unexpected.

I did dismiss probably twenty-five or thirty of the cases in the months of January and February. Some of those dismissals were the decision of the prosecutors, who in part reassessed cases involving issues similar to the one

I had resolved in the *Baker* case. Some of the dismissals were on evaluation by my law clerks and me of information given by the prosecutors as to whether on its face a case appeared too weak to be worthy of a trial. But the rest of the existing cases moved slowly because of unexpected hazards.

A chief target of the government appeared to be Allen Cooper. Hanging over all efforts to schedule trials was the message from the defense team that the trial of Allen Cooper would last four or five months. Rumors began floating as early as March 7 that Cooper was in negotiations for a plea of guilty to at least one of the charges against him. The U.S. marshals said he would never plead guilty. In fact they said "the Plan" would wither and die. Ray Gartner, my go-to man among the marshals, remained loyally optimistic. By March 22 Defense Counsel Albert Krieger was saying that Cooper wanted to plead guilty to one count and his counsel recommended it, but "there [was] much social pressure against it," so Krieger thought there *would* be a Cooper jury trial. On May 13 I took from Cooper a plea of *nolo contendere* (the equivalent of a plea of guilty, except that the plea cannot be used as evidence against him in any future civil matter) to a charge of assaulting a federal officer.

I didn't learn why the government's interest in Allen Cooper was higher than for some others, but I speculated that it was because he was a non-Indian and deeply committed to the Indians' cause.[7]

The second motion to suppress, involving the same roadblock, took even longer than the first. By March 14 I had heard a total of five weeks of testimony, all on two motions to suppress. The prosecuting attorneys, including Joe Butler, Carleton "Tex" Hoy, and Ron Banks, who were private practitioners in South Dakota hired by the government as special prosecutors for the Wounded Knee cases, took the position from the outset of the hearings that the cross-examination by the defense attorneys was irrelevant. Perhaps it was, but I chose to let the defense team try to build a case of a planned pretextual search as part of their defense. If they failed—and they did—I would use the failure to stymie any future effort to try again. I denied the motion to suppress.

On March 14 I wrote in my journal, "Today's denial is the first glimmer the government has that I'm not pro-defense, I suppose. After 5 weeks of testimony, Al Krieger, a defense counsel, made a telling admission that only 10 pages of the transcript were pertinent and *they were questions asked by the judge!"*

I was surprised that highly competent counsel failed to develop the critical facts of the actual searches. My journal noted that I guessed they "were enamored of their pursuit of hoped-for facts to support their theories to the point of distraction." My take on the matter was that the defense was digging and scraping to find some illegal acts by the government. All in all, it was not successful, but once in a while it was.

My willingness to listen to what would probably be irrelevant evidence, as well as to accommodate proposals to have the courtroom used for a worship service, allow a defendant to say a prayer before the jury, and let oaths be taken on a sacred pipe were not relevant to the legal elements of any crime, but I considered them important to a continual building of respect for the traditions of a slice of humankind who had experienced rejection and had complained of not being heard. The least I could do was listen to what they had to say and accommodate their wishes with respect. The *most* I could do for both sides, however, was to be stoutly fair. Without that, no plan would work and all proceedings would be tarnished. Respect and fairness do not require each other, but they are good companions.

By mid-March 1974 word had come from the leadership trial in St. Paul that an FBI wiretap had been installed in the Wounded Knee trading post during the occupation of 1973. The wiretap covered as much as a month of the occupation. I talked with Judge Nichol about it and learned that he had heard two days of testimony and expected to hear two days more. The issue was whether such a listening device was illegally installed and thereby tainted the FBI investigation,[8] at least pertaining to facts occurring during the month the wiretap was in operation. The judge considered the issue "extraordinarily troublesome," particularly because FBI witnesses had previously testified and declared privately that no wiretap ever existed.

Because the issue would probably be applicable to cases I was or would be trying, I offered to send one or both law clerks from my office to help research the law. Judge Nichol thanked me and said he thought that would not be necessary.

When Joe Beeler filed a motion in the *Ackerman* case that was before me at the time, asking for a week's delay of the trial, I granted it so that the transcript of the evidence Judge Nichol was hearing would be available to the attorneys and me for use in that case and any others. (Use of the transcript would make unnecessary the witnesses' coming from St. Paul to testify wherever my trials were being held. Such an understanding existed as a part of "the Plan"—that testimony from the St. Paul trial would be usable in succeeding trials without the presence of the witness or witnesses.) Ackerman's counsel had already said a motion would be filed in his case to dismiss on the ground of governmental misconduct. I was aware that use by the prosecutors of evidence that had been obtained by illegal wiretaps was the kind of "governmental misconduct" that could result in a dismissal of the charges. The transcript arrived two days later, and I spent several hours reading it.

Matters in St. Paul reached "fever pitch," I wrote in my journal on March 27. Judge Nichol reported that a meeting was to be held in his case with R. D. Hurd, the chief prosecuting attorney, Director Clarence M. Kelley of the FBI, U.S. Attorney General William B. Saxbe, and Assistant U.S. Attorney General Henry Pedersen to decide whether the FBI would tell Hurd who the informant or informants were who had been inside Wounded Knee and whether they listened to communications between attorneys and clients. I wrote that if the FBI wouldn't budge, Judge Nichol said he would dismiss the case. "If he does," I added, "I suppose all mine will go, too."

Attorney General Saxbe overruled the director of the FBI. Informant information went to the chief prosecutor. Judge Nichol didn't dismiss the case, and neither did I dismiss any case when I resolved the same issue, because there was not persuasive evidence of any harm to the defendants by the presence of any informant. But having to resolve the issue had cost us five weeks.

Planning the move to Lincoln did prolong the proceedings. We anticipated the presence of nonresident American Indians in Lincoln, but we had no idea of the probable number at any given time. To let the people of Lincoln know of our plans and what accommodations we thought might be needed, Deputy Marshal Gartner and I held a series of meetings with various law enforcement officers in Lincoln: U.S. marshals and deputy marshals, probation officers, Lincoln police, University of Nebraska campus police, FBI, postal service workers, Nebraska Wesleyan University security personnel, the county attorney and deputies.

In early April I met in Lincoln with representatives of the press for the same purposes. They asked for a press room, but I thought the one available room in the Lincoln courthouse probably would be needed for the court reporters making daily copy.[9] I agreed to look further into the subject, but was unable to find a room for their sole use. Months later, during the hearing on the Fort Laramie Treaty of 1868, I arranged for a sound system to be installed to pipe the proceedings from the large courtroom to a secondary courtroom on the third floor for the overflow of spectators. It held about two hundred.

My official position was that I was neutral as to whether the Lincoln community should assist the Indians. I had no objection to community involvement, but would not help with it because doing so would be helping one side of the trial participants. At my request John Moseman, one of my law clerks, did attend meetings involving the community and reported developments to me.

Senator Carl Curtis telephoned to inquire about why the trials were being moved and suggested that the mayor's office be briefed. I did brief Mayor Sam Swartzkopf and Governor Jim Exon together. The mayor was concerned about food and housing for the influx of Indians. The governor seemed interested but not worried. Members of AIM had a meeting at Lincoln's Indian Center about food and housing and establishing communication with the police; Deputy U.S. Marshal Ray Gartner was invited and ready to attend, but his superiors in Washington disapproved. I telephoned Dale Williams, Ray's superior, after the meeting, but found only that he and Washington had a different philosophy from mine about the roles of marshals.

Throughout the dozen months I was engrossed in the Wounded Knee trials I relied on Ray Gartner for many things, all related to security. He was peerless in his responses, I think to his detriment. He did what I asked him to do, unless he was directed by his superior officer not to comply. His responsibilities in Sioux Falls were minor, but he organized the Lincoln proceedings and put in place what I wanted.

By the time we moved the proceedings to Lincoln I felt that any tension between the Indians and the court had subsided to the point where no obvious security devices were warranted. I asked that no magnetometer or other similar device be present and no other security be visible, except the presence of one or more deputy marshals. That was instituted. I thought there was readiness but no visible signs of safety concerns.

Ray Gartner established security at the level I wanted and by means that worked well. If there was more than one incident of danger, I didn't know it. The one I did know about was when Ray learned that one of the prosecuting attorneys, Alan Kirshen, had a pistol in his briefcase in the courtroom. I talked with Kirshen, who said he needed the gun for his protection when he walked between the courthouse and his car. I offered him a deputy marshal as an escort. He refused that, and I ordered him not to possess any weapon while in the courtroom. Ray emptied the gun of shells, and the prosecutor agreed not to have the gun in the courtroom. As far as I know, he complied with the order.

After Ray had been told by his superior not to communicate with AIM, I met with Wayne Colburn, director of the U.S. Marshals Service. He said he would send Reis Kash, another member of the Service, to meet with Ray and me. I can't remember whether he did. I do know that Kash approved, albeit reluctantly, the low-level security plan I wanted.

Ray Gartner did have regular contact with John Thomas, a spokesperson for the Indians, and developed a relationship with him whereby I would know when the Indians expected to ask for something special or unusual. When the Indians wanted a religious ceremony to precede the first trial in Lincoln—a ceremony that would last two hours and feature the presence of three separate tribes—I was able through Thomas and Ray to have the details in advance and to have a conference about the worship service before it happened. I approved it and attended it. I required that the service be completed before 9 a.m. and it was. The trial started on time.

Because I was told in advance that some witnesses wanted to take their oaths on a sacred pipe, I could consider it and approve it without restraint. I saw no problem with the request, because the purpose of an oath is to impress the *witness*, not the judge or jury, with the importance of telling the truth.

When I learned that one defendant wanted to ask the jurors to stand and pray with him while he led a prayer preparatory to his opening statement, I was able to fashion an appropriate method for it: I told the jury of his plan to pray; that each of them could pray or not pray with him as each chose; and that to avoid any embarrassment, they should remain seated.

I cannot say that other changes were directly brought about by Ray Gartner's relationship with John Thomas. I do say that the relationship had a contributing effect on the atmosphere that allowed those events to happen smoothly and without objection by anyone.

I fear that the general dissatisfaction of the Marshals Service with the way I handled the judicial proceedings related to Wounded Knee worked to the detriment of Ray Gartner. Promotions or other benefits he sought after the experience were held from him. I'm sorry about that. I felt that he performed in a way that could be held up as a model for deputy marshals.

Concerns for housing the Indians attending Lincoln trials and hearings were allayed in good time by a Lincoln resident, Bud Irons, who donated use of a barrack extant from the former Lincoln Air Park, only a few miles from the federal courthouse. Estimates from representatives of the Indians were that there might be an average of twenty-five Indians present in Lincoln from elsewhere during the trials, and probably five hundred during a hearing on the 1868 treaty. Transportation from and to the barrack would be needed, as well as availability of medical care and food. The Lincoln Committee of Concerned Citizens, formed under the inspiration of Beatty Brasch and chaired by Reverend Bob Jeambey, responded with vigor and insight. Churches and individuals provided free transportation to and from the barrack and food through food stamps, for the most part. All are entitled to high praise for the smooth operation of providing the defendant Indians and their families and friends with the necessities and more.

However, by the end of the trials and the 1868 Treaty hearing there were reports of some subtle bigotry toward Indians by white residents, including poor or no service to Indian customers at eating establishments and taverns. At least one arrest was reported by the press, of an Indian from Buffalo, New York, named Mike Clifford.[10]

We began hearings in Sioux Falls on the *Ackerman* case on April 29. A lawyer with the defense team testified to the government's failure to make timely delivery to the defense of available evidence. That's a legitimate complaint and one that is sometimes valid, but this time the slow delivery had not been prejudicial to the defense, and I urged the defense not to make any further showing of discovery failures because it would undermine harmony between lawyer camps, and I did not intend to dismiss any case for untimely discovery without a strong showing of prejudice. They understood.

No sooner had we finished that matter on April 30, than we received word of violence that had broken out in the state courthouse a few blocks from where we were in the federal courthouse. The state court trial was of five Indians and had grown out of an earlier incident in Custer, South Dakota, not Wounded Knee. At the beginning of the state court trial on about April 23, we learned, the Indian defendants had refused to stand when ordered to do so. Judge Joseph Bottom had the defendants carried out of the courtroom and ordered the court closed for a week. On returning on April 30 the defendants again refused to stand. Judge Bottom had brought in a SWAT Team from the State Safety Patrol, and this time the result was fighting, smashing of windows, trashing of the courtroom, and injuries to some participants, though none serious enough to be life-threatening.

Within a few minutes after our first word of the violent action in the state courthouse, we were told by the deputy marshals that Indians were said to be headed in the direction of the federal court. We waited as calmly as we could. (Nobody was in our court facilities at the time, except court personnel and the deputy marshals.) We saw no arrival of disgruntled Indians that day, Wednesday, April 30, but my journal entry for Thursday, May 1, was this: "Rumblings around town Wednesday night—Indians around, in Holiday Inn, looking upward from outside, claiming FBI was aiming rifles at AIM headquarters across the street."

I remembered our "no standing" incident of January 14 and felt good about its outcome. But uneasiness remained, and my staff and I were relieved to be returning to Lincoln for the weekend.

On Saturday, May 3, in Lincoln I met with Ray Gartner and learned that Reis Kash had approved the plan for minimal security for the Lincoln courthouse—no parcel check, no magnetometer, low visibility of security people. It was to be a pilot project, so we would be carefully monitored by the Marshals Service and the Federal Protective Service.

The residents of Lincoln appeared to be edgy about the move to Lincoln. That mood wasn't eased by statements we heard that weekend that somebody purporting to speak for AIM members was saying that if they didn't get what they wanted under the "treaty defense," there would be a revolution.

The next day I heard from KELO-TV that radio station KFOR in Lincoln had reported that residents near Willard School in Lincoln were protesting a proposal to house Indians during the Wounded Knee trials in the Willard schoolhouse and wondered if the government couldn't "more economically move [families] to Sioux Falls and keep the trials there than move 200 Indians to Lincoln." In Sioux Falls on May 7 I told Chris Cunningham of radio station KFOR that moving my family and me to Sioux Falls would entail also the moving the four members of my staff and their families and would deter the resolution of my regular Lincoln docket of cases. These were being handled only in part by visiting judges, and I could help manage them more effectively from Lincoln than from Sioux Falls. I assured the people of Lincoln, "Not a single incident arising from the hearings and trials which I have held in Sioux Falls during the past three months would forecast any reason for Lincoln residents to worry."

The first actual trial of a Wounded Knee case began in Sioux Falls on Tuesday, May 7, 1974. It was *United States of America v. Ackerman, DeCora, and Gilbert,* indicted together for burglary and larceny. I had denied the motion to suppress evidence, and we were geared to receive evidence in this nonjury trial. James Shellow of Milwaukee, John Thorne of San Jose, and Joe Beeler of Miami Beach were defense counsel. Ed Carpenter and Joseph Butler were prosecuting. On Thursday, May 9, we were in recess until Monday while Krieger and Shellow were at a meeting of the National Association of Criminal Defense Lawyers in St. Louis, recruiting lawyers for service in Wounded Knee cases. From the beginning the report was that the Indians wanted to take advantage of the lawyers' willingness to serve without pay, so I did not appoint any except Beeler, who served for the better part of a year. Monday, May 13, featured two, perhaps three, things: the beginning of a novel theory of defense, Allen Cooper's plea of *nolo contendere,* and standing by the Indians.

The novel defense was that the owner of the trading post, from which the defendants were alleged to have stolen property, was not licensed to do business; therefore he could not own the property allegedly stolen. John Thorne gave a two-hour argument on the issue, citing the long, sordid history of parts of humankind. I listened. Al Krieger made the same argument in five minutes in legal terms and with a more powerful impact. My journal says that the point of the Krieger argument would "be the harder one to deal with." The journal continues: "Dave [Pedersen] and I worked till 10:00 on it—he researching legislative history at Augustana [College] and the public library." On the basis of that research I decided that the license defense was not a valid one and denied the motion.

The plea by Allen Cooper was significant. It avoided what had been predicted to be a four- or five-month trial. Henry Crow Dog, a spiritual leader of the Sioux, attended the plea-taking to voice his approval of the plea agreement process. My journal note says, "A large crowd stood when Cooper pleaded."

The "standing" note raises a baffling question: Is standing by the Indians at Cooper's plea tied in some way with the Indians' *not* standing on January 14? I'm not sure. Here's what I know: by the time we neared the end of our stay in Sioux Falls, some three months after the beginning of my stay, the Indians usually stood at the opening of court. I was pleased with that. I didn't know why they stood, but I was willing to give credence to the thought that it was to show respect for me and the legal system at large. That seemed to be the essence of the matter and of Krieger's assurance of its essence to me directly on at least two occasions. His detailed version, however, is beyond any knowledge of mine. He asserts that he came into the trial of his client, Lorelai DeCora, a day late, sat beside her, and then heard scuffling of feet of some 150 Indians in full native regalia charging up the stairs into the courtroom and with gun-drawn marshals aghast at the sight. Krieger said he was frightened, fearful he was going to die, until his client told him, "Albert, it's all right." The Indians took seats, he says, until I entered the courtroom and began to take my seat at the bench, whereupon the Indians, "as one," rose to their feet in honor of the system of justice they were experiencing, thus marking a new era of relationships between two peoples.[11]

I have no memory of a rush of regalia-laden Indians up a flight of stairs, nor do I think I would forget what would have been an incomprehensible scene of U.S. deputy marshals guarding the outer door of the courthouse, being ineffective in obstructing entry to the second floor, and being befuddled about what to do in a melee in the courtroom. The courthouse was tightly secured. Such a scene of turmoil is unthinkable without memorable consequences. There is simply nothing like that in my memory. Neither the official record nor my journal declares anything of such a ruckus. My journal does say that the only trial that Lorelai DeCora faced was begun on May 7; on that day my journal says merely, "Albert Krieger is absent but on his way." I also noted that court was in recess from Thursday noon on the 9th until Monday the 13th because of Krieger's and Shellow's being in St. Louis to recruit attorneys to defend Indians in these ongoing trials. The journal's notes for the 13th speak of the license defense and of Allen Cooper's plea: "Allen Cooper pleaded nolo [contendere] to assaulting a federal officer. . . . Crow Dog, spiritual leader, was here at the plea, giving hoped-for assurance to others of his approval of the plea agreement process. A large audience stood when Cooper pleaded; prosecuting attorneys did at first, later reconsidered and sat!"

My journal mentions no crowded courtroom during any days of that trial, except at Cooper's plea-taking. Does all that mean that the event of Indians' standing for some reason other than Cooper's plea didn't happen, or happened on some other day and wasn't noted in my journal? I don't know. I think the most likely account is that the standing of the Indians in large number happened at the Cooper plea-taking, and that because of Krieger's absence from Sioux Falls for four days, he was unaware of or had temporarily forgotten the scheduled plea on Monday until he walked into a courtroom and was told about it by his client, DeCora. That fits well with the skeletal facts in my journal, treating kindly the wonderfully dramatic hyperbole at which Krieger is an unmatched master.

Who or what was the standing in honor of? I don't know. I choose to say it probably was in honor of Allen Cooper, a white man paying a price for his people's past wrongs to Native Americans. But I'm comfortable with sharing some of the honor with him, because, whether or not they stood for the system of justice that day, they did stand thereafter many times when we opened court as I walked in. That's thrilling enough for me.

The description by John Thorne meshes well with my memory. In an unsolicited letter from him to Chief Judge Carolyn Dimmick of the Western District of Washington, dated July 17, 1995, Thorne spoke of "an incident that came up in the first trial [of the Wounded Knee trials]." He continued:

> Many of the Indians did not want to stand when the Judge walked in. One of my clients, who was to be in the second trial, told me this and asked if it was mandatory. I told her I thought the best thing to do was to talk to the Judge, so I made an appointment and we met in his chamber. She explained her position, and Judge Urbom immediately understood. He then instructed his bailiff not to say "please rise," and told my client none had to stand in his courtroom. They didn't. After we finished the first trial and started the second, when the Judge entered I suddenly heard a noise behind me, and as I turned around I saw the entire audience standing. I went over to one of the hard working leaders and asked what had happened, the reply being, "We just decided this man was entitled to our standing when he came in to the court."

Eight months later, at a sentencing hearing during the afternoon of January 24 and the morning of January 25, 1975, Allen Cooper gave extensive testimony about his background and his role in the Wounded Knee episode. He testified that on March 11, 1973, during one of the cease-fires, he arrived inside Wounded Knee village, bringing medical supplies, food, and clothing for the Native Americans. Some ten hours later, four men were escorted into the museum with their hands up. Cooper arrived at the museum about the same time as the four, who said they were postal inspectors, which the persons inside the museum didn't believe. The four were required to sit on a bench facing a wall; they may have been tied to the bench. Cooper was handed a rifle by an unidentified Indian with directions to see that the four men not leave the building. Cooper retained the rifle, which he examined and found to be unloaded, for perhaps an hour and a half or two hours, part of the time resting the rifle against a wall. He was about thirty feet from the four. He did not speak to any of them; he did not give orders and did not tell them that the rifle was not loaded. On

those facts Cooper acknowledged that I could find him guilty of assault of the four postal officers. I did.

Cooper testified at length about his previously frequent participation in civil rights actions. He testified that he had left the University of New Mexico after three semesters to work as a community development worker in Venezuela for sixteen to eighteen months. He returned to the United States and spent time in Washington DC, learning about racism and spending three months investigating the death of a black man in jail, concluding that the man had been beaten to death. There was an inquest, after which the U.S. attorney recommended there not be an investigation, which Cooper did not understand.

Cooper said he then worked with the Southern Christian Leadership Conference in Atlanta, Georgia, for four months, then joined a group of "passive activists" in a walk through Georgia and into Florida to protest the conflict between Cuba and the United States. He was arrested several times. All this, he said, was a "very intensive learning process," not just a physical process, but "a process of reading and learning and talking, and . . . not a one-dimensional thing." After "several months of jail and fasting and bringing pressure to bear on the community of Albany, Georgia, . . . [the group] won the right to picket and it was rather a historic right to picket and walk on the sidewalk and leaflet."[12]

After Georgia, Cooper and others went into Florida, he said, where efforts were made to persuade the government to allow passage to Cuba to lessen tensions through exchange of students, trade, and cultural exchange. The group boarded a boat for Cuba, where they would walk to Guantánamo. The boat was seized by the Coast Guard, people were arrested, and the project ended. Cooper returned to Albuquerque, soon to join a march from Selma to Montgomery, Alabama. From there he went to Mississippi for a couple of years, doing "voter registration work" by starting a reading program for kids and a literacy class for adults, among other things. In 1965 he was taking some black workers to a meeting to organize for higher wages when he was attacked by white persons and injured about his back and kidneys; he was taken to the hospital in Greenville, Mississippi, and then to Washington DC to be under a doctor's care for three months. It was here that he began to think seriously about pacifism, nonviolence, and self-defense.

For several years from 1969 on he taught at a university and in a public school, got married, got expelled from the University of New Mexico for his activism regarding the Vietnam War, lived for several months with his wife in Israel on a kibbutz, got divorced, and on the invitation of a friend wound up in Wounded Knee on March 10, 1973. Persons who had known Cooper many years described him as a nonviolent young man of deep commitment to help the disadvantaged.

Because the crime for which he had pleaded *nolo contendere* involved use of a gun, I remained concerned about whether he had some tendency toward violent behavior. I sought advice by ordering a psychological study of Cooper with a report to me within three months. The study, by Thomas A. Gonda, MD, professor and chairman of the Department of Psychiatry and Behavioral Sciences at Stanford University Medical Center, was reported to me with the conclusion that the prognosis was good that Allen Cooper would not commit acts of violence in the future.

On April 8, 1977, after completion of Cooper's unsuccessful appeal on jurisdictional grounds and the Supreme Court's denial of *certiorari*, I sentenced Cooper to three years of probation, with conditions to be prescribed by the probation officer. In the meantime he had purchased ten acres of land in the mountains of New Mexico, had hand-built a house on that site, and had been in no trouble with the law.

On reflection, I suspect that Cooper's counsel was saying a several-months-long trial would be necessary if he didn't plead guilty or *nolo contendere* because he would want to get before the jury or judge all the details of Cooper's past protests—not merely by his own testimony, but by the testimony of many corroborating witnesses. I think I would have found it necessary to take measures to shrink that effort. I was willing, however, to let his past be told at sentencing, where it belonged.

Meanwhile, in May 1974 trial in the *Ackerman* case proceeded, the government resting its case on May 21. I observed that the evidence of the value of the property taken by the defendants from the trading post was probably no more than $100, and a conviction could only be a misdemeanor. I queried whether I should dismiss the case because we had more important matters to tend to than misdemeanors. The defense agreed, but the prosecutor, Ed Carpenter, was adamant that "the people of South Dakota deserve a decision." Nearly three months had passed, though only two weeks and two days had actually been spent in the courtroom on that case.

We went forward with the defense's case, and I heard what I called "splendid arguments by all counsel," and then granted a motion for judgment of acquittal of all three defendants. Other than Cooper's plea of *nolo contendere,* the government had gotten no conviction in any of the cases before me, so I'm sure it was a devastating loss for the prosecution, but I had a reasonable doubt that these defendants had committed either burglary or larceny.

As hard as the ruling in the *Ackerman* case was for the prosecution, an even more upsetting decision—not by me—was in the immediate offing.

A feature of federal criminal cases is that the judge must not participate in negotiating a settlement. The parties and the attorneys alone work out plea agreements, then present them to the judge for approval or disapproval. On the morning of the day of dismissal of the *Ackerman* case, John Thorne told my law clerk Dave Pedersen that the prosecution had offered to dismiss all remaining Wounded Knee nonleadership cases (there were more than a hundred) if five named defendants would plead guilty or *nolo contendere.* It was an exciting idea. The next morning, Wednesday, May 29, I met with counsel and learned that the offer as stated was genuine, but the U.S. Justice Department might not be able to give final approval until later in the day. The five who were named in the offer were located in various states and were expected to arrive in Sioux Falls for negotiations soon.

William Clayton, the district attorney for the District of South Dakota, said on Thursday that the Justice Department would not have its answer until the first of the next week, so my staff and I drove to Lincoln. On Saturday I wrote, "Lincoln is already sighing with anticipated relief over the threatened demise of Wounded Knee trials here."

By Monday, June 3, rumors from the U.S. Marshals' office said that District Attorney Clayton had exceeded his authority in announcing negotiations; Washington would not approve the proposed settlement; neither would AIM leadership. At 11:30 a.m. Joe Beeler called to say that Clayton had just told him that he had not heard from Washington. Beeler said that the five named defendants had agreed to plead *nolo contendere* as offered. Whatever truth the rumors held, approval of the settlement proposal never came.

Settlement efforts did not end, but faded as the months went by. A letter from Albert Krieger on November 30, 1974, to Assistant Attorney General Henry E. Petersen of the Department of Justice in Washington recounted, "[Within] hours of the acquittal of the three defendants in *United States v. DeCora (Means), Ackerman and Gilbert,* I was approached by Edward Carpenter, Assistant United States Attorney for the District of South Dakota, and Joseph Butler, Special Prosecutor in the Wounded Knee cases. They proposed to me . . . a disposition of all non-leadership cases predicated on pleas of nolo contendere by the five defendants, Going, Westerman, Onco, Escamilla and Mulhall." In another letter Krieger said he was writing with "a deep sense of outrage" because of a "total lack of communication between the Government attorneys in South Dakota and the Department of Justice in Washington or a total misunderstanding of the true facts on the part of the Department of Justice." All was to no avail.

We moved the trials to Lincoln with "the Plan" still in place, even if we were behind schedule. Except for disappointment that the settlement proposal seemed to be dying, we had some satisfaction with the progress of "the Plan." I had disposed of a reasonable number of cases and issued several opinions on issues that would probably be applicable to future cases: search and seizure, the invalidity of the license defense, whether the Major Crimes Act had to be defined by common law, and whether the government violated the attorney-client privilege and the defendants' right to effective counsel by having an informant inside Wounded Knee and within the inner workings of the defense attorneys and their clients (defendants-to-be) during the stand-off at the village.[13] More major legal issues remained, one of which was faced in the first Wounded Knee trial in Lincoln, *United States v. Jaramillo.*[14]

The two defendants in the *Jaramillo* case were indicted for attempting to interfere with a law enforcement officer "lawfully engaged in the lawful performance" of official duties during a civil disorder. One defense was that officers surrounding the village of Wounded Knee at the time of the charged offense were *not* performing their lawful duties in a lawful manner because the intrusion of the army in those duties had been without the approval of the president of the United States or Congress and therefore had been in violation of the doctrine of *posse comitatus*. That doctrine, described in a law passed by Congress, made it unlawful to willfully use any part of the military forces to execute the laws in civil matters, except as expressly authorized by Congress. Congress had given the president power to approve use of military forces to execute the laws in civil matters, but the president had not approved use of military forces in the Wounded Knee fracas. I ruled that the issue of whether there had been a "use" of the army was a factual one, and had to be decided by the finder of fact, which in this nonjury case was the judge.

In abbreviated form, these are my findings of the facts shown by the evidence: On March 9, 1973, the date of the defendants' attempted entry into Wounded Knee through the armed roadblocks, a "civil commotion" existed beyond a reasonable doubt; that is, there was, as the law stated, a public disturbance involving acts of violence by three or more persons, which resulted in damage to property and immediate danger of damage or injury to the property or persons of others.[15]

The investigating of reported crimes and the operation of the post office at Wounded Knee were federally protected functions. Reports had been made of holding of hostages and a forcible entry of the post office by the Indians. Sporadic shooting from within Wounded Knee toward the law enforcement officers' roadblocks prevented the officers from investigating these reports, except by forcible entry at least through March 9, the date of the attempted entry by Jaramillo and Sturdevant. Therefore, there was interference of the officers in the performance of their duties by the occupiers of Wounded Knee, beyond a reasonable doubt. The remaining issue was whether the FBI or USMS had "used" any part of the army.

Col. Volney Warner, chief of staff of the 82nd Airborne Division of the U.S. Army, arrived as ordered at the Pine Ridge Reservation on March 3, 1973. His primary role was to advise the Department of Defense as to whether federal troops should be used at Wounded Knee. He constantly advised against such use. And he did more. He approved requests by the Department of Justice (FBI and USMS) for military supplies and equipment. He urged the Department of Justice officials to change from a shoot-to-kill policy to a shoot-to-wound policy. That change was made. Colonel Warner suggested use of other tactics that were part of the rules of engagement for civil commotions. The suggestions, at least in part, were adopted. He also urged negotiations with the persons occupying the village. He approved a request for armored personnel carriers at the roadblocks on the conditions that they be used only by way of defense, only at the perimeter without moving the carriers more than one hundred meters, and not as an aggravation to attack.

A single reconnaissance was made by air by the Nebraska National Guard, and South Dakota National Guard mechanics did the maintenance work on the armored personnel carriers.

Based upon the evidence, I could not find beyond a reasonable doubt that no part of the army was "used" by the FBI, the USMS, or the BIA in relation to a civil disorder in enforcing the law. Such use was contrary to the *posse comitatus* statute, 18 U.S.C. § 1385, because use at Wounded Knee had not been authorized by Congress or the president of the United States. Therefore, the government had not met its burden of proving beyond a reasonable doubt that the enforcement officers *were* performing their lawful duties in a "lawful" manner. Dismissal of the charges was the only option.

In making that ruling, I assured the men on the ground—the FBI, the USMS, and the BIA—that they were not being told *they* had done anything improperly.

My ruling in the *Jaramillo* case set a precedent on the military involvement issue, affecting other cases in obstructive ways. If the issue was one of fact—thus determinable by a fact finder—it meant that in future similar cases a trial would probably be necessary. Since I as the fact finder had found that the use of the military was excessive without the authorization of Congress or the president, the likelihood was that the government would opt for a different fact finder, namely, a jury in each trial containing the issue of use of the military. On the other hand, if the issue were a matter of law, as Judge Nichol had ruled, the judge could make the decision and the decision could be based in some cases, at least, on evidence already received by the judge, and any trial could be without a jury and shorter in duration. Hence the government, the loser in the *Jaramillo* case, sought to find a way to appeal my decision, but found it unlikely that an appeal was possible. We were in a bind: either have a nonjury trial to me with the likely outcome of a government loss, or have a jury trial that would be lengthy. The government chose the latter in *United States v. Iron Cloud,* which would follow the nonjury trial of *United States v. Dodge.*[16]

"Ford: Nightmare Is Over," declared the headline of the *Lincoln Journal* on August 9, 1974. Wounded Knee prosecutors, who had labored for five months before me and were yet to win a conviction, might have sensed from the headline a moment of relief, but found none. The announcement was not of Wounded Knee matters at all, but of Richard Nixon's resignation from the presidency and Gerald R. Ford's succession. So the only two signatures on my commission—Richard Nixon's and John Mitchell's—were now symbols of shattered lives.

The prosecuting attorneys in all the Wounded Knee cases had an incredibly hard job for many reasons. A large part of the records were imprecise and incomplete because they were made at the roadblocks *outside* the village of Wounded Knee by the marshals and FBI agents while shots were being fired at them from the *inside.* Recovery of the records a year later for a specific trial or trials was difficult because of the unreliability of the filing systems. Most of the witnesses who knew the facts of the activities *inside* the village were uncooperative because they had been indicted and chose not to give evidence possibly usable against themselves, or because they were stoutly loyal to the cause that had brought them to Wounded Knee, or because they were frightened of those against whom they might be giving evidence. A goal—sought by both sides—was to get a precedent for the resolution of a particular type of case, one in which the military use was a claimed defense, for example. That precedent would be used as a guide in working out a settlement of other, similar cases. Negotiations were constantly in progress on individual cases. Many cases were settled that way, most of them by voluntary dismissal if the defendant did not accept the government's offer of a settlement, which usually was an offer of a plea of *nolo contendere* or guilty to a single count of a multicount indictment.

Scheduling was a major problem. Attorneys from other parts of the country, asked on short notice to come for a lengthy trial, were not easily enlisted, especially when no fee and only twenty-five dollars a day for expenses were being offered.[17] I did authorize payment to researchers for the defense at a modest rate, and that relieved the trial lawyers to a fair degree. Sometimes dismissal would happen two or three days before the trial was to begin; not unexpectedly, a week or two would be necessary to find a defense attorney and witnesses available to begin the next trial. These were rarely cases where an attorney knew more than a week or two before trial even the name of his or her client or anything about the facts. Time was precious, but reasonableness reigned. Virtually everybody cooperated, but time rolled on, albeit somewhat jerkily. By early August Alan Kirshen reported to me that only forty-nine cases remained and that the government would dismiss fourteen of them and would dismiss more if trial became imminent.

By mid-August 1974 the circuit court committee overseeing the movement of the trials was leaning toward assigning multiple judges to try cases simultaneously to push toward quick resolution. I made my recommendations in a letter of August 16. I discouraged any plan to use more than two trial judges simultaneously because of the massive number of records that had to be available to each trial judge in courtrooms in different cities. (There were no multiple federal courtrooms available in any city in the region.) My recommendations came to this: that we begin having two simultaneous trials; that both trials be held in Lincoln, unless both trials were jury trials, whereupon one of them be held in Sioux Falls; that I schedule cases for both judges; that some other judge and I try the remaining cases, and that the other judge be one who could commit to being constantly involved in Wounded Knee cases for a period of four to six months, preferably a senior judge.

The trial of *United States v. Iron Cloud* was one that carried a bundle of unusual twists: it was the first *jury* trial after spending five months in Sioux Falls without a jury trial; it was the first use we'd made of the jury-selection plan I'd adopted very early in Sioux Falls; witnesses refused to testify; a defendant wanted to pray with the jury; I drew my first experience ever of a serious challenge to the makeup of a jury panel; and I was criticized publicly by a prosecutor.[18]

The fact that the *Iron Cloud* trial was the first jury trial was consistent with "the Plan." True to "the Plan," some dismissals had been had, some nonjury trials had been completed, and one plea of *nolo contendere* had been processed. Consistent, yes; spectacular, no.

The jury-selection method used in the *Iron Cloud* trial had been developed in February, when I first arrived in Sioux Falls. The defense attorneys were particularly eager to have ample time to interrogate the prospective jurors as part of the selection of the jury. In view of the fact that publicity of some notorious trials had featured jury selection lasting several weeks, the government lawyers and I were leery of a wide-open method of selection. So the attorneys on both sides were invited to bring experts who had studied the pros and cons of the alternatives to testify to their opinions. I listened to four experts.[19] Their preference was for questioning of an individual to be allowed outside the presence of the other prospective jurors, because that permitted a more comfortable ambiance and likely yielded more information of possible biases, tendencies, and feelings. They acknowledged that such questioning in isolation would be more time-consuming than questioning in a group setting. My conclusion tried to give heed to both factors by letting each attorney choose to use his or her time with jurors either singly or in one or more groups, but the total time for questioning of all prospective jurors would be limited.

I allowed the United States six peremptory challenges, the defendants jointly ten. That was the usual allowance in all criminal trials. A group of fifty prospective jurors were chosen by lot at the outset. I then orally questioned all fifty on such subjects as occupation, residence, spouse's occupation, children, acquaintanceship with defendants and possible witnesses, past criminal history, past jury service, knowledge of the parties' attorneys, political affiliation, and relationship with the United States, AIM, and the Wounded Knee confrontation. I touched lightly, if at all, on possible racial prejudice and pretrial publicity but essentially left this issue to each counsel to resolve. The first thirty-five chosen of the fifty would be the group from which the jury ultimately would be chosen, supplemented from the remaining fifteen by replacements of those dismissed on challenges for cause.

The government was allowed two hours to question the group of prospective jurors. The defendants' counsel had a total of four hours collectively. Each counsel could request additional questions for the judge to ask or to decline to ask. All questions were to be put to a prospective juror in the presence of all other of the nonexcused prospective jurors.

Three alternate jurors were chosen, the government having two peremptory challenges and the defendants collectively having two. The government used less than one of its two allotted hours. The defendants collectively used all of their four hours and made no request for more time. I was satisfied, as I believe counsel were.

In the *Iron Cloud* trial two witnesses were subpoenaed by the government and came to the trial but refused to testify. One, Melbert Cut Grass, a twenty-four-year-old Indian who lived on the Rosebud Reservation in South Dakota, testified in an identification hearing outside the presence of the jurors that he had seen and spent time with all four defendants inside Wounded Knee on April 27, 1973, the day of the events of which the defendants were charged. Cut Grass also testified that he had made identifications of the defendants to FBI agents on the day of or the day after April 27. Twice in interviews in late 1973 Cut Grass had picked out pictures of two defendants, Iron Cloud and Wallace Little, from among several pictures furnished by the FBI agents.[20]

Nevertheless, after testifying at the identification hearing, when Cut Grass returned to the witness stand to testify before the jury, his version of events had changed. He said he saw the defendant Red Boy in the village of Wounded Knee on April 27, 1973, and saw him shooting. He said he saw other people shooting, but didn't know who they were. When shown notes of an FBI interview with him, he acknowledged that the notes refreshed his memory, but said, "I can't say it [for] personal reasons." He then asked that the courtroom be cleared so he could "have words with the jury and the judge and defense counsel." On being questioned about his reasons for not answering more questions, he said, "I'm afraid." He said he was afraid of AIM and specifically "Mr. Pin," who he thought was in the courtroom, but "Mr. Pin" proved to be William Thomas.[21] I took Cut Grass to my chambers and was told by him that he was afraid of what might happen to his wife and his family, both after and during the trial, because family members of defendants were in the courtroom.

The witness protection program was explained to Cut Grass by Deputy Marshal Jack Douglas, who was in charge of the program in the region, and Deputy U.S. Attorney Alan Kirshen from Sioux City, who had joined the prosecution team in Lincoln.[22] Cut Grass also conferred with the lawyer I had appointed for him.

I told Cut Grass that if anything happened to him or his family from then on of an unusual or suspicious nature I would direct the U.S. attorney to make immediate investigation; if prosecution was warranted, it would be the U.S. attorney's job to prosecute.

When Cut Grass resumed the witness stand and reviewed the statement handed him, he testified that he saw Iron Cloud and the Littles in a bunker, but saw just their clothing and wasn't sure it was them. At that point, Cut Grass refused to testify further, even after a conference with the prosecuting attorneys and his own attorney.

The prosecutors opted to question Cut Grass no more before the jury. I gave them an hour to find whatever other identification witness they hoped to have. Cut Grass was excused as a witness. The defendants made motions for an acquittal; I overruled them, awaiting the prosecution's effort to produce another identification witness.

Two U.S. marshals, Andrew J. Snyder and Francis A. Hammer, were called by the prosecution to testify. They said that on April 27 they were fairly close to the bunkers erected by the occupiers of the village and caught fire from three of the bunkers. Neither marshal identified anyone firing from the bunkers.

I instructed the jury to disregard all evidence that had been given by Melbert Cut Grass. That is a typical consequence of a witness's refusal to be cross-examined on the testimony he or she has given before the refusal to continue.

The last witness called to place the defendants at the scene of the occupied village on April 27 was Bernie Nichols, a twenty-year-old woman who grew up in the Pine Ridge area and whose counsel promptly announced that Nichols wished to invoke her right under the Fifth Amendment. The government asked for and received from me an order of immunity, a status that would prevent use of any testimony she gave in this present prosecution against her in any future prosecution against her. Again she refused to testify. The prosecution asked me to order her to testify. I did. For the third time she refused to testify, and I was asked to hold her in civil contempt. I refused, because she told me in the quiet of my chambers that she was afraid of other people who lived on the reservation, and because civil contempt would allow, at the most, her placement in jail until she testified or until the trial of that case had been concluded. Here, by the end of the trial day, at five o'clock, she was the last witness the government had with any possibility of evidence of any defendant's being in Wounded Knee on April 27. If the government didn't produce more evidence the next morning—and lack of any looked probable—I would have to dismiss the case because no evidence identifying the defendants as being at the Wounded Knee scene on the day of the crimes charged had been given. The sole purpose of civil contempt is to cause a witness to do what he or she had been ordered to do. I saw no chance of her agreeing to testify after a single night in jail. When the need for the testimony was gone—by dismissal of the case, for example—the witness could no longer be held. I saw no good that would come out of putting her in jail for one night.

The defendant Roger Iron Cloud is the one who asked to have the jury stand and pray with him at the outset of the trial. After reading the written prayer, I approved of its being said aloud by Iron Cloud, but said that I would tell the jury to remain sitting and to pray or not to pray, as each of them chose. He agreed. Here is Roger Iron Cloud's prayer: "O Great Spirit, we pray to you at this time to help us and guide us throughout this court, and give guidance to these jurors and their deliberations, their quest for the truth and justice."

Strangely, the jury in the *Iron Cloud* trial was composed entirely of women—twelve women as the regular jury and two alternates. The strangeness of that led the defense to challenge the method of selecting the persons called to jury service. The clerk of the district court, Richard Peck, who was responsible for producing the jury lists for the district, testified that the method used was in strict compliance of the court's master plan. The result was a pool of forty-two women and twenty men from which the jury was chosen. A statistician testified that the chances of getting a jury of fourteen women were about one in two hundred.[23]

I could have ordered a new array of jurors, drawn with extra care to see that more balance existed, but I doubted that the law required it. So I denied the motion. Ultimately any error was rendered moot by the dismissal of the case.

Judgment of acquittal was granted on September 12, 1974, at the end of the government's case-in-chief. There was simply no evidence that any of the defendants in the *Iron Cloud* case had committed a crime. The only evidence putting any of the defendants inside the Wounded Knee village had to be stricken because of Melbert Cut Grass's refusal to submit to a complete examination and cross-examination.

Alan Kirshen, the prosecutor, criticized my refusal to hold Bernie Nichols in contempt of court. It is quite all right for an attorney to criticize a judge's decision, as long as it is done privately. But to do it to the press is another matter, generally viewed within the legal profession as unbecoming to the legal profession. Kirshen was quoted in the *Lincoln Journal* on September 13 and the *Omaha World-Herald* on September 14 as saying, "If the criminal justice system continues to be thwarted in the way it has been the past couple of days, we're going to have anarchy." The *Journal* reported that Kirshen said the government was considering an appeal to obtain an order from the Eighth Circuit Court of Appeals making contempt citations more mandatory than discretionary at the district court level. It is "a very rare situation," he said, "where a judge overlooks contempt of court."

I have a copy of John Thorne's response of September 16 to the *World-Herald*'s story. It is a letter to U.S. Attorney General William Saxbe berating Kirshen's remarks to the press and insisting that Saxbe "immediately investigate this entire situation." Attorney General Saxbe's response was made through Assistant Attorney General Henry E. Petersen and signed by Carl W. Belcher, chief of the General Crimes Section, on October 21: "This matter has been investigated and appropriate steps have been taken to limit Mr. Kirshen's public statements." Thorne was not satisfied. In a letter of October 30 he demanded more answers and urged that Kirshen "be removed from these [Wounded Knee] cases" and "be removed from U.S. employment in view of the statements."

Alan Kirshen continued as a prosecutor of Wounded Knee cases until mid-December. The press dutifully reported conflicting theories of why he was reassigned shortly before the beginning of the hearing on the 1868 Treaty and replaced by Duane Nelson.

Of course, criticism of a judge's performance is not rare and is fully expected by every judge. Judges are like most other people. They prefer to be praised. They cringe at disapproval. They cannot possibly have the approbation of everyone, because trials are contests, where almost always somebody is a loser who feels the loss keenly. We judges know that, and most of us, I think, try to treat praise and criticism as equally exaggerated.

In the midst of the *Iron Cloud* trial in Lincoln I received word from Judge Nichol in the Wounded Knee leadership case in St. Paul that he had dismissed all charges against the defendants, Russell Means and Dennis Banks, because of government misconduct that the judge considered to be so aggravated that a dismissal had to be entered in the interests of justice. It was a stunning end to the leadership trial.

Judge Nichol pointed to five acts of the government's prosecuting team that cumulatively meant bad faith that justified the dismissal of all charges: (1) presenting false evidence by Louis Moves Camp that the government had reason to distrust but did not adequately check for trustworthiness and failed to offer an explanation or correction of that false evidence, despite overwhelming evidence of its falseness; (2) deceiving the court and the defense by withholding evidence of the possible involvement of Louis Moves Camp in a rape incident; (3) failing to furnish the defense with documentary evidence that could have been used to attack or qualify the evidence of a witness, Joseph T. Sneed, called by the government to testify about the extent of military involvement at Wounded Knee; (4) eliciting testimony from a sixteen-year-old boy, Alexander David Richards, that was contradictory to information given by him to the FBI earlier and put in an interview form that was not produced to the defendants' counsel for impeachment; and (5) refusing to agree to accept a verdict from eleven jurors after the eight-month trial had been submitted to the jury for a verdict and one juror had become too ill to continue. The defendants (Banks and Means) had agreed to accept a verdict by the remaining eleven jurors. The prosecution refused, because, the chief prosecutor told the media, he felt the chances of getting a conviction to be "slim" from the eleven-person jury. The judge considered the refusal to be a "blatant attempt to obtain a retrial and thus correct the many errors of the past eight months." Those acts were detailed in Judge Nichol's October 9, 1974, Memorandum Decision.[24] None of the acts cited by Judge Nichol in the Banks-Means case were problems, as I remember, in any trials we held in the nonleadership cases. I doubt that Louis Moves Camp or Alexander David Richards testified in our nonleadership cases, though I can't be certain of that. Joseph T. Sneed did testify, I think, about the extent of the military in the Wounded Knee incident, but I recall no successful claim that cross-examination was hampered by failure to deliver documentary evidence that might have helped the defense. There was no time that an issue arose in our trials of having fewer than twelve jurors. The prosecutors in the St. Paul trial were not the same persons as the prosecutors in the Sioux Falls or Lincoln trials.

The nonleadership trials proceeded apace after the ending of the leadership cases. One was that of Robert Charles Onco, a twenty-five-year-old American Indian from Lawton, Oklahoma, who was indicted on May 10, 1974, on two counts of having possession of an assault rifle that had not been registered. He was one of five who had agreed to plead *nolo contendere* to a crime pursuant to a proposed agreement to settle all the pending cases in late May and early June 1974, but the proposal was not consummated. When his case came before me in December for trial, his attorney presented a stipulation that admitted facts necessary to warrant finding him guilty of those two crimes. A cover sheet for a transcript says, "Trial before the Honorable Warren K. Urbom, Chief Judge, commencing at 4:00 p.m., December 3, 1974, in Lincoln, Nebraska." The court minutes say, "Defendant agreed to waive his trial and entered an oral agreement that if the treaty defense is ruled against, he will enter a plea of guilty to Ct. I and Ct. II will be dismissed."

A presentence report was prepared, but the probation officer who prepared it, Burton Matthies (later to become chief probation officer of the

District of Nebraska), was suspicious of Onco's military history. Onco claimed that he had served in Vietnam for thirteen months and had won the Silver Star and Purple Heart; his verified military records disputed this. The records reflected that Onco entered the air force on February 4, 1970, and was discharged under honorable conditions as "unsuitable" on September 3, 1971, after having attempted suicide by an overdose of sleeping pills. No indication of his having served in Vietnam appeared in his military record. After the overdose, he was transferred to Sheppard Air Force Base in Texas and was admitted to the psychiatric ward on April 25, 1971, showing signs of "severe personality disorder, personality pattern disturbance, schizoid personality, chronic, severe, unchanged as manifested by over-sensitivity, seclusiveness, avoidance of close or competitive relationships, eccentricity and shyness."

A handwritten note of mine says that before the trial and before the sentencing, Onco's attorney informed me of his psychological problem and recommended that I not send him for a study and report (by a psychologist or psychiatrist at government expense) about it, because such a study would probably do more harm than good. He emphasized that Onco's past problems related to tendencies to hurt himself rather than others. I wrote in the note, "I'm willing to take the chance." I reasoned that sentencing would probably not occur until June, and a one-year probation after that would give a reasonable time for seeing whether he was reasonably stable. On June 30, 1975, I sentenced Robert Charles Onco to probation for one year on one count and dismissed the other count. I have not heard of him since.

This above all: to thine own self be true,
And it must follow, as the night the day,
Thou canst not then be false to any man.[25]

From the beginning of our hearings in Sioux Falls in January 1974, the defendants made it clear through their counsel that they were depending upon the terms of the Fort Laramie Treaty of 1868 to form their major defense and to have a massive effect on future relationships between the Sioux and the United States. All counsel agreed that any hearing on the status of that treaty would be held after many of the pending cases from the Wounded Knee incident of 1973 had been resolved, probably by late 1974. Any judgment against any Native American would be made subject to a determination of the status of the treaty.

The treaty hearing was held over twelve days from December 16, 1974, through January 2, 1975. Duane Nelson, Kenneth Fields, and David Gianapp, assistant U.S. attorneys, appeared for the prosecution; John Thorne and Sandra Terzian for the defendants.

Preceding any testimony, John Thorne summarized the jurisdictional defense in an opening statement, declaring dramatically, "A decision will be made in this court that will have in my opinion the greatest impact of any decision . . . rendered by any court over any issue."[26] The Indians wanted me to declare that the Sioux Nation was fully sovereign at the signing of the Treaty in 1868, that the Supreme Court of the United States had wrongly built an immoral law on the false basis that the Sioux were uncivilized savages, and that the Fort Laramie Treaty of 1868 should be interpreted as retaining for the Sioux Nation full control over crimes committed on their reservation.

Twenty-six witnesses testified toward the goal of showing, in the words of John Thorne, that "all federal courts have no jurisdiction over any Indian for an alleged crime committed in Indian country, even as this court ha[d] no jurisdiction over a Brazilian or a Frenchman . . . over any alleged crimes which they might commit within the boundaries of their territory."[27]

Acknowledging that the law as declared by the U.S. Supreme Court was contrary to the Indians' position, the assertion nonetheless was that I had but two choices: to "reaffirm dehumanizing language" of earlier Supreme Court opinions—most notably *Johnson v. McIntosh*'s referring to the Indians as uncivilized savages—or to say "within the matured conscience of our judicial system" that the Supreme Court was wrong in *Johnson v. McIntosh* and its offspring, just as it admitted in *Brown v. Board of Education* in 1954 that it had been wrong in *Plessy v. Ferguson* in 1896.[28]

In *Johnson v. McIntosh* in 1823 Chief Justice Marshall recounted in great detail the centuries-old international understanding of the potentates of Europe, including England, regarding rights to land by a nation when it discovered a land not previously known to it and occupied by another. Such land could be held for the "discoverer" itself from the time of its discovery of that land, with an exclusive right "to extinguish the Indian title of occupancy, either by purchase or by conquest; and . . . also a right to such a degree of sovereignty, as the circumstances of the people would allow them to exercise." "The potentates of the old world found no difficulty in convincing themselves that they made ample compensation to the inhabitants of the new land by bestowing on them civilization and Christianity, in exchange for unlimited independence." The chief justice acknowledged, "The title by conquest is acquired and maintained by force. The conqueror prescribes its limits." Marshall's opinion declared, "The United States . . . have unequivocally acceded to that great and broad rule by which its civilized inhabitants now hold this country." He said that usually when conquest is complete, the conquered inhabitants blend with the conquerors and "make one people." But the Indians were "fierce savages, whose occupation was war. . . . To leave them in possession of their country, was to leave the country a wilderness; to govern them as a distinct people, was impossible, because they were as brave and as high spirited as they were fierce, and were ready to repel by arms every attempt on their independence." The inevitable consequence, the chief justice said, was "frequent and bloody wars, in which the whites were not always the aggressors."[29]

Then, in plain and forceful words, the chief justice summarized: "However extravagant the pretension of converting the discovery of an inhabited country in to conquest may appear; if the principle has been asserted in the first instance, and afterwards sustained; if a country has been acquired and held under it; if the property of the great mass of the community originates in it, it becomes the law of the land, and cannot be questioned."[30]

Much of the testimony at our hearing was by persons who had experience with oral history. For a traditional Sioux, oral history was common, because for most of the tribes composing the Sioux no written language existed. A Sioux depended upon those leaders specially chosen because of their good memories and their holiness. They became custodians of the tribal traditions.[31]

Some of the witnesses testified in Lakota, a Siouan language, with translators furnished by the Indians. The transcript is in English, the court reporter having reported in English as recited by the translator. Leaders of the tribes made an effort to have a live recording of that testimony made, but thought of it too late to get it accomplished.

After hearing from historians and many Indians who were familiar with oral history, I was persuaded that oral history is an excellent tool for gaining the essence of events of the past, both near and distant. The details of an event are not the stuff of oral history; the meaning is.

It is the evidence elicited at the eleven-day hearing on the Fort Laramie Treaty of 1868 that I necessarily had to rely on.

It is, now January 2, 1975. For six hours I've listened to the closing arguments of John Thorne and Duane Nelson. I've bidden the lawyers good-bye and now have dropped into the large leather-covered swivel chair that sits majestically behind the oak desk that has been the zone of reflection for two brilliant judges who preceded me. A long minute passes. Then another. Then ten more. I agonize over Thorne's challenge to resign my judgeship unless I can reject the concept that "might makes right" by declaring my court has no jurisdiction to try these criminal cases against American Indians. Silently I say again the oath I took when I lifted my right hand before Judge Van Pelt on May 5, 1970:

> I, Warren Urbom, do solemnly swear that I will administer justice without respect to persons, and do equal right to the poor and to the rich, and that I will faithfully and impartially discharge and perform all the duties incumbent upon me as a United States District Judge under the Constitution and laws of the United States. So help me God.

Once more I study the words "perform all the duties incumbent upon me . . . *under the Constitution and laws of the United States.*" I know now what I have to do.

I come to my feet, make my way to a straight chair that sits at the end of the matching table, pick up a pencil, and start to write on a yellow legal pad. The words come surprisingly easily, almost nonstop: "The Sioux people were once a fully sovereign nation. They are not now and have not been for a long time. Whether they ever will be again is dependent upon actions of the Congress and the President of the United States and not of the courts. There is a residue of sovereignty, however, a part of which reserves for the Sioux partial criminal jurisdiction."[32]

That's the conclusion. Now the rationale. The conclusion, I write, "is irresistible, if I am to follow an unbroken line of decisions of the United States Supreme Court, extending from the early 19th century until the year before last."

As I continue to write, I note to myself that I must drop back later to cite with the assistance of my law clerks the "unbroken line of decisions" that we've already analyzed. I know that the Indians' counsel is aware of that unbroken line because he has characterized it as arrogant and unjust and asks me to shunt it aside. Is it arrogant or unjust, and if it is, may I either push it aside or change it?

By now I have three goals. First, I must make a clear statement that I know the Native Americans have had shabby treatment by the United States for at least two centuries and the law of discovery and conquest has not enhanced the treatment, insofar as it has been based on the declaration that the Indians are "fierce savages whose occupation is war." More needs to be said about that. A distillation of the testimony about the history of the Indian people and the relationship with the United States seems to be in order: I write:

> It cannot be denied that official policy of the United States until at least the late 19th century was impelled by a resolute will to control substantial territory for its westward-moving people. Whatever obstructed the movement, including the Indians, was to be—and was—shoved aside, dominated, or destroyed. Wars, disease, treaties pocked by duplicity, and decimation of the buffalo by whites drove the Sioux to reservations, shriveled their population and disemboweled their corporate body. They were left a people unwillingly dependent in fact on the United States.
>
> It is an ugly history. White Americans may retch at the recollection of it.[33]

Second, I must explain why I cannot change the history or the law that has developed around it, nor should I try. Third, I must say that I have listened and heard and watched the building of a record on which the Supreme Court or the Congress can change at least in part the long-standing law, if either chooses to do so.

As to the nature of the Sioux, the evidence by the experts and by the recitation of oral history of traditional Indians made an unequivocal declaration that the Sioux were both knowledgeable and restrained, both intelligent and peaceful, and civilized in the development of and devotion to their own culture, including their culture's attitude toward rivals. They were supremely religious, ample in their own governmental design, and respectful of humanity and the source of their sustenance.

While the Sioux Indians had been once sovereign, nothing in the evidence has persuaded me that the Sioux were fully sovereign when the 1868 treaty came to life. They were, rather, dependent upon the United States for their continued survival but retained internal sovereignty only—that is, the power to control their own people within their own land territory. From 1821 on, the Supreme Court of the United States has been unrelenting in its assertion that Indian tribes have only limited sovereignty. Having sworn that I would comply with the law, I cannot ignore or disobey the law as decided by the Supreme Court unless I am as faithless as the United States has been to the Indians.

The urging of the Indians' counsel is that the Sioux's full sovereignty could be lost only by discovery (which they say was by the Indians, not the Europeans), or conquest (they assert that if there was conquest, it was by the Indians, not the Europeans), or treaty (none of which, they say, diminished the signatory tribes' sovereignty). The argument is unavailing.

Discovery in the annals of European-English-American legal history has to do with that stream of law bred by "the potentates of Europe" centuries ago and thereafter recognized by the Supreme Court of the United States early on and today. Within it is the proposition, explained by Chief Justice John Marshall in *Johnson v. McIntosh*,[34] that the first European discoverer (tightened by the English to mean a Christian discoverer) instantly acquired in the name of the European discoverer's sovereign the right of title to and occupancy of the land found. Quite aware that occupancy might bring to the European discoverer-occupant the challenge of the previous occupant, the European discoverer was expected without compunction to deal with the previous occupant as it chose: to live with it in mutually acceptable ways, or to conquer the previous occupant, or to abandon the place.

In commonly known history, affirmed by the evidence at the hearing on the Fort Laramie Treaty of 1868, the European discoverers, for centuries now known as Americans or the United States, have made efforts to live with the American Indians in mutually acceptable ways. Those efforts have taken various forms, none thoroughly or mutually acceptable. The United States has not abandoned the place. Conquest has been a fact, though ugly in form, as I have acknowledged. At this point, the Indians' counsel argued, conquest regarded in terms of "might makes right" is rationally immoral. Whether I accept that or reject it, I arrive at the same place: nobody—neither counsel nor myself—has found anything in the Constitution or federal or state law or moral law itself that gives me as a U.S. district judge the go-ahead to mind moral law, as I may define it, and defy the law of the Constitution of the United States and law as announced by the Supreme Court of the United States.

With that skeletal background the citizenry of the United States by means of the Constitution placed the power to make treaties upon the president with the advice and consent of the Senate. Interpreting the treaties, as well as statutes by Congress, was assigned to the Supreme Court and other, lesser federal courts, including this district court. Treaties and statutes of Congress were given equal status by the Constitution, thus the most recent one, whether treaty or statute, takes precedence over any other. In terms of recency, the Major Crimes Act of 1948 and the Act of June 2, 1925, granting Indians citizenship in the United States (even though not necessarily wanted by the Indians) have the clear edge.[35] They are acts of Congress that give to this court jurisdiction over these cases. I am compelled to follow their lead until there has been a change of interpretation by the Supreme Court of the United States, or by a statute by the Congress, or by a treaty, or by an amendment to the Constitution. None exists.

In fairness, perhaps I can suggest where some relief may lie. I try to say:

> [White Americans] may . . . ask themselves questions: How much of the sins of our fathers must we rightly bear? What precisely do we

> do now? Shall we pretend that history never was? Can we restore the disemboweled or push the waters of the river upstream to where they used to be?
>
> Who is to decide? White Americans? Those traditional people who testified here? Those Sioux of a different mind who did not testify? The officials elected by the Sioux on the eight reservations?
>
> Feeling what was wrong does not describe what is right. Anguish about yesterday does not alone make wise answers for tomorrow. Somehow, all the achings of the soul must coalesce and with the wisdom of the mind develop a single national policy for governmental action.[36]

John Thorne argued for the Indians that I did not need to wait for the Supreme Court to speak again, saying that the Supreme Court has been wrong regarding jurisdiction over Indians, just as it admitted it was wrong about equality in education in *Plessy v. Ferguson*. I am not persuaded.

In the *Plessy* case the Supreme Court had rejected the argument that "the enforced separation of the two races stamps the colored race with a badge of inferiority."[37] Thus was established the "separate but equal" doctrine: if the elements of education, except for the fact of separation by race, are equal, enforced separation of the races does not stamp the black race with a badge of inferiority.

The Kansas trial court in the *Brown* case found that the elements of education *were* equal in the Kansas schools *and* found that "segregation in public education has a detrimental effect upon Negro children," but denied relief on the ground that the black and white schools were substantially equal with respect to the elements of education, aside from the fact of separation by race.[38] The Kansas court was following the holding of the Supreme Court in the *Plessy* case, explaining, "As a subordinate court in the federal judicial system, we [the Kansas court]. . . do not substitute our own views for the declared law by the Supreme Court."[39] I agree.

My conviction is that the testimony of witnesses in this case should go far to dispel the assertion that Indians are or were "fierce savages, whose occupation was war." Following is what the evidence showed:

Beginning some fifteen thousand years ago, Native Americans migrated from Asia to what are known now as North and South America. They occupied all ecological zones from northern Alaska to the southern tip of South America. Their adaptability was remarkable, according to the anthropologist William S. Laughlin, because they adapted to "high altitudes, dry deserts, jungles, river conditions, arctic cold. In this way they performed one of the most interesting and significant experiments in human evolution. . . . People from one continent successfully going to another continent and occupying every ecological zone is significant."[40] They built societal structures in keeping with the environment. Some were simple; some were complex. All the items of civilization, including monumental architecture, the concept of zero, mathematics, astronomy, and writing, were present, though not in every subset of groups.

The Sioux, as an identifiable group, probably began with a split in the Siouan-speaking people who dwelled in the Ohio Valley at about the time of the landing of Christopher Columbus. The Sioux migrated to the head of the Mississippi River, where they were forest people. They lived in a semipermanent settlement with dwellings made of earth, poles, and bark, and their hunting was done on foot. Game, berries, and fish were the basic food supply. In approximately 1700 they moved, perhaps under pressure of one or more other Indian tribes, into the Great Plains, and specifically west of the Missouri River. They tamed the horse at about that time, permitting them to become a hunting society. Their notion of a tribal land base was influenced by their dependence upon the buffalo. A tribe would fasten to a moving buffalo herd and remain with it as long as it supplied the tribe's needs. The concept of private ownership of real estate was unknown to them. All land was owned by Wakan Tanka, known also as the Great Mystery or Great Spirit.

The Sioux developed no written language. Their history was learned, retained, and transmitted orally from one generation to the next by persons especially adept at memory and trained for the task.

The living Sioux Indians, says Professor William Laughlin, are "related to earlier Indians who were here in what is now the United States many thousands of years before any Europeans arrived anywhere in the Americas.

... The genetic continuity between the living Indians and their antecedent populations is firm and is demonstrable with the highest level of scientific proof."[41]

The religion of modern Sioux has remained much as it was in antiquity. Some conversion to Christianity has happened, but the traditional Indians remain true to the beliefs, ceremonies, and traditions imbedded in the age-old ways of their ancestors.

The Sioux religion was and remains monotheistic. To the traditional Indian in the modern era the Great Spirit still permeates all, and there is no distinction between sacred and secular. At some unknown point in history, the Great Spirit sent the White Buffalo Woman, who delivered to them the sacred pipe, a connecting link with the Great Spirit, through which prayers may be offered and promises made. Any promise made on oath taken on the sacred pipe is to be unending.

The earth is Mother Earth, supplying whatever her children need, and is to be respected as such. No buffalo or tree or other item of nature is to be killed unnecessarily or without the uttering of a prayer. With earth as their Mother, land can no more be sold than their Mother can be sold. Occupancy might be changed by agreement, but title cannot be.

The evidence from the hearing on the Fort Laramie Treaty of 1868 is persuasive that the Sioux were at the time of the signing of the treaty of 1868 no more ignorant, no more savage, and no more warlike than were the European or American whites.

But to go further and say that acceptance of the doctrine of "discovery and conquest" is wrong would be deliberately disrespectful of the Supreme Court of the United States. I will not do that.

I then jot down four possible reasons for saying that the law regarding the public policy as to relationships between the Indians and the United States is not for the district courts to decide, and perhaps not for the Supreme Court to decide. First, the elective process best reflects the conscience and wisdom of the people. Second, legislative bodies have tools for wider investigation than courts. Third, relations with American Indians are rooted in laws about shifting power from one group to another, developed over centuries, now better changed by broad participation. Fourth, this court has been given no power to set national policy regarding relations between the Indians and the United States. The courts may hold the government to the policy once set, but cannot set the policy. Accordingly I must deny the motion to dismiss for want of jurisdiction.

Writing a tailored final version of the treaty opinion took some time, but my journal for January 14 is this:

> Complications arose about the opinion on the treaty defense, but by late p.m. Dave Pedersen and I had them resolved. Marlene and I got the opinion to the post office about 7:00 p.m. It is not to be released to the press until John Thorne in San Jose says he has it. I'm afraid the Indian community—if not the press itself—will be enormously let down because they've billed this as such an "historic" hearing. The holding is against the Indian community and their hopes were soaring, I'm afraid. I've fretted since last summer that they were building on false hopes, but I couldn't warn them without prejudging the defense evidence and arguments.

I was right about that. Thorne was so confident that he wrote a letter addressed to me *before* he received the opinion, but didn't mail it until *after* he got the opinion. (That's proper; he shouldn't communicate with a judge after the arguments are finished and the case has been submitted for decision but before the decision has been made and communicated.)

My duties in the Wounded Knee cases were then complete, except for sentencing those who had been convicted and arranging for the transfer of remaining cases to another location and another judge or judges. Now that the treaty defense had been rejected, all agreed that the sentencing could go on, even though an appeal from my treaty decision would be taken.

I did the sentencing, as I've previously set out. The defendants found guilty did appeal my treaty ruling. The Eighth Circuit affirmed my ruling, doing it in a way seldom seen but pleasing to me. Judge Heaney, writing for the circuit court, said, "No useful purpose would be served by attempting to improve on the thoughtful opinion of Judge Urbom. We, therefore, adopt it as our own insofar as it applies to the appellants before us, with the exception of the determination of jurisdiction over Fleury for his conviction of second degree burglary."[42] Mark Joseph Fleury, a non-Indian, was convicted of violating a South Dakota statute, and absent a treaty provision to the contrary, the court said, the state has exclusive jurisdiction over the crime.

Application was made by the Indian defendants to the Supreme Court, but the Court declined to take the case.

I was sorry that the Supreme Court bypassed. This was an opportunity for the Court to review the issue of sovereignty and the status of treaties between the Indians and the United States. On the other hand, the substantive issue of sovereignty of another nation and the other nation's relationship to the United States are probably political questions, assigned wisely by the Constitution to the legislative and executive branches of government.

My final report to the Eighth Circuit's committee dealt with dispositions during my stint from February 11, 1974, through the date of the report, December 9, 1974, and not including the treaty hearing. The sum of the report was that cases against forty-nine persons had been completed, resulting in dismissals of forty-three and convictions of six.

Of the eleven trials and hearings I presided over, twenty-two defendants were involved, six of whom were either found guilty or pleaded *nolo contendere* and then were found guilty. Charges against the rest were dismissed. Four of the six who were found guilty had their cases reversed on appeal. I sentenced six persons.

On about February 15, 2008, I visited with Duane Nelson, who prosecuted Wounded Knee nonleadership cases in Lincoln and later in Council Bluffs, Iowa. He told me that a few cases had been tried in Council Bluffs and Sioux City and that the cases "just seemed not to be there any more." And that's the way the Wounded Knee criminal cases ended. At least one case was transferred to U.S. District Judge Edward J. McManus in the Northern District of Iowa, Cedar Rapids Division.[43] The remaining cases were then transferred to the Southern District of Iowa for trial in Council Bluffs and Sioux City.

A letter dated March 4, 1975, from Kenneth Uhl, U.S. attorney for the Southern District of Iowa, says that a review of the pending cases had been made after the transfer of the remaining cases to that district. He said that, based on that review, a recommendation was made to the U.S.

attorney for South Dakota that approximately fifty of the cases should be dismissed, and that dismissal was then being processed. He reported that approximately thirteen cases involving twenty-eight defendants remained for trial or other disposition.

I didn't follow through to find out whether those charges were dropped, but I am led to believe that probably two or three trials were held and the rest just faded away.

Assessment of my Wounded Knee experience is complex. There is no question that it was one of the richest of my life. Issues were new and hard. The lawyers were amazingly dedicated. The Indians were deeply engaged in a cause.

The massiveness of the court's docket lay heavily on everybody's mind. The inability of the lawyers to have smooth communication with their opponents because of a need for all decisions about potential settlement to go through Washington left the subject of settlement a dismal hope. The work of my staff members—Dave Pedersen, John Moseman, Marlene McGuire, Deputy Marshal Gartner, court reporters Joe Pasquale and Allen Tewes—was exceptional.

It would be presumptuous of me to try to evaluate the worth of the takeover of the village of Wounded knee to the American Indians. The residents of the Pine Ridge Reservation were not of one mind, if I heard the evidence right, and the different minds are better equipped than I to speak authentically of the value. I can say that I know of no benefit and no improvement in condition that has arisen because of the occupation of the village of Wounded Knee in 1973. That's not to say there is none; it is to say I know of none. I can speak of the value to *me* of my part in the trial episodes that followed the takeover.

Elliott Taikeff, one of the top-notch defense lawyers who volunteered for one or more trials, wrote me after the trials were over, suggesting that I tell lawyers to be cautions about taking part in a political trial because "it might change your life!!" It changed mine. The trial experience engaged me almost totally for a year. Of course it affected me. I wrestled with it. I grew from it. It challenged me to honor my judicial oath to follow the law completely or not at all. It caused me to think again: What is the role of law? What is justice? What is the role of a judge? Out of the Wounded Knee experience I have been driven to prepare my own answers to those questions—for myself, not for anyone else.

Defining law, its role and its boundaries, isn't easy. After living in law's domain for almost sixty years, I still love it. I shall cherish it. I shall respect it. I shall not worship it.

Law is the work of lawmakers and represents the *lowest common denominator* that a society, as voiced through its representatives, is willing to live by. Each of us can do better than the law requires. Said another way, law sets a *floor* not a *goal* for our behavior. It does not ask that we reach upward; it demands only that we not sink below the floor. A lawmaker's job is to set that floor. A judge's job is to acknowledge it, interpret it, and apply it.

Where does that leave me after the whole Wounded Knee experience? It's fair to say I wanted justice, whatever that means.

Learned Hand, a great judge who never was a justice on the Supreme Court of the United States, said, "Justice, I think, is a tolerable accommodation of the conflicting interests of society, and I don't believe there is any royal road to attain such accommodations concretely."[44] I like that, but when I sit back and try to describe it for myself in terms of a particular case, I choose to use slightly different words that are more familiar to me, and to add a few words about procedure and attitude, so the statement looks like this:

> Justice, I think, is (1) a reasonable accommodation (2) of the competing interests—insofar as those interests are clearly not destructive of society—of persons and entities likely to be affected by the accommodation, (3) achieved respectfully by rules applied with careful speed, economically and evenhandedly, the competing interests being weighed for value and accommodated proportionately among the holders of the competing interests, and (4) given by a court authorized by a state or nation to give it.

My revised edition provides no "royal road" to attain accommodations concretely, but suggests at least a cobblestone path for me to tread day-to-day.

29. Edward Carpenter, one of several prosecutors in the Wounded Knee nonleadership trials. Photograph by *Lincoln Journal Star*.

30. Duane Nelson, one of several prosecutors in the Wounded Knee nonleadership trials. Photograph courtesy of Duane Nelson.

31. Alan Kirshen, one of several prosecutors in the Wounded Knee nonleadership trials. Photograph courtesy of Alan Kirshen.

32. John Thorne, one of many defense counsel in the Wounded Knee nonleadership trials. Photograph courtesy of Nancy Thorne.

33. Albert Krieger, one of many defense counsel in the Wounded Knee nonleadership trials. Photograph courtesy of the Florida State Bar Association.

34. Ray Gartner, deputy U.S. marshal, worked closely with Judge Urbom on the Wounded Knee nonleadership trials. Photograph by Lifetouch Church Directories and Portraits.

Was there justice in what I did regarding the Wounded Knee event, as gauged by my revised edition of "justice"? Let me try to analyze it.

First, regarding the occupation of the village of Wounded Knee by AIM, I offer no view as to the wisdom or lack of wisdom of it. I know too little about the results of the agreement made to end the occupation.

Second, as to the nonleadership trials I conducted, the competing interest of the United States was to prosecute the charged defendants fairly. The basic competing interest of each defendant was to have the opportunity to defend himself or herself fairly. Was each interest accommodated reasonably, respectfully, under rules with careful speed, economically and evenhandedly? Yes, I think so. Were there additional accommodations made to the defendants? Yes: not requiring people to stand during the opening of court, permitting the taking of the witness oath on the sacred pipe, allowing

35. John Thomas, liaison of AIM in the Wounded Knee nonleadership trials. Photograph by *Lincoln Journal Star*.

36. Madonna Gilbert, a defendant, explained why Indians did not stand up at the Wounded Knee nonleadership trials. Photograph by *Lincoln Journal Star*.

a prayer service preceding an opening of court, letting a defendant pray with a jury, and allowing witnesses to testify in the Lakota language, even though the witnesses were knowledgeable of the English language. These accommodations were afforded as appropriate to the societal background of the requesting defendants. The United States did not object.

Not included in my definition of justice but always considered intuitively is the question of whether an appropriate verdict or ruling as to guilt was provided. The Eighth Circuit Court of Appeals said the verdict was not appropriate for four of the defendants. I have no quarrel with that. The same evidence was applicable to all four in the same trial, so either all four or none was guilty. The weighing of evidence is a matter upon which reasonable persons can differ, and I was neither surprised nor ruffled by the ruling of the court of appeals.

Of the approximately 150 defendants I dealt with, I dismissed the charges

37. Circuit Judge Gerald Heaney monitored the Wounded Knee trials. Photograph courtesy of the Eighth Circuit Executive Office.

of about 101 without a trial, and I tried forty-nine. Of those, forty-three were found not guilty or had their charges dismissed for lack of evidence, six were found guilty and sentenced. Of the six, four had their convictions reversed by the Eighth Circuit Court of Appeals, and two (Cooper and Onco) were sentenced to probation—three years for Cooper and one year for Onco. Were the appropriate sentences given? Yes, I think so.

Third, as to the hearing on the Fort Laramie Treaty of 1868, the sole interest claimed by AIM, the Sioux Nation, and the individual defendants, except the "additional accommodations" awarded in respect of the social backgrounds of requesting defendants, was a finding of lack of jurisdiction of an American court to try an American Indian for any crime committed within the Pine Ridge Reservation. The grounds for that claim were that (1) the Sioux were a sovereign nation that had occupied, long before the arrival of the Europeans, the land now known as the Pine Ridge Reservation, and that sovereignty could not be taken from the Sioux Nation without its agreement, which had not been accomplished, and (2) the Fort Laramie Treaty of 1868 remains in effect and provides that only the Sioux Nation

38. U.S. District Judge Andrew Bogue, District of South Dakota.
Photograph courtesy of A. Stevenson Bogue.

39. Chief U.S. District Judge Fred Nichol, District of South Dakota, tried the Wounded Knee leadership trial in St. Paul. Photograph courtesy of the clerk of the U.S. District Court, District of South Dakota.

40. Judge Urbom being interviewed by a *Lincoln Journal Star* reporter after the 1868 Fort Laramie Treaty hearing. Photograph by *Lincoln Journal Star*.

shall have jurisdiction to try an Indian charged with having committed a crime on the reservation.

The short but clear answers to these claims are (1) part of the full sovereignty of the Sioux Nation can and has been taken by conquest and legislation by the United States; only partial sovereignty, over internal matters, remains; and (2) the Treaty of 1868 does not provide that only the Sioux Nation shall have jurisdiction to try American Indians for crimes charged to have been carried out by Indians on the Pine Ridge Reservation. Legislation by Congress provided jurisdiction to the court.

41. Indian chiefs and headmen in the jury box during a hearing of the 1868 Fort Laramie Treaty. Reproduced by permission from Roxanne Dunbar Ortiz from *The Great Sioux Nation Sitting in Judgment on America*, photograph by Melinda Rorick.

While I had authority to try the defendants, I did not have the authority to grant the full sovereignty claimed on behalf of the Sioux Nation, AIM, or the individual defendants.

There was no accommodation to be made regarding sovereignty, except to permit the Sioux Nation, AIM, and individual Indians to make an extensive written record that could be used by the appellate courts and the president and the Senate of the United States to review and perhaps to change the relationship of the United States with the American Indians. That accommodation was made. The Eighth Circuit Court of Appeals did use the record and agreed with my findings. The Supreme Court declined to provide a hearing on the matter. Whether the Senate has any thought of doing anything on it I do not know.

42. Associate Justice Samuel Alito of the Supreme Court of the United States, Chief Judge William Jay Riley of the Eighth Circuit Court of Appeals, and Senior Judge Warren K. Urbom of the District of Nebraska (*from right to left*) lay a wreath at a small monument at the cemetery at Wounded Knee, South Dakota, memorializing the 1890 Wounded Knee massacre. The ceremony was arranged by Chief Judge Karen Schrier of the District of South Dakota as part of an Eighth Circuit Judicial Conference during the week of August 15, 2011, in Rapid City, South Dakota. Photograph in author's possession.

8

The Progressive Farmers Association Trial

Nationally the 1980s had the look of peacefulness. The Vietnam Veterans Memorial, conceived by a twenty-one-year-old architectural student, was dedicated in 1982 and became Washington's most popular attraction. If you've visited it, you know why: that flat, black granite wall seems to drive itself into the earth, emblazoned with name after name after name of the dead and missing.

The toppling of the Berlin Wall in 1989, a wall that had divided Germany into West and East for almost thirty years, symbolized the end of the cold war, an icy peace that represented distrust between the Soviet Union and the United States and its allies. Added to that was the fact that the 1980s enjoyed the longest economic boom to that time in American history, supporting an overall sense of tranquility.

But in my judicial life the 1980s were not peaceful. They began with a trial inordinately long and featuring deceit, surprise, and uncertainty. They then dived into a swamp of hardened issues that would not recede: abortion, the death penalty, control of crime by sentencing, and the long *Nebraska Public Power District* trial.

In ancient Greece criminal trials had to be completed in the span of a single day. Such was the case in Socrates' trial for impiety, punishable by death, by 501 jurors in 399 BC. In eighteenth-century England the tradition of long standing was that every felony trial ended within a day. One trial that was remarkable for its breaking that tradition was the trial of Thomas Hardy for high treason in 1794 in Old Bailey that lasted eight days. Nowadays a month-long trial in the United States is commonplace. I don't know the length or name of the longest jury trial in the history of the United States, but I think one I had that took ten and a half months comes close. It was in Kansas City, Missouri, and I never expected it to run that long.

In the spring of 1979 I telephoned John Strong, dean of the law school of the University of Nebraska–Lincoln, and reminded him of his invitation to me to teach a class in trial advocacy. I told him I was ready to take it on, if the offer was still open. He said it was, and I began making lesson plans for the fall semester. I was eager to try such a class.

Class sessions began on August 28. Two weeks later I was asked by the chief judge of the Eighth Circuit Court of Appeals, Floyd Gibson, to accept an assignment to the Western District of Missouri to try a criminal case that appeared to have such close political implications that the federal district judges of Missouri had disqualified themselves. I explained to him my teaching responsibility, but said I would see what I could work out.

I soon discovered that the charges involved twenty-two defendants (another was later added), part or all charged with 175 separate counts, including conspiracy to violate the Racketeer Influenced and Corrupt Organization Act (RICO), actual violation of RICO, use of the mails to commit fraud, fraudulent sales of securities, and failing to file and evading income taxes. In early conferences the attorneys told me that the trial would take as long as three months; I told them that I could free myself for no more than thirty days of trial time.

The defendants' lawyers urged me to require the government to choose for trial any ten of the fraud charges and have the rest of the charges severed—that is, split off and at least postponed for trial. The prosecution resisted. I did choose to sever all but six counts, but made the mistake of allowing two of those counts to be the RICO counts, that is, one count of conspiracy to violate RICO and one count of actual violation of RICO. That mistake swept open the door to the prosecution to prove 158 charged predicate acts of the conspiracy, that is, illegal acts in carrying through with the conspiracy. My failure to realize the enormity of my decision resulted in my thirty-day estimation being a gross, almost comical miscalculation.

Pretrial events reduced the number of defendants to ten by the time the trial started on October 2, 1979, and when the case was submitted to the jury ten months later, five defendants remained,[1] but the lesser number of defendants made little difference in the time needed to complete the trial.

The distance between Lincoln, Nebraska, and Kansas City, Missouri, is about two hundred miles and took about three and a half hours to drive. To keep my commitment to teach at the University of Nebraska I drove to Kansas City with my staff on Sunday afternoons, held court from 8:30 a.m. to 4:30 p.m. Mondays through Fridays, drove back to Lincoln Friday evenings, taught the class at the law school in Lincoln for three hours on Saturday mornings, and returned to Kansas City Sunday afternoons.[2] It was grueling, but I enjoyed it, except for the motels. After about four months of motel living, I sought out friends from Lincoln.[3] I stayed with them for about six months, until the trial was nearing its end. That didn't change the routine of commuting, but I could stay in a comfortable home instead of a motel.[4]

The focus of the trial in Kansas City was the alleged setting up, principally by a handful of men, and arranging for the operation by others, of four agricultural cooperatives in three states—Missouri, Oklahoma, and Arkansas—and selling securities in the form of annuities and mortgage notes to farmers. The government's case was that there was a raking off of substantial amounts of the income for the personal use of defendants and making of fraudulent promises, all leading to the crippling and financial demise of the cooperatives. The financial losses were alleged to be nearly $13 million by some seven thousand farmers who bought the securities. The principal target of the prosecution was Russell Phillips, who established the Progressive Farmers Association (PFA) and Progressive Investors, based in Springfield, Missouri.

Other cooperatives and managing corporations were important, but for ease of reference the press spoke of the trial as the PFA trial, as I shall. Donald H. Gibson, an attorney, was prominent in advising Phillips and forming the intertwining corporations. He avoided prosecution by agreeing to cooperate with the United States in prosecuting the defendants, including testifying against them.

Before trial began, pleas of guilty or *nolo contendere* to one or more counts or dismissals in return for agreements to testify for the prosecution

43. Russell Phillips. Photograph courtesy of the *Springfield (Missouri) Daily News.*

were made by a dozen of the indicted men. The trial opened on October 2, 1979, with ten defendants, including four who soon were either dismissed or pleaded guilty.[5] Months later Donald E. Burks was severed, and the remaining five stayed for the full trial.

The case was originally assigned to U.S. District Judge William R. Collinson of the Western District of Missouri. From October 27, 1978, when the indictment was handed down by the grand jury, until August 16, 1979, when Judge Collinson disqualified himself from further participation in the case, he was flooded with and resolved dozens of motions designed to ready the case for trial. His rulings included changing the venue of the trial from Springfield, Missouri, to Kansas City, ordering appointment of counsel for the defendants, and resolving motions of many kinds—for production of documents, to sever, to suppress evidence, to dismiss counts, to reveal informants, for separate trials, and to compel handwriting exemplars—as well as other requests. The case was then passed to me by Chief Circuit Judge Floyd Gibson. At least one day-long meeting in Kansas City of all the attorneys and me resulted in final plans for trial.

On the morning of October 2, 1979, Courtroom No. 5 in the old federal courthouse at 811 Grand Avenue in Kansas City was crowded. Seated at one counsel table were two prosecuting attorneys, Assistant U.S. Attorney Robert Schneider of the Western District of Missouri and Senior Trial Counsel Peter B. Shaeffer, Chicago Regional Office, U.S. Securities and Exchange Commission. Their notes were stacked in front of them, and microphones were positioned to ensure their words could be heard. Around two other tables ten defense attorneys were similarly gathered. The ten defendants appeared in various degrees of restlessness, sitting just behind their attorneys, within easy reach for consultation purposes. My two law clerks, Kerry Kester and Brian Riepen, the deputy courtroom clerk Steve Navarro, and the court reporter Joe Pasquale filled chairs directly in front of the bench.[6] A lectern stood in the center of the space between the bench and the railing that separated the working area (the "well") of the court from the spectators' seats. Many—at least 120—prospective jurors, also showing some nervousness, filled the spectators' area. Deputy U.S. marshals, at least three of them, stood conspicuously in separate locations near the bench, the exit, and the spectators' seats.

To a trial judge a courtroom is like a honeycomb to a bee or an inferno to a firefighter or a sanctuary to a preacher. There is an instant challenge, an invitation, a dare, an opportunity for doing good things. It is a temple where justice can live.

Facing a trial predicted to last three months, we spent the next four days reducing the number of prospective jurors from 120 to 16. Twelve were regular jurors and four were alternates to serve in the event of disqualification or some inability to serve by one or more regular jurors.[7] After preliminary instructions were read aloud to the jury and lawyers had given their opening statements to alert the jurors to what each counsel expected the evidence to show, the prosecution tromped into its case-in-chief.

No facts—none at all—were stipulated for use at the trial, so each one had to be proved by a knowledgeable witness or witnesses. Proof in the main consisted of paper trails of countless financial transactions through one or more of at least a dozen corporations traceable from or to one or more of the defendants. Each had to lead toward the charged conclusion that fraud was rampant in the formation or operation of one or more of the cooperatives. Each document was identified by a person, often a corporate officer, with great care. Each examining and cross-examining counsel inquired of the genuineness and meaning of the documents. Day after day, week after week, the droning went on.

Jurors were driven toward sleep. There were occasions when I invited the jurors to rest their heads on the backs of their chairs, but to be careful not to sleep, because they needed to hear the testimony. I allowed them to take notes, which may have helped somewhat to keep them awake. I suggested they might politely elbow the juror next to them into awakening if it appeared necessary. They generally took all this in stride; they sometimes insisted they weren't asleep, but were just resting their eyes and listening carefully. Although the lawyers objected freely to many things, nobody objected to the efforts I made to help the jurors be able to listen.

I also permitted the jurors to ask questions, directed to me and transmitted to the witness by me, if I deemed the question appropriate. Quite a few questions were asked, and one juror, Paula Osborn, a very bright, young black woman, was apparently designated by the other jurors to be the spokesperson for asking questions to be answered by the witness. She was artfully articulate.

One Friday evening, probably in early May 1980, Osborn came to my chambers to say that she and her fiancé wanted to be married by the county judge the next Monday morning, but the county courthouse didn't open until 8:30. Since our trial was to start at 8:30, she might be a half hour late. "Would that be all right?" I said yes, we could accommodate that. "Unless," she said, "*you* would marry us. You could do it some evening after court, and I wouldn't delay the trial." I thought it would be interesting and agreed to do it.

Weeks later, after she had made all the arrangements, I walked into a regal ballroom—not a county judge's chamber—crowded with mostly black and some white guests in tuxedos and stunning gowns, surrounded by gardens of flowers. A few other jury members attended. I did my thing, following a contemporary ritual, pronouncing the couple husband and wife, lingering a respectful amount of time, and departing. It was a beautiful affair.

Shortly thereafter the defendants Stafford and D. Cloninger, joined orally by the defendant Phillips, filed separate *pro se* motions to disqualify me or, in the alternative, to strike jurors, sever the particular defendant from the trial, or declare a mistrial because of my performing the Osborn wedding.

The law is careful, as it should be, to protect the litigants from a judge's having or appearing to have personal bias or financial or other interest that could be substantially affected by a trial's outcome. If the judge's impartiality might "reasonably be questioned," the judge "shall disqualify himself."[8]

Research by my law clerk Brian Riepen satisfied me that my actions relative to the wedding were appropriate and did not call for any of the remedies suggested by the movants. I said so orally from the bench and in writing by a memorandum and order dated May 28, 1980.

I have conducted other wedding services occasionally, almost always for people who wanted a nonclergy person to perform the ceremony or for a mixed-religious-faith couple or one connected to me by family or other specific ties. Once a couple I didn't know well asked me to perform their wedding. When I asked what sort of ceremony they wanted—thinking religious or nonreligious—the groom said something like, "It doesn't matter about that, but we've been together for a long time and we have a wonderful relationship. Just don't do anything that'll spoil it!" They've stayed happily together for over thirty years now. Others have also survived; I'm not sure about all of them.

Several months after her wedding, Paula Osborn Harston appeared to be sleeping in her juror's seat, but denied it, saying she didn't like the juror next to her to jab her as if she were really asleep. I cautioned her that she must remain awake or I would release her from jury duty. It happened again, a few weeks later, during the prosecution's closing argument. I softly announced a recess and asked the other jurors to leave quietly. They did, and Harston remained seated in an obvious state of slumber. I awakened her, talked with her, and heard from her that she had hardly slept the night before and couldn't help being tired. She said that had been true for weeks. I considered it necessary to excuse her from further service on the jury. I was sorry to do that, because she had all the attributes of a careful, intelligent, and willingly active juror. In fact I had talked with her previously about what she would like to do with her life. She had expressed some interest in becoming a lawyer, but had been told by her college counselor that she was not smart enough to go to law school, so she had abandoned the idea.

Then, she said, she had been so exhilarated by her jury experience in this trial that she again wanted to be a lawyer. I urged her to try to do it. I heard from her a couple of times after the trial ended, and I believe she joined the army. I have not heard of her since.

Not all the hours of a day or days of a week were dull. As the weeks droned on, the feel of the ponderous creeping of a lava flow of evidence began to make its impact—pressured sales of "estate builders," exaggerated assurances of imagined interest payouts, flowery claims of company success, unrevealed financial slippage, secret agreements unknown to the investors, consulting fees scraped off the top of the invested monies, and sinking of cooperatives.

Most of the jurors were in my chambers at least once for assistance or telephoned for temporary release from jury duty because of some unexpected experience that crowds an ordinary life: one juror was in a bicycle accident; several had an illness in the family; several became ill themselves, and one was hospitalized for four days; one had an abscessed tooth with a lump on her jaw that the attorney said was "as big as a golf ball"; one left to attend a funeral of a family member; and one was threatened with loss of her job if she didn't leave the jury at once. She continued after I told her employer that federal law forbade an employer to take any such action against a juror, whereupon the employer said she had to replace her but would do her best to rehire the juror as soon as the trial was finished. I heard nothing further about the matter. Of the four alternate jurors we used only two to replace jurors who could not complete the trial. In most instances the problem was resolved by recessing the trial for a few hours or days and then proceeding when the juror could return to duty. In all ways I was favorably impressed by the admirable performance of the jurors during this long, grueling trial.

Not unexpectedly the defendants and their lawyers were not immune from mishaps during their out-of-court lives. One of the defendants was hospitalized for thirty days and authorized us to proceed with the trial in his absence. We did, and he came back in due time. One attorney's wife had surgery, delaying the trial, I believe, for only a day. One of the attorneys,

James Crabtree, lost out on a vacation trip to Europe for which he and his wife had prepaid. He let me know my refusal to recess the trial to enable him to go raised Mrs. Crabtree's ire to unfriendly heights.

Problems between attorneys and clients were almost nonexistent, but any problem may threaten not only time but quality of service. Two such matters were present in this trial. The first was the displeasure of Thomas Moffitt with his attorney's behavior: (1) the attorney's sleeping during the trial (the attorney said it was done purposefully for rest when the other attorneys were at the bench in conference with me pertaining to issues that had nothing to do with his client); (2) the attorney's not making objections or taking part in conferences at the bench (the attorney's answer was that Moffitt had instructed him to keep a low profile, not to make an objection unless he, the client, specifically agreed to it); (3) the attorney's pressing Moffitt to accept a plea agreement (the attorney did not respond to that); and (4) disagreement over Moffitt's signing a waiver of his right to be in the courtroom. I had allowed defendants to be out of the courtroom if they signed a waiver. Moffitt had not signed one on one occasion when he had to go to the bathroom urgently and the counsel had asked me to excuse him to do so. I did excuse him, but said he would be excused in future only if he signed a waiver. Moffitt did sign and turn in the waiver to his attorney, but demanded it back, whereupon the attorney handed it to him and said, "I hope you shit in your pants." In a letter to me, dated October 14, 1979, the attorney's version of his statement to Moffitt was this: "I handed him the waiver, telling him brusquely that in the future his physical problems were going to be his, not mine."

It seemed that the easy communication wanted and expected between client and counsel was not likely to develop between this pair, but the trial had already been in progress a week, and ability to find a lawyer who could get ready for a trial of monumental complexity was next to nothing. I said I'd see what I could do. Remembering that just before the trial began a defendant named Charles Hoose had pleaded *nolo contendere* to a misdemeanor in the PFA case and had been represented for several months by Mark Slatkin, who had shown considerable knowledge of the general claims and facts of the case, I telephoned Slatkin and asked him to represent Moffitt. He said he would, if he could be given a week to get ready. I gave him that week, and he then came aboard as Moffitt's appointed counsel. He remained so to the end of the trial ten months later. I think Slatkin was a sole practitioner, and because of that there was some hardship during those ten months, but he accepted it as a committed professional.

The second incident of unrest between client and counsel occurred five months later. At the end of March 1980, some two weeks before the government rested its case-in-chief, Thomas Bradshaw came to my chamber with his client, Russell Phillips. At Bradshaw's request Phillips explained to me that he had several concerns about how the case was proceeding and how his defense ought to be handled. He was not finding out, he said, "what the language of the law means." He had concerns about the legality of the RICO statute. He thought he should call a number of investors as witnesses, and then he should testify to answer all of the questions elicited by the prosecution. He said the prosecution's evidence had been put in "all out of order." He feared that all of the original counts that had been severed were still charged against him because they had not been dismissed. There were, he said, many investors who sold their securities for a profit and needed now to say so. He worried that not just interstate but intrastate transactions were charged against him, improperly. He wanted it to be known that in the past seven or eight years he had spent about $200,000 on legal fees to be sure what he was doing was legal. He feared that the jury was not being made to understand the role of commissions in business. Furthermore Phillips was of the view that Bradshaw was not asking questions that were effective in getting the truth out. Accordingly Phillips asked to be permitted to "co-counsel" his attorney and "call the shots . . . about who [would] be called as witnesses and how they [would] be examined."[9]

I rejected his request, saying the responsibility rests upon counsel to exercise his or her best professional judgment in how to proceed in the interests of the client. The carrying out of the counsel's judgment must be done competently in consultation with the client, and, if it is not, the client is entitled to relief.[10] Phillips asked for time to consider asking me to permit him to represent himself without the assistance of counsel. I said he could make that request any time. I heard nothing further from him on that subject.

The trial offered some snarly procedural problems. The government rested its case-in-chief on April 14, 1980, and the defense began its case-in-chief after a two-week recess. Presentation of evidence concluded on August 14, and closing arguments began on July 31. Then came a bruising event that mauled the dynamics of the trial.

When the prosecuting attorney, Robert Schneider, was in the second day of his four-day closing argument, word came that the Eighth Circuit Court of Appeals (to which any appeal from this trial would necessarily go) had issued an opinion in another case, *United States v. Anderson*,[11] that changed the law from what we had thought it to be. That change affected the two most sweeping charges: the RICO-related counts. Upon reading that court's opinion in the *Anderson* case I was aghast at what we were facing: an almost certain reversal of any conviction under either of the RICO-related charges.

The case we were trying had been tried on one theory; the *Anderson* opinion seemed to say a different theory was the only acceptable one. The difference lay in the meaning of one word, "enterprise," a key word in the RICO statute. If there was no "enterprise," there was no RICO crime. The *Anderson* case said the statutory meaning was different from what we had thought. To be an "enterprise," the Eighth Circuit three-judge panel seemed to say, there had to be one entity or group of people having a common purpose and a continuing and ascertainable structure that is different from the pattern of racketeering activity, that is, different from the claimed fraudulent selling of securities of the four agricultural cooperatives, different from the cooperatives themselves.

The Eighth Circuit's ruling sent shivers down the spines of the prosecutors, melodies of joy through the minds of the defendants and their attorneys, and a mule's kick to my stomach. My reaction wasn't because of any ill feeling that the defendants might not be convicted of two of the crimes charged against them, but because I had let the RICO charges be a part of the trial at all. We had spent perhaps a third of the trial time—three and a half months—trying the RICO counts, all probably wasted time. I hated that I had been shortsighted.

Each participant in the trial did what could be done to adapt to the ruling in the *Anderson* case. The prosecutor, Schneider, abruptly altered his closing arguments in a scramble to accomplish what we all felt was a nearly impossible feat of avoiding a reversal on appeal of any conviction under either or both RICO-related counts. I changed the instructions to the jury by telling them that they could determine whether there was an "enterprise," using the definition in the statute. Maybe, I thought, that would satisfy the circuit court. The prosecutors argued more pointedly that the band of defendants, not the cooperatives they created and ran, were the "enterprise." And the defendants demanded that there was no "enterprise" at all.

The government attorneys and the five defense attorneys finished their closing arguments over a period of six more days, a total of eight, counting the two already used by the government. In the final few seconds of his rebuttal Schneider broke down, crying. He quickly turned away from the jury and took his seat. I promptly called a recess. A motion for a mistrial was at once made by the defense, but I denied it out of hand. I could see no reason to think the breakdown was intentional. Schneider was obviously tired, worn out, and emotionally drained.

Paula Osborn Harston, while still a juror, made a phone call to Steve Navarro, the deputy courtroom clerk, asking about Robert Schneider's "breakdown" at the end of his closing argument. Navarro told me of the call, and I then held a hearing at which he reported on the record what had occurred: that Harston had called on August 5 at about 6:10 p.m. (about two hours after Prosecutor Schneider had had his "breakdown"), asking whether Schneider was "like that in the courtroom always," and had said, "What Mr. Schneider did was very touching . . . [and] bothered me a lot." Navarro testified that his only response was that she should call the judge. (She did not call me.) She also said, according to Navarro, that some other jurors "started laughing" in the jury room because they "really didn't know what was going on." Navarro said he "felt he, Schneider, was really sincere."[12] I concluded that no damage had been done by the telephone call and denied the government's motions to excuse Harston as a member of the jury.

Shaeffer completed his part of government's closing argument on August 13. Five hours were then consumed by my reading aloud to the jurors 147 pages of instructions (of which each juror had a copy for following along), describing the law they were to apply. Some 2,500 exhibits had been received into evidence and were available for use by the jury. The exhibits remained in the courtroom while the jurors deliberated in a separate room. When the jury wanted to study any exhibit or set of exhibits, the foreperson would make a request for it. From the way the jury made its requests we could tell the orderly way it was proceeding—calling for exhibits first that dealt with Count 1, then calling for exhibits pertinent to Count 2, and so on through all six counts. The jurors' discussions continued during eight days before reaching a unanimous verdict on August 25, 1980, that found all five defendants guilty of all counts against them.

But a clear, unanimous verdict did not mean a smooth ending of the trial. Immediately following the reading of the verdict, I asked the jurors to remain for another hearing. Between the beginning of closing arguments and the finding of guilty of the five defendants, Paula Osborn Harston was released from jury duty, as I have described. After her release, she was reported to have telephoned an active juror, Ms. Albright, despite my instruction to Harston not to have any contact with any juror until the verdict had been received. The hearing was necessary to learn whether there had been some interference with the deliberations of the jury, but I found that the call had been one of curiosity arising from Harston's hearing there *was* a verdict before there was one.

Once the trial had ended, the sentencing of five defendants who had pleaded guilty or *nolo contendere* earlier—Beaver, Canaday, G. L. Cloninger, Harmon, and Morrison—and sentencing of the jury-convicted defendants, Phillips, Bledsoe, Stafford, Moffitt, and D. Cloninger, proceeded on August 29, 1980.

There were other odd happenings at the PFA trial. The first was when Richard E. Anderson announced at the very outset of the trial that he was concerned about proceeding. My memory is that he said he was not "competent" to defend his client, Burks. I have not seen that statement in the transcript, and I doubt he used that word, but my thought (that he had used that word) stuck with me because in previous years I had handled habeas corpus actions of convicted defendants claiming their counsel had not met the requirement of the Sixth Amendment of the Constitution, that a defendant shall have "the assistance of counsel," by which courts have said it means "competent" assistance. I wondered whether he was setting a cautionary scene for a later similar claim in the event his client were to be convicted. Somewhat later Anderson again asserted, though not in terms of "competency," that he had said before beginning the trial that he "felt unprepared to handle the case" because he had been under the impression that the federal public defender's office would assist him but he had received "absolutely no assistance."[13] I did not relieve him of his duties, nor did I explore the intentions of the public defender to help Anderson. I heard nothing more on the subject. It is possible that these disclaimers by Anderson were a prelude—even an unintentional one—to the second odd episode.

The Patty Click switch drew the attention of everybody because it came dangerously close to aborting the trial. Every drama has a cast of characters, some in leading roles and others in supporting roles. The leads in this one were Donald Gibson, the principal witness favorable to the prosecution; Russell Phillips, the targeted defendant; Richard E. Anderson, defense attorney for supporting-role player Donald Burks and nephew of Donald Gibson; and Patty Click, an attractive woman who had known both Gibson and Phillips for several years and who, she testified, had slept with both.

To tie Phillips to the Arkansas cooperative, CFA-Arkansas, the prosecution needed whatever it could find to overcome Phillips's efforts to obscure any CFA-Arkansas connection with his frequent visits to Arkansas.

When Defendant Phillips's turn came for presenting evidence at the trial, Phillips's lawyer, Bradshaw, subpoenaed Patty Click with the expectation that she would testify to the same event in the same way she had recounted before. Three times, at least, she had declared in the past three years—once under oath by affidavit to an attorney in Greene County, Missouri; once by testimony before a grand jury in Greene County; and once by a recorded oral statement taken by telephone by Phillips's attorney—that a certain $1,500 check (that was traceable to funds of CFA-Arkansas) had been given to her by Gibson, not by Phillips, when she had telephoned Gibson and asked him for a loan to cover some personal expenses.

On Wednesday, April 16, 1980, when she appeared in Kansas City in response to the subpoena, she repeated the story to Bradshaw. However, on the next evening, Thursday, she had dinner with Richard Anderson and later in the evening visited with Donald Gibson at a disco, telling Gibson that she knew she had lied about the check. He told her that if she didn't tell the truth at the trial she would be in trouble. She also told Anderson, when he drove her to her hotel that evening, that her religious upbringing now told her she must tell the truth—that she got the check from *Phillips, not Gibson*. She expressed some fear of Mrs. Phillips, who had put some pressure on her at the time of the Greene County grand jury inquiry (perhaps because Mrs. Phillips had learned of and resented a Phillips-Click affair). Click said she didn't know what to do, but with the encouragement of Gibson and Anderson she went to Bradshaw the next morning and told him she was no longer going to say she got the check from Gibson.

That put Bradshaw in a dilemma. I think he figured she would be called to testify by the prosecutor or by one of the other attorneys if he did not. The question was, if she were to testify that the check came to her from Phillips, not Gibson, would the impact on the jury be less harmful to Phillips, his client, if the switch were revealed when he questioned her about it than if she were called and questioned by some other party's lawyer? He chose to take the chance that the answer was yes. He knew, though, from conversations with the other lawyers in my presence, that if he called her as a witness and then felt compelled to call all others who knew something of the Thursday-evening conversations with Gibson and Anderson, it meant he would call Anderson to testify, and that would jeopardize Anderson's ability to continue to represent Burks in this trial and might reflect badly on the other defendants.

The expected reaction of presiding judges, including me, is that there is an obvious conflict of interest when an attorney of a defendant testifies during a trial to a matter of some importance to the parties. The role of the attorney in protecting the interests of his or her client is in danger of being compromised. The solution is to remove the attorney from the case.

Another reason for Bradshaw's uneasiness was that if Anderson testified, he might give testimony favorable to the government's position on the feebleness of Click's credibility and the strength of Gibson's credibility. That would be at odds with the vibes the defendants and their lawyers wanted to be wafted about and inhaled by the jurors, namely, that the defendants and their lawyers were aligned together in one harmonious assembly against the government and the government's witnesses, especially Gibson, and that the defense lawyers were a close-knit group in tune with each other. But having hopefully built a favorable impression, the defense lawyers would feel betrayed by what might seem to be a loose cannon, Anderson, in their midst, and the jury might feel that the good vibes they felt had been inaccurate.

Bradshaw *did* call Patty Click as a witness. One thing in her favor was that the prosecuting attorney from Greene County had obtained immunity for her from prosecution for perjury she may have committed in testifying before the Greene County grand jury. Now she could switch versions of the check delivery without that impediment. When she took the witness stand in Kansas City at the PFA trial, she testified that she got the check from Phillips, not Gibson; that she had lied whenever she said it came from Gibson; that she had lied because she loved Phillips—and still did, and still hoped to be with him on a permanent basis.

Bradshaw also called Gibson and Anderson as witnesses. Both largely agreed that Click's testimony of the Thursday-evening conversations was reasonably accurate. Gibson added that on Friday morning, when Click was leaving Bradshaw's office after telling Bradshaw in Phillips's presence that she was going to testify that the check had come from Phillips and not Gibson, she walked out of the office and was met by Phillips at an outer door. There, Gibson said, Phillips told her he loved her and that when the trial was over, they would be together. That elicited a shout from Mrs. Phillips in the spectator section of the courtroom, "You are a god damned liar!" and she stomped out. That resulted in a motion by Schneider, the prosecutor, to hold Mrs. Phillips in contempt of court. I refused, but told the jury to disregard what Mrs. Phillips had said.

However, when we discussed the question of Anderson's continuing to represent Burks in the trial, no one asserted that he could. I excused him from continuing to represent Burks in this trial. Because the trial was in its latter stages, I knew that trying to appoint someone else to represent Burks was hopeless, so I severed Burks from the trial, meaning that Burks could be tried later. Anderson indicated that he could be available to represent Burks at a later trial, after the current one was finished. I responded to that by reading to him a memorandum I had prepared: "You have demonstrated insensitivity to or lack of discipline about the problems inherent in your association during the trial with a witness considered important by the prosecution . . . and causing yourself to become a witness in this case, whether intentionally or unintentionally, and the resultant disqualification of you as counsel in the trial and the severing of your client." Furthermore his familial relationship with Donald Gibson had not changed, and I could see no reason to think he would be any more sensitive or disciplined than he had been. I then relieved him of his appointment as Burks's attorney and said I would inform any judge entrusted with a later case of Burks's that Anderson should not be involved in the case except as a witness.[14]

The third odd episode was the testimony by Michael Chapman on May 1, 1980. He said that sometime in 1976 or 1977 he had been offered $30,000 by Donald Gibson and Charles Luna to kill Russell Phillips, but no money was exchanged and nothing more came of it. Chapman also said that Gibson had offered him $500 to "break the fingers" of Phillips. Again, no action was taken to carry that out, he said.

The fourth and final oddity involved mention of the Mafia and organized crime. In May 1980, well into the trial, Prosecutor Schneider asked the witness Michael Chapman, "In November of 1974, . . . did you come up to Kansas City and meet with members of the Mafia or organized crime?" That brought defense lawyers to their feet, making motions for a mistrial or severance, because of fear that the jury would read into the question the hint that these defendants had some friendly connection, at least, with a large and notorious criminal element.

On May 23 I issued a memorandum and order denying the motions. The reference to "the Mafia or organized crime" was infinitesimal in the melee of a seven-month trial to be expected to cause a reasonable juror to give weight to some suspicion of any of the defendants or the witness having connections to some criminal element—particularly when no answer was given to the question and an instruction was given by me to the jurors to ignore the question.

The PFA trial was another milestone for me. Its length, of course, was noteworthy, but its dominating characteristic was the relentless hammering of surprising problems. Each one left me counting myself lucky with its outcome. At its end, however, I felt that I had been walking in a den of thieves, but saved by magnificent people around me. The lawyers for the most part were superior in doing what they were supposed to do, representing their clients by making me maneuver through every legal pothole and offering every persuasive phrase in favor of *their* option. My law clerks, Kerry Kester and Brian Riepen, were brilliant, level-headed, and loyal. The court staff were courteous, careful, and undemanding. I felt "seasoned," ready for whatever came next.

I received from Judge Van Pelt a note dated July 31, 1980, when I was winding down, but hadn't completed the PFA saga. It was addressed to "Warren" from "Bob." This is the complete text:

> I trust that you are giving consideration to taking a vacation of substantial duration. Leaving out family obligations, which you alone should pass upon, I think you owe it to yourself to completely divorce yourself from judging for such period as you can live without worry or undue pressure later on.
>
> I think you should consider not taking any court files with you and not taking or reading any reports or legal articles of the nature which we all promise ourselves to read "when we are not so busy." May I also suggest, and as you know by now I make many suggestions, that you not make any speeches or prepare any speeches. I think it would be proper for you to permit your monthly checks to be deposited but beyond that I would hope you would have no connection with the courts for such period. I am sure it would be good for you and thus good for all of us if you could take a vacation of that kind.

I was grateful for his caring advice and told him so. But in all seriousness I did not feel washed out by the PFA trial, hard as it had been. Under the circumstances, I decided that the greater need was the disposition of cases that had accumulated on my docket. So I bypassed the vacation and set a bundle of cases for trial. By the end of the year I had probably disposed of a dozen cases, including four that were tried over fifteen days. I had no feeling of being a martyr or a workaholic. I thought then and think now that I was just doing what a reasonable judge would do. Robert Van Pelt in his younger days would have done the same.

Still, there's more to be said about the PFA case. An appeal was taken by the convicted defendants. The panel of Judges Donald Lay, Gerald Heaney, and Donald Ross (Judge Ross dissenting) vacated the convictions of all the defendants on the two RICO counts. It also vacated the convictions of Bledsoe and Cloninger on the securities fraud counts and remanded those charges for a new trial. It affirmed Phillips's convictions on the four securities fraud counts and remanded his case for resentencing on those counts.[15] I resentenced Phillips to the same sentence as before: five years of imprisonment and $5,000 on each of three fraud charges, the prison terms to run consecutively, and one five-year term of probation and a $5,000 fine on another fraud count. An appeal was taken by Phillips to those sentences, but they were affirmed by a panel of Judges John R. Gibson, Myron Bright, and Pasco M. Bowman II.[16]

There were no further trials related to the PFA case. The cases against Bledsoe, Cloninger, and Stafford were reassigned to Judge Scott Wright. Each of those defendants pleaded *nolo contendere* to one count of securities fraud. Bledsoe and Cloninger received five-year sentences and Stafford a two-year sentence, negotiated to avoid a long and expensive trial. Moffitt pleaded guilty to one count of securities fraud and was placed on probation for three years and required to contribute three hundred hours of community service. He had served eight months in prison before entering his guilty plea.[17] No appeal was taken by Bledsoe, Cloninger, Stafford, or Moffitt from their sentences after remand.

That year, from September 1979 through August 1980, was probably the busiest I have ever been. Aside from being occupied with a riveting trial in Kansas City and commuting nearly two hundred miles on weekends to teach a three-hour class in trial advocacy at the University of Nebraska in Lincoln, I was doing my best to keep abreast of the duties of being president of the Board of Governors of Nebraska Wesleyan University in Lincoln. That included monthly meetings of the board. (I didn't make all of them but talked frequently with the college's president, John White Jr., who had succeeded twenty-year president Vance Rogers and in the course of time would serve twenty himself.)

All this meant that my family was experiencing a part-time father-husband. During October 1979 through May 1980 Joyce and I supplemented our shortened and periodic times together by her enlisting "jurors" for the final exams of my trial advocacy class. Each exam was a mock trial three or four hours in length; students or friends of the class members were recruited by the student "attorneys" to portray witnesses. With textbook sets of facts, the trials were held in Lincoln in the courtroom of the law school or the federal courthouse on Saturdays and Sundays at the end of each semester, which meant December and May. I acted as the judge and critiqued and graded the performances. Joyce's getting the twelve jurors for each trial, attending the trials, and acting as bailiff added fun to the experience.

Our daughter Joy was in her senior year of high school in Lincoln and the only child of ours living at home that year. I was able to attend her installation on June 1 as honored queen of Jobs' Daughters, an offspring of the Ancient Free and Accepted Masons. She and her mother gave me a special treat in July by visiting Kansas City and having dinner with me and my staff, eating (not coincidentally) at Michael's Plum Restaurant, where the Patty Click episode had taken place. Joy, multitalented and quietly careful with both oral and written words and a natural leader, had chosen Nebraska Wesleyan University, Joyce's and my alma mater, for her undergraduate work and was registered for the fall semester of 1980. She later chose law as her profession, without urging by me beyond my suggesting she not overlook that possibility because I was sure she had all the qualifications for the profession, or virtually any other she might choose.

Tornados struck Grand Island, Nebraska, on Tuesday, June 3, 1980, seven of them in one vicious day, wrecking much of the town, including causing considerable damage to Joyce's parents' home. After learning that they were unhurt, we hurried to Grand Island on Friday evening, but found the town literally unrecognizable in the darkness. We retreated twenty miles east to the town of Aurora. Unable to find any sleeping facilities, we spent the night in the car, sleeping a few hours, and made contact with Mom and Dad Crawford the next morning. The wreckage of Grand Island was horrendous. The need for repairs of the damage to the Crawfords' home, which was mild in comparison with the destruction of many properties, led to our taking Joyce's parents to our home in Lincoln and inviting them to stay as long as necessary.

January 1, 1980, is touted in our household as the birthday of Joyce's and my first grandchild, Aaron Rager, son of Kim and Scott. Aaron was the first baby born in the new year in Sioux County, Iowa.

9

Back to Normal

Returning from the PFA trial to what I supposed would be a slower and easier pace in the fall of 1980, I met instead an avalanche of work. Abortion, the death penalty, bid-rigging, sentencing alternatives to imprisonment, and sentencing guidelines engulfed my time and energy. My docket seemed bloated during most of the 1980s, at times showing more than six hundred pending cases, which was more than enough.

When the Supreme Court of the United States handed down its decision in *Roe v. Wade* in 1973,[1] acknowledging a constitutional right of privacy of women to decide to abort pregnancies and to abort pregnancies, Nebraska's legislature, like many others, responded boldly. A set of laws was adopted in 1977, framing restrictions the legislators hoped were within the constitutional standards of *Roe v. Wade* and pronouncing criminal penalties on violators. In turn, pregnant women, parents of pregnant minors, physicians available to perform abortions, and clinics equipped to furnish services for performing abortions took up legal arms to challenge the restrictions. They typically sued the governor, the attorney general, and a county attorney—the authorities whose duties included prosecuting violators of the laws. The resulting face-off put me in the middle of the disputing parties for a piece of 1979 and parts of the next two decades.

The midst of the abortion melee was in one sense a notable time for our family. Our son, Randy, and our daughter Joy graduated from law school in 1981 and 1988, respectively. Though I have no memory that any of us noted it, I think we all could see a parallel between a law school's agony of "birthing" a putative lawyer and a mother's agony of birthing a putative child. The worry, tension, fright, expectation, hope, and uncertainty are ample in both, and the result may be positive or negative, success or failure, joy or despondency. I too had those feelings through the law school adventure and again had them when resolving the emotionally charged issues inherent in abortion legislation.

The first set of challenges to the constitutionality of portions of Nebraska statutes came before me in the form of three consolidated cases, two labeled *Women's Services, PC v. Thone* and one labeled *Ladies Service Center v. Douglas,* appearing in print as *Women's Services, P.C. v. Thone.*[2] The plaintiffs in the three consolidated cases were two professional corporations who provided services to physicians who performed abortions, two physicians who performed abortions, the friend of a pregnant minor, and interested interveners.

Nebraska's statute left no doubt of the goal of the legislature. The legislation of 1977, it declared, was motivated by the "legislative intrusion" of the Supreme Court of the United States in its seminal case of *Roe v. Wade* four years earlier. The interest of the people of Nebraska, its legislature said, was that "every precaution be taken to insure the protection of every viable unborn child being aborted, and every precaution be taken to provide life-supportive procedures to insure the unborn child its continued life after its abortion."[3]

Two attacks were made on the legislation in these cases: first, that the statute offended the U.S. Constitution's clause in the First Amendment that forbade the making of a law "respecting an establishment of religion or prohibiting the free exercise thereof," and second, that parts of the statute violated the Fourteenth Amendment's due process and equal protection clauses.

The First Amendment claim sprang from the statute's use of the term "unborn child" and in the definition of "pregnant" as being "the condition of a woman who has unborn human life within her as the result of conception." Additionally the defendants, who were state officials with the responsibility to enforce the statute's requirements, admitted "without qualification" that the statutes would "be enforced in the interest of unborn children from the moment of conception."

Because many consider the belief that life begins at conception to be a religious belief, the plaintiffs argued that a law favoring it constitutes an "establishment" of religion—that is, a putting an approving hand of the state government on that religious belief, thus violating the First Amendment. I sought to analyze that contention by examining the parameters of both theistic and nontheistic beliefs, and concluded that in the context of the religion clause of the First Amendment and the legislation in this case the belief that life begins at conception could be as capably labeled *philosophical* as *religious*.

The legislature said that it had a nonreligious purpose, namely, protecting the life of the mother (to say nothing of protecting fetuses), quite aside from any religious idea. Furthermore there was no indication that the legislators thought that this legislation should be adopted to bring the law into closer harmony with the will of a Supreme Being or to be in accord with a nontheistic principle. All this enabled me to say that the idea that life begins at conception is not necessarily or always a religious idea and did not appear to have been a significant religious force in passage of the statute. For that reason, I held, the establishment clause of the First Amendment was not violated by passage or enforcement of the statute.

Neither was the statute in violation of the free-exercise branch of the religion clause, I ruled. The decision to have or not to have an abortion is one to be made by the individual woman as a personal preference, depending on the ingredients of each woman's life situation. To have or not to have an abortion may be considered by some to be a religious duty, but that does not make *every* abortion decision a religious act.

Aside from the religion clause of the First Amendment, the claims of the plaintiffs were aimed at specific sections of the statute. Although much of the statute was held to be constitutional, I held five separate parts unconstitutional under the due process clause of the Fourteenth Amendment.

One section of the statute, 28-343, mandated that a written form prepared by the Bureau of Vital Statistics, Department of Health, be used to report every abortion "performed or prescribed" in the state and include "only" certain listed items, none of which included "prescribed" abortions. Section 28-344 made failure to comply with section 28-343 a criminal act. The two sections were inconsistent: one made reporting of "prescribed" abortions mandatory, while the other said that "only" reports that did not include "prescribed" abortions were to be reported. I found both sections void for vagueness because they failed to give a reasonable person in the position of the physician clear notice of what he or she must do or not do to avoid criminal prosecution for not complying with the requirements of the statute.

Another section, 28-333, forbade an abortion on a minor under the age of eighteen without her informed consent unless an emergency situation existed. It then said that the informed consent of the minor must be retained as part of the permanent record of the attending physician "for *no more* than ten years" (italics added). Because the statute said nothing about how long the informed consent *had* to be kept, but only the longest it *could* be kept, which seemed to mean that it could be destroyed immediately after it was received, I held that section also void for vagueness.

Still another section, 28-326(8), subsection (a), required a woman seeking an abortion to state in writing that she had been advised, among other things, of "the reasonably possible medical and mental consequences resulting from an abortion, *pregnancy and childbirth*" (italics added). Testimony at the trial was that several hours would be required to "advise" a pregnant woman of the reasonably possible medical and mental consequences of, not just an abortion, but of pregnancy and childbirth. With criminal charges facing a physician for failure to carry out the complete package of advice, I found it convincing that the provision put the physician in an "unconstitutional straitjacket." I declared that it went beyond the boundaries of *Roe v. Wade* and hence was too broad—that is, outside the appropriate interests of the state. I held subsection (a) of the statute unconstitutional and permanently enjoined its enforcement.

Last, I held that section 28-327's requirement of a forty-eight-hour waiting period between the getting by the physician an informed consent from the woman and the performing of an abortion imposed an undue burden on the woman's freedom to have an abortion and therefore was unconstitutional under the due process clause. Evidence at the trial was that the distance between western Nebraska and the only abortion clinics in the state, in Omaha, would cause not only added waiting time, but the additional expense of a second trip to Omaha or the expense of staying in

Omaha during the entire forty-eight hours of waiting time. The waiting period, I found, was a substantially increased risk to the woman's health.

My decisions holding these parts of the statute unconstitutional were appealed by the defendants, who were the officials duty-bound to enforce the abortion statutes. The Eighth Circuit Court of Appeals affirmed my holdings.[4] Appeal was taken to the Supreme Court of the United States, which responded with these words: "*Vacated and Remanded on Appeal. . . . Thone v. Governor of Nebraska v. Women's Services* . . . Appeal from . . . 8th Cir. Judgment vacated and case remanded for further consideration in light of *H. L. v. Matheson*, 450 U. S. 398 (1981). Justice Brennan, Justice Marshall, and Justice Blackmun dissent and would affirm the judgment. Reported below: 636 F. 2d 206."[5] In short the Supreme Court sent the case back to the Eighth Circuit Court of Appeals, and the Eighth Circuit sent it back to me "for further consideration in light of *H. L. v. Matheson and Planned Parenthood Association of Kansas City, Missouri, Inc.* and *Planned Parenthood Association of Kansas City, Missouri, Inc. v. Ashcroft* . . . 655 F. 2d 848 (8th Cir. July 8, 1981)." I did reconsider in light of both cited cases and came to the same conclusions as before—that the specific sections of Nebraska's statute were unconstitutional.

The defendants again appealed, and the court of appeals again affirmed my decision,[6] noting that this time on appeal the defendants were no longer claiming that the parental consultation requirement of the statute was constitutional.

Once more the case returned to the Supreme Court. Again the Court vacated the judgment and remanded the case to the Eighth Circuit "for further consideration in light of *City of Akron v. Akron Center for Reproductive Health, Inc.*, 462 U.S. 416, 103 S. Ct. 2481, 2499, 76 L. Ed. 2d 687 (Part V)(1983)."

The Eighth Circuit court received the remand from the Supreme Court on June 23, 1983, and by August 25 had granted motions by all parties to dismiss the appeals with prejudice, except as to the matter of attorneys' fees and costs, which I then resolved. My original opinion remained in force.

The remands are good evidence of the flurry of abortion cases that were alive in the dockets of the courts at the time. None of the cases cited by the Supreme Court or the court of appeals—the *Mattheson* case, the *Planned*

Parenthood case, or the *City of Akron* case—had been available to me or the Eighth Circuit Court of Appeals when we made our decisions in the *Women's Services* consolidated case, because they had not been decided by the Supreme Court. They and other abortion cases were running almost side by side, so remands were the way of making those cases available to me and the Eighth Circuit Court of Appeals for immediate guidance and reconsideration if necessary.

The *Mattheson* case made no difference in my decision during the first remand, and a glance at the *City of Akron* case doesn't give me any clue that it would have affected my decision if the consolidated *Women's Services* cases had been remanded to me for reconsideration a second time. The *City of Akron* case involved a twenty-four-hour waiting period from receiving informed consent to performing an abortion (holding it unconstitutional, just as I had done in *Women's Services*). The Supreme Court gave the lower courts, by the remands, an opportunity to decide whether the recent Supreme Court case would have made a difference. The circuit court had the remanded case first, but sent it back to me to decide whether availability would have made a difference to me. The Nebraska statute appears to have been revised since 1983 to comply in all respects with my decisions in the *Women's Services* cases.

On July 30, 1981, I issued an opinion in *Schulte v. Douglas*,[7] finding four more sections of the 1977 abortion law of Nebraska unconstitutional. The definition of viability in sections 28-326(6), 28-329, and 28-330 as "that stage of human development when the unborn child is potentially able to live outside the womb of the mother by natural or artificial means" was found to be deficient because it omitted the words or ideas of a "meaningful" and "sustained" life outside the womb. Both of those words were used by the Supreme Court in *Roe v. Wade* and *Colautti v. Franklin* to assure the aspect of survival to mean more than momentary.[8]

Another section required use of certain methods in postviability abortions. I said the state could do that as long as the statute did not interfere with medical judgments as to the method necessary for the saving of the life or health of the mother. But section 28-330 *did* interfere in that way, I held, even when in the physician's judgment a different course should be undertaken to preserve the mother from a *nonimminent* peril that endangers her life or health *less than substantially*, or from an *imminent* peril that endangers her life of health *less than substantially*. The state had no authority to do that, according to the Eighth Circuit's *Planned Parenthood Association of Kansas City, Missouri, Inc. v. Ashcroft*.[9]

More yet, I concluded in the *Schulte* case that all three sections pertaining to postviability health decisions—sections 28-329, 28-330, and 28-331—were unconstitutional because they failed to include on the part of the physician performing the abortion any requirement of scienter. By "scienter" I meant that intent or knowledge or a culpable mental state was necessary to be held guilty of a crime. Due process insists upon such a requirement. The Eighth Circuit affirmed my order.[10]

As judicial decisions declared various portions of abortion statutes unconstitutional, Nebraska's legislature continued to find revisions that would meet the standards of *Roe v. Wade* and its followers. Important revisions occurred in 1979, 1984, 1986, 1991, and 1993. Litigation then waned, but the emotional battle over abortion itself did not.

A clear swerve in the road of abortion litigation appeared in the mid-1990s. Instead of relying on legislation to discourage abortion, objectors began using other means to the same end. Picketing the doctor who did the aborting was one technique.

In September 1995 and May and June 1996 three residents of Omaha—Melissa Abbink, Sharon McKee, and Larry Donlan—ran a picketing campaign to discourage Dr. Winston Crabb from using abortions to terminate pregnancies, as he did regularly in his medical practice in Lincoln and elsewhere. In the June incident the three protestors arrived at Dr. Crabb's residence at 7 a.m., followed him to and into a local restaurant, were seated at their request near Dr. Crabb, talked loudly of the awful nature of abortions, left when Dr. Crabb did, followed Dr. Crabb's car in their car to his place of employment, and there joined other protesters in picketing that clinic. Abbink, McKee, and Donlan were cited for the June incident and for picketing peacefully at Dr. Crabb's residence on September 22, 1995, and May 10, 1996. Charges were under Nebraska's Revised Statute section 28-1317(e), which made it unlawful to picket the place of residence of a person, or interfering, against the person's will, with his or her right to work. The three were fined $300 each. They remained in jail for ten days rather than pay their fines. They then filed suit against Donald Stenberg, the Nebraska attorney general, for a judgment that would declare that the statute violated the Constitution's First Amendment's freedom of speech clause.

A protective order had been entered earlier by a state court against Abbink, McKee, and Donlan for violating Nebraska's stalking laws, sections 28-311.03 and 42-924(1). That court found that the protestors' campaign had consisted in part of blocking entry to the doctor's car, attempting to block the path of his car, following him when he left his residence in the morning, following him into eating establishments, following him from his place of employment, and surrounding his car at a stop sign. Dr. Crabb then began wearing a bulletproof vest, looking around his car before getting into it, checking his rearview mirror for anybody following him, and feeling anxious. The background of the state court's protective order made doubtful the protesters' claim in the case before me that they had intended in the June incident to be a symbol of nonviolence and peacefulness.

Audra Hamilton, my law clerk from Arkansas, at my urging and approval, wrote at length of the strength and importance of the right of free speech to Abbink, McKee, and Donlan, as well as the colliding interest of the state to keep a citizenry free of living in fear of harassment and to protect one's right to work without obstruction. When the plaintiffs argued to me that their actions toward Dr. Crabb were symbolic speech that carried the nonviolent and peaceful message to stop doing abortions, I doubted that was the intended message. I ruled that the conduct of Abbink, McKee, and Donlan had ceased to contain any expressive value and had become only brutish conduct, thereby not being "speech" protected by the First Amendment. Moreover the statute was obviously so broad it forbade "picketing . . . any . . . place, where . . . [a person is] in the exercise of his or her right to work." I permanently enjoined enforcement of the statute.

In 1998 a suit challenged a Lincoln ordinance regarding "focused" residential picketing.[11] "Focused" picketing meant, according to the ordinance, picketing directed toward a specific person or persons. The area not allowed for such picketing was in the street in front of or within fifty feet on either side of a targeted dwelling. The plaintiffs, Monsignor Timothy Thornburn, Pam

Tabor, Dominic Pynes, and Mary Adam, wanted an injunction prohibiting enforcement of the ordinance. They asserted that the ordinance was constitutionally vague, ambiguous, and violated the freedom of speech clause of the First Amendment, as well as the equal protection and due process clauses of the Fourteenth Amendment.

These plaintiffs alleged that they had not picketed in the vicinity of Dr. Winston Crabb's residence for fear of being prosecuted for violation of the ordinance. Plaintiff Mary Adam said that she had refrained from walking or standing on the sidewalk in front of Dr. Crabb's residence holding a sign of protest about abortion, or walking around the block on the sidewalk by which his residence was located, or kneeling in prayer in the grassy median of the street in front of his residence. Monsignor Thornburn complained that he had thought about going near the Crabb place to quietly stand, kneel, or walk on the sidewalk in front of the home without a sign, to pray for Dr. Crabb's salvation and that the doctor would quit performing abortions. Dominic Pynes feared prosecution if he were to deliver leaflets to homes, knock on doors of homes, and speak with the people who live in the homes. Pam Tabor had similar concerns.

I reviewed the ordinance in detail and found it constitutional. The ordinance was content-neutral; that is, it neither prohibited nor permitted speech because of the city government's liking or disliking what the speech said. It was narrowly tailored to fit the city's substantial interest—protecting residential privacy and tranquility—and was not substantially broader than necessary to achieve the city's interest. The ordinance allowed ample alternatives for people to communicate their opposition or approval to abortion: they could picket, march, walk, preach, or pray directly across the street from the targeted home and the home on each side of the one targeted. It was specific enough to give a person of ordinary intelligence notice of what was prohibited. Furthermore, I wrote, the ordinance gave adequate guidelines for law enforcement officers to determine what conduct was in violation of the ordinance. My ruling was affirmed on appeal.[12]

One employment belch came from the abortion intake. In 1997 Dr. LeRoy H. Carhart, a physician who performed abortion procedures and provided fetal tissue from his abortion patients to researchers at the University of

Nebraska Medical Center's Department of Pathology and Microbiology, challenged in court the constitutionality of Nebraska's statute making criminal the performance of a "partial birth abortion."[13] Shortly thereafter he was appointed volunteer adjunct assistant professor (clinician) in that department. Thirty-four months later he was terminated from that faculty status, and he claimed in a suit that came to me that the termination was in retaliation of his having filed the lawsuit challenging the "partial birth abortion" law.

He was successful in his challenge. District Judge Richard G. Kopf, the Eighth Circuit (Judge Richard Arnold writing), and the Supreme Court of the United States (Justice Breyer writing) held Nebraska's "partial birth abortion" law unconstitutional.[14] Justice Breyer's opinion summarized the reasons for the unconstitutionality: "First, the law lacks an exception 'for the preservation of the . . . health of the mother.'" (The statute prohibited a "partial birth abortion" when the fetus was capable of living for a period more than momentary, unless the "partial birth abortion" was necessary to save the *life* of the mother; it did not add "or the *health* of the mother.") "Second," said Justice Breyer, "it 'imposes an undue burden on the woman's ability' to choose a D&E abortion, thereby unduly burdening the right to choose abortion itself."[15] (D&E is the most commonly used abortion procedure when the fetus is capable of living for a period more than momentary; if the statute clearly prohibits D&X, which is the term often used for "partial birth abortion," and may prohibit the more common D&E, it goes too far in restricting the woman's right to an abortion.)

I concluded that Carhart's bringing the lawsuit that resulted in the Supreme Court's saying that the statute was unconstitutional was a right he had under the free speech clause of the First Amendment. If the University of Nebraska terminated Carhart for exercising that right of speech (litigation), he would be entitled to relief. Upon hearing evidence on a motion for a preliminary injunction, I found that the greater weight of the evidence supported his claim and that he would likely be successful if a full trial were held. Shortly thereafter the parties agreed to settle the case, whereby Carhart would be reinstated to his faculty role, effective the date of his termination, and subject to the same policies applicable to all other members of the volunteer faculty of the University of Nebraska Medical Center. Judgment was entered accordingly.

No more abortion cases have come before me since the turn of the century.

In 1972 the U.S. Supreme Court brought to a standstill the use of the sentence of death. In a 5–4 decision in *Furman v. Georgia* the Court declared that as to the three defendants convicted in a Georgia court of murder or rape, "imposition and carrying out of the death penalty in these cases constitute cruel and unusual punishment in violation of the Eighth and Fourteenth Amendments" of the Constitution.[16] The words of the Court's majority opinion spoke only of "these" cases, but their scope abruptly stopped executions in every state. No resumption of execution was seen until the case of *Gregg v. Georgia* had wended its way to the Supreme Court in 1976 and the Court held that the death penalty as such is not unconstitutional. The plurality opinion of the Court in the *Gregg* opinion said:

> We hold that the death penalty is not a form of punishment that may never be imposed, regardless of the circumstances of the offense, regardless of the character of the offender, and regardless of the procedure followed in reaching the decision to impose it. . . .
>
> . . . .
>
> . . . Because of the uniqueness of the death penalty, *Furman* held that it could not be imposed under sentencing procedures that created a substantial risk that it would be inflicted in an arbitrary and capricious manner.[17]

Between the *Furman* decision and the *Gregg* decision, four years apart, it became "evident that a large proportion of American society continue(d) to regard . . . (the death penalty) as an appropriate and necessary criminal sanction," said the Court in the *Gregg* plurality opinion, noting that some thirty-five states had enacted new statutes that provided for the death penalty for at least some crimes that resulted in the death of another person.[18] In addition, in 1974 Congress had enacted a statute providing the death penalty for aircraft piracy that resulted in death. Post-*Furman* statutes had made clear that capital punishment itself had "not been rejected by the elected representatives of the people."[19]

Although Nebraskans have had some misgivings about the death penalty, Nebraska remains in the majority of states in providing the death penalty for first-degree murder. In 1981 the unicameral legislature passed a proposal to abolish capital punishment, but a veto by Governor Charles Thone scrubbed it. Three executions have been carried out since then.[20] In one of them, leading to execution by the electric chair, I was called upon to decide whether the protections of the Constitution of the United States had been observed.

After announcement of the holding by the Supreme Court in the *Furman* case, the Nebraska legislature took prompt steps to formulate guidance to the sentencing judges in determining sentences that might pass the scrutiny of the reviewing courts.[21] Section 29-2523 of the Nebraska Revised Statutes set out eight "aggravating" and seven "mitigating" circumstances by way of guidance. Section 29-2522 required the sentencing judge or judges to determine in criminal homicide cases a penalty of death or life imprisonment based upon "(1) whether sufficient aggravating circumstances exist to justify imposition of a sentence of death, (2) whether sufficient mitigating circumstances exist which approach or exceed the weight given to the aggravating circumstances, or (3) whether the sentence of death is excessive or disproportionate to the penalty imposed in similar cases, considering both the crime and the defendant." That statute had to be churned through the state and federal courts for many years before any of us knew how successfully state legislatures were able to draw lines clearly enough to satisfy the Constitution of the United States.

Death sentences bring massive work. The almost inevitable process can be illustrated by the typical path of a death case in Nebraska as follows: conviction and imposition of a sentence of death in a state district court, an automatic appeal to the Nebraska Supreme Court, a postconviction proceeding begun in the state district court, an appeal of the postconviction decision to the Nebraska Supreme Court, filing of a habeas corpus action in the federal district court, an appeal of the habeas corpus decision to the federal circuit court of appeals, and an effort, at least, to reach the Supreme Court of the United States. Added to that may be one or more remands at any point by one of the reviewing courts to a previous court before resuming its forward march.

Usually a very long time is expended—ten, fifteen, twenty years—of moving through the labyrinth of court proceedings. Culminations may be execution of the defendant, retrial of the case with a repeat conviction, release of the defendant because of some major error in the process, a new trial with a verdict of not guilty, the death of the defendant from some natural disease process, suicide of the defendant, or a reduction of the sentence to life in prison. All these have happened in death sentence cases I have been involved in, except release of the defendant for any reason. In my experience all defendants sentenced to death have been executed or have had their sentence reduced to life imprisonment or have died by means other than the carrying out of the death sentence.

The length of time spent moving through the courts has been a regular target for lawmakers, but without notable success of reduction.[22] The search for justice strains the system. Our natural goals—justice and speed—are at war with each other. They will continue to be at war as long as we retain the sentence of death.

Every death case coming to me brought a swarm of issues. All or almost all the issues brought to the federal court on habeas corpus are constitutional issues, including whether the defendant received all of the following rights specified by the Constitution of the United States: due process of law, a speedy trial, an impartial jury, the assistance of competent counsel, protection from unreasonable searches and seizures, and a sentence that was not "cruel and unusual punishment."

It is the avoidance of the "cruel and unusual punishment" statement of the Eighth Amendment of the Constitution that the Supreme Court says may be fulfilled by the use and weighing of "aggravating" and "mitigating" circumstances set up by a state legislature and applicable to the specific facts of the case at hand. Of the eight "aggravating" circumstances set out by the Nebraska legislature the most difficult one to assess, in my experience, has been the one denominated 1(d): "The murder was especially heinous, atrocious, cruel, or manifested exceptional depravity by ordinary standards of morality and intelligence."

That sounds simple enough—until a person puts it alongside a set of facts, either actual or imagined. Circumstance 1(d) speaks of two ideas. One, the "especially heinous, atrocious, cruel" prong, goes to the nature of the acts of violence that led to the murder. The second, the "exceptional depravity by ordinary standards of morality and intelligence" prong, goes to the mind-set of the defendant at the time of the murder. Facts of the case fitting either prong will permit the sentencer (judge or judges) to use and weigh 1(d) as an aggravating circumstance that points toward but does not require the imposing of a sentence of death.

A trio of necessary questions follows from this: Using the words of the statute for guidance, can there be reasonable consistency about what is "especially heinous, atrocious, cruel" among various sets of facts about first-degree murders later judged by different judges? Can a judge or group of judges determine that one accused person's mind "manifested exceptional depravity by ordinary standards of morality and intelligence," while another accused person's mind didn't, though both minds committed first-degree murder? Do the words of the statute give adequate guidance, without further definition, to mark clearly the appropriate sentence—death or imprisonment for life? If any of these questions is answered with a no, there is a fourth: If the statutory words don't objectively guide the sentence, what descriptive words could be supplied by a legislature or court that would?

I have never had to sentence someone who faced a possible sentence of death, but sometimes I have known that what I would decide *could* result in the carrying out of a sentence of death. That is because cases have come to me by way of habeas corpus from state courts that already have sentenced the defendant to death. One of the deciding issues sometimes has been whether the trio of questions should be answered yes. When the questions were directed to the second prong of aggravating factor 1(d), my answer was usually no. The goal set by the U.S. Supreme Court in the *Gregg* opinion was to offer guidance that would assure that a sentence of death would not be given arbitrarily or capriciously.

The first prong of the statutory wording of 1(d) ("especially heinous, atrocious, cruel") was freed from my no by the Nebraska Supreme Court. That court has the authority to define the words used in Nebraska statutes. In 1977 it defined the phrase "especially heinous, atrocious, cruel" to mean a pitiless crime where torture, sadism, or extreme suffering existed.

Those defining words, especially "torture," seemed to me narrow and objective enough to protect against capricious and arbitrary imposition of death sentences.[23] I said so in *Holtan v. Black* in 1986 and again in *Harper v. Grammer* in 1987.[24] In the *Harper* case there was evidence of torture by poisoning extending over several days and accompanied by vomiting, loss of appetite, extensive internal and external bleeding, loss of consciousness, and eventually death. I affirmed the sentence of death because the sentence had appropriately applied the first prong, finding that the murder involved torture and therefore met the meaning of "especially heinous, atrocious, cruel" language of the statute.[25] The Eighth Circuit Court of Appeals affirmed my decision.[26]

In the *Holtan* case, on the other hand, I did not affirm a sentence of death because the *second* prong of 1(d) was the only basis used by the sentencing judges for applying an aggravating circumstance. The *first* prong of 1(d) did not qualify because there was no evidence of torture, sadism, or extreme pain of the victim. Regarding that second prong, the Nebraska Supreme Court was not as successful in describing it objectively as it had been in describing the first prong. It said in *State v. Holtan* that the words of the second prong applied when the murder was "so coldly calculated as to indicate a state of mind totally and senselessly bereft of regard for human life."[27] I found those descriptive words "no more specific than the words of the statute, which are ambiguous."[28] The sentence of death could not stand, I held, if based on the second prong of aggravating factor 1(d), even as defined by the Nebraska Supreme Court, because the definition did not cut a sharp line between a mind that qualified for death and a mind that did not. It could reasonably be said that virtually any first-degree murder was committed by someone whose mind was "totally and senselessly bereft of regard for human life." When guided by such a phrase a sentence would have a wide angle from which to view the facts, rather than one tightly drawn.

In the *Holtan* case the evidence was that Holtan, the defendant, entered the Dugout Bar in Omaha on October 31, 1954, pulled out a gun, robbed the cash register, forced the bartender, the bartender's girlfriend, and the other patron into a restroom, ordered the bartender to tie up the other two, and fired four shots, killing the bartender with two of the shots, wounding the bartender's girlfriend with one shot, and missing the patron with one. Holtan was charged with one count of first-degree murder while in commission of a robbery and one count of shooting with the intent to kill, wound, or maim. Holtan pleaded "no contest" to both counts, was sentenced to death for the murder of the bartender, and was sentenced to fifteen to forty-five years for shooting the others with intent to kill, wound, or maim. Ultimately, in 1989, the sentencing panel ended his thirteen-year stay on death row by reducing his death sentence to life imprisonment on the murder count because of the inability to find that condition (d) was applicable under either prong.

Harold Lamont Otey, on the other hand, fit the description of the first prong of aggravating condition 1(d). The murder involved torture, thus qualifying for the first prong, and making Otey eligible for the death penalty. The second prong had not been objectively limited by the Supreme Court of Nebraska, I said, so was not available for use.

The charge against Otey was that he entered the sleeping victim's apartment in Omaha, took her stereo outside, reentered the apartment, told the now-awakened victim that he was going to rob and rape her, slashed her forehead with a knife when she resisted him, raped her, dragged her upstairs, struck her in the head with a hammer, and strangled her to death with a belt. The first prong of aggravating condition 1(d) *was* satisfied, I held, by the fact of the rape and torture. Otey was found guilty of first-degree murder in 1979 and was executed in 1994.

The status of the second prong remains in a state of limbo to this day, although the Supreme Court of Nebraska continues to try to find more concrete terms that will provide sentencing judges with guidance on interpreting the statutory "exceptional depravity by ordinary standards of morality and intelligence."[29]

The climax of the legal struggle in the *Otey* case came over a different set of issues. It was not circumstance 1(d) that perplexed the lawyers and me but troublesome issues arising from Otey's request that the Board of Pardons commute his death sentence to life imprisonment. The problems came partly from the fact that the Board of Pardons' procedure had been rarely used in death sentence cases and partly from the makeup of the Board of Pardons.

The claims were that the rights of equal protection and due process of the law were denied Otey by the Board of Pardons in two ways: (1) the decision maker—that is, the Board of Pardons—was unfairly composed because the attorney general, who was the chief prosecuting official and defender of the sentence throughout the proceedings, sat as a voting member of the three-person Board; and (2) Otey was treated differently than others similarly situated by being subjected to testimony and argument by two assistants of the attorney general, as well as by the Board of Pardons' direction to the Board of Parole not to give the Board of Pardons a recommendation as to commutation.

I held that neither claim could be sustained. Simply put, Otey had no right to commutation or even to fairness in the process. He had a *right* to the *process*, but no *right* to *fairness* in the process. That's brutal, but arises from the Nebraska legislature's giving no clue that it *intended* a person seeking some relief from the Board of Pardons to have any expectation of an enforceable right to get relief.

The state statute created for persons the right to petition for commutation, but it offered no assurance of mercy and set no limit on the leniency—or lack of leniency—the Board could give. Under the statute the Board of Pardons had complete discretion to award or not to award commutation for any reason or no reason. Accordingly neither due process nor equal protection of the laws attached to Otey's request for reducing his sentence from death to life.

I added a personal note to my written opinion. I said that writing an opinion like this one was painful for me. "I do not like the prosecutor's being judge of his own cause; I would abolish it if I could. I do not like the death penalty; I would abolish it if I could."

On appeal, my ruling was affirmed on a two-to-one vote, Judge John R. Gibson dissenting, saying, "Substantive due process protects individuals from government contact and that 'shocks the conscience.' [Citations omitted.] The idea of a prisoner pleading for his life before a board that includes the very official responsible for his prosecution and conviction is shocking to the judicial conscience."[30]

Harold Lamont "Wili" Otey was executed by electrocution in the early morning of September 2, 1994, while an estimated 1,200 to 1,500 people crowded outside the Nebraska State Penitentiary in two fairly evenly divided groups, one favoring the death sentence, the other deploring it. The reporter Al J. Laukaitis wrote in the *Lincoln Journal* on that day's front page, "Death penalty supporters waved signs reading 'Fry Wili' and 'Nebraska State Pen First Annual Animal BBQ.' . . . People on both sides . . . screamed and cursed each other. . . . Someone on the anti-death penalty side of the crowd even burned an American flag in protest. . . . At one point, tensions were so high that the State Patrol called out its SWAT team and police dogs as a safety precaution."

Rarely do I hear from people who comment on my decision making, but sometimes they write me. Sometimes it's somebody I've sentenced; usually it isn't. As a rule, a letter writer thanks me or berates me. Then I answer and that's the end of it. But there are repeaters.

One particular person repeatedly let me know of his (or her, it might have been) displeasure at my judicial behavior. From sometime in the 1970s until at least the mid-1990s, the writer scolded me bluntly, vehemently, rudely whenever I ruled in favor of the position of a person charged with or convicted of a crime. For at least ten years he snorted at me for my not sending "these murdering bastards to the chair." He (I think it was a man) chided me for not caring for victims. He urged me to retire from the federal bench and "go to small claims court." He regularly accused me of taking bribes. In one of his final blasts, in September 1993, he culminated his discontent by declaring, "Just once I would like to see one of these bastard(s) rape and kill your wife and daughter and then maybe you liberal assed judges would get your damn head out of the sand." And he accused me of cowardice.

He never signed his name.

I must have had this fellow in mind when I wrote an answer to a request from Roger Welsch. Roger, whom I know well enough to call him a friend, wrote asking me whether writing letters to judges affected the judge. This was my tongue-halfway-to-my-cheek response:

Dear Roger:

Judges are a different bunch. We are supposed to be influenced by nothing but the law, the facts and our good judgment. Figuring out what the law is is hard enough. Learning what the facts are is twice as hard, because peo-

ple don't always tell us the truth. Letter writers aren't likely to be any more forthright than other kinds of people, so we think that fairness requires us to treat them like everybody else: come in person. Take an oath or affirmation, face the people whose conflicting interests are at stake, and let them ask you questions about what you claim the facts are.

My good or bad judgment is fair game for letter writers. But evaluation of my judgment is of no weight unless it is made in light of the facts and the law. If it is, I'll read it and ponder it.

The optimum length of a letter, I'd say, is about one and one-half pages if it's double-spaced or handwritten, one page if it's single-spaced. That gives space enough to tell me what the writer knows, not just what he or she wants me to do.

Letters that are unsigned and accuse me *of having no nerve put me off. So do letters that rail about a hoped-for result without reflecting any awareness of the facts or the law.*

My advice for prospective letter writers is this: I need to know what you know much more than what you think. Even what you know won't be of much help until it has been sifted for trustworthiness. Be willing, therefore, to follow up with your personal testimony. I like getting letters; I read them all. If you enjoy writing, write. But if you expect to influence me, do it with facts that will withstand a courtroom testing. That's what everybody else has to do.

Good luck, Roger, with your "Roger, Over and Out." Joyce and I love your "Postcard" on Sunday mornings.

Sincerely,
Warren

Passing sentence on someone found guilty of a serious crime is the most difficult part of the job of any trial judge. The reason is easy to note: excepting the death penalty, nobody knows how the sentence is likely to affect the defendant, or his or her family, or the victim, or others. Worse yet, the judge probably will never know how the sentence actually *did* affect the people it touched. It is true that sometimes the judge gets a clue when the defendant comes back on another charge, but the clue is weak at best. The truth is we don't know what causes crime to happen or what causes crime to stop. With a straight face and earnest heart any of us can say a crime was committed because the actor made "wrong decisions." But what caused him or her to make the wrong decisions? Or we can say he or she had poor "moral standards." But why did he or she have poor moral standards? Family background? Inadequate education? Lack of religious experience? Why do people of like familial, educational, and religious upbringing fare so differently in the legal offense arena?

We can speak of the goals of sentencing: punishment, deterrence, rehabilitation, safety to the public, and recompense. But evaluation and application to specific human beings under specific circumstances are slippery and thorny. The ghostly presence is that, however carefully reasoned, a sentence may be absolutely ineffective in reaching its intended goals, and the judge may go on time after time making the same mistake, because the judge has no way to learn what is right for *this* offender.

In my early judicial career sentencing was largely unguided, except by the judge's lone sense of decency and the advice of a probation officer who at least had some experience in the criminal field. A judge would probably have some knowledge from reading about criminology and from some experience with criminal law in law school and the practice of law, but that's about all. In the federal court system there were no guidelines to suggest what we should do in sentencing people. Nor did we have appellate courts to help, because in those times an appeal of a sentence was seldom useful because the sentence was affirmed by the court of appeals if that court considered the sentence to be within the sentencing court's "sound discretion," that is, I suppose, a reasonable sentence. Hence this was the process: A probation officer assembled the facts of the defendant's background and the details of the crime and presented them to the judge, together with the probation officer's recommended sentence. The lawyers for the government and the defendant gave their arguments for why the sentence should be the same or higher or lower than recommended by the probation officer.

Once the sentence was passed, it was expected to be final. If the sentence was imprisonment it was usually served in a federal prison, but the time actually spent in prison was likely to be between one-third and one-half of the number of months or years stated in the sentence, because a parole commission was authorized (unless a specific time was set by the judge) to put the defendant on parole at such time as it chose for the rest of the term of the sentence. If the defendant misbehaved during parole, the parole could be revoked by the judge and the sentence completed in prison.

My early sentences, from the early 1970s to the late 1980s, often featured use of probation. Rarely was that a "straight" probation—that is, a period of time when the defendant spent *no* time incarcerated in jail or prison. Rather I often sentenced the defendant to a specific length of time to be in jail or prison—say, four years—but I would immediately suspend the imprisonment and would place the defendant on probation for a period of time, probably four or five years, with several conditions. One condition required the offender to spend time in jail—say, thirty days. Another condition was to commit no crime, federal, state, or local; another, to keep in close touch with the probation officer and follow the probation officer's instructions. Other conditions, among many, were to hold a job and to perform a set number of hours or weeks or months in a certain project of community service. If a breach of one or more conditions occurred, the result could be revocation of the probation and incarceration for the remaining time of the original sentence.

This technique was by no means unique to me, but I do not know of anyone who used it more than I did. This was my rationale: the number of years or months in prison announced by me or any judge would signal to the defendant what to expect if he or she failed to comply with the conditions of probation. The conditions were designed to modify the defendant's behavioral problems by getting his or her life on a routine of honest work and decent actions or by providing treatment for medical or other needs, such as drug or alcohol addiction, all under the guidance of a probation officer. Not only, I thought, was there expected improvement of behavior and other needs, but the expectation was underlined by the constant threat of imprisonment if one or more conditions were not met. I expected strict compliance by the defendant with the conditions and strict application by me of the hammer of incarceration upon breach of conditions of probation. I thought using the probationary period *first* might be better than using incarceration first. The threat of incarceration could stand as a deterrent to misbehavior.

During the 1970s and 1980s, until the arrival of the established validity of guidelines of the Sentencing Commission authorized by Congress in the late 1980s, I imposed approximately 413 sentences on convicted defendants. Of that number at least 286 (69 percent) included probation in whole or in part. Community service was the principal tool of usefulness embodied in the conditions of probation. I was aware that rehabilitation was losing force among some criminologists as a legitimate goal of imprisonment, but I chose not to give up on the possibility of helping a convicted person to change for the better, even if only a small bit, by alternatives to imprisonment.

My first sentence was in *United States v. Sheets* in 1971: five years of imprisonment on each of six counts of securities fraud, to run concurrently, and an additional two years on each of three other counts, the latter two being suspended and followed by three years of probation. The expectation was that Sheets would spend about one-third of the five-year sentence in prison, then be released to comply with the conditions of probation. If he did not comply with all the conditions, he was subject to revocation of the probation and a return to prison for up to three years. Sheets's codefendant received only a probationary sentence because he had less involvement in the crimes. All parts of the sentences were affirmed on appeal.[31]

Probation always contained conditions, such as no committing of any crime, caring for the needs of his or her family, no excessive using of alcohol or illegal drugs, no associating with any felon, working at a job, taking treatment for drug or alcohol addiction, living only in a particular county or city, not moving to a different address without permission of the probation office, and other conditions particularly relevant to a defendant.

But more than that, I was determined to find a way for defendants to repay the community for what it had suffered because of their criminal behavior and permit the defendants to feel they had done something constructive during the probation. Community service was my preferred answer.

One of the early such sentences was for the crime of failure to report as required by the Selective Service Act. I sentenced a young man to three years of probation, two of which had to be spent working for Lincoln Housing Authority at two dollars an hour, of which thirty-five cents an hour was to be withheld as savings until completion of probation. The other usual and pertinent conditions were added. In another case I sentenced a man for filing false and fraudulent income tax returns to three years in prison, suspended, and probation imposed on conditions of spending thirty days in jail, paying a fine of $5,000, and spending eight hours a week for twenty-five weeks doing a community service, such as heading a YMCA fund drive or setting up a drug counseling program or some program determined by the probation officer. Sometimes I said that jail time was to be served on weekends, to enable the defendant to hold his or her job to support the family.

In 1982 through 1984 I saw an opportunity to spread the practice of "alternative sentences," that is, sentences that relied more on alternatives to imprisonment than imprisonment itself to reach the goals of sentencing in cases of nonviolence. The opportunity arrived in a coincidental joining of two events. One was a blizzard of criminal charges against prominent contractors in Nebraska who were accused of rigging bids for state construction contracts. The other event was my learning of two organizations, Crime and Community, Inc. and Nebraska Center for Sentencing Alternatives, devoted to designing proposals for sentences featuring alternatives to imprisonment. The particular persons of inestimable value to me in my expansion excursion were Gregory Lamm, Gary Meers, and Kathy Shada. I say that unashamedly.

Fifteen contracting firms and an official of each firm (except one) were charged under the Sherman Act of rigging bids for construction projects of the State of Nebraska and committing mail fraud in the process. Eleven "sets" (a set being the offender and the offender's firm) pleaded guilty to the charges.[32] One firm stood trial alone and was found guilty by a jury.[33] Two sets stood trial and were found not guilty by their juries.[34] One official of a firm was tried separately and found not guilty.[35]

At sentencing of the defendants found guilty I received proposals worked out by Crime and Community or Nebraska Center for Sentencing Alternatives at the request of the defendants and their counsel. The sentences were similar in form, but different in scope. The goal of the sentence on the offending company *official* was to sentence him (no women were charged) to prison for a specific amount of time, suspend most of the time of imprisonment, fine him, and suspend most of the fine, all on condition that he spend a certain amount of time in jail, spend a specific amount of time in community service for a certain charity or educational institution, and give to that charity or educational institution most of the amount of the fine. The conditions of his probation were to be reviewed and approved or altered by the probation officer and me. The goal of the sentence on the *company* was to sentence it to probation for a specific amount of time, fine it a substantial amount of money, but suspend most of the amount of the fine if that amount were given to a charity or educational institution, usually the entity for whom the official was to perform community service.

The first seven of the bid-rigging sentences of the early 1980s came by way of guilty pleas by the firms and the officials of the firms charged. In a memorandum to each of the defendant's lawyers I explained my thinking and described the nature of the crimes, the background of the offenders in general terms, the purpose of the sentences, and the techniques of sentencing. It named only Missouri Valley Construction and its officer, Joseph Thoendel, because I considered them the most influential in the bid-rigging practice. The memorandum said:

I. NATURE OF THE CRIMES

Each of the individual defendants in these seven cases, including United States v. Missouri Valley Construction and Joseph Thoendel, has been charged with one count of restraint of trade through bidrigging and one count of mail fraud, the latter being a part of the transaction encompassed in the first. Each corporation except Missouri Valley is charged with one count of restraint of trade through bidrigging; Missouri Valley was charged with two counts.

Each person's and each company's involvement differs in some particulars, but they all involve all the features that make these crimes unusual.

First, they involve collusion—secret agreements secretly arrived at for fraudulent purposes. No one undertook any of the criminal acts for beneficent purposes or with beneficent results.

Second, they involve people of splendid reputation, of strong talent, of excellent education, with proven leadership qualities. Each defendant lent that reputation, talent, education and leadership to provide to their peers an aura of respectability to an illegal enterprise, thereby dulling each other's sense of propriety and lulling persons with whom they dealt into a habit of trustfulness.

Third, they involve a defrauding, not of strangers, but of friends, customers, the defendants' own state government.

Fourth, there is no sign of sudden passion, no fit of temper, no grudge to square, no desperate need for drugs, no alcoholic lessening of judgment, no psychopathic sign of illness, no pressure of poverty, no rudderlessness of broken homes; but deliberate acts by people well equipped to live by the accepted ways of society.

Fifth, there is repetition—each defendant admits to doing the same or similar illegal acts over and over again.

Sixth, there is a large amount of money involved in each case.

Seventh, there is difficulty of detection. Unlike most kinds of crimes, even the victim did not know it was a victim until long after the act was done.

Eighth, there is no violence or threat of violence involved.

Ninth, every defendant has admitted guilt. I do not say that each has readily admitted guilt, because the bidrigging practice is old enough to have become a custom, but no defendant came forward until a federal investigation was undertaken and no defendant, as far as I know, invited the investigation. All have been highly cooperative since admitting guilt.

Tenth, the money lost by the state did not directly inure to the benefit of the individual defendants, although all relied in one degree or another on it and shared it indirectly.

Eleventh, none of the defendants has been convicted of any crime before this.

II. PURPOSE OF SENTENCES

Retribution, deterrence, incapacitation, and rehabilitation are the usually stated reasons for punishment. As applied to the cases before me, I accept the views (1) that society does have a right, perhaps a duty, to balance its universe, to speak in clear terms that it has been offended, (2) that punishment has some effect in deterring some persons from similar crimes, (3) that the likelihood of future repetition by these particular defendants is remote enough to rule out incapacitation—that is, the need for rendering them unable to do further damage, and (4) that rehabilitation is to be sought in reforming whatever bents of mind rationalized the practice of bidrigging to be acceptable behaviors.

III. TECHNIQUES OF SENTENCING

Several factors should be and have been explored in each case—the nature of the offense, the background and nature of the particular defendant, the probable (or possible) effect on each of the kinds of people who will be touched by the sentence, and the likely efficacy of different kinds of sentences in reaching the appropriate purposes of sentencing.

Incarceration is not a preferred form of sentencing and should be used only if justified by explainable reasons. I am persuaded that in these cases a total lack of incarceration would fail to reflect the seriousness of the crimes. I have noted the unusual features of these crimes, most of which point to a period of incarceration as the lowest level of clemency that is tolerable under our present societal state. These sentences must speak for society, dramatizing its congressionally declared intent in not having its free market manipulated covertly and unfairly, especially by those who are a part of it and presumably claim to want the competitive process kept intact. Additionally, a dispassionate and hard-to-detect crime like bidrigging, like income tax evading, calls for a sentence that shocks, to gain the attention of those defendants and other contractors who may be tempted. No sentence but prison or jail can provide the appropriate shock effect.

But other qualities in a sentence are also to be found, if possible. A sentence should be consistent—that is, it should be similar to other sentences in similar circumstances or the variations should be reasoned ones. The sentences in the cases before me have been compared with one another and with other kinds of crimes and will continue to be.

A sentence should be constructive, if possible. I have been pleased to have the imaginative assistance of defense counsel and of Gregory Lamm of Crime and Community, Inc., and Gary Meers of Nebraska Center on Sentencing Alternatives in developing ideas for causing the defendants to give back to the society they have offended more than merely an expensive idleness in prison or jail, while at the same time causing the defendants to be disrupted in the usual routines and styles of life. The alternative sentences will be designed to be firm, specific, unpleasant for the defendants, and constructive for them and others. They have the additional strength of being aimed in most instances at helping directly people who are in the criminal justice population or are prime candidates for it. If the community service features of the sentences are correctly devised, they will not have decreased the amount of punishment, but will have increased the usefulness and decreased the expensiveness of it.

The fines, some of which are to be channeled into community service projects, will be tailored to the defendant's culpability and financial condition, care being taken to preserve the ability of each individual or corporate defendant to continue as a viable participant in the business community. No monetary restitution to the State of Nebraska is likely to be within the sentences, because no agreement exists as to the exact amount of loss by the state.

The term of imprisonment (that could be spent in full if the offending official violated conditions of his probation) was in each case three years on each of the counts. Jail time varied for the officials from none to sixty days. Length of probation was five years for most of the offenders; three for one of them. Fines levied against officials ranged from $3,000 to $10,000; they were suspended if given to a specific charity for which the official was to perform community service.

Community service ranged from none to performing work for specified numbers of days or hours to, for example, the Santee Indian Reservation, Independence Center, Houses of Hope halfway house, Tabitha Home, Adams County Fair Association, Good Samaritan Village, North Platte Opportunity Center, Nebraska Youth Leadership Development Center,

Christian Heritage Children's Home, and the YMCA. Probation terms for the contracting companies were five years, and fines ran from $20,000 to $2 million, most of it to be suspended upon its donation to the charitable or educational entity.

Every guilty official was required to spend some time in jail, and each was required to pay a fine or, as a condition of probation, to donate money. I felt strongly about that. The sentences were welcomed by the press and the public generally. An editorial titled "A $2 Million Message" noted that Missouri Valley Construction Co. had been sentenced to pay a $2 million fine and observed, "Highway bid-rigging—reportedly so widespread in parts of the state as to be considered institutionalized—also may be purged from the Nebraska scene." The writer suggested that my sentencing had made it clear that I was speaking to a still larger audience: people who trim or even break the law because of the pressures of an employer who either blinks at or condones such activity. "None of us is perfect. None ever will be. But perhaps Urbom's action may be regarded as a shove towards prospective self-improvement."[36]

The government appealed the first batch of seven corporations I sentenced for the bid-rigging scandal. The three judges of the Eighth Circuit Court of Appeals were Gerald Heaney, John R. Gibson, and Edward Dumbauld, a U.S. senior district Judge of the Western District of Pennsylvania, sitting by designation.[37] Judge Dumbauld wrote the opinion affirming the sentences. No objection was made as to the sentences imposed upon individual officers of the corporations, but objection was made that the statute authorizing probation, 18 U.S.C. § 3651, did not permit the paying of fines to any entity other than the U.S. Treasury or to "aggrieved parties for actual damages or loss caused by the offense":

> [A]ny court having jurisdiction when satisfied that the ends of justice and the best interest of the public, as well as the defendant will be served thereby, may suspend the imposition of sentence and place the defendant on probation . . . upon such terms and conditions as the court deems best.
>
> . . . .

While on probation and among the conditions thereof, the defendant—

May be required to pay a fine in one or several sums; and
May be required to make restitution or reparation to aggrieved parties for actual damages or loss caused by the offense for which conviction was had; and
May be required to provide for the support of any persons, for whose support he is legally responsible.

The government argued that the words "upon such terms and conditions as the court deems best" are limited by the next series of permissible conditions—payments to "aggrieved parties" and "actual damages or loss caused by the offense for which conviction was had" and "for the support of any persons, for whose support he is legally responsible."

The appellate panel unanimously rejected the government's argument, saying:

> The general terms of the first paragraph of § 3651 authorizing probation "upon such terms and conditions as the court deems best" authorize the terms and conditions specified by Judge Urbom.
>
> . . . .
>
> . . . When specifying certain particular terms as includible "among" the conditions of prohibition, the statute simply wishes to put beyond question . . . the propriety of the particular terms specified. The meaning is the same as if the familiar corporate draftsman's locution "including but not limited to" had been used.

Even more, the government argued that since "a corporation is but a fiction existing in contemplation of law, it can do nothing but pay money, and hence can not be subject to conditions designed to promote rehabilitative behavior." The response of the appellate panel was swift and scoffing. "The formalistic contention smacks of medieval antiquarianism," Judge Dumbault wrote. "It resembles the argument that a corporation could not be a trustee because it had no soul and was therefore not subject to enforcement by a chancery court of obligations based upon the requirements of equity and good conscience. . . . Their . . . decision-making processes, acting through human agents, affect for weal or woe the daily life of many communities. That such decision-making process can not be affected, in the area of collusive or monopolistic pricing . . . by rehabilitative measures and punitive sanctions is an argument divorced from reality."

I liked one other declaration by the appellate panel's opinion: "It would seem that Judge Urbom's sentencing objectives are in full accord with current penalogical philosophy and that his carefully formulated scheme of sentences deserves the praise of being described as 'creative,' innovative, and imaginative."[38]

The government was not easily daunted by the *Anderson* holding. When a sentence I had earlier imposed on the convicted bid-rigger Missouri Valley Construction Company reached the Eighth Circuit (but was delayed because of procedural problems), the case was assigned to the entire eight members of the court, because at least a majority of the members thought it appropriate to do so and because one three-member panel cannot overrule another three-member panel's decision—which is to say a three-judge panel of the *Missouri Valley* case could not overrule the three-judge panel of the *Anderson* case. All eight members participated (not including Judge Dumbauld, who was not a member of the Eighth Circuit Court of Appeals). The result was a reversal and largely a destruction of my "creative, innovative, and imaginative" idea.

United States v. Missouri Valley Construction Company was the government's chance to strike again at sentences that set as a condition of a corporation's probation the paying of all or part of a fine to a charitable organization. I had sentenced Missouri Valley Construction Company to a fine of $2 million, but suspended all but $325,000 and put the corporation on probation for five years on the condition that it contribute $1,475,000 to the University of Nebraska Foundation for permanently endowing and supporting a chair in ethics. The government appealed.

Sitting *en banc*, all eight members participating, the Eighth Circuit Court of Appeals held in an opinion written by Judge Myron Bright that district courts have no authority to "impose on a willing corporation as a condition of probation, in lieu of a fine, the requirement that it contribute money to a charitable organization that has not suffered actual damages or loss from the corporation's criminal offense."

The arguments were the same as in the *Anderson* case, but the full court adopted the government's position on statutory construction—that here, where the statute's specific language puts limits on three types of money payment as conditions of probations, those limits apply also to the statute's general language granting use of "such terms and conditions as the court deems best." That principle of construction, the court said, is in keeping with what "other courts have applied." Furthermore the three types of payments the statute expressly authorizes are limited to "payments to the treasury (fines), to persons for whose support the defendant is legally responsible, or to aggrieved persons who suffered actual damage or loss caused by the offense for which conviction was had, in the amount of such damages or loss." Since the payments to the University of Nebraska were not to be made to the nation's treasury, or to support persons for whom the corporation was legally responsible, or to aggrieved persons who suffered actual damages from the corporation's crimes, the order for those payments were outside the district court's authority to order.

One other notch was cut in the sentencing court's timber: "The courts are ill-equipped to pick and choose, among countless worthy causes, which nonaggrieved charitable organizations should receive large sums of money that would otherwise be paid to the treasury as fines. In the absence of clearer authorization from Congress, we reject the concept here that the general grant of discretion in section 3651 empowers the courts to dispense largesse to nonaggrieved parties, however worthy their activities."

The two circuit judges who were members of the three-judge panel in the *Anderson* case, Heaney and Gibson, concurred and dissented in the *Missouri Valley* case. Each wrote an opinion. Each joined in the other's opinion. Each specifically said he agreed with the *result* in the *Missouri Valley* case. Each said he dissented from the majority's overruling the *Anderson* case.

It appears to me that Judge Heaney's opinion means that he agreed that my decision was incorrect in requiring Missouri Valley to pay to the University of Nebraska as a condition of probation money that would otherwise be a fine. I'm not sure why. It probably is because the one feature of the *Missouri Valley* case that differs from the *Anderson* case is that payments by the Missouri Valley corporation were to go to the University of Nebraska, which had no connection with the harm caused by Missouri Valley's bid rigging or the funding or supporting of the community service to be done by the official of Missouri Valley involved in the bid rigging, whereas in the *Anderson* case the payments by the Anderson corporation were connected with and supportive of the community service to be provided by the corporation's officer involved in the bid rigging.

Judge Gibson's opinion decries the majority's reliance on a principle of statutory construction that is questionable (that where a statute contains both general and specific language on a subject, the specific language governs) where it rests on a negative implication. More important, perhaps, Gibson's opinion clarifies the factual distinction between the *Anderson* case and the *Missouri Valley* case. In the *Anderson* case the corporation was required to fund community service to be done by its officer, whereas that was not so in the *Missouri Valley* sentence. Gibson pointed out a supportable reason for tying the corporate sentence with the officer's sentence, saying, "[Corporations'] management and functioning are intrinsically that of the individuals managing and controlling the organization. Insofar as the conditions of probation in *Anderson* affect the managers and decision makers and recognize the interrelationship between these individuals and the corporation, the *Anderson* conditions are in full accord with the purposes and goals of section 3651."

When there was no tie between the payment of money to the corporation and the probation of *individuals*, wrote Judge Gibson, the view of the majority of the court was correct in the *Missouri Valley* case. But he continued, "I believe the Court makes a great mistake in failing to distinguish the limited situation in *Anderson*, and in discarding the valuable role that it can play in corporate probation."

Judge Gibson went one step further, excoriating me for allowing "the corporate defendant to choose a favorite beneficiary for the receipt of those funds. The selection in this manner runs contrary to the purpose of imposing punishment on the defendant."[39] I am not persuaded.

Our son, Randy, had moved to Lincoln and in March 1985 landed a job with the law firm of Mattson, Ricketts, Stewart, and Calkins. I knew of no group of persons I would rather have Randy associate with, and I told him so. Our family celebrated with champagne.

In that same week Allison, the star nursing student at Nebraska Wesleyan and Bryan Memorial Hospital in Lincoln, passed the nursing boards in Texas, where she lived, and took a position at Baylor University Medical Center in Dallas.

By July 1985 Joy had enrolled in law school at Washington University in St. Louis. Having our last child leave us was hard, of course, but Joyce and I were joyous to have two daughters enter or make ready to enter the professional world.

In October 1985 Marlene McGuire, my secretary for over twenty years of both my lawyer years and judicial years, died suddenly. She had ruled the reception offices with as much tender or brittle efficiency as the occasions seemed to her to deserve, had little forbearance of slackers, slickers, or dimwits, enjoyed her own clever and sometimes acerbic tongue, and loathed the new device called a dictating machine, insisting that direct oral dictation from human to human was the superior method. She was a single mother and loved all children. She collapsed on the west steps of the federal building in Lincoln as she was returning to the office from lunch. A heart attack was the killer, though she had long been almost morbidly fearful of what she envisioned to be probable consequences of her insulin-dependent diabetes. She and my law clerks were good friends; she shared the responsibility of interviewing and selecting them, one new one each year.

Ellen Lefler, Marlene's successor, was selected easily and began work on November 18, 1985. My journal of that day says, "She seems bright, eager, altogether competent, though I worry about her shorthand. Or is it, as one applicant wrote, 'I take fast notes'?" In truth, she rarely needs shorthand, uses it when necessary, but counts the dictating machine as a blessing. Ellen is exceptional. In every quality needed she glistens. She has dived into the electronic age, has taught me what I think I need to know about computers, and generously rescues me from my miscues. I rely upon her more than she should have to bear, but she never complains. Her official title of judicial assistant is a fitting one. Her organizational skills, her intelligence, her dedication make her invaluable. Ellen would have made a first-rate lawyer if she had chosen to be one. I learned from her early that

44. Marlene McGuire, Judge Urbom's secretary from 1965 to 1985. Photograph in author's possession.

her family members are her top priority and I should consider every minute after 5 p.m. her personal time. I react to that with enthusiasm, because she is right. She has finished her twenty-fourth year with me, during which her children have grown and have children of their own, all products of her and her husband Glen's love and care.

In 1984 Congress passed the Comprehensive Crime Control Act, creating the Sentencing Commission to build a set of guidelines to further the purposes of crime control, which are commonly known as punishment, incapacitation, deterrence, and rehabilitation.[40] The members of the Sentencing Commission were to be appointed by the president with the advice and consent of the Senate. Three of the members were to be chosen from a list of six federal judges recommended by the Judicial Conference of the United States, of which the chief justice was the chair.

For the four years beginning on March 28, 1982, I had some experience with Chief Justice Warren Burger. He was chair of the Board of the Federal Judicial Center, of which I was a member. From that experience I barely escaped becoming a member of the Sentencing Commission, or so I think.

In Williamsburg, Virginia, on March 9, 1985, a few months after Congress

45. Ellen Lefler, Judge Urbom's judicial assistant from 1985 to the present. Photograph by *Lincoln Journal Star*.

had passed the legislation to construct the Sentencing Commission, I attended a gathering sponsored by the Brookings Institution and consisting of representatives of all three branches of the federal government. The purpose was to discuss the administration of justice. Attendees included, according to my journal, "the Chief Justice, the Attorney General (newly sworn-in Ed Meese), the Solicitor General, the Senate and House Committees of the Judiciary or their staff representatives, a half dozen federal judges, a half dozen state supreme court chief justices, and other think-tank people." I had been asked to speak and did speak at some length on my experience with alternatives to imprisonment—that is, sentences that involved little or no incarceration. My journal says, "I spoke on alternative sentencing and all discussed it for half an hour. Wonderful experience. But I felt (woke up at 2:30 a.m.) I'm on a limb for membership on the sentencing commission."

After rising from my short sleep at the Williamsburg Lodge, I walked to the Convention Center, where breakfast was to be served. As I approached the Center's front entrance, I saw a limousine pull up to the curb and stop. Out stepped Chief Justice Warren Burger. He waved and called, "Warren!" (He usually called *me* Warren; I never called *him* Warren.) "Let me speak to you. Do you know some judges who could do both a job on the Sentencing Commission *and* their regular assignments? I have to turn in the list in a few weeks." I was able only to say that I noticed that the legislation spoke of the position as full time, and I didn't know of any active judge who could do two jobs at the same time, though perhaps a senior judge (retired) could. I said I would think about it. At that moment Judge Gerald Tjoflat of Florida joined us to speak with the chief justice about something. I took advantage of the opportunity to slip away. I avoided the chief justice and had no further conversation with him at the meeting.

About six weeks later, on May 1, 1985, I was in North Platte, Nebraska, substituting as trial judge for the hospitalized, cancer-ridden Judge Albert "Duke" Schatz of our district court, when I received a call from the White House. The caller, Mark Sullivan, on behalf of the Department of Justice asked if I would approve having my name submitted to the president for appointment to the Sentencing Commission. I had not wanted the assignment, but I suspect I would have said yes, except for the fact that on the very day before, Judge Schatz had died, leaving only one other active judge, Arlen Beam, and two senior judges, Richard Robinson and Robert Van Pelt, to carry the load of the district for the next many months it might take to get a successor if I were entangled in Sentencing Commission business. I told that to Sullivan and said it would seem unfair for me to leave my fellow judges (women had not yet been a part of our district bench) with such a docket load.[41] He said he understood and agreed. But that wasn't the end.

On May 22 Mark Cannon, the administrative assistant to the chief justice, called, asking if I wanted to be on the Sentencing Commission. I said I would much rather not be a member, but wouldn't refuse to be. I explained to him my overload problem. He said the position would require "something less than full time" and the chief justice wanted somebody who was familiar with alternative sentencing. He said he would talk with the chief justice, and in view of my case load my name might well go on the list of nine or ten being submitted to the president. But he assured me, "We won't press your name." I said that would be fine.

I heard no more about the matter, and I do not regret not having served. A few years later I did serve for a year on an advisory committee to the Sentencing Commission on alternatives to imprisonment. The committee's recommendations were to expand opportunities for probation, with and without conditions of short-term incarceration other than in prison, such as at home, a public work center, or a treatment center.[42] The impact of the recommendations has been little or none, but I have no reason to think my membership on the Commission would have improved its work.

The Sentencing Commission interpreted the mandate of Congress to be formulation of guidelines for judges in reaching three objectives of crime control: (1) *honesty* in sentencing, that is, making the length of the sentence announced be the sentence actually served, or nearly so; (2) reducing *disparity* in sentencing by creating like sentences for like criminal acts by persons of like criminal history; and (3) *proportionality*, that is, recognizing that some sentences should differ from other sentences, depending upon the culpability of the offender and harm or danger caused by the offense.[43]

The Sentencing Commission was organized in October 1985, and by April 1987 its original sentencing guidelines and policy statements were submitted to Congress. The Sentencing Guidelines became effective November 1, 1987, following congressional review.[44] They applied to all offenses committed on or after that date, but enough litigation stalled them to make any calculations about them sensibly start with 1991.

In interpreting its role the Sentencing Commission recognized that Congress sought to avoid "confusion and implied deception" that arose from the preguideline sentencing system.[45] That system permitted the Parole Board, after the offender had served a portion of his or her sentence, to decide when the offender should be released from prison. Frequently the amount of time served would be only a fraction of the amount of prison time announced by the judge.

The *Stephenson* case is an example. I sentenced Dana Stephenson in 1985, before the Sentencing Guidelines arrived, for a series of cocaine-related crimes. I sentenced him to ten years in prison, followed by five years of probation to begin when the imprisonment ended. Under the system of the then-existing Parole Board in 1985, the actual time of imprisonment under a ten-year sentence would likely be somewhere between two and three years. I knew that and told Stephenson so.[46] That meant that approximately one-third of his ten-year sentence would actually be spent in prison. It is possible that the average member of the public would suppose that a ten-year sentence of imprisonment would mean that ten years or nearly so would be spent in prison. Thus there could be "confusion and implicit deception."

The Sentencing Commission went about its journey to "honesty" by seeing to it that parole and the Parole Board be abolished. In the Sentencing Commission's words, "Honesty is easy to achieve: the abolition of parole makes the sentence imposed by the court the sentence the offender will serve, less approximately fifteen percent for good behavior."[47] That may have the sound of "honesty" but is pricey to the inmate and lacks rationality.

By eliminating parole and by reducing the amount of good time an inmate could earn in prison to fifty-four days a year, the time actually to be served in prison on any sentence suddenly sky-rocketed. For a crime committed one day *after* the Guidelines went into effect the sentence for the same type of crime—committed exactly the same way as a crime committed the day *before* the Guidelines went into effect—more than doubled. No longer would a ten-year sentence mean thirty months spent in prison; now a ten-year sentence would mean at least eighty-five months spent in prison.

The Sentencing Commission reported in November 2004, "Under the guidelines, punishment became not only more certain but also more severe. The proportion of probation sentences declined, use of restrictive alternatives such as home confinement increased, and the rate of imprisonment for longer lengths of time climbed dramatically, compared to the pre-guidelines era." Between 1984 and 2006 the average time spent in prison (by persons sentenced by federal judges) almost doubled, increasing from an average of just under twenty-five months to almost fifty months.[48]

Parole had been designed to help the offender upon a reentry of out-of-prison life. The newly devised supervised release has the same task, but the supervisor has no authority to cut short the sentence of imprisonment. The term of supervised release is fixed by the judge as a part of the sentence, and the judge alone is empowered to reduce it. During the period of supervised release following release from prison, the supervising officer (probation officer) monitors the defendant for violation of any condition of supervised release, including commission of a crime, and at the same time assists the offender in avoiding the enticements that led to imprisonment. When appropriate, the judge may terminate the supervised release. Usually that is prompted by a recommendation of the probation officer.

The starting point for the Sentencing Commission in the late 1980s was the estimates of what judges had been doing before the Guidelines came into effect, as revealed in summary reports of some 10,000 convictions and a sample of 10,000 presentence reports, parole guidelines, and policy judgments.[49] The average amount of time actually served in prison on sentences of a specific kind of crime was used as an approximation of what would be the "base offense level" in the Guidelines for that kind of crime. Adjustments then were made for victim-related features (such as whether a firearm was brandished or the victim was injured), the defendant's role in the offense (whether the offender was a leader or a follower in the offense), obstruction of administration of justice (such as whether the offender lied to law enforcement officers), and acceptance of responsibility (whether the offender admitted guilt and fully described everything he or she did in committing the crime).

The base offense level, modified by the applicable adjustments, then became the "total offense level." Coupling the total offense level with a numerically fixed "criminal history" of the offender determined the recommended span of months of imprisonment the Guidelines offered as the sentence the judge might announce.

Sentencing judges like me, I believe, are disappointed in the "honesty" limb of the goal search, because of the upward spurt in the length of time actually served in prison. If the upward spurt had arisen from an empirical study to determine what length of imprisonment was required for reasonable punishment or rehabilitation, then it would have a ring of rationality to it. But if the Commission made such an empirical study or relied on someone else's empirical study, it has not given notice of it.

If the Commission began its computations with the averages of time actually spent in prison under the preguideline system, as it says it did, where did the rise come from? Was it from adding the four adjustments—victim-related features, the defendant's role in the offense, obstruction of administration of justice, and acceptance of responsibility? Was it supposed that sentencing judges took none of those adjustments into account until the Sentencing Guidelines announced them, so that the averages were of the raw crimes and all adjustments ignored? It is impossible to accept that assumption if it were made in the pursuit of "honesty." If the adjustments are not the answer, what was the rationale for nearly doubling the actual time spent in prison on each sentence? It could have been, of course, a demonstrated need or command of Congress to double the average amount of time a prisoner is to spend in prison. If that had been the case, it could have been argued that it was a move triggered by "honesty." No such demonstration or command has been mentioned by the Commission.

My take on the matter is that the Sentencing Commission simply boosted the "actual time to be spent in prison" from about 30 percent to about 85 percent of the sentence without any demonstrated need. The boost has the feel of a PR scam.

A second goal of Congress in creating sentencing guidelines was uniformity: specific rules or suggestions to judges would result in similar sentences for a particular crime for those with a similar criminal history. It's a goal with some appeal. Probably most think convicted defendants should be treated similarly if they acted similarly. The Sentencing Commission has examined many different characteristics of persons and circumstances in which particular crimes can be committed. The Guidelines recommend to the judge the amount of slack there may be in a sentence by the presence of a particular characteristic or circumstance. If all judges follow the applicable suggestions in about the same way, near uniformity may be expected.

Statistics show, I think, that judges have done a fairly faithful job of following the Guidelines, even while departing from them on occasion. Nationally in fiscal year 2008 59.4 percent of cases sentenced were *within* the recommended Guideline range. Of all federal cases sentenced that year, 25.6 percent were sentenced *below* the Guideline range on a motion filed by the government; 13.5 percent were because the defendant rendered substantial assistance to the government in prosecuting other persons. Some 1.5 percent of all sentences were *above* the recommended guideline range.[50]

Drug cases (controlled substances) form the largest type of criminal activity sentenced in the federal courts, accounting for 32.6 percent of all offenders sentenced in fiscal year 2008. Crack cocaine, powder cocaine, marijuana, and methamphetamine were the prime targets and have been for at least the past twenty years. The average length of imprisonment sentences for crack cocaine offenders that year was 114.5 months. That trumps all other crimes, except murder (221.6 months), kidnapping/hostage taking (205.3 months), and pornography/prostitution (119.8 months).[51]

Congress has played a significant part in the upward climb of the severity of drug sentences. It did so partly by adopting mandatory minimums for certain amounts of trafficked drugs. Indeed in fiscal year 2008 about two-thirds (66.3 percent) of all sentenced drug offenders were convicted under statutes bearing a mandatory minimum sentence, some of which (27.3 percent) required by statute at least a five-year prison sentence and some of which (39 percent), at least a ten-year prison sentence.[52]

One feature has eased for some the effect of the increased length of sentences for drug trafficking offenses. Since 1994 Congress, by adopting a "safety valve," has permitted offenders with little or no criminal history to be free of the mandatory minimums, and the Sentencing Commission has amended its Guidelines to permit qualifiers for this safety valve to receive a decrease of two levels, which could average about twenty months of decrease for drug trafficking offenders. In fiscal year 2008 over a third (37.9 percent) of drug offenders had the benefit of this reduction.[53]

The third objective to controlling crime is proportionality of sentences, signifying that not all crimes cause the same severity of harm. Some crimes are similar in kind but have or tend to have different results. The sentence, we say, should "fit the crime." In my view, the Sentencing Commission has done a remarkable job in fitting the sentence to the crime—not just the kind of crime, but the way the crime is committed and the specific harm it causes. I feel no need to speak further of that.

Are the Guidelines working to meet the goals of sentencing? I think that depends on what "goals of sentencing" are meant. If reduction of "disparity" and establishing "honesty" of sentences are meant, I think the answer is a qualified yes as to disparity, bearing in mind that there is enough natural variety in judges and offenders that there will not be—nor should there be—actual eradication of disparity. As to honesty? No, I think not. If the goal of sentencing, in whole or in part, is reduction of *crime,* I see no way that the statistics reported by the Sentencing Commission can be said to answer yes.

The statistics do say that the number of persons *sentenced* during the seventeen fiscal years of 1991 (the practicable first fiscal year of Guideline sentencing) through 2007 has *more than doubled,* increasing above the preceding year "by on average, five percent per year."[54] Add to that the fact, as the Commission's report shows, that the average amount of time prisoners spent in prison during the Sentencing Guidelines' life has "almost doubled." That does little to show a positive effect of all efforts to reduce the amount of crime.

If the information we have from the Sentencing Commission is an indicator of anything, it is an indicator that we are marching boldly toward an unannounced goal of bloating the federal penitentiary population. In 1991 the federal prison inmate population at year's end was 71,608.[55] On January 7, 2010, the federal prison inmate population was 208,104.[56]

In the first dozen or so years on the bench I visited many prisons, mostly federal. I was impressed with the physical facilities and the decency of the administrators. Perhaps the most indelible statement of wisdom I heard was from a warden who explained that misbehavior in prison was rare, and he capped his explanation by saying, "We know how to make a good prisoner. We don't know the first thing about making a good citizen."

I think the searing question remains the same today: Do prisons know how to make good citizens? Paradoxically the Sentencing Commission's Guidelines are telling us to put the offenders in prison for an increasingly longer time despite a continuing directive that the Commission "shall insure that the guidelines reflect the inappropriateness of imposing a sentence to a term of imprisonment for the purpose of rehabilitating the defendant or providing the defendant with needed educational or vocational training, medical care, or other correctional treatment."[57] We, the judges, are sending more offenders to prison for increasingly longer periods of time despite a statutory direction in 18 U.S.C. § 3582 to recognize that "imprisonment is not an appropriate means of promoting correction and rehabilitation." Then who and what is to "correct" or "rehabilitate" the offenders? The probation officers, undoubtedly. They are the ones who are in charge of the offenders temporarily while the offenders aren't in prison. That's a huge burden to leave to them.

The Sentencing Commission has prodigiously worked to be helpful to judges. The output has been flawed, partly by the intrusion of Congress, partly by the Commission's starting on an unstable base (treating as tentatively reliable what the unguided federal judges did before the Sentencing Guidelines came into being), and partly by its unwavering adherence to its conception that criminals can best be brought to heel by imprisonment. I say that respectfully. The Sentencing Commission is held with tight reins by Congress, and this book is no place to analyze in detail the enormity of the problem (art or science) of sentencing. I shall offer only a few thoughts of mine and continue to look to the Sentencing Commission for more careful studies of the human psyche for answers.

Every judge knows that, even if he or she does not know what causes crime, there probably are a bundle of conditions or characteristics that cluster around people who commit crimes. The presence of those conditions or characteristics may offer some clue as to whether a particular criminal offender is likely or not to commit a future offense. Knowing that about the person to be sentenced may be important in the type of sentence the judge may be wise to tailor. One of the earliest efforts of the Sentencing Commission in exploring predictability of human behavior produced a paper that offered connections for consideration by the judge to gauge the likelihood of future criminal activity of categories of offenders.[58]

Criminal history categories (CHC) run from a low of 1 to a high of 6. A result of the study is that risk of recidivism under each of the definitions increases with each CHC; there is more likelihood of a high CHC offender's committing a new offense within two years of beginning probation or leaving prison than an offender with a lower CHC. If criminal history "points" are used rather than CHCs, the predictability is somewhat more precise.[59]

Offender characteristics that the study highlights, not as causes but as possible factors of predictability in assessing risk of recidivism, are gender, age at time of sentencing, race and ethnicity, employment status, educational attainment, marital status, illicit drug use, Guideline instant offense level, Guideline applied for the instant offense, sentence type (probation, alternatives, or prison), length of sentence imposed for instant offense, departure status, and type of the recidivating event.

Perhaps it can fairly be said that the report suggests that the best candidate for *not* recidivating within two years after reentering the community would be (1) a man (2) over fifty, (3) white, (4) employed during the year before being sentenced for the instant offense, (5) having a college education, (6) married, (7) not a user of illicit drugs, (8) being sentenced for fraud or larceny or drug trafficking, (9) receiving a straight sentence of probation on the instant offense or probation combined with confinement alternatives, (10) receiving a downward departure for substantial assistance to the government in finding others who may be in line for prosecution, and (11) with a CHC of 1. Those conditions or characteristics carry lower recidivism rates than their counterparts.[60]

The report finds no connection between recidivism and the Guidelines' offense level because the offense level was not written to predict recidivism. On the other hand, the report highlights illicit drug use and offender's education level as having "interesting relationships" with recidivism. It also calls the offender's age a "pertinent characteristic," and points to the U.S. Parole Commission's recidivism predictor, the salient factor score, as having incorporated offender age, "thus improving its predictive power."[61]

I am hopeful that the Sentencing Commission will find it worthwhile to continue study of the possible connection between both the offender's education level and illicit drug use, on the one hand, and recidivism, on the other. Given the report's suggestion that the offender's age is "a pertinent characteristic," I am inclined to the view that district judges should reasonably take age into consideration whenever prediction of recidivism is a genuine factor in setting a sentence. The other characteristics, except race and ethnicity, may be useful to a judge in appropriate sentencing situations if a connection is shown by future studies.

I am confident that sentencing judges will look with great appreciation to publications on the subject of recidivism because it is of much concern to them. I am especially interested in information about recidivism because it has to do with the likelihood of an offender's committing another crime in the future. That's the heart of the sentencing task from a sentencing judge's perspective.

The purposes of sentencing, it is often said, are deterrence, incapacitation, just punishment, and rehabilitation. I think the most critically important of these is rehabilitation. By "rehabilitation" I mean remolding, remaking, fixing, or changing. I don't mean putting back as it was before. Each part of imposing a sentence has something to do with remolding or remaking or fixing or changing the people affected by the crime to be better people, including the offender, of course. Prisons probably change all prisoners, but not necessarily for the better. Attention and monitoring by probation officers may help change offenders, hopefully for the better. We should have more opportunity to find out.

Reconciliation, bringing together the offender and the victim, is an idea of interest. I do not know that penal systems have tried it. I've known of its being done, for example, with a fifteen-year-old boy who was a ward of the State of Nebraska, and in custody of a state facility, Whitehall. The boy stole a car and drove it toward Omaha before it ran out of gas. He was arrested and put in lock-down at Whitehall. His counselor there learned the identity of the car's owner. She suffered constant fear, imagining the offender as a vicious, burly, repeat offender. She was nonetheless willing to meet her offender. The youth, also frightened to come face-to-face with one he had wronged, agreed to meet her. The result was relief to both, made effective by an agreement by which the boy did chores for the owner.

As I shall recite in a later chapter of this memoir, my meeting the widow and offspring of the man I accidently killed furnished relief from anguish of her family and mine.

Just a week ago I received a call from the father of a young man who was the driver of a car that rammed another car, killing its twenty-two-year-old driver. He asked me to spend some time with his son to help relieve his anguish. I agreed to do it, not as a part of the judicial system, but as a human being with an experience similar to his. That's a part of reconciliation and, perhaps, rehabilitation. The Guidelines cast little help for either. But judges' sentences can't ignore things that may have an effect on offenders.

Can reconciliation efforts be made in selected situations within the penal systems?

Settling or trying to bring about a settlement in civil cases is an important part of a federal trial judge's role. Not necessarily the most skillful, but the most fervent in my experience was in 1984, in the case of *Nebraska*

Public Power District v. Austin Power.[62] It was a civil case arising from the construction of Gerald Gentleman Station, a coal-fired power energy plant near Sutherland, Nebraska. One hundred million dollars were at stake. The owner, Nebraska Public Power District, claimed that over the four-year construction process overruns had been caused by lost time attributable to the contractor, Austin Power. Austin Power, on the other hand, pointed at NPPD's delays in providing materials at the site as the cause of the losses.

I met with all counsel during the several weeks before trial was to begin. The participating trial lawyers had forecast that the trial would take between five and seven months. The number of exhibits expected to be used at trial was staggering, and I could see us slogging through another trial of PFA length. More than that, we in the district court in Nebraska were using at the time a civil jury of six persons. I was sure that the jurors, especially with only six of them, would have had no experience in the constructing of a huge building such as a power plant. The parties to this case, on the other hand, were experts in such an endeavor.

I learned that the parties had made repeated efforts to settle the case, and further attempts would probably be futile. I nonetheless invited the two boards of directors to come to the courthouse for a final push to keep the decision regarding settlement in their own experienced hands. They came dutifully. I spoke as persuasively as I could to point out the time, expense, and other costs likely to be suffered throughout a long trial. No success.

To guard against a runaway trial I decided to set a time limit. I asked for and got the lawyers' common opinion of the required time. It was declared that each side would need three months of trial time from jury selection through closing arguments. I broke six months into minutes and ordered a time limit of half the total on each side. Pat Nelson, a deputy courtroom clerk, was assigned as timekeeper, checking every minute used by each side, keeping counsel informed as often as they asked for the status, and counting against the side using the minutes from opening statement to closing argument. Time used in arguing an objection was charged to the side losing the argument. It worked. The trial ended almost exactly six months of hours and minutes used by counsel after it started.

My journal tells the tale:

TUESDAY, JANUARY 3, 1984

I've ordered the boards of directors to attend all the trial. Now five of the NPPD directors asked for and received excuses for some days in January—mostly for illness or check-ups or surgery. Today I decided to excuse the defendants' board members, except the three executive committee members, who have full authority to negotiate and settle. NPPD has appealed the order to attend; against [for settlement] is 1–9.

I've set 325 hours as a maximum for each side for trial. I became apprehensive because the NPPD has identified 4,500 exhibits it wants to use at the trial; Austin, 45,000. I've spent five days in pretrial conferences with counsel, just to try to work out problems on exhibits. We got through NPPD's, a few of Austin's. If they use anywhere near all of the exhibits—most need testimony—we'll be here beyond exhaustion. We can get in only about 5½ hours a day—that'll take 118 days. We'll miss [January] 16 to 20, 30 & 31 & 2 holidays. So if we miss no more, we'll finish June 29.

WEDNESDAY, JANUARY 4

Jury selection today. Thirty-two came, after answering questionnaires that they could stay six months. Questioning by me began 10:30, 30 minutes late for lateness of a juror, ending 2:30. . . . Have four alternates. Jurors are from Lincoln, Hastings, Crete, Syracuse, Pleasant Dale, Elk Creek and Aurora; one has a B.A., two have one year of college, the rest high school; two are unemployed, two are secretaries, one a homemaker, one a work leader, one a postal manager, one assembler, one a technician, one a ceramics business operator.

THURSDAY, JANUARY 5

Opening statements and testimony. Both sides have resisted the time limitation on the trial but present no good reasons.

FRIDAY, JANUARY 6

Testimony. Plodding. Anton Divis was witness. Very cautious, pausing 10–15 seconds before beginning most answers, but answers well. He nicely explained the model of Gerald Gentleman Station that is in the courtroom, which takes up most of one side of the spectators' area.

MONDAY, JANUARY 9

At 4:30 counsel in chambers told me that NPPD's counsel in St. Louis had reported by telephone at 4:00 that the 8th Circuit had ruled from the bench that my order of attendance of the boards of directors was improper, but said that perhaps requiring a representative to be present would have been permissible.

I admit that I am surprised at the jolt I felt. I had supposed I could be philosophical.

The 8th Circuit has so little confidence in district judges.

TUESDAY, JANUARY 10

The 8th Circuit called at 9:30 to say that Judge Heaney is drafting an order amending mine to have only one director and one management official other than the project director to be at trial for NPPD. The testimony of Anton Divis continues on direct.

No word from the 8th Cir. by quitting time as to its final wording.

WEDNESDAY, JANUARY 11

The Circuit's order arrived by phone. It limits my discretion to ordering continuous attendance of only one board member of NPPD and one senior management officer. I decided, after talking yesterday with counsel, that one board member present would be worthwhile, but not a management person, so I've signed an order accordingly, effective Jan. 23 (no trial next week). And I provided for substitution—either of two designated board members may attend. And I provided the same attendance requirements for Austin Industries.

Divis' testimony continued. Cross-examination by Steve Yungblut began shortly after 4:00.

THURSDAY, JANUARY 12

Cross-examination of Divis by Yungblut continued. We lost 1½ hours from 1:30 because Yungblut's boy fell at school, breaking a tooth. Yungblut couldn't find his wife so had to take the boy to the dentist. Appears tooth is probably a baby tooth, so loss not serious. . . . Stayed in session till 5:00 to make up part of lost time.

FRIDAY, JANUARY 13

Juror Vicki Cartwright's car had a flat tire, so we lost time getting started . . . but only 15 min. . . . We're keeping time on everybody—each side gets 325 court hours. Defendants mention that we spent about three days on plaintiff's exhibits in pretrial conference—not chargeable time—but only one or so on def's. So I agree I can't very well charge defs with similar time spent at the trial on exhibits defs want in evidence. Today is the only time it's been a problem—we spent ½ hour on defs' exhibits in argument. But next week the magistrate will spend at least a day and a half on defs' exhibits. That'll help.

At 4:30 the blow came. NPPD*'s counsel presented a letter from Fred Herrington,* NPPD*'s board chairman, saying none of the board members could agree to be present all or most of the time. Maybe, it said, if any one of the members could attend any time, the board could have some members there all the time & the board would meet telephonically weekly to discuss the trial. I felt a very hollow hole in my stomach. They'll resign, the letter intimated, if they don't get their way. I'm tempted to let them, but I've decided to say o.k. Something may be better than nothing. But when 1 out of 5 citizens summoned at random said they would come every day of trial for six months and not one of eleven* NPPD *board members—who want* NPPD *to collect $100 million by the trial— will agree to come except spasmodically, my confidence in their dedication to this cause is destroyed.*

SATURDAY, JANUARY 15

Joyce & I are off to Phoenix for a workshop & Indio to see [sister] Bev. et al. It'll feel good.

TUESDAY, JANUARY 17

The workshop begins tomorrow, but an 8th Circuit committee to draft model jury instructions assembled today to review work of the subcommittees. We met all day, adjourning at 6:00 with still some work to do tomorrow afternoon. We got along well—Scott Wright, chairman, Ross Roberts, as reporter, and Bruce Van Sickle, Andy Bogue, Bob Renner, Hal Vietor.

WEDNESDAY, JANUARY 18

I had hoped to talk with Don Lay about some judicial help in Lincoln during my long NPPD trial, but he wasn't at the workshop. . . . Andy Bogue is willing to come, but Don has been an obstructionist in the past as to Andy's coming to Nebraska—other places need Andy more, so Don has said. . . . Fred Nichol says he's willing to come during good weather (it's been icy & snowy in Nebr.) if his wife is willing to come. They spend about 7 mos. in Sioux Falls and 5 in Sun City now that he is on senior status.

THURSDAY, JANUARY 19

The workshop was splendid. Arthur Miller took notice of my effort at settlement of NPPD by requiring trial attendance, but merely apologized for having only press accounts. I think what he meant was that the National Law Journal carried an article about my order and the reversal and Miller's reaction to it was "unusual but not irrational . . . not surprised at the reversal." The committee on jury instructions listened but only with forbearance to my suggesting they try letting jurors ask questions to be put to witnesses. The planting of a seed is all I expected.

FRIDAY, JANUARY 20

. . . Joyce and I picked up a Hertz car at the Phoenix airport and drove to Indio . . . , about 250 miles. Bev cooked a neat Chinese dinner and we talked until we were exhausted.

MONDAY, JANUARY 23

Testimony sailed along until 11:45, when [NPPD] ran out of available witnesses.

TUESDAY, JANUARY 24

Counsel for [Austin Power] wanted to have a new notice-of-witnesses arrangement. We settled on: have a pool of at least three always & give it at least 24 hours' notice of who will be next—but let's be reasonable about it.

My first meeting with the trial advocacy class for this semester. . . .

Allison says she hopes to move to Dallas upon finishing nurses' training at Bryan in September.

THURSDAY, JANUARY 26

... The second class session in Trial Advocacy went well. It is fun to work with kids who are eager but unknowing of trial techniques. They catch on quickly and grow greatly.

FRIDAY, JANUARY 27

A quite ordinary day of testimony in NPPD *v. Austin. I was able to accomplish quite a bit of progress in other cases while keeping one ear on the testimony—well, maybe two ears and one-half my mind—on* NPPD*. . . . I have an Episcopacy Committee meeting at 5:00. . . . Tomorrow is a Federal Practice Committee meeting here and Sunday. Tuesday I'll be in Williamsburg, Va. for a Federal Judicial Center board meeting.*

SATURDAY, JANUARY 28

Randy, Kelli, Grant [son, daughter-in-law, grandson] here to take Marilyn [Kelli's mother] to flight [from Omaha to] Maryland—a study to learn whether her diagnosis of Alzheimer's disease is warranted. She seems much better from a few months ago.

SUNDAY, JANUARY 29

Williamsburg, Va., for a Federal Judicial Center board meeting. Then cocktails at Lightfoot House, reserved by the Colonial Williamsburg for use of VIPs*—visiting heads of state [Shah of Iran], presidents* [Nixon]*, chief justices [Burger].* C.J. *Burger took my order—vodka & orange juice, mixed it himself. He . . . stayed at Lightfoot House Dinner at Williamsburg Inn—$35.*

MONDAY, JANUARY 30

FJC *board met. The* C.J. *was in a mild mood. He's so forcefully opinionated that on some matters there's no invitation to discuss them, such as whether bankruptcy judges should be Article III judges. But by and large it was an open meeting with good exchange.*

WEDNESDAY, FEBRUARY 1

Back at the ranch . . . NPPD *drones on. We've had some challenging legal questions, such as whether statements by a member of* NPPD*'s board of* *directors are non-hearsay under 801(d)(2)(C) or (D). I held evidence insufficient to show it was within scope of his agency, but for the most part the proceedings are slow, dominated by documents, each witness testifying about many documents generated by the . . . project. . . .*

Joyce and I saw a thriller—Nebraska beat Oklahoma State in basketball—54 to 52 in overtime on a last second lay-up by David Ponce.

THURSDAY, FEBRUARY 2

Breakfast at Village Inn with John White [Nebraska Wesleyan president] brought a good discussion of the status of the religion department, the NWU liquor policy, and the [United Methodist] Conference's inquiry about it, tuition increase, John's future. . . . He asked me to give NWU's commencement address May 6. I am honored to do it. . . . John said Dottie Shapiro, an instructor at Bryan, has high praise for Allison. I passed it on to Allison. She's not surprised.

Trial as usual.

Class went very well. They strain to understand foundation and proper form of a question—I strained to explain.

[Daughter] Joy wants to take a one-week internship in Wash. DC thru Geo. Wash. U. I think she should.

MONDAY, FEBRUARY 6

Paul Douglas, Attorney General of Nebraska, issued his own report re his role in the Commonwealth fiasco. He admits to mistakes but no illegalities. Maybe he's right, but his relationship with Marv Copple and Commonwealth—no payment of principal for years, selling lots to Copple's secretary for much profit, providing services to Copple—smells. He's been greatly damaged in his reputation at least.

TUESDAY, FEBRUARY 7

Andy Bogue has agreed to come [to try cases] for a week in April, 2 in May. . . . Arlen [Beam] can't take a rape case set for next Mon. . . . I may have to interrupt NPPD to try the criminal case. Lunch with Joy. She's enjoying her internship with State Senator Rod Johnson.

WEDNESDAY, FEBRUARY 8

J. Van Pelt agreed to try a rape-on-an-Indian-Reservation case beginning Monday, so I needn't interrupt NPPD-*Austin case to try it. . . . [Circuit Chief Judge] Don Lay has asked for a senior judge outside the circuit to come to help.*

THURSDAY, FEBRUARY 9

A long day of boring testimony. . . . But tonight at Trial Ad. I was exhilarated by the performances of the students. Everybody seemed to know what to do and how to do it and did it—all re introduction of exhibits. They understood the technique better than the NPPD *lawyer.*

SATURDAY, FEBRUARY 11

We have 45 over-sixty-days-old motions. I got rid of about 15 of them. Kim called, wanted to come with [her son] Aaron & [daughter] Nicole a day or so. I said great.

TUESDAY, FEBRUARY 14

. . . We got to opinion evidence today. Dr. Thomas, a professor from Penn State, opines that $25 million of loss came from [Austin's] inefficiencies.

WEDNESDAY, FEBRUARY 15

. . . Mr. Driscoll detailed his opinion that both parties were responsible for delays in completion of the project—[Austin] 186 days, fewer for NPPD.

TUESDAY, FEBRUARY 21

. . . This is trial day No. 25.

WEDNESDAY, FEBRUARY 22

Judge Van Pelt turned me down on my request to preside at the bid-rigging trial scheduled for 5 days . . . March 5. So I've told counsel I'll interrupt NPPD *v. Austin to try U.S. v. Land Paving Co. March 5. [Criminal cases have priority, partly because the Speedy Trial Act requires trial within certain deadlines.]*

I'm impressed with counsel in the NPPD *trial. Philip Fortune, Chas.*

Surasky & James Butler of the Smith Currie firm in Atlanta, Ga., are knowledgeable, experienced, courteous and sensible in representing NPPD. *Jim DeMars, also able, is the only active counsel from Lincoln.*

On [Austin's] side Gil Lundstrom, Ed Tricker, Steve Yungblut and Chas. Lowe do the talking—all to good effect. There is no animosity; all counsel are honorable and forthright.

WEDNESDAY, FEBRUARY 29

Monday [my secretary] Marlene [McGuire] was in depression over a clouding in her right eye. The left one for many months has been so deficient she can't use it in reading. Yesterday she saw an associate of Dr. Statton's—he said she's had a hemorrhaging of her good eye; that it's a natural result of her diabetes; that nothing can probably be done but he'll schedule her visit to U. of Iowa Medical Center. She says she's on the fringe of being unable to work.

FRIDAY, MARCH 2

Pat Nelson suffered chest pains yesterday afternoon and went to the hospital. She's been relieved [in the timekeeper role of NPPD *trial] by Carol Reitz for the time being.*

MONDAY, MARCH 5

It's good to get to a trial other than NPPD *v. Austin. Land Paving Co. of Omaha is charged in two counts with bid rigging and mail fraud. A motion in limine held us up only slightly—the government moved that the defense be prohibited from bringing up the homosexuality of one of its witnesses. I held a hearing [and granted the motion.]*

TUESDAY, MARCH 6

The lawyers in U.S. v. Land Paving are nearly all from Chicago—Mary Jones and Morris Pasqual for the government and Thomas Mulroy, Jr. for the defense are from Chicago. All are o.k. Jones is inexperienced and hesitant; Pasqual a bit sharper, and Mulroy very accomplished and cooperative. The defense is "Don't believe them."

WEDNESDAY, MARCH 7

At 8:00 I heard a frivolous civil rights case, dismissed the case and taxed the costs to plaintiff's counsel, Wm. Chapin.

THURSDAY, MARCH 8

Young Mr. Chapin was waiting for me at 8:00 this morning. His question was "Shall I remain in the practice of law?" I said yes but urged him to take his irritations out on a punching bag or running tracks or something other than in court. He's young and, I think, sincere, but victim of the syndrome that courts can solve all human problems.

The Land Paving jury was ready with a verdict and I was ready to go to class, so rather than be late to class, I asked Magistrate Dave Piester to take the verdict. "Guilty."

SATURDAY, MARCH 10

Joyce's mother was taken to St. Francis Medical Center. The report was congestive heart failure. Joyce left for Grand Island.

SUNDAY, MARCH 11

The EKG *today shows Joyce's mother had a heart attack, maybe more than one. Joyce will stay in Grand Island a few days.*

TUESDAY, MARCH 13

NPPD *says it should be finished with its case in 3 weeks. Today is its 35th day.*

FRIDAY, MARCH 15

The legislature impeached [Nebraska Attorney General] Paul Douglas, and voted a resolution of condemnation, too. I expected censure or condemnation, but not impeachment.

TUESDAY, MARCH 20

10:45 a.m. I've just seen the morning mail. John White's letter shows the Board of Governors on March 2 voted to grant me an honorary doctor of laws degree and asks for my response. Well, I'm deeply honored. I mean deeply honored! The college's policy has been not to grant honorary degrees to people still on the board.

WEDNESDAY, MARCH 21

Marlene is back from 2 days at Iowa Univ. Med. Center about her diabetic retinopathy. . . . She has, they say, a maximum of 2 years of sight, a minimum of 1 day. She's depressed but brave. [She died a year and a half later, on October 15, 1985.]

SUNDAY, MARCH 31

A judges' meeting . . . in Omaha mostly re case management—what to do to plan for a heavier docket while awaiting another judgeship. We're reeling now. . . . I want to try parallel trials—one from 8:00–1:40; one from 2:00 to 7:40. That can be only temporary, of course.

MONDAY, APRIL 9

[Judge] Andy Bogue was to come today for a week but the cases he had set for today settled, so he's to come Wednesday. He's caused a stir—from saying at first he'd take jury and non-jury [cases] to later saying non-jury only, to sending a 3-page list of things he must have, such as ice water twice a day, to raving at Marlene about the clerks' refusal to renumber all exhibits and the marshal's not having somebody available in the courtroom all the time or to swear-in the jury during deliberations. He'll not bring his secretary and wants secretarial service.

I'm ready to send him home. The last thing I need is a disruption of our smooth operation. We terminated 71 cases last month. We've averaged 66 each of the last 9 months—more than Omaha with their 2½ judges [two district judges, one magistrate judge]!

FRIDAY, APRIL 12

Allison cried last night . . . about her stress, the first time that's happened for several months. She's in a particularly hard rotation, where the patients may be terminal. She feels, not so much inadequate, as unable to bring herself to write plans for hopeless patients whom she's been trying to care for all day. . . . We feel for her. . . . Joyce is very good about helping her. . . . Today was the first day of the defense's presentation.

SATURDAY, APRIL 14

. . . Joyce spent the morning taking a test for endorsement in Art, found it very hard. She teaches but has little training in Art . . . & doesn't expect to pass this time.

MONDAY, APRIL 17

The NPPD trial bumps along. This is day 57. We should be about half way through.

SATURDAY, APRIL 21

The first two of five final exam trials for my Trial Advocacy class were today at the law school. Joyce helped, of course, as she always does. The jurors this time are primarily from a business women's organization, raising money for scholarships.

THURSDAY, MAY 3

Philip Fortune, lead counsel from Atlanta, Ga., for NPPD, came in to tell me that he's scheduled to be fitted with a hearing aid. He suddenly lost his hearing in both ears on February 15; it gradually came back in the left ear but is gone in the other. His right eye is black and blue. I asked him why and he said he was attacked last weekend in the Kansas City Airport. His plane was diverted to K.C. on his flight from Atlanta to Omaha and as he walked off the ramp a man screamed that Fortune had abducted his wife and child, and he then beat up Fortune. Fortune was hospitalized for 3 hours and on a doctor's instruction, his partners kept him awake all that night. He says he's o.k. The man is a drifter from N.J., has no wife or child, apparently is a wacko.

FRIDAY, MAY 4

I announced the summer trial schedule yesterday and excused [juror] Vicki Cartwright because her husband has won a trip to the World's Fair in New Orleans and she needed a two-week hiatus. I'm declaring two weeks off, a month between the two, both being times when a juror and I have scheduling problems with unchangeable vacation dates and I with a [Federal Judicial Center] conference in Wash., DC, and an 8th Cir. Judicial

Conf. in [Kansas City]. Up to now we've lost 18 [trial] days. . . . I hate to lose more than that during the last half of the trial.

TUESDAY, MAY 15

Beginning of parallel trials experiment. NPPD *began 8:00. Ten-minute recess at 9:50 & 11:50; finis 1:40. U.S. v. Clark begins 2:00; 10-min. recesses at 3:30 & 5:10; finis 6:30 (we can extend that to 7:40 if need to).*

WEDNESDAY, MAY 16

8:00 a.m.–7:15 p.m. was the time consumed by the 2 juries.

THURSDAY, MAY 17

The murder case goes along nicely. The defendant, a 22-year-old Indian, is accused of a child-abuse murder of his 3-year-old son. His wife and his mother have testified to prior bruises on the boy and lack of bruises on the morning of the day of death when the boy was with his father. Many bruises, severe head injury and bowel injuries . . . Allison listened and says the case is open and shut.

FRIDAY, MAY 18

The NPPD *trial fizzled at 9:30 for the day—no witnesses available. The Clark murder trial was to begin at 1:00, but . . . Defense Counsel Dan Wherry fears his client isn't competent to stand trial. So I ordered an exam by Dr. Osborne for 4:45 this afternoon. Dr. Osborne reported about 7:15 that Clark is competent & if he's withholding info from his counsel, it' s by choice.*

SATURDAY, MAY 19

Joy left for Wash. DC *for a week's seminar at Geo. Wash. U. on government.*

WEDNESDAY, MAY 23

I had 3 trials going at once today. NPPD *8:00–1:40; U.S. v. Clark, 2:00–4:30 and the jury deliberated until 5:35 (guilty of 2d degree murder); and Esquivel v.* LAP *4:30–7:40. Gets to be a circus.*

The sentencing of David Scott Clark is set for July 6. I let him out on a $4000 cash bond because he and his family can't raise any more. I put him in the custody of his father, who seems to be a responsible man.

FRIDAY, JUNE 1

Allison's graduation from Bryan Hospital.

SATURDAY, JUNE 9

Scott Rager called about 6:30 p.m.—Elizabeth has a penis! Kim has been so sure the baby would be a girl that she never considered a boy's name, and Elizabeth is the favored girl's name.

MONDAY, JUNE 25

Monday at 3:30 the defendant [in NPPD *v. Austin Power] rested—on the 99th day of trial. Rebuttal next.*

FRIDAY, JULY 6

On our early morning walk, our dog Tosca was coming back west from the east side of 56th Street at Van Dorn, responding to my whistle, and was struck by a van. She was killed instantly.... The young man driving the van felt terrible.... She was a loving dog, shy, impetuous. She never learned to watch for cars or find her way home. Her greatest triumph came... on Monday or Tuesday [just before her death] when she caught a rabbit, the first ever. She didn't know what to do with it—brought it to us, decided to leave it in the weeds west of 56th, revisited it each day we walked by the place.

The other bad news of the day—I must try McCurry v. Tesch, in which persons were carried or dragged by the sheriff and his deputies from a church building following a court order to close the church as a school in Louisville. I'd ruled the sheriff and his deputies had absolute immunity because of the court order, but the panel of the 8th Circuit—two-thirds of the panel—say not.

Today I had to sentence David Scott Clark for second degree murder of his 3-year-old son. I sentenced him to 30 years. He still claims to be innocent and showed his first emotion (he's shown none to the probation officer any time, it's reported) when he made a little statement at the sentencing. The child was battered brutally.

MONDAY, JULY 9

Two trials a day again for two [more] weeks. The Federal Judicial Center asked me to write my experience of parallel trials for "Chambers to Chambers," but I've done them only 3 weeks, so I'll try 2 more before assessing the idea.

SATURDAY, JULY 14

[Wilhelm and Elke Rathjens of Germany, the host family for Randy's year-long venture through Christian Youth Exchange in 1973–74, visited us in Lincoln for the past couple of weeks.] This evening we got word that Wilhelm Rathjens had a heart attack yesterday, I believe, in New York City. He and Elke had finished their U.S. journey, had checked in their car and had said goodbye to [friends] in Hartford. They decided to have one more look at New York City and boarded a train to do it. The attack came on the train. Wilhelm was taken to Bellevue Hospital, where he had another attack. He's in intensive care, of course. Elke is . . . frightened and confused and wants Randy to come. He says he will on Thursday of next week, as soon as he finishes a trial that begins Tuesday.

WEDNESDAY, JULY 18

At 10:15 Surasky asked the last cross-examination question of "Patsy" Scoville, thus ending the trial evidence in the NPPD-Austin Power case: 113 days' worth.

I figure there were about 4 million words spoken on the record during these 113 days and we're ready to be through. Now the lawyers will check exhibits, I'll confer with them about instructions and go next week to the 8th Circuit Judicial Conference. The jury will come back July 30 for final arguments, instructions, and deliberations.

THURSDAY, JULY 19

Met with NPPD & Austin lawyers to complete the work regarding exhibits.

Joyce is in South Sioux for a golf tournament! She'll be back tonight.

Unable to reach her to tell her that her father is in the hospital, having been pushed or fallen in Lincoln Street Manor, operated by [her sister] *Phyllis.*

A lawyers' poll—Nebraska's first—was published today. Robert Van Pelt got the highest overall approval rating; I got second according to the Lincoln Star. I hope I can rate at all when I'm 86. Good grief, that's nearly 30 years away!

[Worked all day July 27, August 1 and 2 with counsel on jury instructions.]

FRIDAY, AUGUST 1

Closing arguments at last. 16½ hours allowed to each side.

MONDAY, AUGUST 6

Closing arguments continue all day.

FRIDAY, AUGUST 17

Joyce and Mom Crawford and Phyllis and Kenneth Schmidt moved Dad Crawford into the Veterans Home in Grand Island. Mom hasn't been able to take care of him for several weeks—he's been at Phyllis' Lincoln Street Manor and when an opening came, in he went. It was hard, but, I think, a good idea.

WEDNESDAY, AUGUST 22

The Star and the Journal reporters called mid-afternoon to say the 8th Circuit en banc overturned my sentence in Missouri Valley—the alternative sentence whereby the corporation was to fund a chair in ethics at the University of Nebraska.

A few minutes later the jury in NPPD v. Austin reported it had a verdict. When everybody assembled, the verdict was received—$12 million plus for NPPD, $26 million plus for Austin. I think there's justice in that. NPPD offered $3 million just before trial began. As I recall, Austin at that point offered to settle for about $14 million. NPPD withdrew its offer & demanded about $14 million for itself.

I entered judgment accordingly and taxed costs in the amount of $797,386.45 against NPPD as the losing party.

Both sides appealed to the Eighth Circuit Court of Appeals. Judge Gerald Heaney wrote a forty-five-page opinion for a unanimous panel that affirmed the judgment in every respect. Included in the opinion was a summary of the numbers that gave a fair description of the massiveness of the trial, quite aside from the money damages awarded by the jury, "Thus, after a trial that consumed 117 days over a seven-month period, in which ninety-nine witnesses testified, resulting in over 20,000 pages of trial transcript, and in which 6,862 exhibits were received into evidence, the matter went to the jury with Nebraska Power contending it was entitled to a verdict of $35.6 million, and Austin contending it was entitled to a verdict of $31 million."

Judge Heaney also observed, "The jury obviously followed the court's instruction carefully, and conscientiously considered the matter for over three weeks before returning its verdicts."[63]

THURSDAY, AUGUST 23

Dad Crawford died about 10:45 last night. Phyllis called about 6:30 or so, saying he'd apparently had a stroke, wasn't responding to anyone and was on oxygen. We went, arriving at the Nebr. Veterans Home . . . about 10:15. He made no sound or movements except breathing. Phyllis, Kenneth, Verne Schroeder were there and Jennifer came a few minutes later. Mom C. held his hand. . . . About 10:45 he just quit breathing. It was perfect. He died as quietly as he lived and had his family around him, as he did in life.

In the summer of 1987 Harvey Perlman, dean of the University of Nebraska Law School, suggested I establish an organization patterned after the English Inns of Court. Chief Justice Burger, he said, was impressed with the English version and was speaking favorably about a growing American version.

By September I was sending word to selected judges, lawyers, and senior law students letters of congratulations for having accepted an invitation for the birthing of Lincoln Inns of Court. It explained that a committee—Judge Jeffre Cheuvront, J. Arthur Curtiss, Susan Jacobs, Virginia Johnson, Con Keating, Theodore Kessner, Kirk Naylor, Harvey Perlman, and I—were gathering by invitation a group of fifty lawyers, judges, and students. The purpose was to promote an intermingling of persons of all levels of experience to continue education of members whose primary professional interests were trial and appellate practice.

The Lincoln Inns of Court was an instant success. Seven inns of seven persons each met monthly during the school year, each inn having responsibility for presenting one program at a late-afternoon meeting, preceded or followed by a light meal. Membership and leadership rotated appropriately, and the members enjoyed and grew from the practical interchanges among judges, lawyers, and students.

In March 1990, after some nudging by the American Inns of Court Foundation, we, as the Robert Van Pelt American Inn of Court, had applied for and been accepted as a member of that foundation. We felt comfortable enough with the structure and operation of our local group that we kept the original structure rather than adopt the Foundation's.

The Robert Van Pelt American Inn of Court meets seven times each year to participate in trial demonstrations, appellate arguments, and discussions of ethical issues and advocacy techniques, to receive critical evaluations, to share insights into the judicial process, and to enjoy a light meal together. The mentoring program is of particular importance. Its goal is to bring about a close relationship between members of the individual inns or teams by experiencing special activities on a one-on-one basis and the frequent meeting of the members of each individual inn.

The structure that has existed from at least 1992 has been, by and large, retained, but with slightly increased membership. The Robert Van Pelt American Inn of Court has seven individual inns, each having one master of the bench (a judge), three masters of the bar (experienced lawyers), three barristers (less experienced lawyers), and one associate and two law students. Additionally there are as many emeritus members as choose to be; they have completed their terms as masters or barristers and have asked to be emeritus members, supporting the program financially and otherwise. I was the administrator for fifteen years, 1987 to 2002, then yielded to Judge Richard Kopf, who served from 2002 through 2008 and now has been succeeded by Judge Kenneth Stephan of the Supreme Court of Nebraska.

On May 6, 1995, at the annual meeting in San Francisco of the American Inns of Court Foundation, I was presented with the Lewis F. Powell Jr. Award for Professionalism and Ethics. I was impressed with the excellent turnout at the banquet, which featured, as the only banner or plaque, a prominent 26-by-20-inch plaque announcing the award. Justice Antonin Scalia was the speaker. He rendered a scholarly explanation of his theory of originalism of statutory construction. It was interesting and long—long enough to permit me comfortably to respond to my award with a two-sentence "Thanks for the award" speech. I am grateful for the award. It has a special place in my chamber.

My experience in the Robert Van Pelt American Inn of Court has been a genuine thrill. I retired from my official position in 2002 and was richly honored by the ceremony in Lincoln. More significantly, the Inn has left its mark on hundreds of students, lawyers, and judges of all levels of position and experience, and continues to do so.

The law clerks make the judge look good. Law clerks are generally young lawyers who have recently graduated from law school. For whatever reason, the judge may ask the law clerk to write a proposed opinion or order. The final approval comes from the judge, either in original or altered form. The approval usually comes after consultations between the law clerk and the judge. The important thing is that the finished product reflect the judge's best judgment.

In advance of trial the chief mission of the law clerk is to write a proposed memorandum that, if adopted by the judge, will grant or deny a motion designed to affect some issue in a pending case. The most significant motions are for summary judgment that, if granted, may end the case or dispose of one or more issues. The law clerk usually attends the trial, listening to testimony, taking notes, and researching issues at the judge's request.

My experience with law clerks has been a happy one. Until 1993 I chose two law clerks to serve two years with staggered terms, the one with a year's experience to help choose and tutor his or her successor. After 1993 and until 2001 I employed one law clerk each two years; since 2001 the same law clerk has remained. With care we (the law clerk and the secretary, now more fittingly designated the judicial assistant) would interview the top four or five applicants in the fall of each year, usually when the applicants were beginning their third year of law school. I would choose the one who appeared to be the best fit to work with the rest of us. Often, but not always, that was also the one at the top of the heap in academic standing. The appendix of the book lists these law clerks and a brief description of their experiences with me and following their term.

10

Judging throughout the Nation

The futurist Alvin Toffler in 1980 had predicted the world was undergoing a transformation so dramatic it could only be compared to that of 10,000 years ago, when the agricultural revolution took hold, or of the Industrial Revolution of the nineteenth century. Toffler dubbed it the Information Revolution and claimed it would be achieved primarily through the mysterious device known as the computer. It was the arrival of the personal computer in 1977 that made turning the world around possible, and turn it around it did.

In 1995 the Internet stormed in. In the 1930s H. G. Wells envisioned a "World Brain" in which the entire range of human knowledge would be stored for easy access. Well, the Brain was here!

To be in the midst of this monumental change has been almost dizzying. The legal profession has been touched by it—and is still reeling from the effect and awestruck at the wonder of it all. We rely much less on law books; to an extraordinary degree we do research on the computer. We prepare documents of almost any kind on word processors. We see newspapers and magazines, including, of course, those we have relied on for so long, shrinking in size and number. The effect has been dazzling. One example is evident in the announcement in December 2010 of the retirement to senior status of my successor in office, Judge Richard G. Kopf. Our district's chief judge, Joseph E. Bataillion, wrote in a press release, "[Judge Kopf] has been a pioneer in the development of innovative programs, such as digital court recording, which has made court records more accessible to the public." District Judge Laurie Smith Camp added, "Judge Kopf created the first paperless federal court in the nation. In 2002, under Judge Kopf's leadership, for the first time in history, lawyers began filing federal civil and criminal cases electronically, and then managing these cases on line." Since 2002 dozens of federal district courts have followed suit.

By the end of 1990 I had been on the judicial bench for more than twenty years and had reached the age of sixty-five. That permitted me to retire, if I chose. Congress offered two ways it could be done: retirement from the office or retirement to senior status.[1] Retirement from the office meant I would no longer be a federal judge, but I would receive "during the remainder of . . . [my] lifetime an annuity equal to the salary" I was receiving when I retired. Retirement to senior status meant I would retain the office but retire from regular active service, and would continue "to receive the salary of the office," meaning the salary with whatever increases Congress voted for district judges. To qualify for the "salary of the office" I would have to receive from the chief judge of the circuit each calendar year a certificate that I met the requirements of the statute, including doing in the preceding calendar year judicial work equivalent to what an average active judge would do in three months.

I wanted to continue to work to help our district, but I wanted at an appropriate time to help other districts in need by traveling to districts other than the District of Nebraska and districts in circuits other than the Eighth Circuit. Title 28, section 294 of the United States Code made provision for such work.

My taking of senior status was effective January 1, 1991. My successor, Richard G. Kopf, was nominated by President George H. W. Bush and was awarded his commission in May 1992. The choice was an excellent one. Judge Kopf is a sterling judge—intelligent, even-keeled, hardworking, and a natural leader. I am proud to have him as a successor and as a colleague and friend.

I retained a full case load in Nebraska until 1993. By then I felt our district was in good hands without full-time service from me, so I reduced the number of cases I would be regularly receiving in the District of Nebraska. At the same time I let it be known that I was available for assignments elsewhere. The Judicial Conference Committee on Intercircuit Assignments is a source of help in joining available judges with help-needed requests from districts across the country. The committee has been helpful to me, but my finding assignments outside Nebraska has been principally by my reaching directly chief judges of districts who have given some indication of a need for assistance.

My first assignment outside the Eighth Circuit came from a telephone call from Judge Anne C. Conway of the Middle District of Florida. She had attended a seminar for new judges that I helped conduct, and I think she learned there that I was amenable to an invitation to help. I then reached Chief Judge Elizabeth A. Kovachevich of the Middle District of Florida, and upon getting her approval and arranging for the necessary paperwork, I was sent a bundle of that court's files for which I was to be responsible.[2] A few weeks later my staff and I had readied some of the cases sufficiently for trial. Then in May and June 1993 we spent four weeks in trials in Tampa, interspersed with one week when Joyce and I went to Washington DC for meetings of the Federal Judges Association and a National Workshop for Judges. The staff and our families agreed immediately that a stretch of four or five weeks was too long a time to schedule being away from home. After that, we were smart enough to plan for a two-week slice of time, expecting that one or two trials could be completed in the two weeks. Of course, some trials took more than one week, but rarely. Preparation for trial of every case involved telephone conferences with the lawyers several times in resolving motions, so I knew from them about what time a particular trial would take. At least we were sure to schedule a weekend at home at the end of every two-week session.

That was the beginning of my working at least a quarter of my time on cases from districts other than Nebraska from 1993 through 2004. I was usually assigned a bundle of perhaps fifteen to twenty cases, for which I was responsible for resolving all issues, such as discovery issues, motions to dismiss, motions to suppress evidence, motions for summary judgment, and other motions *in limine* (motions at the outset of a trial). Then I would assist in settlement efforts in the civil cases, set dates for trials, and preside at the trials if settlements were not achieved. In most instances, my staff and I worked largely independently from the staffs of the court we were assisting, because those staffs were already busy. We were there to help, not to add to the burden of the staffs of the receiving court.

Between 1993, when I began taking out-of-Nebraska cases as a judge on senior status, and 2004, the last year I accepted such assignments, I resolved 321 cases (253 civil and 68 criminal), of which 70 were tried (60 civil and 10 criminal). The others were either settled or dismissed on the motion of a party or parties. During the same eleven years I also had on my docket in the District of Nebraska 1,945 cases (1,534 civil and 411 criminal), of which I tried 84. Depending upon the need, I usually took one or two staff members—one secretary (now called a judicial assistant) and one law clerk. Joyce almost always went with us, not at government expense, of course. She was adept at enjoying cities, scouting for the current attractions, including plays, concerts, movies, and sports events, for filling our free evenings.

Outside our Eighth Circuit we tried cases in Tampa, Chicago, Phoenix, and Dallas. Inside the Eighth Circuit but outside Nebraska we tried cases in Minneapolis and St. Paul, Minnesota; Des Moines, Cedar Rapids, and Sioux City, Iowa; and Little Rock, Pine Bluff, and Batesville, Arkansas.

What do federal trial judges do when they retire? The answer is simple for many of us: we prepare cases for trial and try cases, the same as active judges do, but we have fewer cases over a larger geographical territory. I don't know what percentage of cases tried in the federal courts are tried by "retired" judges like me, but I have read that it is nearly 20 percent. Whatever it is, we do it because we want to, and if the others are like me, we feel good about it. My feeling is that I was hired for life, so I should contribute for life, but only as long as I genuinely contribute.

I have picked out some of the cases I've had during senior status, and I'll share them with you. They are a variety, not all of great public notice, but ones of some peculiarity that makes each special to me.

United States v. Chong Ha Chang was tried to a jury in Tampa for six days in May 1993. Chong Ha Chang, also known as Jake Chang, was charged with four counts relating to cocaine, including conspiracy to distribute it. The testimony of three men who were indicted co-conspirators of Chang's and had pleaded guilty to similar charges, the testimony of five law enforcement officers, and the physical evidence—credit card receipts, toll records, and cocaine—pointed directly to the defendant Chang as the one who financed the operation. Involved were about 2½ kilograms of cocaine, probably worth some $75,000 on the street at the time.

The defendant Chang testified he had nothing to do with it. The jury found him guilty of conspiracy and two substantive counts, and not guilty on one. When the verdict was read, Chang, his live-in girlfriend, and his brother howled, and Chang cried out loudly to me that he wanted to be put into the electric chair immediately rather than go to jail. Instead, three months later I sentenced him to prison for 103 months, with five years of supervised release to follow. The sentencing was without commotion.

For the first time ever I had in the *Chang* trial a challenge by a party (here, the government) that a prospective juror did not understand the English language well enough to be a juror. I agreed that he lacked fluidity in the language, but refused to excuse him from serving. Instead I hired an interpreter to interpret for the Vietnamese juror throughout the jury selection, the trial, and the deliberation of the jurors. It worked very well. Chang appealed to the Eleventh Circuit Court of Appeals on several grounds. One was that I erred in permitting the Vietnamese juror to serve. The circuit court noted that Chang had not objected at the trial to the use of the Vietnamese juror but had insisted that he be used, so Chang could not complain after the trial was over. Both the conviction and the sentence were affirmed.[3]

Herbert Marvin Feinberg was an associate of Reuben Sturman, a key player in the porn industry in the 1980s. Sturman was a supplier who "furnished the requisite smut to countless porn retailers across the country. Sturman became so powerful that he was able to demand (or extort) large sums from the retailers that he serviced."[4] When retailers in Phoenix, Cleveland, and Chicago refused to pay, Sturman hired Feinberg to "send them a message." Feinberg, in turn, hired Jay Brissette, Donald Mares, and Paul Mahn to vandalize the Phoenix store's video machines. Baseball bats and hammers were the weapons of choice in Phoenix, but when Brissette and Feinberg agreed on a price of $7,500 for each of eight jobs in Chicago, the decision was made to use another kind of persuasive device. Feinberg told Brissette a story about how effective stink bombs were, saying it took weeks for the victims to get the smell out. Brissette decided to use them. He prepared two kinds of bombs—metal pipe bombs and plastic pipe bombs with "stink vials." The bombs were designed to be triggered by remote control. Brissette planned to plant bombs at six of the Mays' Chicago stores. He left to Mares and Mahn to place five. They placed one successfully, but on the way to plant a second bomb Mares took a bomb from his bag and put it on his lap. The bomb was triggered by something, perhaps by electrical current from Chicago's downtown traffic system. The bomb exploded in the car and the car burst into flames. Both men got out of the burning car, and Mahn escaped, but Mares died from the explosion.

Feinberg and Sturman were indicted together in ten counts that included conspiracy to extort money from retailers in Phoenix, Cleveland, and Chicago, causing others to use or carry a destructive device in the commission of extortion, and related crimes.

Sturman had been convicted of some of the counts by the time I presided at Feinberg's trial in Chicago in March 1994. The jury found Feinberg guilty on all counts. Judge Paul E. Plunkett of the Northern District of Illinois sentenced him to a mandatory minimum of thirty years on the conspiracy count and ten years on the remaining counts, to be served consecutively, for a total sentence of 481 months. Both the conviction and the sentence were affirmed on appeal to the Seventh Circuit Court of Appeals.[5]

In an opinion for the three-judge panel Circuit Judge Jesse Eschbach spent time discussing the defendant's objection to my having permitted the jurors to ask questions addressed to me to be put to the witness. Feinberg's counsel had not objected to any of the questions asked by jurors or to the practice of permitting such questions. Judge Eschbach noted that this was the first time the Seventh Circuit had faced the issue. He wrote that every circuit to consider the practice, including the First, Fourth, Fifth, Eighth, and Ninth Circuits, had found it permissible in some circumstances, but that the same courts expressed grave concerns about the practice. Judge Eschbach's opinion made it clear that his panel did not condone the practice, but thought it was acceptable in some cases, such as conspiracy or antitrust cases, where the facts are so complicated, that questions should be allowed by jurors. This was a conspiracy case, and I'm of the view that the jurors probably considered it complicated. Failure of the lawyers to object suggests a similar view by them. Judge Eschbach pointed to *United*

States v. Bush,[6] where procedures are laid out for courts to follow to ensure against prejudice.

I continue to disagree with the negative assessment. I know the risks. Having used the practice extensively for thirty-five years, I think that most cases have little or no likelihood of risks that outweigh the benefits. I have had no case overturned because of jurors asking questions. More than that, no case was cited from any circuit that found use of the practice so edgy as to dislodge the verdict. Every trial carries risks. Virtually anything a trial judge does, if carried to an extreme, can be a ground for prejudicial error. Every trial judge knows and accepts that. I appreciate all efforts to suggest procedures that may help ensure against harm. But abandoning in all but a handful of cases a useful technique that is a source of genuine assistance to the jury's finding of the facts in many cases and is rarely, if ever, misused, is too heavy a price.

The second bombing case I had in the 1990s was tried to a jury in Tampa in May 1996. The defendant, Samuel Gentile, was charged in four counts with possessing an unregistered pipe bomb, conspiracy to use a weapon of mass destruction, attempt to destroy or damage a vehicle, and carrying a firearm during and in relation to a crime of violence.

The evidence introduced by the government, including the testimony of co-conspirator Mark Viscome, was that Viscome made a pipe bomb at Gentile's request but refused to fasten it to the underside of a pickup truck that Gentile's ex-wife, Deanna, regularly used in her job. Gentile, Viscome said, hooked the pipe bomb to the underside of the pickup. The bomb stayed there for several months without exploding. It was noted by a woman passerby to be dangling from the truck, so she notified the Tampa Police Department, and the bomb squad removed it and defused it.

Viscome admitted making the bomb, had pleaded guilty to all four counts of the indictment and testified that Gentile planned to kill his ex-wife. Strong evidence showed that Gentile was involved in a bitter custody fight. Statements were made by Gentile incriminating himself before the trial.

Gentile's defense was that he had nothing to do with the bomb, except that he knew it had been made and was in his father's possession. He testified that his father told him he had "taken care" of the problem with Deanna, from which Gentile concluded that his father had placed the bomb. The father did not testify, but I believe he was in the courtroom when his son testified. Gentile testified that his father had a mental or emotional problem. Gentile's sister, mother, and girlfriend testified to Gentile's innocence.

The jury deliberated about three and a half hours before finding him guilty on all counts. I sentenced him to imprisonment for a total of 560 months (more than forty-seven years) on October 11, 1996. Both the conviction and the sentence were affirmed on appeal to the Eleventh Circuit.[7]

On June 11, 1999, Gentile filed a motion to vacate the conviction and sentence under 28 U.S.C.§ 2255. He charged that his counsel at trial had not provided him with adequate service by failing to move for a mistrial because of a frightening scene erupting in the courtroom. Gentile's description of it was as follows: "Gentile was handcuffed and shackled in the courtroom by gun-wielding marshal's [*sic*] in the very presence of every juror because of a supposed bomb-threat and the building [was] evacuated." I denied the motion, saying, "Although the courtroom was evacuated during the petitioner's trial, there is nothing in the record to suggest that the petitioner's counsel knew or should have known that the jury was aware that the evacuation was due to a bomb threat. . . . After all, the evacuation was not overly disruptive since it was called off before the jurors even got down the stairs, and the trial resumed only six minutes after it was interrupted. As to the drawing of weapons and handcuffing and shackling Gentile in front of the jurors, there simply was no such event." My denial of his section 2255 claim was affirmed on appeal with an unpublished opinion.[8]

Civil rights lawsuits have been abundant during my life on the court. Discriminations in favor of white persons over persons of color and in favor of males over females were seen quite often. One suit of both was *Hollins v. N. P. Dodge Management Co.*[9]

Mary E. Hollins made application to N. P. Dodge Management Co. of Omaha for a position of part-time leasing agent. Her testimony was that on the telephone the company's agent was eager to have her come and excited about her qualifications, but upon Hollins's arrival to make a written application, the agent was changed, hesitant and argumentative. The agent asked how her small children would be taken care of during the day and resisted each suggestion Hollins made, such as that her mother or a neighbor or her older children would care for the younger children. A white male was hired. Hollins sued. The claim was that because of her race and gender, a black woman, she was not hired.

The jury deliberated several hours, then asked for my definitions of "race" and "gender" and asked whether "single parent" fell within the definition of either race or gender. I said that, as applied to this case, "race" meant being black, that "gender" meant being a woman or a man, and that "single parenthood" had in law no relationship to race, and whether it had a relationship to gender depended upon the facts, which they would need to determine.

The verdict was in favor of the plaintiff on the bases of both gender and race. The award was for $344 for loss of wages, $20,000 for other damages, such as emotional distress, and $250,000 in punitive damages.

Less frequent, but real, were claims by a white person of discrimination in favor of a minority, that is, reverse discrimination. That was the claim in *Roberts v. University of South Florida.*[10]

Two positions of assistant professor were advertised by the University of South Florida in Tampa in 1988. Cleora Roberts and Aaron Smith applied. Smith, a black male, indicated he could not leave the higher paying position he held at Stanford University for the money being offered by the University of South Florida, $26,000 compared to $28,500, for each of the advertised assistant professor positions. Thereafter one of the assistant professor positions was re-advertised as an associate professor position, tailoring it to Smith's qualifications, and the position was offered to Smith at $40,000. Smith accepted it. Roberts accepted the other position of assistant professor at $29,518.

Roberts sued the University of South Florida, charging violations of her civil rights on account of (1) reverse discrimination—that is, discrimination by treating a black male more favorably than a white woman, and (2) paying her less than Smith for the reason of gender. Roberts added claim (3) to her suit, a charge that, because she had filed the suit on charges (1) and (2), the university retaliated by delaying a granting of tenure to her.

Because the case was under three acts of Congress, part of the fact finding had to be by me and part of it by the jury. The part I was to decide was submitted to the jury; the jury's decision was advisory to but not binding on me.

Probably the key evidence was that the School of Social Work of the University of South Florida had no black faculty members at the time Smith was offered the position. The school was scheduled for a reaccreditation evaluation by the Council on Social Work Education, and the accrediting process would place significant weight on a program's effort to recruit and hire ethnic minority faculty members. A program had to demonstrate a commitment to that effort in order to be reaccredited.

The jury specifically found on the first claim that Cleora Roberts was as qualified as Aaron Smith for the position he received, and that the race, but not the sex, of Aaron Smith was a determining factor in the university's decision to employ him at a higher rank and higher salary than Roberts's rank and salary. Roberts was entitled to back pay, defined as the difference between the salary and fringe benefits she actually received as assistant professor and the salary and fringe benefits she would have received if she had been employed at the same rank or salary as that of Smith. That amount was recommended by the jury and adopted by me to be $68,212.

The jury also found that the discrimination was with malice or reckless indifference to her rights and that the amount of money that would reasonably compensate for her emotional pain, suffering, inconvenience, or mental anguish was $70,000. I declined to accept that, because the Civil Rights Act of 1991, under which this claim was made, had not been enacted when Roberts was hired, and the Eleventh Circuit Court of Appeals, which has Florida within its jurisdiction, had not declared that act to be retroactive.[11]

The jury also found for Roberts on her equal pay claim but awarded no damages for it. On the claim of retaliation the jury awarded Roberts $250,000 for pain and suffering. I adopted the jury's findings and made the award accordingly. I also awarded Roberts an attorney's fee of $74,295. I denied her request that I direct the university to grant her tenure, saying in my Findings of Fact and Conclusions of Law, "While it can be argued that such a finding would be warranted in this case, I do not make the finding. An opportunity remains for the plaintiff to be awarded tenure by the university. She has not been denied tenure, although she has been delayed in obtaining it."

An appeal was filed by the university on January 4, 1994, but was dismissed on August 14, 1995, by the Court of Appeals on a joint stipulation of the parties, filed May 18, 1995.

Cleora Roberts wrote a letter to me and the jurors, dated June 21, 1996, three years after the trial. She said in part:

> We have never really met, but you have played a very important role in my life. My purpose . . . is to thank you and to let you know how my lawsuit was resolved.
>
> You might recall that right after my trial and your verdict there was a great deal of press coverage. University officials were quoted as saying they would appeal my case to the Supreme Court. Well, their legal tactics drew it out for nearly two years but no appeal was ever filed. [Perhaps she didn't know of it, but an appeal to the Eleventh Circuit Court of Appeals was filed, as I have stated, but nothing was addressed to the Supreme Court that I know of.]
>
> . . . One year ago the lawsuit was settled for $323,000, which was slightly above the jury award of $318,000. [The 3.38 percent per annum interest decreed by the judgment would account for more than the settlement amount over the jury award.] I also received the promotion, was given the raise in salary and was awarded tenure (along with Dr. Aaron Smith) in 1994. . . .
>
> . . . .
>
> I am still on the social work faculty and enjoying my teaching and research. I keep a low profile. . . .
>
> . . . .
>
> When I filed my lawsuit in 1990 it was politically incorrect, but I am amazed at how much change there has been in affirmative action policies since that time. Your verdict may have played a role. I have become an avid supporter of our jury system (although the O.J. trial shook my faith). . . . Before my trial, I told my attorneys I felt like David versus Goliath, but I came to appreciate that in the Courtroom each side is treated equally. . . .
>
> . . . As jurors you made many personal sacrifices . . . to spend those seven days in the courtroom. . . . I deeply appreciate all that you have done. And to Judge Urbom, . . . a special thank you for your decisions and rulings. My attorneys tell me that your flawless handling of the

case was likely one of the reasons the University did not file an appeal. [Surely the attorneys would know of the appeal!]

Discrimination by a city is not rare. It may result in hiring, firing, promotions, or, as in *Bolden v. Jacksonville, Arkansas,* the giving of services to its inhabitants.[12]

Jacksonville, Arkansas, had a population of about two thousand, of which about 17 percent were black. Of the ten parks in the city only Johnson Park was in the predominantly black area of Henry Estate. Pleasure Park and Dupree Park were in predominantly white areas. Paradise Park and Reuther Park were in nonresidential, strictly industrial areas. The other five parks were in areas that could not be categorized as being in either predominantly black or predominantly white areas.

A class action was filed on behalf of the residents of Jacksonville who claimed to have been subjected to discriminatory providing of municipal services. The defendants were the City of Jacksonville and the various officials charged with being in care of the parks and recreation areas of the city. A nonjury trial was held on October 19, 1994, in Little Rock.

The defendants could be held liable if it were shown by the greater weight of evidence (1) the existence of a racially identifiable neighborhood in the municipality; (2) substantial inferiority in the quantity or quality of the municipal services or facilities available in that neighborhood; and (3) motive or intent to discriminate.

I found all three elements proved. The only real dispute was over the issue of motive or intent, that is, whether the Parks and Recreation Department of Jacksonville had motive or intent to discriminate. Its director had been appointed by the city to oversee the operations of the parks and had been delegated by the city the authority to make the decisions on what maintenance or care would be provided to the parks. She admitted at trial that it was her belief that "[w]hen there is a park that is not being used properly, the people who should be in the park are not, because of the illegal activities and the undesirable activities that are going on": "[W]e chose not to put a lot of more effort in there than was required because it was not being used as it was designed to be." Earlier she had said at a meeting of the department heads, "We deliberately let it (Johnson Park) go because there was so much illegal acts and fighting and drinking, carrying on, over there that nobody was going to go to the park." At the trial she testified, "I may have said that, but it was in the context that we chose not to put good money into a bad situation until the situation was remedied."

The city and its responsible agents, I wrote after the trial, did "little or nothing" to remedy "the situation."

At another meeting another member said she would not spend any more money on Johnson Park "until them people learned to take care of it themselves."

I held, "Although the evidence is not voluminous, I find that in light of the testimony and statements of the Director of the Parks & Recreation Department the amount of disparity between maintenance of Johnson Park and the parks in other areas of the City of Jacksonville gives rise to the inference of discriminatory intent." I said that injunctive relief was necessary to prevent future discriminatory actions by the defendants regarding Johnson Park, noting, however, that the maintenance "appears to be about equal to the maintenance of the other parks," "because of actions taken by the defendants (the city and its officials) since the filing of this suit."[13]

I entered an order on October 25, 1994, permanently enjoining the city and its officials from discriminating against the black inhabitants in the delivery of municipal services concerning the maintenance of Johnson Park. I also required the Jacksonville Parks and Recreation Department to regularly make a written log evidencing the date, time, and type of work performed and the names of the workers doing the work and to deliver the log to the City Council weekly as a public record. On appeal, the Eighth Circuit affirmed my decision.[14]

About seven years later, in 2001, a motion was filed, asking that the city and its responsible officers be held in contempt of the court's order. I asked that it be assigned to another judge because that case was the only one I had pending in Little Rock, and the expense of having me fly to Little Rock seemed unnecessary if another judge were available. It was reassigned to Senior Judge G. Thomas Eisele of Little Rock, whom I had known since 1970, when we both were sworn in as federal judges. I had the utmost confidence in him. On October 10 Judge Eisele found that the defendants were not in contempt of the order I had entered. I take it that the city and its responsible officers were doing their job correctly.

To illustrate the care with which cases needed to be scheduled for trial, and the attorneys to be notified and organized, I quote a letter I wrote to six lawyers in four Arkansas cases on August 10, 2001, including the *Bolden* case:

> Following my telephone conference with you this week . . . this is the way things look. We should be able to try the *Bolden* case, if it is not previously resolved, on October 1 and 2; the *Allen* case on October 3, 4 and 5; and the *Caston* case on October 9 and 10 or 10 and 11, if mediation is not successful; and the *Smith* case on October 11 or 12. . . .
>
> The above assumes that in the *Allen* case Mr. Carney's trial before Judge Wright will be finished before October 1 or that the *Bolden* case is resolved thereby freeing October 1; and that Ms. Murray's appearance in the Polaski Circuit Court will be completed by October 2; and that the coming motions for summary judgment will be filed soon and resolved in good time.
>
> Of course, if one or more of the cases are resolved, that may open time that will allow some more flexibility.
>
> In any event, that is the way I see it at this time and I shall make plans accordingly. I ask that you do the same.
>
> Please keep me informed of any happenings that may affect this schedule.

Scheduling is an art. Even using art can leave a tangle, because many people are involved, even in short trials: lawyers, witnesses, jurors, judges.

Cases with some celebrity came my way during senior status. Barney, the famous plush toy, was the subject of one, a major league baseball player was the subject of another, and a U.S. senator of still another. The trials didn't have the bounding headlines of, say, a murder or kidnapping, but they let us see some of the inside tensions of the commercial and political realms.

The celebrity in *Ganz v. Lyons Partnership LP* was Barney, a plush toy, the creation of Sheryl Leach of Allen, Texas, in 1987.[15] It was boosted as a dinosaur of sweet nature and became a stunningly successful sales item in the early 1990s, particularly through a television series, *Barney & Friends*, aimed at children between two and eight.[16] Baby Bop was a companion plush toy added fairly early by the makers of Barney. Intellectual property rights engrossing both Barney and Baby Bop toys by the time of the lawsuit were owned by Lyons Partnership, LP, a U.S. limited partnership. Ganz, a Canadian toy distributor, had obtained from Lyons the right to distribute Barney and Baby Bop plush toys in Canada.

Ganz and Lyons arrived at an agreement of sorts in March 1993 for Ganz's buying toys. The purchase order for 264,000 toys was accepted by Lyons. That purchase order was changed more than once, increasing the number of toys to 720,000. Both Ganz and Lyons wanted a formal written contract, and they worked toward getting one written, but none was signed.

Ganz sued Lyons for breach of contract, relying on the oral agreement and a written document of March 1993. Ganz claimed Lyons delayed the shipping of the toys beyond the required delivery date, and also claimed Lyons failed its duty to use its "best efforts" to protect the Canadian toy market from sales of "knock-offs"—that is, imposter toys or infringements that looked like but weren't the real things. Thus, Ganz argued, because of Lyons's delay and the invasion of the Canadian market by knock-offs, only slightly resisted by Lyons, Ganz was left with 174,000 unsold toys, on which it lost profits. Ganz claimed also that it had lost profits on another 204,000 toys on which it did not take delivery.

Lyons counterclaimed that Ganz had failed to take delivery of and to pay for 204,000 plush toys it was obligated to buy under the agreement. The trial to a jury in Dallas took nine days to complete.

The pieces of evidence were strongly at odds. For instance, Ganz changed the required original shipping date from an unspecified day in April 1993 to May 15, 1993. Delivery was completed on July 10. Lyons's evidence was that Ganz had set up a letter of credit on March 25 to cover the original order of 264,000 toys. Ganz amended that letter of credit on June 3 to provide for a shipping date of July 10. Therefore, Lyons argued, the amending of the letter of credit to July 10 also amended the original order's shipping date to July 10. Because Lyons complied with the July date, Lyons argued that it did not violate the contract. Ganz, to the contrary, contended that the jury could find from the evidence that amending the letter of credit did not amend the parties' understanding that time was of the essence and did not change the shipping date of the original order of the 264,000 items.

I agreed with Ganz's position, because the central principle of letters of credit is the "independence principle," by which letters of credit are recognized in law as being by their nature separate transactions from and not controlled by the performance of the sales on which they may have been based.

Evidence was complex and stretched widely from the specific to the general. Experienced persons in the toy industry calculated the number of sales of Barney plush toys that would probably have been made if the delivery had been made by the contracted delivery date, in light of the knock-off invasion, the depressed Canadian economy at the time, and how much of the sales of knock-offs was probably made to the detriment of sales of the legitimate Barney toys, all in the months of May and June 1993. Such was the nature of the goal we expected the jury to grapple with and reach from the necessarily speculative evidence produced.

One witness estimated that Ganz could reasonably have anticipated that 275,000 Barney toys would be sold in the two months, if delivery had been timely. Another time the same witness estimated 720,000. The sales manager of Ganz's toy division made a projection of 315,000. An economist and professor testified sales would be fewer than 420,000. He began his calculation by including all children under five years; in 1993 this number was 2,013,900. Because, however, not all of these spoke English or had access to Barney's television show, he reduced the figure to about 1 million. However, he concluded that the market group for Barney was only two- and three-year-olds, further reducing the figure to 420,000.

Yet other testimony was that Barney's popularity and demand might extend to children up to eight. Another's opinion fixed the interested age group at five. Another questioned whether Canada's bad economy at the time would affect spending for children's toys. One knowledgeable witness opined that some toys claimed to have been in competition with Barney in May and June 1993 were not yet available in Canada or had not yet begun to rise in popularity until late 1993.[17] You can see how difficult a jury's task sometimes is. And our trust in them is often less than our demand of them.

The jury in the Ganz case awarded Ganz a total of $3,821,268. Of that, $1,120,070 was for loss of profits on the 204,000 toys Ganz never took delivery of because of lateness of projected delivery. I reduced that amount by $272,965 because that figure represents what was calculated from loss on Baby Bop toys, but Ganz had offered no evidence of loss on Baby Bop sales. The technique I used was to say that Lyons's motion for a new trial was denied if Ganz were to accept the reduced award, but the motion for new trial was granted if Ganz refused the reduction (called a *remittitur*). The record does not reflect whether there was acceptance of the lowered amount, but the parties obviously settled the case without a completion of the appeal, because on August 27, 1997, an order was entered, dismissing the case in accordance with the stipulation of dismissal by the parties.

The remittitur in the *Ganz* case calls my attention to another case tried in North Platte, Nebraska, in May 1989. In *Nelson v. Production Credit Association of the Midlands,* the jury awarded a plaintiff $1,278,000 on a breach of contract claim. The defendant filed a motion for judgment notwithstanding the verdict. After thoroughly examining a transcript and the exhibits of the ten-day trial, I set aside the verdict, holding the evidence was insufficient to permit any award to the plaintiff. On appeal, the Eighth Circuit agreed with me in a split decision, 2 to 1, Judge Gerald Heaney dissenting.[18] As I recall it, the plaintiff's attorney expressed to the press consternation that I was making such a decision at the time, that is, after the verdict was reached. At least, he seemed to be saying, I could have done better by dismissing the case without submitting it to the jury at all.

I could empathize with the plaintiffs and their attorney. It was true that for a short time Mr. and Mrs. Nelson had the excitement of a huge financial award for what they believed was fair and reasonable. They also understandably were shocked at the sudden loss of the award.

My reason for not announcing a judgment for the defendant before submitting the case to the jury was twofold. First, I wasn't confident of the absence of sufficient evidence to support a finding for the Nelsons until the trial was over and I had read the transcript of the trial, where I could scrutinize all the evidence rather than just hearing the witnesses once, and having studied the exhibits. If I had dismissed the case without a jury's verdict and then, after study of the transcript of the trial, I had decided I was wrong in dismissing it, or the circuit court had decided I was wrong in dismissing it, a full retrial would have been necessary—starting again with a second trial. Second, if the appellate court were to decide there was sufficient evidence to support a verdict for the plaintiff and I was wrong in ruling to the contrary, the case would have to be remanded for a second trial. Second trials consume time and money, of course. That time and expense can be avoided by the method I used: letting the jury decide, then setting aside the verdict, and if the appellate court were to decide I was wrong in setting the verdict aside, the case would be at an end. The same would be true if the appellate court were to decide I had been right in setting aside the jury's verdict: the case would be ended. So in either event, the time and expense of a second trial would be avoided. That may seem harsh to a plaintiff but is generally considered the preferable procedure, and the ultimate result is the same: a loss for the same losing party without a second trial.

In *Terrell v. Childers* a professional baseball pitcher, Charles W. (Walt) Terrell, was the plaintiff celebrity.[19] He worked his way to the major leagues through the minors, first picked up by the New York Mets; he spent most of his best baseball years with the Detroit Tigers. His highest salaried years were 1985 through 1992. Those were the years Talent Services, Inc. (TSI) was contract-bound to receive Terrell's checks from the Tigers, pay his bills, give him financial advice, provide tax and estate planning, and make investments for him and his wife, Karen. John Childers was the principal owner of TSI. Michael Childers was John Childers's son and the recruiting agent for TSI. Frank Schuette was the clone of John Childers and regularly reported to Terrell that things were "fantastic" or "super," even when the investments were at their worst. Terrell probably provided TSI about $1 million to invest. Most of the investments were in annuities and in a real estate undertaking known as the Pine Street property. On each investment JoAnn Childers, John Childers's wife, received a commission, allegedly without being employed by TSI or performing any services.

The accounting firm of Bercoon, Weiner, Glick & Brock, of which Elwood Kreger was a senior partner, was contracted to give tax advice to the Terrells and prepare tax returns. Kreger and his firm were charged with knowing of the ill-directed commissions to JoAnn Childers but never telling the Terrells of them. The Kregers learned too, it was claimed, that the investment in Pine Street property was deteriorating but did not tell the Terrells.

Walt and Karen Terrell sued seven defendants in twelve counts.[20] An eight-member jury was selected in Chicago on September 3 and 4, 1996. Evidence was presented for ten days, and closing arguments and jury deliberations covered three days. The verdict was for the plaintiffs, awarding in compensatory damages a total of $187,000 ($12,000 against TSI and John H. Childers, another $175,000 against John Childers, JoAnn Childers, and Elwood Kreger) and in punitive damages $15,000 against John Childers and $60,000 against JoAnn Childers. In all other respects the jury found for the defendants.

I have no doubt the Terrells felt devastated by the verdict. I say that for two reasons. First, their attorney, Gary Lee Starkman—who, I could tell from his rapport with the opposing counsel, was a highly respected lawyer—told the jury from the beginning, "We are asking for more than a million dollars in this case."[21] And the evidence might have supported such a number, if the jury had accepted Terrell's version of all the facts. Second, after the verdict was read, Starkman asked for a polling of the jury. That's entirely permissible and is often requested in criminal cases, but not as often in civil cases, and virtually never when the request is by the "winning" plaintiff. Polling was done by my asking each juror individually whether he or she did or did not agree with the verdict in each of its questions and answers. Each juror answered that he or she agreed with the verdict in each of its parts.[22]

One count had not been submitted to the jury. Count VIII requested a declaratory judgment by me that TSI and John Childers were liable to the Terrells regarding the Pine Street investment. I made a written finding that they were liable, but the amount of the loss could not yet be known. I wrote that the defendant TSI breached its contract with the Terrells and that TSI and John Childers violated their fiduciary duties to the Terrells and committed fraud upon them. I said, "It appears likely that the plaintiffs or the plaintiff Charles W. Terrell will be damaged and suffer liability because of such breaches and fraud regarding the . . . Pine Street property. Defendants Talent Services, Inc. and John H. Childers are therefore liable to the plaintiffs for such loss as the plaintiffs suffer as a result of the breach of contract, breach of fiduciary duty, and fraud of John H. Childers and Talent Services, Inc." Only time will tell what liability will come to Walt and Karen Terrell by way of the Pine Street property.

Problems with the jury's verdict weren't over when it was read and polling had affirmed what it said. The verdict form was long—seven pages long—and complicated. Indeed when the jurors were leaving the courtroom after the verdict had been received, the foreperson said quietly to me, "I suggest you not use that form of verdict again!" I had no wish to disagree with her, but the complexity of the issues and the number of defendants made an easier form virtually impossible. I smiled, nodded, thanked her, and bade her good day.

Fourteen days after the verdict, a motion on behalf of the Terrells was filed for a new trial and for modification of the judgment because of inconsistencies in the verdict form. I granted the motion for a new trial on all issues regarding Count IV as to the Bercoon firm and Elwood Kreger; on Count VI as to John Childers and TSI; and on Count VII as to Elwood Kreger and the Bercoon firm; and I denied the motion for modification of the order of judgment.

The problem with the verdict on Counts IV, VI, and VII was that in each of them the jury found for the Terrells and found there was damage to them, but also found that the amount of damages was "$0.00." But under the law, as set out in the instructions to the jury, in order for a defendant to be liable on each count, there had to be damages to the plaintiffs. If there was no damage, there was no liability. So a finding by the jury of liability but "$0.00" in damages created an inconsistency, for which there was no remedy but a new trial.

Accordingly I ordered a new trial on those three counts. A new complaint was filed, answers to it were filed, motions were filed and resolved, and arrangements were made for a second trial. I hoped that on a second try I could devise a less complicated verdict form that a new jury could understand. (I probably could and the jurors probably could, because fewer issues and defendants would be involved.) Before the second trial could start, an appeal from the first trial had been filed, but before it was heard by the Seventh Circuit Court of Appeals, the appeal was dismissed. Obviously a settlement was reached, ending the lawsuit.

Before embarking on the next "celebrity case," I shall insert a little case that immediately followed the *Terrell* trial in Chicago. It was brought as a claim that a hospital had violated the Family Medical Leave Act by discharging the plaintiff from her job for taking a justifiable leave to care for two children who were ill with chicken pox.

At the very end of a trial day I suggested we recess until the next morning, but the plaintiff's counsel asked to be permitted to call to the witness stand "just one short witness." I glanced at the defense counsel and saw no sign of resistance, so I nodded yes. A moment later in walked a new witness, two feet tall. A "short witness" indeed! But he didn't testify long and was fully supportive of his grandmother's case, for he was one, he said, who had been taken care of by her when he had the "chicken pops." The jury awarded his grandmother $58,000.[23]

David F. Durenberger was a United States Senator from Minnesota who had won in a special election in 1973 the right to finish out Senator Hubert Humphrey's term. Durenberger was elected twice more. Sometime before April 2, 1993, he had appeared before the Senate Committee on Ethics for investigation of possible misconduct in falsifying his request for reimbursement of lodging expenses. The Committee's report led to the Senate's denouncing him for bringing "dishonor and disrepute" to the Senate. A criminal indictment followed, charging he conspired with two others to commit fraud on the United States by seeking reimbursement from the Senate of rent he claimed he had paid when he stayed in a condominium he owned, and by preparing and backdating documents to make it appear, falsely, that the condominium had been sold before he occupied it. The indictment was handed down in the District of Columbia. The case was transferred at Durenberger's request to the District of Minnesota, and it was assigned to me.[24]

One of the defenses was that the case should be dismissed because the prosecution had presented to the grand jury eleven selected pages from a Report of the Select Committee on Ethics and the Report of Special Counsel on Senate Resolution 311, pertaining to Durenberger's alleged misconduct. That, the defense argued, was a violation of the speech or debate clause of the U.S. Constitution.[25]

In a decision that caused headlines and controversy I ruled that there was a violation of the speech or debate clause. After examining the facts and the law, I decided that *United States v. Gravel,* decided by the U.S. Supreme Court in 1972, was the controlling law. The *Gravel* case said that "the Speech or Debate Clause was designed to assure a co-equal branch of the government wide freedom of speech, debate, and deliberation without intimidation or threats from the Executive Branch." The clause, the Court declared, "protects Members against prosecutions that directly impinge upon or threaten the legislative process."[26]

The Senate, I wrote, has a duty to discipline its members, according to the Constitution. "The defendant contends and I agree that if a member of the Senate believes that his statements to the Committee or the findings of the Committee and its Special Counsel could be introduced as evidence against him one day in a grand jury proceeding, then the intimidation caused by the prospect of criminal liability will chill senators and severely undermine the ability of the committee to effectively investigate and discipline members."[27] I wrote that the speech or debate clause's purpose is fundamentally different from other constitutional guarantees, because in the words of the Supreme Court of the United States in *United States v. Helstoski,* "[The] purpose [of the speech or debate clause] was to preserve the constitutional structure of separate, coequal and independent branches of government."[28] Accordingly I found that to protect the integrity and independence of the Committee, I should dismiss the indictment against David Durenberger. What that meant in this case was not that a grand jury cannot charge senators with a crime, but that what is said to or by the Senate's Select Committee on Ethics or its Special Counsel of the committee cannot be used as evidence of a crime when the matter about which the Ethics Committee is investigating comes before a grand jury in charging the senator with a crime.

Writers took sides on the argument. Said an editorial writer in *Roll Call,* the newspaper of Capitol Hill, "We applaud the logic of Judge Warren Urbom's decision."[29] On the other hand, an editorial in Minnesota's *Star-Tribune* fussed, "[Durenberger] has stretched [the] reasonable protection [of the clause] beyond all bounds. He has used it to shield himself from federal prosecution on charges that he essentially falsified expense claims to the Senate. Incredibly, U.S. District Judge Warren Urbom has bought Durenberger's arguments."[30] What this writer apparently feared was that senators, particularly this senator, couldn't be prosecuted. He need not have feared.

My dismissal was "without prejudice," thus keeping the door open for the government to indict Senator Durenberger again on the same charges. He was indicted again, on February 25, 1994, in the U.S. District Court for the District of Columbia. The selected pages of the Committee couldn't be used against him, but he properly was still vulnerable to prosecution. Pursuant to a plea agreement he pleaded guilty to five misdemeanor counts of conversion of public monies under title 18 U.S.C. § 641, set out in a superseding information filed on August 21, 1995. He was sentenced on November 29, 1995, by Judge Stanley S. Harris to probation of one year on each count to run concurrently and to pay a fine of $1,000 total and on each count a special assessment of $25. As a special condition of his probation, he was required to perform seventy-five hours of community service at the direction of the probation office.[31] David Durenberger did not stand for reelection in 1994.

Aside from fears, whether based biblically or otherwise, that the world would come to an end when the new millennium arrived, people's scariest and most reliably grounded worry was the "Y2K problem." The aggravation came from the computer; the cause was its human makers. As I understood it, many computers that had been around a few years had been made to be receptive to two-figure years rather than four-figure years. When a period of time was written as, say, 12/17/25, the two-figure "25" usually meant the year 1925, but upon reaching 2000 the older computers were likely to be unable to discern whether the 25 meant 1925 or 2025, thus causing befuddling problems for gigantic businesses, small businesses, governments, and individuals. The problem was no secret. Expert users, at least, knew of it at least as early as 1970, when thirty-year mortgages were being written and might well be in for trouble when calculating the effect of the mortgage into or beyond 2000. So massive efforts were undertaken before 2000 to fix the problem. For lack of knowledge or money, many computer users did not replace the old with new computers or otherwise avoid the problem. The White House Office of Management and Budget reported in its 1999 report that the government spent—just in moving to fix the Y2K problem, even before the assault of 2000—$8 billion.[32] The Y2K problem was worldwide, but fortunately it inconvenienced the federal courts in Nebraska little, if at all, as I remember it.

My judicial problems in the first decade of the new millennium had a similar cause (human) but a lesser scope, though they were as nettlesome to fix. They included a charge of kidnapping and rape, a claim for a landlord's offering rentals for sex, carelessness with ethical obligations, and sexual harassment in the workplace.

In the early evening of April 6, 2001, Anthony Steven Wright, who preferred to be known as Anthony Steven Zappa, approached Anne Sluti in the parking lot of the Hilltop Mall in Kearney, Nebraska. After getting her into his blue Suburban, he drove north into South Dakota, then west into the hinterland of Montana. Fourteen months later Tony Zappa stood before me in a federal courtroom charged with two felonies: kidnapping Anne Sluti and brandishing a firearm in furtherance of the kidnapping.[33] Zappa was an imposing thirty-one-year-old, in both physique and manner. He stood six feet tall and weighed 247 pounds. Sluti was a petite seventeen-year-old.

Having learned that Zappa's criminal history included at least two convictions of burglaries of dwellings, one in Minnesota and one in Iowa, both classified as crimes of violence, as well as an attempted escape from custody in Lincoln a few days before trial began (involving his somehow being able to unlock his security shackles, leap from a marshal's van, and lead a chase across a highway before being overtaken), a report of a wild chase by Zappa from the FBI in the Mall of America in Minneapolis, and his attack on a man in Louisiana, I ordered that the trial be held in Omaha's federal courthouse, which was more secure and modern than Lincoln's.

During the trial, Zappa was reasonably docile but had moments of unrest. He was shackled at the ankles but free at the wrists in order to be able to take notes. Early on, he swore at the jury, called me a kangaroo judge, and in a separate incident slapped his attorney, Federal Public Defender David Stickman, in the face. At the sound of the slap deputy marshals pounced on Zappa and slammed him face-down on the counsel table so hard I thought he might well have a broken nose. I ordered him taken to a hospital for whatever medical treatment he needed. He was shortly returned, and he assured me he was not injured. I banished him from the courtroom with permission to watch the trial by closed-circuit television from the marshal's facilities until he told me he would be on good behavior. He returned to the courtroom the next morning and caused no further disruption.

At the end of a two-week trial and after deliberating for two hours, the jury found Zappa guilty of kidnapping and brandishing a firearm in furtherance of the kidnapping. I set September 16, 2002, as the date for sentencing. The revised presentence investigation report from the probation officer was received in due time, making a full description of Zappa's background, including familial, legal, medical, educational, and employment history.

His attorney, who at the sentencing was James Martin Davis, asked that Zappa not be classified as a career criminal and sought a downward departure from the range that the advisory Sentencing Guidelines recommended—anywhere from 360 months to life in prison. I heard the arguments and denied the motions.

At the sentencing hearing I selected phrases from the trial evidence and the revised presentence investigation report that enabled me to classify Zappa as a career criminal and to sentence him at the upper edge of the recommended sentence. I said that Zappa's treatment of Anne Sluti had been unusually cruel, brutal, and degrading to her. I cited the following acts:

Pointing a handgun at her
Beating her with his fist to get her into the car despite her screams
Forcing her to lie on the floor of the car
Chaining her hands behind her back and chaining her feet together
Tying a shirt over her eyes
Duct-taping her hands behind her back and her legs together at the ankles, knees, and thighs
Telling her she would be let go if she could free herself, and watching her cut herself on a barbed-wire fence in trying to free herself
Attempting to burn duct-tape from her wrists by a lighter, but burning her wrist
Ordering her to make telephone calls, monitoring them, and being unhappy when she did not say exactly what he told her to say
Again duct-taping her arms behind her back and her legs at the ankles, and taping her mouth and eyes shut

Cutting off her clothes with a knife and raping her despite her pleas not to and her saying truthfully that she was a virgin
Telling her he would take her to the mountains, where they would spend their lives together
Telling her he would make her like him and they would have sex three times a day
Telling her, after she found a way to call 911 and report her whereabouts, that it was all over for her and he might as well kill her now
Forcing his way into a cabin, smashing the telephone, burning her clothes that he had cut off her, and telling her some chains he took were for her
Raping her again
Taping her arms and legs together, taping her mouth, and putting her in the trunk of a Toyota Tercel
Forcing her to sleep in a bedroom with him with the door jammed shut by a coat hanger
Again chaining her and telling her he had better not hear the chains move
Telling her, "If they're going to catch us, we might as well have some fun," and again raping her
Telling her, when a law enforcement officer walked toward the door, "If you make a noise, I'll kill you. If I die, you die."
Using her to communicate with law enforcement officers during a ten-hour standoff with members of the sheriff's department
All in all, terrorizing for six days a seventeen-year-old girl who had done him no harm, violating her body, and leaving her with jagged emotional scars

During the trial Zappa was being held at the Nebraska Department of Correctional Services. He was overheard making comments to other inmates, such as "Wait until next week, make sure you watch the news. The shit is going to start to fly. I'm going to go into that courtroom with a machine gun and kill all of the guards, all of the cops, and then kill that fucking judge."

Upon examination at the Federal Medical Center in Springfield, Missouri, to stand trial, he was found to meet the criteria for antisocial personality disorder. The presentence report said that he had displayed a failure to conform to social norms by repeatedly engaging in criminal activity. "He displays," the report said, "no remorse for having hurt or mistreated others in the past."

I said, "While Mr. Zappa has complained of his medication having been responsible for some of his activities in the courtroom of the trial of this case, he has offered no evidence or claim that his six-day rampage of Anne Sluti was influenced by medication, illegal drugs, mental illness or alcohol." I then overruled the objections to the presentence investigation report, listened to the allocutions of counsel, and heard the defendant. He complimented his attorneys, apologized for disrupting the courtroom, apologized to Stickman for slapping him in the courtroom, and insisted that he did have remorse for things he had done. He did not identify the things for which he had remorse.

In my sentencing statement I said:

> I have reviewed . . . the background of Mr. Zappa. And all that background . . . results in a sense . . . of a person bent on committing crimes—unpredictable, irresponsible behavior. . . . And I've heard no sensible explanation of why . . . [the crimes before the kidnapping or during the kidnapping] happened. . . .
>
> His antisocial personality disorder, schizophrenia, . . . depression, are concerns . . . because one of the factors I have to consider is rehabilitation. And my experience only is that changing a person's makeup from those conditions is unlikely and dreary at the best. . . . [P]unishment is [not] the primary factor in this case, but it is an important one. . . .
>
> What sentence will help deter other persons who give some thought to committing crimes . . . similar to these? . . . I suppose the question is whether a life sentence will be important in deterring other people. I don't know, of course, . . . what any sentence would do in that regard. . . . [M]y judgment is that a life term would come closer

> to deterring other people than a period of a lot of years. And I remember . . . that Miss Sluti testified that Mr. Zappa at one point explained that he was a fugitive and that now that "we're across state lines, . . . I face a life sentence." So life [sentence] has . . . an impact, I think, on people. Even though it didn't stop him in . . . the continuation of his rampage, it stuck with him as having some significance to him. . . . Will it rehabilitate him, the life sentence? I don't—I don't think so. . . . I agree that age and time affect everybody, but . . . I can't count on age and time to rehabilitate Mr. Zappa, given his past and the difficulty he has produced for people in the past, culminating in this awful crime against Miss Sluti. The seriousness of the crime has to be considered, and I've already spelled out why I consider this to be a serious crime.

I continued, "[T]he sentence will be that Mr. Zappa is sentenced to the custody of the Bureau of Prisons for"—I paused for an instant, to be sure I said what I meant—"life on Count I. On Count II, the sentence is seven years and it is to be run consecutively to the life term. I understand that seems out of . . . the realm of possibility, but the law requires that it be consecutive, and so it will be."[34] The convictions and the sentences were confirmed on appeal.[35] Zappa filed thirty motions, some after the trial and some after the circuit court had affirmed his conviction and sentences. All were denied.

A once-in-a-lifetime story occurred in *Jennings v. King*.[36] Robert Lee Jennings was incarcerated in the Santa Cruz Unit of the Arizona State Prison System. In 1995 he filed suit against A. W. King, who was the grievance coordinator of the Santa Cruz Unit. Jennings claimed that King had denied him access to the courts, denied him due process of law, and retaliated against him for using the prison's grievance system and for writing to congressional representatives and the press about prison conditions.

Chief Judge Robert Broomfield of the District of Arizona assigned the case to me in March 1998. I granted summary judgment to the defendant, but on appeal the Ninth Circuit in August 2001 reversed my decision and remanded the case for trial of the retaliation claim.

In early April 2002 Jennings filed a motion to set the case for trial, and I set it for May 21 in Phoenix. Jennings, who had no lawyer, filed motions between May 2 and May 15 to change judges, for King to furnish Jennings information of the whereabouts of several people Jennings wanted to call as witnesses if he could find them, and to have counsel appointed for him.

Jennings, King's lawyer, and I had a telephone conference about the motions and other pretrial and trial matters on May 16 for trial on the 21st. Jennings was devoid of witnesses, except for himself, and, though he said he was trying hard, he insisted that King, King's lawyer, and I surely could furnish enough help to provide him a case. It seemed clear to everybody but Jennings that at that late date little, if anything, could be done for him. He said he did not want a delay of the trial, because any delay granted by me would be months, probably years long.

Also Jennings wanted me removed as the judge in the case because I had not granted a single one of the many motions he had filed, I had wrongly granted the other side a second chance to file a motion for a summary judgment, and, as was plain from the fact of reversal by the Ninth Circuit, I had wrongly granted the defense's motion for summary judgment. He was almost right about his facts. I hadn't granted any of his motions, except the one to set the case for trial. But I denied his motion to recuse me because I sometimes may be wrong, but not always. I then directed the defense counsel to provide to me the last known addresses of the three people Jennings said were critical to his case. She did, and I had subpoenas issued for them to appear at the trial. I also told Jennings I saw no way I could expect to be able to find any lawyer to represent him at a trial five days away, but I would try.

Finding a lawyer to be appointed to handle the case would be fruitless, I was sure. I called Stephen McNamee, by then a chief judge, who referred me to James McKay, staff attorney for the District of Arizona, who scooted me to Michelle Hamilton of the Federal Bar Association. None provided more than a breath of hope, but Hamilton said she'd do what she could.

Joyce, my judicial assistant Ellen Lefler, and I flew to Phoenix on Monday, May 20. Michelle Hamilton phoned me that afternoon at the hotel, saying she believed she had somebody who was willing to do the job. He was Larry Debus. I called him at once. He told me he had some connection with Omaha, had previous experience with civil rights cases, and would try to interview Jennings that evening. Unfortunately he was not able to find Jennings until the trial was under way the next day.

Tuesday morning, May 21, at the federal courthouse I told Jennings of my efforts and rising hopes. Jennings hadn't known until then that Debus had been located and, of course, hadn't talked with him. After half an hour of discussion with Jennings and the defense counsel about trial procedure, we gathered the prospective jury panel and proceeded with jury selection. When questioning of the jury panel was completed and peremptory challenges were set to be exercised, a new face entered the courtroom, looked wonderingly around, and said, when I asked him who he was, "I'm Larry Debus."

From that moment Debus assumed the representation of Jennings with Jennings's full cooperation. Debus had not met Jennings, had seen no part of the court file, had seen none of the papers Jennings had accumulated, and knew nothing of the nature of the case, except what I had told him: it was a section 1983 action by a prisoner for retaliation for exercising his First Amendment rights. I granted Debus's request for a fifteen-minute break to meet and talk with his client. Then we went forward with the trial.

Debus's representation of Jennings was nothing short of remarkable. He made a sensible, clear, fact-dominated opening statement immediately after lunch, and over the next two and a half days called and examined King as a witness, called and examined a Captain Brown (one of those Jennings wanted subpoenaed), and examined Jennings in excellent detail. He cross-examined the defendant's witnesses and made a splendid closing argument. It was a premier performance.

The jury found for the defendant, King, though I was a bit surprised. The jurors' questions to me for the witnesses had signaled an inclination to award Jennings something for King's taking away, during a house-cleaning search of Jennings's cell, his compilation of addresses and a stack of receipts for things he'd bought. Jennings was gracious in defeat, wishing me well, inviting me back to Phoenix, and obviously pleased with the help he'd been given in finding witnesses—only one of whom did him any good—and finding counsel for him, who had helped him a great deal, even in losing.

The defense counsel was Susanna Pineda of the Arizona Attorney General's Office, who taught me that residents of middle Spain pronounce the "d" in her name as "th." She won the case. There was no appeal.

When I first heard of having "model jury instructions," by which I visualized a set or sets of standing instructions prepared by a committee of lawyers, capable of being plopped down in front of a judge to apply in the case at hand, I sniffed at the idea. Every trial lawyer, I reasoned, needs a set of instructions tailored for the immediate case by counsel who were cognizant of the exact issues being raised in view of the specific facts of the case. I couldn't have been more wrong.

Happily I was asked by Chief Justice Paul White of the Supreme Court of Nebraska to serve on such a committee to prepare model jury instructions for the Nebraska bar. I served for more than twenty years and enjoyed it. When I took the federal bench, I served on a similar committee for preparing model instructions reflecting federal law for use in federal courts. I was on that committee from its inception in 1983 until early 2010, all because I learned to see the value in such a piece of work.

The goals and values of model jury instructions are, first, to be patterned after the applicable law of wide-ranging and often-litigated legal subjects, saving hours of time in research for practicing trial judges and trial lawyers; and, second, to use words in common usage to express the law for clarity of understanding by the jurors. Nothing is more important in a trial than that the jurors understand the law they are to apply.

What I didn't have the vision to see when I first heard of the proposal was that much of the work can be done by small committees of practicing lawyers—civil and criminal, plaintiff and defense—professors, and judges, thinking, reading, writing, huddling together, talking, debating, not to create law but to find and express for lay jurors law already made by legislators and judges. Of course, the versions of the committee's product will need to be tidied up to fit the peculiarities of the case on trial, but the product lets the trial lawyers and judges do the tidying up without having to do all the groundwork. Revisions to reflect changes in the law are made by the committee as needed. I am an avid supporter of model jury instructions.

(Entirely as an aside, the last of the Urboms' derring-dos was a whitewater rafting trip on the Arkansas River through the Royal Gorge in Colorado on July 7, 1991, with others of the Eighth Circuit Committee on Jury Instructions.)

In the federal system punitive damages—that is, damages in money for the purposes of punishing or disciplining a person or entity for bad behavior—are often allowable in civil cases, depending on how egregious was the conduct of the defendant. If the applicable law allows it, the jury as the fact finder decides whether money for punitive damages is to be awarded against the defendant and, if so, the amount. Generally the jury is left with little or no guidance as to how the amount is to be determined, but jury awards of punitive damages have sometimes been so huge that the court has stepped in to reduce the amount in a particular case. Not only the trial judge, but the appellate panel or full court on appeal may reduce the figure.

Little was done by the Supreme Court of the United States to restrain judgments of punitive damages until about the mid-1990s. At that point the Supreme Court entered the fray with decisions in *BMW of North America v. Gore* and followed with *State Farm Mutual Automobile Insurance Co. v. Campbell.*[37] In these cases the Court laid down three guideposts for setting punitive damages: (1) the degree of reprehensibility of the defendant wrongdoer, (2) the disparity between the actual harm and the potential harm suffered by the plaintiff, and (3) the difference between the punitive damages and the civil penalties that could be awarded in similar cases. It said that the U.S. Constitution's due process clause requires some proportionality between the compensatory damages awarded in a case and the punitive damages awarded. Indeed the Court declared that, although mathematical ratios are not binding, they "demonstrate what should be obvious: Single-digit multipliers are more likely to comport with due process, while still achieving the State's goals of deterrence and retribution, than awards with ratios in range of 500 to 1 . . . or, in this case, of 145 to 1."[38] That's helpful to a judge in deciding whether a jury's punitive damage award has been excessive. But what about letting the jurors know before they make a decision what the Supreme Court has said? I've had a fairly recent case in which punitive damages in my view had the prospect of being large if the jury accepted the plaintiffs' testimony in its entirety.[39]

The United States sued John R. Koch, a landlord, under the Fair Housing Act for allegedly trading or offering to trade rent for sex.[40] The suit was on behalf of nineteen women who rented or tried to rent houses from him. Most of the renters were single black women who were financially strapped, so I took the precaution of giving to the jury an addition to the usual punitive damage instruction. I said, "The amount of an award of punitive damage should have a reasonable relationship between that amount and the amount awarded an aggrieved person for actual damages as described in a previous instruction. Ordinarily, the relationship should be calculated in terms of a ratio, and in this case probably should not exceed a ratio of 7 to 1—that is, no more than punitive damages of 7 times the actual damages." Having heard all the evidence before I mentioned the 7-to-1 ratio to the jury, I would be in as good a position to make an assessment as I would be at any later time. It was made as my estimate of a maximum award if the jury were to decide punitive damages were warranted.

Maybe I needn't have been concerned. The trial before jury deliberations filled nine days, with each of the nineteen women telling of her encounter with the landlord: unwanted physical and verbal sexual advances, unwanted sexual touching, terms of a tenancy conditioned on the granting of sexual favors, and threats to take and then taking adverse action against them when they refused or objected to the sexual advances. The women testified to a variety of damage: embarrassment, loss of self-esteem, loss of trust in male landlords, contemplation of suicide, and loss of enjoyment of sex, in one case resulting in the breakup of a marriage. The jury deliberated thirty-two and a half hours over a five-day period. The verdict was for ten of the women who had rented or tried to rent houses owned by the defendant. Those ten were awarded a total of $16,967 in compensatory damages and $49,185 in punitive damages. The total punitive damages award was a ratio of slightly less than three times the compensatory damages awarded. One of the women received a punitive damages award of about 50 percent of the total punitive damages awarded for all ten women. She was the one who, at the government's request, wore a microphone and taped her conversation with the defendant, in which he suggested sex from her if she didn't have enough money to pay the rent.

The government moved for a new trial on the ground that the damage awards for the ten were too small. Although the awards were smaller than I expected, I concluded that they were not "plain injustice" or a "monstrous" or "shocking" result, which appeared to be the Eighth Circuit Court of Appeals' standard.[41] There was no appeal.

A couple of years earlier another case was notable, not only for its sexual harassment tone and my concern about what could be an extreme verdict of punitive damages, but also because of the number of plaintiffs. It was *Equal Opportunity Commission v. Dial Corporation*.[42] Having nineteen plaintiffs (or "aggrieved persons," as the Fair Housing Act calls them) in the *Koch* case was a jarring enough challenge for a jury. Having 101 plaintiffs in the *Dial* case raised challenges to a new level. Like the nineteen in the *Koch* case, the 101 made both pattern and practice claims and individual claims, and not as a class action. They sought compensatory and punitive damages and injunctive relief. That necessitated, I decided, a phased approach for disposition by trial, and not just one trial but several trials and several juries. The workplace was a plant in Aurora, Illinois. The trial was to be in Chicago.

The purpose of a "pattern or practice" case is to cast liability on the employer who creates or ignores policies that allow shoddy sexual advances against its employees. The individual claims of the women were for compensation for harms done to individuals by discrimination. I held before trial that deposition testimony of women workers was sufficient to show legitimacy to the claims of physically invasive behavior by male employees, touching women's breasts and buttocks, grabbing a woman employee by the crotch and jerking upward, males exposing their genitals while making suggestive or threatening remarks, repeated comments and conduct of a sexual nature, and open displays of sexually offensive pictures and calendars about the workplace—and that supervisors knew of the conduct but did little or nothing to stop it.

Working toward trial, a specific plan was developed and announced. It featured four trial phases. Phase I would decide whether a pattern or practice of offensive behavior by workers existed at the plant and, if so, when (the women's employment covered several different time periods). A jury would decide those issues. If Phase I found a pattern or practice had existed, Phase II would decide whether the pattern or practice was done with malice or reckless indifference on the part of the company management and, if so, what amount, if any, of punitive damages to the whole group of complaining women employees would be appropriate, using an assumption that all the women had been paid compensatory damages in full. The jury in Phase II would not learn how many women had filed claims or that some of them had signed releases. The question for the jury would be what amount of punitive damages, if any, would be needed for punishment and deterrence of Dial and deterrence of other employers who might be tempted to act as Dial had.

Phase III would decide the compensatory damages (sometimes called "actual damages," the amount of money that would compensate each woman for harm suffered from the pattern and practice) for the individual claims; this would require multiple juries, perhaps eight or ten claimants per jury. (I know now from the *Koch* case, but didn't know then, that nineteen claimants in one trial may be too many.) Each jury in Phase III would also arrive at an amount for punitive damages for each plaintiff whose claim was tried to that jury. Phase IV would consist of the apportionment of the punitive damages. The trial judge would decide the apportionment of the punitive damages to each plaintiff who had been awarded compensatory and punitive damages by a jury. The punitive damage award set for the entire group would serve as a cap; that is, the total of awards of punitive damages to individual plaintiffs in Phase IV could not total more than the punitive damages the Phase II jury had set for the entire group.

I concluded that the apportionment by the trial judge—with the appellate judges always being at hand on appeal—would be compatible with past practice and the rationale of the Supreme Court in cases of *State Farm Mutual* and *BMW of North America, Inc. v. Gore.*[43] Having the benefit of two juries' decisions and having heard the evidence on all issues, the judge would be in a position to comport with the Supreme Court's insistence that judges are to have a key role in holding punitive damages to an award "based on an 'application of law, rather than a decision maker's caprice.'"[44]

The *Dial* case was settled without a trial. A decree in accordance with the settlement was entered, providing for protection from coarse sexual acts by employees and monitoring of management's duties. So we didn't get to use the plan I'd developed. Not yet.

It is no secret that I have high regard for lawyers, particularly trial lawyers. It arises out of long experience with them. I see them in their special role—to stand beside the victim of child abuse, the child abuser, the drug dealer, the smut peddler, the consumer, the powerful, the powerless, the insolent, the shiftless, the helpless, the poor, the rich, the injured, the wrongdoer, the innocent, the guilty, the government, the governed—and not to leave that place until the search for equal justice has run its course. That's the charge for the trial lawyer.

Trial lawyers are not faultless. Sometimes they fumble or stumble. The manner of the fumble or stumble varies, of course. Some lawyers do commit crimes, and when they do, they must be treated like anyone else, and probably more harshly if the crime involved a breach of trust. Trial lawyers are held to a standard higher than the strictures of the law—by codes of conduct established by organizations to which the lawyers belong, such as the American Bar Association, state bar associations, the American College of Trial Lawyers, the National Association of Criminal Defense Lawyers, and others.

Many opportunities lie in wait for a lawyer to fumble or stumble. One showed its face in a case in the District of Arizona, a case that was filed in 1997 and ended in 2001.

The lawsuit was filed by California Public Employees Retirement System (CALPERS) and others against Arthur Andersen LLP, who was the defendant and third-party plaintiff. Three companies, collectively known as the National IPF Company (NIPF), were third-party defendants.[45]

In the *CALPERS* case, discovery—the gathering of business papers of each party by every other party—was formidable and exacting. Court orders directed that each party make available to other parties huge amounts of documents. Mindful that some business documents would undoubtedly contain confidential information, such as communications between a client and the client's attorney, a system was carefully worked out for protecting confidential documents from being received, for example, "[A]ll [NIPF] documents must be Bates-labeled and copied on site by NIPF personnel [to be eligible for receipt]."[46] The ethical question was this: What should attorneys in the case do if they find they are accidentally in possession of a document that clearly contains confidential information relevant to the case being worked on but not marked, as required, with a Bates stamp?

At least one such confidential document of the NIPF Companies was found in the accidental possession of an employee of Snell & Wilmer, the law firm representing Arthur Andersen. It was a memorandum written by Michele DiPasquale, an employee of NIPF, to NIPF's attorneys, dated August

25, 1997. About five copies were made of the memorandum and distributed to other employees or officers of Snell & Wilmer or Arthur Andersen. Five persons read the document. They discussed returning the document and destroying all copies, but the document was not returned to NIPF until the Tuesday after the Thursday it was received. At least five days elapsed between the memorandum's being recognized as a confidential document and its return to its owner. All copies were destroyed promptly after that.

CALPERS's and NIPF's attorneys quickly filed motions for sanctions against Arthur Andersen and Snell & Wilmer. After presentation of evidence and briefs for all parties, I wrote a memorandum and order dated March 19, 1999. I reviewed the various sources of law entitling a court to impose sanctions, made findings of the facts from the evidence presented, and wrote the following concluding paragraph:

> I think the prevailing view of the profession is that receiving a confidential document when it was not supposed to have been received must be treated much as having a red hot poker. When the poker is in hand, there is but one proper course—let go of it. Waiting to see if it will soon be cool holds no appeal. Deciding to think about it because it may not really be as hot as it seems is a poor choice. Letting go of it—at once—is the appropriate behavior. So, holding a confidential communication inappropriately received calls for the same treatment. Failure to follow it is enough indication of bad faith to warrant a remedy under the inherent powers of this court.

The remedy included barring from any further activity in the *CALPERS* case the six persons who were directly involved in the receiving or reading of the DiPasquale document. Most of the fees and expenses incurred by CALPERS and NIPF as a result of the receipt of that memorandum by the defense were chargeable to Snell & Wilmer. The DiPasquale memorandum could not be used in any way in the defense of the lawsuit or the prosecution of Arthur Andersen's cross-claim. The time spent by Snell & Wilmer's members or associates related to the DiPasquale memorandum and the motions prompted by its possession would not be deemed compensable by Arthur Andersen or Snell & Wilmer or their associates.

There was no appeal.

In October 2001 Professor Jeffrey B. Morris of Touro College in Huntington, New York, visited me in my office to talk about a book he was writing, *The History of the Eighth Circuit*. His hope, I think, was to get some variety in his exploration of the circuit by having brief conversations with some district judges.

After a few friendly exchanges, he asked me what it takes to make a first-rate trial judge. I pondered long enough to give him my off-the-cuff answer. But later I wrote him, rephrasing parts of what I had said. The letter read:

> Here is what I think makes a first-rate trial judge:
>
> A sense of the importance of fairness.
>
> A willingness to flesh out the legitimate interest of all the parties, honor them and deal with them respectfully.
>
> A willingness to honor the law. Sometimes the law is not what the judge would like it to be, but there is no more excuse for a judge to violate the law than for anyone else.
>
> Knowledge of the law, of course, is important, but most of the time a judge is well-advised to listen to the lawyers and be guided by them.
>
> A trial judge must be adjustable, particularly in procedural matters. Conversations between the judge and lawyers must be open, honest and trustworthy. The judge sets the tone for the way lawyers treat each other and their clients.
>
> Jurors are key decision makers, and the judge must carefully see that they are given the information they need in a form they understand.
>
> I am indebted to you for making me think about this.

That's a pretty good statement of what I believe. Appearing as a lawyer before judges, who have been my tutors, watching those judges perform, and listening to them, as well as analyzing my own experiences and trying to be the best I can be have affirmed the nub of that statement.

I've been lucky beyond measure. A letter to J. Marvin Weems gives an example:

Dear Marv:

For anybody to consider seriously—and follow that with a recommendation to the Attorney General—that I be named to the Supreme Court of the United States is heady stuff. No position in the world is more respected by me.

I wish I were attracted to the appointment for something other than the honor of it.

The fact is that I would not enjoy the work. Perhaps I can best explain by comparing prime duties of a District Court judge with those of a Supreme Court justice:

A district judge deals with people; a justice, with ideas. A judge presides at trials; a justice hears arguments. A judge makes decisions; a justice renders opinions. A judge's decision is effective unless on appeal enough others disagree; a justice's opinion is not effective unless enough others agree.

A judge's look at a controversy is first; a justice's is last. You see, I love where I am, and this is where I want to remain. You have complimented me beyond measure, but please pursue the matter no further.

Sincerely yours,
Warren Urbom

Luck has come my way in torrents. I was born to a good family. I married a perfect wife and have loving children and grandchildren of wide passions and goals. I have been in a noble profession with people I admire. For the past forty years I have had a job I loved.

There are perks that go with being a trial judge. No free membership to an exclusive country club, no free season tickets to the Husker football games, no special seats at the symphonies. Nothing of the sort has ever been offered, I'm pleased to say. But there have been better ones:

Like conducting wedding ceremonies for each of our four children—Kim, Randy, Allison, and Joy—to young persons they were in love with: Scott, Kelli, Jeff, and Tony.

Like an evening off to watch the Rager "Grands" play a streak-of-lightning card game of Nertz and proclaiming themselves World Champions.

Like going on Saturday mornings to the courtroom at the federal building to play "Court" with grandchildren and our own made-up-on-the-spur-of-the-moment cases, taking turns being judge, lawyer, defendant, witness, and juror, and finding the defendant guilty or not guilty.

Like being blown away by grandson Grant's dazzling drums.

Like oohing and aahing at grandson Alex's high school performance as the Ugly Duckling in *Honk*.

Like being invited by granddaughter Georgi to attend her second-grade class, there being introduced by her and talking with the class about being Georgi's "Papa" and about solving cases.

Like being invited by granddaughter Tommie to attend her second-grade class, there being introduced by her, talking with the class about being a judge, about being a lawyer, and about being Tommie's "Papa," and listening to Tommie and her quartet sing a song they'd composed about saying no to drugs.

Like walking hand-in-hand with grandson Joe Warren to get our first glimpse at his brand-new baby sister, Samantha.

Like being in the delivery room and seeing grandson Jacob lifted from his mother's womb.

Like playing Wii bowling with grandson Jacob.

Like taking a day off to play caroms with Joe Warren and Sami and Jacob or playing Wii with Joe Pat, and another day watching two-year-old great-granddaughter McKhenzie joyfully spraying her face with a water stream at the Children's Museum.

Didn't I say this being a judge is the best job in the world? Maybe now you can see why I love it so!

Diminuendo

Closing Down

Given my questionable youthful experience with music, it may seem odd to use a musical term to summarize my closing phase. But my early musical efforts had to do with trying to *make* music, nothing more. *Listening* to most music is easy and a joy, but making it is drudgery for me. On the other hand, whether musical or not, a word that exudes the right message is a treat for me.

"Diminuendo" means "diminution," and diminution means, musically, "variation of a theme by shortening, usually halving, the time value of the notes."[1] There you have it: varying the theme by shortening the time value of the notes. That's what happening in my life, but not by my design. Cancer, the killing of a man, advancing years—they gang up on a person to shorten the time value of the notes of life. Let's talk about that.

The first clue came on Friday, February 7, 1997. Joyce's routine physical examination uncovered a suspicious-looking left breast. A biopsy ten days later showed cancer. If the nipple was involved, we understood, at least a mastectomy of the breast would be required, and a reconstruction with an implant would be done at the same time.

Our three daughters—Kim, Allison, and Joy—flew in to give assurance of family concern and support. For all of us the whole scene was an emotional collision.

I spent the week of February 10 trying a lawsuit, *Callins v. Seven L's*, to a jury in Tampa.[2] On Friday the 14th at noon I submitted the case to the jury and flew back to Lincoln, two days before the scheduled biopsy. Judge Steve Merryday agreed to receive the verdict when the jury had made a decision.

Nobody knew what Monday the 17th would bring. The check-in was at 7:30 a.m. The surgery began at 10:20, and by 2 p.m. it was over. The surgeon, Dr. "Bad News" Reed, as he dubbed himself, reported immediately after the mastectomy that he had removed thirteen lymph nodes, of which five had tumors. That meant, we were sure, chemotherapy at least or chemotherapy and radiation at worst were in store. The breast had to be removed, but the surgery had gone well. Joyce was rolled into room 773, groggy and eyes half open. I took her hand and she murmured, "Oh, Warren, they had to take it!"

"I know."

"I never thought they would."

"Neither did I. But it'll be all right."

Within moments she regained her composure, as well as her great sense of humor. Our friends Jackie Robertson and Fran Bates had been with us from early morning. When Jackie picked up the phone to talk with her husband, Bud, she told Joyce that Bud had been there all morning too.

"Good," said Joyce, "Bud owes me one," referring to her having sat with Jackie during some of Bud's surgeries. (We had been friends for some sixty years.) Jackie held the phone to Joyce's ear, and Joyce said, "We've spent a lot of time talking about your testicles. Now we'll have to talk about my breast."

After a pause listening to his response, Joyce said, "No, Bud, but maybe when we get to know each other better, you can show me your testicles and I can show you my breast."

The next sentence we heard was, "Come to think of it, I can't, because I don't have anything to show."

And a moment later she chuckled, "Oh, Bud, that's right. Neither do you! So that puts us back to just *talking* about it."

All this in her groggy state. Their inside joke, stemming from his previous cancer surgery, lived on.

Dr. Scot Sorensen, an oncologist, proved to be enormously reassuring—realistic but reassuring. Chemotherapy, he said, will be the regimen. Four treatments, each three weeks apart. Joyce will lose her hair, but whether it will otherwise adversely affect her nobody knows. When the final tests have been completed in perhaps ten days, he will schedule the treatments. She is essentially cancer-free; all the lymph nodes on the left side had been removed. But there may be other malignant cells somewhere in her body, so the recommendation is that systemic treatment be given intravenously to kill them, wherever they are. Probably 80 percent of women who have Joyce's symptoms will have a recurrence without treatment. We agreed that the treatment was to be done. The road was fixed.

Friends were wonderful. They came, cheered us, cried with us, prayed with us, laughed with us. All available shelf space was filled with flowers and plants.

The eight-member jury I had left in Tampa was having a hard time with deliberations. Judge Merryday reported to me by telephone, and I fed him ideas to try, such as yielding to the jury's request to have a witness's deposition read to them, allowing the lawyers to reargue the case, asking for ideas from the jury. None of the suggestions resolved the deadlock. Merryday was on the verge of getting an agreement, he said, that I would decide the case without input of the jury. Instead he received approval of the lawyers and their clients of a majority verdict of the jurors. The result was a majority verdict for the defendants on the claim of racial discrimination and a majority verdict for the plaintiff on the claim of retaliation for $15,000. It was a good verdict, I thought, and one that closely matched what I would have done. The resilience of the lawyers and parties to wrestle with many alternatives to find a satisfactory end to a difficult dispute was a heartwarming rarity.

Joyce's first night's sleep at home, Wednesday, was somewhat fitful but otherwise okay. Randy arrived on Thursday, after a frustrating and unsuccessful day at the Phoenix airport to get on standby. Determined to look and feel her best for her family, Joyce was driven by Randy to Kevin Moore's shop for a hair appointment on Friday noon. She looked and felt great. Allison helped us, as did the home health care nurse, drain the excess fluid from the breast and bandage the breast-long incision and the drainage outlet.

Coping wasn't easy. Joyce was bedeviled by the memory that many of her friends and acquaintances had died from breast cancer. In response she made a list of all those who had *survived* breast cancer. I admired her diligence in finding antidotes for troubling fears.

Joyce said God's gift in all this was the coming home of all our children. Each child—none is a child, except to us—has been special: sad, strong, sympathetic, sensitive, sensible (all those good "s" words), and more. Joyce and I knew we had a beautiful family, and we loved them more than we could say.

Kim used her inquiring mind to probe the feelings of all of us, but especially her mother's. Kim's experience with counseling served Joyce well. Kim wanted to know, several times, how her mother felt inwardly and offered thoughts about handling those feelings. She wisely limited the involvement of her own children by having only twelve-year-old Chris come. The University of Nebraska women's basketball team, of which Chris was the de facto mascot, was playing twice while Chris was in Lincoln, so not only did those games help pass the time, but Charlie Rogers, the starting center though only a freshman, took Chris under her wing and spent hours with him. He idolized her, and she was an untiring friend.

Randy didn't come for the surgery because, when he asked me whether he needed to come, I said no and suggested he come later, when his mother might need some support after others had left. But after getting our reports on the surgery, he chose the better part and came. When he arrived Thursday afternoon, he found her on her bed, and they wept together.

Randy was at his best in doing fix-ups: repairing a limping kitchen chair leg or rearranging the guest bedroom to distance sleepers from the TV and VCR noise in the next room. There were even more challenging projects, like helping me select a new refrigerator from Montgomery Ward, educating me about electric drill tools, and fixing scrambled eggs for his mother.

Daughter Allison flew in from Dallas with Samantha, eight and a half months old. Allison's nursing expertise was good for us all. She was adroit at asking the right questions of the doctors and interpreting the answers for us. She was excellent on the phone, answering our friends' inquiries while protecting Joyce's need for quiet. She learned how to change Joyce's drain and taught us. And she came early to help prepare Joyce for the tough road ahead. She was always reassuring and comforting.

Samantha was a joy. Audra Hamilton, my law clerk, sat with her one day;

Shirley Ekdahl, our pastor's wife, another. The rest of the time, Sam, as we called her, was with one of us, often Aunt Joy. For a time Sam was even in Joyce's hospital room. In the brief week she was here, Sam crawled for the first time, held her own bottle, cut her first tooth, and recognized Allison's distinctive voice and reached for her. We loved having her.

Daughter Joy was picked up at 6:30 p.m. in Omaha, fresh from work and stunningly dressed. She dovetailed into the family setting at once. She had encouraged Allison to bring Samantha and sat with Sam quite a lot so Allison could "do her medical bit." She was, as always, skillful at observing and remembering—like the seating arrangement of our family, who sat where when the kids were growing up. She set up the buffet at our home day after day, did dishes, and greeted callers, always with a smile. She coiffed her mother's hair. She shared her husband Tony's stories with us, prompting Joyce to call Tony to tell him that he could not come to our house again without a "big [engagement] ring." Joy took the teasing with grace.

Chris was a pleasure to have. He stayed at our home, took care of himself a lot, went golfing with Bud Robertson one afternoon, and gave Joyce an "I Love You, Grandma" book. On his last afternoon here, Joyce entertained Chris with her "minute mysteries," which he assured her he needn't write down because he was sure to remember them.

Through all this Joyce was great—strong, realistic, hopeful, devastated but determined, cheerful and sad. Her sense of humor remained. She frequently joshed boldly "This is *my* time" or gave us a wimpy "I've had *surgery*, you know!" to bring us playfully into line.

The rarity of all this—having all our children here for a few days to talk, to mesh, to give, to receive, to love—boggled the mind and made us inexpressibly grateful, even though it took a startling and painful event to make it happen.

As for me, I tried to be single-minded. Being with Joyce was paramount, doing whatever needed to be done for her. Ellen brought or sent work from the office, and I was able to do it at home, but there was not much of it. I canceled a projected three weeks of Chicago trials that were to begin on March 17, and got relieved of a Denver assignment of four to six weeks.[3]

By the end of February Dr. Sam Bryant was cautious about the redness that had appeared around the breast implant. That redness soon burst into infection, postponing the beginning of chemotherapy. Joyce went through three medications, but none halted the infection. Surgical removal of the implant became a necessity and was accomplished on March 31. Chemotherapy was launched the next day.

During the next several weeks, the day after each four-hour treatment was a good day; the next day was usually a downer, reeking of Joyce's depression and doubts. She cried, worried about being a bad patient, and felt she was making it hard on me. She wasn't. She was a wonderful patient—upbeat, cooperative, reliant but never demanding. We were just learning how chemotherapy would affect her.

The idea of getting an aquarium originated with Joyce's admiring Kim's three. I'd been lukewarm about it because of the imposition on others when we would have to ask them to care for the fish during our travels. But Joyce's steadiness in wanting one, Kim's encouragement, and Kayla Kula's (the wife of my law clerk Ken Kula) remembering how her mother felt relaxed and peaceful watching her fish during an illness, convinced me not to obstruct. Kim's visit one weekend provided the occasion for her to pick out the aquarium, the gravel, the ornaments, and other accoutrements. She brought all of it to our house and exclaimed how friendly and helpful the proprietor of the store had been. Two days later the proprietor, Sandy Knox of Fish World, came and assembled everything. A day or so later Sandy stocked the tank with eight tiny fish, and Joyce named them all.

The sunroom, which needed attention, became a place of beauty. Kim and Joyce tossed away the unneeded accumulation, redistributed books, sorted snapshots, and soon had graced the room with a beautiful thirty-gallon aquarium. The room was a place of quiet and contentment for the twelve weeks of chemotherapy. Then I understood how important the aquarium was to her.

The weeks of chemotherapy were a success: hard, tiring, bedeviling with mouth sores, vomiting, and diarrhea, but finally free of all cancer.

And that's the way it stayed for eleven years. We had begun to believe it wouldn't happen again.

On September 8, 2006, I had a car accident. A man on a motorcycle was killed as a result of my not seeing him. That morning I left Dr. David Bigler's office following my regularly scheduled examination and treatment of my head, arms, and torso for signs of precancer growths. My next appointment was for 11:30 a.m. to speak on the subject of "the issues of the Wounded Knee trials" at the meeting of the downtown chapter of Kiwanis at the Windsor Stables. By about 10:50 I was driving my 1990 Buick Riviera west on J Street, a one-way street consisting of five lanes, the one on the far left being for left turns. My intent was to make my way to that lane and turn left onto 13th Street. I looked in my side mirror, saw no moving vehicle, flipped on my left-turn signal, and began my leftward movement. Suddenly I saw a flash outside the left front window. A motorcycle was passing me from the rear. It was just beside my car. In an instant the right side of the motorcycle collided with my car's left front fender. The motorcycle tipped to its left and slid on its side into the intersection of 13th and J. I stopped the car. I ran to the driver of the motorcycle, who was lying on his left side, just to the west of the motorcycle, except for one leg that appeared to be under the motorcycle. I saw blood on his face. I leaned over him. I don't recall saying anything to him. By then one or two other persons were with me. One said, "911 has already been called." The man lying in the street made movements toward getting up. More than one person told him not to move, but he persisted, and within a few seconds one man helped him to a sitting position while another man and I lifted the motorcycle to free his leg. The motorcyclist then put his hands on his helmet and pushed on it. One of the bystanders urged him not to take off his helmet, but he continued to push, and the bystander helped take it off. Someone asked him if he hurt, and when he nodded yes, he also drew his one arm over his chest, signaling, I think, that his chest hurt. Someone said that an ambulance would arrive soon.

An ambulance did arrive quickly—in a very few minutes—and police similarly were on the scene very soon. The ambulance loaded the victim and drove him away. Police personnel were busily viewing the scene, interviewing witnesses, and one officer, a woman, talked with me. I told her what I remembered of the accident. I said I wasn't sure what lane I had been in at the time of the impact, but from the positions of the vehicles after the collision, it was pretty clear that I had not been in the turning lane.

My mind was clear and confused at the same time. As I thought back, I asked myself questions: *Did I really look in the side mirror and not see this motorcycle?* I was sure I had looked but saw nothing—nothing at all. No car, no motorcycle, nothing. *Did I turn my head to the left to look back?* No, I think I didn't. *Didn't I realize I was turning to the left, where my blind eye couldn't see any danger?* Of course I did. But I didn't turn my head. I should have. *Why didn't I?* I don't know. *Which lane was I in?* I'm not sure. I thought it was the turning lane, but where my car stopped was not the turning lane, so I must have been in the lane next to the turning lane when we collided. I'm not sure.

After a few minutes the policewoman told me they had a report that the victim had been administered at least one resuscitation effort and that in cases of serious injury the accident investigation unit of the Lincoln Police Department would be called to investigate. A woman police officer—maybe the same one, I don't know—asked me if I needed anything. I said I was supposed to speak at Kiwanis at the Windsor Stables at 11:30, so I would appreciate someone's going there and telling them of my predicament. She said she would go. I don't know whether she did.

A little bit later she said she needed a recorded statement from me and drove me to the police station, where I answered her questions before a recording machine.

By 12:20 or so the officer said the police didn't need me any more and asked where I wanted to go. I didn't really know what to say. I couldn't do anything to help the man I'd tipped off the motorcycle, but I was sure he was in good hands at the hospital. The officer told me my car would be held for the time being. I said that, although the Kiwanians probably had given up on me, I would like to stop by the Windsor Stables to apologize for missing my commitment. She took me there and drove away. I told the Kiwanians I was sorry but I'd had an accident. They had finished their lunch and were ready for the program. They said that someone from their club had volunteered to present something, but that, if I could, they would welcome my speaking. I said I felt shaky and didn't know the condition of the man I'd hurt but thought I could speak. I proceeded with my speech, though I confess I thought so much about the man I hardly knew what I was saying. I spoke only a little while and sat down. They were very kind. One of the members, Hubert Seng, offered to take me where I wanted to go. I said I had a sentencing scheduled at the federal courthouse at 1:30, so he drove me there. I did the sentencing, finished at about 1:50, and as I reentered my chambers the policewoman came to the outer office door. I asked her how he was. She said he had passed away. My shoulders and head slumped. I felt terrible, annoyed at myself, wishing I had gone to the hospital right after the accident, but knowing I couldn't. The police hadn't said I could leave the scene and were holding my car.

The policewoman said that in cases involving a fatality the law required the taking of a blood sample. I went with her to Bryan LGH West Hospital and gave a blood sample. She offered to take me where I wanted to go. I said I would like to go to Trinity United Methodist Church, where my wife would be, and she could take me home. I met Joyce at the church and told her what had happened. I told her I had decided to quit driving. The fact that my blind left eye made it easier to miss seeing things on my left side and the newly developed dark spot in my seeing eye convinced me that my driving days were over. I stewed that I hadn't decided that one day sooner.

I have not driven since then, and my license has lapsed.[4]

I had learned from the police officer who took me for the blood test and to the church that the victim was Fred McEntarffer; she gave me his address. On the way home I mentioned to Joyce that I wanted to call on the McEntarffer family the next morning. She agreed.

The next morning, the 9th, I found the McEntarffers' telephone number and dialed it. A young man answered. I told him who I was and that I wanted to come to see the family whenever it was all right to come. I could tell that he turned from the phone and asked somebody whether it was all right for me to come; he then answered yes. I asked if it would be all right for my wife to drive me there that morning, leaving immediately. He said, "Yes, that would be fine."

We didn't know what to expect. We felt bad, and we were sure the family, whoever they were, would feel worse. Whether they would be friendly or enraged or in between, we had no idea. Joyce drove me to the southwest area of Lincoln, with which we were only slightly familiar, and we quickly found what we doubted was the correct street. We saw a young man and a young woman standing on the right-hand side of the street we were on, and Joyce slowed down alongside them. I rolled down my passenger's window and began to ask where the address was. Before I could get my question fully out, the young man said, "This is it. You've found the place!" Joyce pulled to a stop and I got out of the car and waited while Joyce parked it. Immediately the man said, "I want you to know there are no hard feelings here." My relief was real.

I approached the young man and the woman with him. He embraced me and said, "Mother is waiting inside for you." The house was a mobile home, comfortably kept. In it were several people, including Mrs. Laurie McEntarffer, two of her sons, one daughter-in-law, and one granddaughter. Mrs. McEntarffer put her arms around me, and I put mine around her. I told her I was so very sad. We both cried. She said, "God knew we both needed this meeting for our healing." I asked her whether she had been able to see her husband in the hospital before he died. She said she had not, that the doctors would not let her see him until he got "cleaned up," and by the time he was cleaned up he was gone. She said she was told he had punctured lungs from broken ribs and they couldn't stop the bleeding.

She wanted to know how the accident had happened because she hadn't heard many details. I told her as completely as I could. I apologized. I told her I was sorry—more than I could describe. She said she hadn't slept the night before, and I said I hadn't either. We cried. The other family members were mostly quiet, but some of them asked questions, and all were respectful and kind. Joyce helped me express my sorrow as well as her own. When we asked about the funeral, we learned that it would be delayed because one son, Fred Jr., was a missionary in New Guinea and probably could not get home for several days. There were four sons, I believe, and one daughter.

As we were getting ready to leave, one of the sons or a son-in-law said something like, "We've been told that forgiveness is a way of life, and we're just trying to walk the walk." We ended our hour together by forming a circle, holding hands, and praying.

As we walked to our car, a woman who identified herself as being from KOLN-TV pulled up in a car and asked me if I would give a statement on camera. I said I couldn't do that. I had no clue as to how she might have learned of my intention to be there. One of the McEntarffer sons walked up and said to the woman, "We've been together as a family, and all we want is for you to leave the judge alone." We drove away. I don't know whether the woman sought an interview with the McEntarffer family.

In the middle of the next week we called Mrs. McEntarffer and learned that Fred Jr., the missionary, had gotten home and that we could come to the family home that evening. Joyce drove us there, and we spoke with the gathered family, including Fred Jr. and his wife and children. We learned the plans for the funeral at the Berean Church in Lincoln, and attended it.

On the Tuesday following the accident Investigator Marlon Hohenstein came to our townhouse and presented me with a complaint charging me with misdemeanor motor vehicle homicide. The hearing date in the county court was set for October 10. A couple of days later Jean Lovell, a member of our church and a county judge, came to our home and explained the workings of the court, saying that usually, in cases of first-time violators, when the charge is a misdemeanor motor vehicle homicide, the county attorney and the offender agree to disposition by pretrial diversion, by which the charge is dismissed and the offender agrees to perform community service of a designated amount and to pay the costs of the prosecution and the pretrial diversion agency. The motor vehicle homicide could be renewed if conditions of the diversion were not performed.

I talked with Robert Grimit, a friend with whom I had practiced law probably a dozen years, about representing me. He thought I didn't need an attorney, but I felt I did, because I was too emotional to speak for myself, particularly if I would need to appear in court. I engaged him and told him that if the usual disposition in cases like this for persons with no previous criminal record was, as I had heard from Judge Lovell, for pretrial diversion, I would like to volunteer to work with the Lincoln Literacy Council, helping people learn to read and write or to learn to read and write better. He called Gary Lacey, the county attorney, who said such an option would be a very good one and agreeable to him. Within a few days I had been interviewed by a young woman at Diversion Services, and an instrument was drawn outlining the plan by which I agreed to work one hundred hours with Lincoln Literacy Council within a year's time. It was soon approved by the county attorney and the charge was dismissed.

On October 9, the day before my scheduled appearance before the county court, I learned that no court appearance would be necessary. That afternoon one of Laurie McEntarffer's sons phoned and asked what time my hearing would be the next day. I explained that no hearing would be necessary. His response was, "Oh, I'm sorry! My brothers and I wanted to be there and stand up for you." I have been overcome with gratitude by the McEntarffer family's kindness.

Joyce decided she too wanted to participate in the literacy endeavor. We attended fifteen hours of training by Lincoln Literacy Council to teach others to speak, read, and write English. Nearing the last session, Joyce and I were asked to work specifically with persons who wanted to become citizens of the United States. We gladly agreed.

Working with eager persons who spoke fair English but needed help understanding the facts and words of American history and government made us feel we were contributing to the health of the country. Most of our citizens-to-be were immigrants from Vietnam, China, Iran, Iraq, Democratic Republic of Congo, Venezuela, Brazil, Mexico, and Kazakhstan. We met with groups ranging from two to six persons, hardly ever consisting of more than one from any single country. They were all adults of varying ranges of experiences and of learning ability. We enjoyed them. The hundred hours and the required one year of community service sped by, and we stayed on for another year, finally yielding to the weight of other demands.

Joyce and I have thought often of the McEntarffers, a beautiful family. We have exchanged Christmas cards and wished each other well. Unhesitating forgiveness is holy. Yes, holy. I know, because I have been touched by it.

After feeling good about Joyce's being cancer-free for eleven years, we were optimistically geared to going for twelve. On Wednesday, March 19, 2008, Joyce had what was thought to be an easy "band aid surgery" for removal of her gall bladder by Dr. Miles Tommeraasen at St. Elizabeth Hospital in Lincoln. It didn't work out that way. The surgery began about 10:30 a.m. and ended at about 2:30, which suggested something unusual. The doctor sent word midway that he had to go "open," which he had explained in our pre-op consultation a week before meant there was not enough room to remove the gall bladder through the belly button incision.

Actually it was more than that. He couldn't see much with the scope, he told us, so he opened a new, larger wound, removed the gall bladder, and, seeing some fluid around the gall bladder that is sometimes a sign of cancer, he dug fairly deeply into the pelvic area. He felt a large mass, forming what he called a "frozen pelvic mass." He took specimens, including a lymph node, and sent them to the lab. The results came Thursday—the cancer had returned.

Our children flew in, not all four at once, but each for several days. Allison flew in from Dallas the day after the surgery. She asked excellent questions of Dr. Tommeraasen and got the available answers. Nausea kept Joyce uncomfortable for a couple of days, but by the Sunday after the surgery she awakened in a much happier state. When Fran Bates talked to her on the phone, she said, "I think I would have been better yesterday, if I hadn't been so sick!" Joyce called it a Joyce-ism; we agreed.

We soon met Dr. Cary Peterson, the oncologist, and heard his proposal for living with cancer. He suggested hormonal treatment, part of a national study being conducted to see whether a regimen of two hormonal units can better be taken together or separately. Joy and I rejoiced at the conference because it assumed the hormonal treatment to be preferable. Joyce was less enthusiastic because the doctor explained that the cancer is not curable; it is only treatable. While we all put on our happy faces, we had our moments of tears. As Joyce was readying herself for bed that evening, she said to Joy, "Now what is it we are happy about?" But by the next morning she favored being a part of a national study to help masses of people fight the cancer fight.

When Randy arrived, Joy had returned home. Kim, Allison, and Randy had rousing fun sitting around the kitchen table, laughing at each other's reactions to life, kidding each other. What a pleasure! It was good to have Randy there. Not only was he funny and clever, but he was more relaxed than we had seen him in many years. More, he saw the confidence and resilience of his mother, and that quieted his jitters. The whole bunch loved solving crossword puzzles, though Kim probably was better characterized as mildly willing to put up with our enthusiasm.

The PET and CT scans in mid-April found the only observable cancer in two small places at the region of the left breast's position before the breast was removed eleven years ago. There had been cancer in the gall bladder and lymph nodes, but they were removed in the surgery by Dr. Tommeraasen. On April 23 I spent half a day at the office—the most time I had spent there for the past thirty-four days.

The summer of 2008 was occupied by driving, Joyce doing much of it, our granddaughter Joy Rager helping when available. Beyond driving me to and from work and elsewhere as needed, Joyce wanted to see her children and grandchildren—all of them—so she and I did. Most of the trips were several-day junkets. All were uplifting to her.

On November 17, 2008, Dr. Tommeraasen surgically removed two small nodules in Joyce's left breast area; both nodules showed cancer.

She'd been having stomach trouble. A C-scan on December 8 showed some fluid in the stomach wall, and a scope examination revealed areas of "nodularity." Some nodules were tested and showed cancer in the stomach lining.

That ended Joyce's part in the national study, and she was shifted to a different kind of hormonal treatment—one injection a month for the cancer, and a fourteen-day dosage of antiviral pills for ridding the stomach of infection.

Joyce drove us to St. Louis on December 23, avoiding the snow and ice predictions. We had a wonderful gathering of the Urbom bunch, including all our children and all their children, except Grant (no job or money) and Alex (moving to a different apartment in Los Angeles, having graduated from UCLA in theater arts). Wii, the latest in toys and a Christmas present from and to the Taylor family, dominated our stay. We spent hours bowling, plus some time on baseball, golf, and tennis, all on the Wii. Jacob and Joe Pat were whizzes at the bowling spree. Jacob had a high of 245, as I recall.

By January 7 in the new year, 2009, Joyce had finished the fourteen days of medicines to curb the infection in the stomach lining. She felt good, and we flew to Tampa to see Bud and Jackie Robertson. After four days (filled mostly with conversation and admiring of the beaches, but no swimming), we returned to Lincoln. By then Joyce was feeling pain in her stomach, stabbing and fitful, separated by five-minute spaces of peace. By the 13th the pain was so insistent she shuttled to St. Elizabeth Hospital, where x-rays indicated a probable blockage of the bowel. A tube forced down her nose relieved the blockage.

By then Joyce and I agreed that we should begin to unload some of our commitments. On January 21 I visited at Lincoln Literacy Council with

Clayton Naff and withdrew our commitment as volunteers. We were sorry to stop working with immigrants who wanted very much to become citizens of the United States, but we had no doubt that replacements for us could be found. Clayton understood our situation and released us.

We decided in mid-March 2009 that we wanted to live at The Landing, a retirement home. When we were shown apartment A211 on April 13, we found it small but nice and just right for us, with its attractive view of Williamsburg Lake. We sold our townhouse on May 20 and moved into The Landing on June 1, 2009.

Meanwhile it was apparent to Dr. Peterson that the hormonal treatment was not working. Chemotherapy was reinstated—a treatment for each of three Mondays in a row, then one Monday off, followed by another three infusions. The first infusion of the series took about three hours; the second, about one hour; the third, one-half hour. I went with Joyce sometimes; Fran Bates or Jan Brockley or Marty White, the other times. The first treatment was done on June 8, during the week we moved into The Landing.

I thought—and I think Joyce thought—the chemo treatment was helping. Indeed on July 27 the lab tests were positive enough that Dr. Peterson exclaimed, "It's working!"

But the pains in the abdomen and stomach, the increasing nausea, the beginning of diarrhea, and the continuous loss of weight were surly omens. In August Joyce had vomiting spells so often she regurgitated nearly every swallowed bite of food before it reached her stomach. Even more, a pill rarely had time to dissolve before she heaved it out.

On August 17 Dr. Peterson was so surprised by our report that he skipped the day's scheduled infusion and directed her to the hospital for tests. Scans showed neither cancer in the brain nor enlarging of any cancer cells.

By Wednesday the 19th (our fifty-eighth wedding anniversary) Joyce had only a little vomiting—probably a reflux—all day and no diarrhea explosion. She stayed in the hospital one more night; the doctor wanted to get the nausea and diarrhea under control before releasing her and before using a new regimen of chemotherapy.

My journal kept track:

WEDNESDAY, AUGUST 19, 2009 [OUR ANNIVERSARY]

Joyce was released from the hospital this afternoon. Apparently the nausea and diarrhea have been controlled.

SATURDAY, AUGUST 22, 2009

More diarrhea. She eats sparsely; tries to eat more.

SUNDAY, SEPTEMBER 27, 2009

Time rushes on, but . . . living with cancer plods. Joyce has been off chemo for three weeks. . . . On the 23rd they took out 2 liters of fluid from around her stomach. On the 25th she had an echo-cardiogram for learning whether her heart is amenable to further treatments. . . . (It is.) . . .

Yesterday she felt "funny" but decided she didn't want "to lie around waiting to die or to get my body healed, so I'd rather do it all." That meant—go to the volleyball game against Texas at 1:00 and the football game against Lafayette-Louisiana at 6:00. . . . We left the football game at halftime.

MONDAY, SEPTEMBER 29, 2009

Dr. Peterson recommends a different chemo, featuring red pills. . . . She began with a chemo treatment today, an infusion tomorrow. She's in good spirits. Thinks it's the thing to do. I agree.

MONDAY, OCTOBER 26, 2009

Fran took Joyce to her weekly chemo treatment. . . . Joyce called me at the office to say that Lisa, Dr. Peterson's nurse, had told her, "You know, don't you, that you should get your things in order—your will, for example. And talking with Hospice to learn what is out there would be a good idea." Joyce was taken aback. So was I. I'm typing this at 4:00 a.m. Tuesday morning. Couldn't sleep after 3:00.

THURSDAY, OCTOBER 29, 2009

My own analysis of all this: if she can't control the continuing loss of weight, her body will eventually become unable to function. Her weight leveled off for a few weeks, but showed loss again Monday the 26th. . . . But if the diarrhea and the vomiting can be reduced, more food can be saved in the body and the body can be resuscitated and remain reasonably healthy.

MONDAY, NOVEMBER 2, 2009

Dr. Peterson decided not to give the chemo treatment and to take a CT *Scan tomorrow and perhaps change the medication to a stronger one—I think . . . the strongest one there is.*

He gave me the impression that if this one doesn't work, she might decide not to suffer any more treatment. Joyce at one point said, "I feel like this is the beginning of the end." Neither Dr. Peterson nor his nurse, the wonderfully capable Lisa, responded. He did say for some persons for whom no other medicine works, this one sometimes does. Tonight Joyce expressed disappointment, sadness. So did I.

TUESDAY, NOVEMBER 17, 2009

Today Joyce is to receive a blood transfusion. She has felt weak the last couple of days. . . . The blood transfusion . . . took from 10:00 a.m. until 5:00 p.m.! . . . [It] went fine, just long.

SATURDAY, NOVEMBER 28, 2009

One of Joyce's better days. Allison, Joe Warren, Samantha, and Jake came from Texas and spent Tuesday, Wednesday, and Thursday with us. We had a great time. The three Raiches and I played pool. Jake and I were partners and didn't win. Joyce played Golf, the card game, with us. It is the perfect game for us. . . . It is simple enough for 8-year-olds like Jacob and near-50-year-olds like Allison to learn and play . . . and win . . . all in the same evening. Yes, Jacob won.

Joyce took a short swim at 6:30 a.m., resting in the afternoon. . . . [Virtually no loss of substantial food] by vomiting during the past two weeks or so. Pain has been her pest. . . . Medicine helps but the severe neck pain doesn't go away entirely. She's very frail, rests a lot.

MONDAY, NOVEMBER 2, 2009

Joyce took another 4-hour infusion of chemotherapy. . . . I began a jury trial (U.S. v. Moore) scheduled for 6 or 7 days, so I didn't go with her.

Our Christmas cards that December trumpeted the oncologist's saying Joyce's condition was "stable." We saw "stable" as good news. We wrote that the side effects of Joyce's chemo were "under control," and she was "virtually without pain!" But we were grasping for straws. As soon as we found one straw, it was blown away, for by January 24, 2010, Dr. Peterson's conclusion was that no more treatment would be useful. We contracted hospice to help us through our pain. Then we waited.

On February 18 Joyce was noticeably weaker but mentally sharp. At hospice's suggestion we had a hospital bed brought into our living room so she would be comfortable sitting up. Though Joyce was helpful to me in solving the morning's crossword puzzle, by midafternoon she was virtually unable to communicate with words. She had to be carried into the hospital bed. She slept the night in that bed.

FEBRUARY 19, 2010

Joyce is unable to speak with words. She lies in a sitting position, responding to me with guttural sounds, watery eyes half-open, looking but not seeing. By dinnertime Daughter Joy, Granddaughter Joy Rager, Daughter Kim and I slip out to the dining room a hundred yards down the hallway for a bite to eat. Daughter Allison stays, lies with her mother, tells of her love, sings to her the songs her mother sang to her many years ago. At 6:34 p.m. Joyce opens her eyes, speaks a single word, "Warren," not calling, not admonishing, but making a simple statement of information . . . and breathes a last breath. She is gone.

A battle like Joyce's leaves its marks—on many. Her journey has been a courageous one. It has drawn our family closer in love and deeper into empathy.

Looking straight at death brings a sense, too, of the changing theme of living. The pace of the notes slows. Each moment grows in worth. Time slows and sound softens. The theme eases up and eases over.

My eighty-fourth year has come and gone. My seeing eye sees less. My ears hear less. I think more slowly.

People notice things like that.

Almanac of the Federal Judiciary is a respected publication, used, it says, as a reference work by attorneys, government agencies, and law students seeking clerkships. It contains lawyers' evaluations of judges, based on interviews.

In the 2006 edition the "Lawyers' Evaluation" section thrilled me, and made me feel sheepish: "Lawyers interviewed raved about Urbom's legal ability. 'He is probably one of the most well-respected judges in the country.' 'His legal ability is excellent. He is the best there is. He is regarded as the best federal judge we have had in anyone's memory.' 'He is an excellent judge all across the board. He is a pillar of integrity.' 'I think he is magnificent. He is great.'"[5] And so on.

But just four years after that, in the 2010 edition, the report plays in diminuendo. It varies the theme, shortens the time value of the notes: "Lawyers interviewed said Urbom is an excellent judge. 'In his day, he was probably the most intelligent judge in the district.' 'He is a master of the rules of evidence.' 'It is an honor to be in his courtroom.' 'He is a model federal judge. He is an old line federal judge. The lawyers really look up to him. You have a sense of awe. He has slowed down. In his day, he was great.' 'At one time, he was an absolutely wonderful judge. He just doesn't seem that interested anymore. He is just not what he used to be.' 'He is an excellent jurist.' 'He set the tone for excellence. He is thoughtful. His mind is still very sharp. He is excellent.' 'I like him.'"[6]

Do you see what I mean? Do you understand now when I say "People notice things like that?" Did you catch the tiny switch from "is" to "was"? "In his day . . . At one time . . . He just doesn't . . . He is just not . . ." They hum the tune, then trash it. It's razzmatazz, then the whammy. From hip-hop to a dirge. They try to put "is" back in, but by now "is" is too wheezy to be heard. Well, there you have it.

Come to think of it, though, they could be right. As I said, I see less, hear less, think more slowly.

So what? What do I have to whine about? Haven't I said over and over again that I've been lucky forever? Haven't I been drawn to the psalms of the lowly as well as the bugles of the mighty? Haven't I basked in the symphonies of justice? Haven't I been driven to my knees by the hymns of sadness? Haven't I leaped to my feet by the drum rolls of the law? Haven't I heard the choir of angels when my entire family has come to pour love on Joyce and me? Have I missed anything? Is there one song I have not heard sung?

When I look around I see a collection of supremely competent judges—three active district judges and two senior district judges, three active magistrate judges, and two bankruptcy judges—each backed by a sterling staff and ready to take full charge of the dockets of this district. I am proud to be shoulder to shoulder with that group, but I am far from indispensable.

I see, too, Joyce's and my children—four of them, who have inherited their mother's model of love—now building four new exciting families learning to take our places. And their own places.

Been there, done that. A diminuendo. A gradual diminishment, a slowing of the pace, an easing up, a smooth exit. Thanks for every moment.

Appendix

I've kept in a scrapbook a picture of each of my law clerks, taken at the time of his or her departure. The information I share now comes partly from that scrapbook, sometimes broadened by a parenthetical remark, and I've added a word or thought significant to me about them and a brief description by or approved by them about their ensuing professional course.

Rodney Johnson, 1970–71. "The benchmark." All law clerks after him have been measured by his service. University of Nebraska College of Law. Rodney had a career as a commissioned U.S. Foreign Service officer, serving as a legal advisor in a variety of overseas posts and in Washington for the U.S. Agency for International Development. Now retired, he serves on the advisory board of the International Law Institute's Center for International Procurement Law and Policy.

George Klippert, 1970–72. University of Nebraska College of Law. Author of books of law, sports, and fiction. Of life since the clerkship he says, "Retired from the law."

Stanley Talcott, 1971–73. "For real, now and then." University of Nebraska College of Law. Special touch: *Ralston v. Volkswagenwerk,* A.G., No. 18763-2 (W.D. Mo. Aug. 23, 1973), 61 F.R.D. 427 (W.D. Mo. 1973). After years of practicing law, Stanley turned to academia. He stepped down in 2003 after six years as a law school dean, and now is professor of law, teaching evidence, scientific evidence, property, and international environmental law and policy.

John Moseman, 1972–74. "The gentlest of men." University of Nebraska College of Law. Special touch: Wounded Knee cases and the Sioux Falls–to-Lincoln transition. In what was headed "In re those matters ordered to be consolidated by order of September 27, 1973 . . . for pretrial purposes with CR73-5019," that is, the "Consolidated Wounded Knee cases," John received a multitude of documents the defense asserted might show governmental misconduct; he then recommended to me whether each document should or should not be sent to defense counsel. It was a rare kind of order and an extraordinary job to give to a law clerk. He did it brilliantly and without objection by any party. After practicing regulatory law, he worked for eleven years in the U.S. Senate, including working with the Alaska delegation for Senator Murkowski and as minority staff director for the Senate Intelligence Committee. Later he directed congressional relations for the CIA and, before retiring from government service, served as chief of staff to CIA Director George Tenet. He now is with a consulting firm, focusing on U.S. intelligence.

David Pedersen, 1973–75. "Uncommon common sense." University of Michigan Law School. Special touch: *U.S.A. v. Consolidated Wounded Knee Cases*, 389 F. Supp. 235 (D.S.D. 1975). Of life after his clerkship David writes, "Partner in Baird Holm law firm in Omaha. Served as legal counsel for the Omaha Public Schools 33 years and was active nationally in education law matters, serving 11 years on the Board of the National Council of School Attorneys and as its Chairman in 1987–88. Retired June 1, 2008, to travel and read philosophy, history and theology."

William Dittrick, 1974–76. "An easy rider." University of Nebraska College of Law. Old courthouse to new. Special touch: *Blackwell v. Wolff*, 403 F. Supp. 759 (D. Neb. 1975). Bill is a partner and trial lawyer with Baird Holm LLP in Omaha. He is a past president of the Nebraska State Bar Association and is a member of the American College of Trial Lawyers. He married Anne Triba of Omaha and is blessed with four children (George, Kathryn, Elizabeth, and John), two granddaughters, and two grandsons.

John Holdenried, 1975–77. "The eternal youth." University of Michigan Law School. Special touch: *Ballew v. Associates Financial Services of Nebraska, Inc.*, 450 F. Supp. 253 (D. Neb. 1976). After clerkship John joined a law firm that is now Baird Holm LLP in Omaha and has been there ever since.

His practice is essentially that of a business lawyer for hospitals and other health care providers. From 2001 to 2009 he was managing partner of the firm. His wife, Lynne, and he have two sons (Jake and Joe), both now out of college and working.

Carl Circo, 1976–78. "Quiet mien, balanced judgment." University of Nebraska College of Law. Special thought: *Broadnax v. Missouri Pacific R.R.*, No. LR-73-C-25, 1978 WL 209 (E.D. Ark. Sept. 6, 1978). Carl says, "Early in my career I taught law at Cardozo, then I practiced real estate law in Kansas City for 20+ years before returning to teaching. Currently, I am a member of the faculty at the University of Arkansas School of Law (Fayetteville). My wife, Bobbi Johnson, and I raised 8 adopted children."

Mary Bausch Snow, 1977–79. "The complete law clerk." Creighton University Law School. Special touch: *Save the Niobrara v. Andrus*, No. CV75-L-96 (D. Neb. Apr. 16, 1979). Mary says, "I worked for the Colorado Attorney General for two years and, then, Mountain Bell for about six years. I have not practiced law since that time. Ron maintains his practice and he and I have raised our four daughters, the youngest graduating from college [in the spring of 2009]."

Brian Riepen, 1978–80. "Eager mind, ubiquitous attention." University of Southern California Law School. Special effort: *Women's Services v. Thone*, 483 F. Supp. 1022 (D. Neb. 1979) and *United States v. Bledsoe*, No. 78-03382-01/22-CR-W2 (W.D. Mo. Sept. 20, 1979), *aff'd and rev'd in part*, 674 F. 2d 647 (8th Cir. 1982). With law offices in Dallas and Kansas City, Brian has litigated cases, more often on the plaintiff's side, in numerous states and represented numerous foreign clients as well as Americans. Brian married Lynn Walker of St. Louis in 1985, and they have four sons: Albrecht, Erich, Dietrich, and Blair. Deceased 2012.

Kerry Kester, 1979–81. "At work he cared for all; at table he et al." University of Nebraska College of Law. Special effort: *Kort v. Western Surety Co.*, No. CV-77-O-208 (D. Neb. Apr. 26, 1980), *aff'd*, 705 F. 2d 278 (8th Cir. 1983) and *United States v. Bledsoe*, No. 78-03392-01/22-CR-W2, (W.D. Mo. May 1, 1980), *aff'd and rev'd in part,* 674 F. 2d 647 (8th Cir. 1982). Since leaving the clerkship, Kerry has practiced law in Lincoln with the firm of Woods & Aitken LLP with an emphasis on public and private construction contracting matters.

Candy Marshall, 1980–82. "The radiant one." University of Nebraska College of Law. Special touch: *Aitken, Hazen, Hoffman, Miller v. Empire Construction Co.,* 542 F. Supp. 252 (D. Neb. 1982). Candy describes her after-clerkship professional life this way: "Law practice in Seattle; then became General Counsel and Executive Vice President with a Seattle software company; joined the Bill & Melinda Gates Foundation in 1995 and now serve as the Director of Operations for the Global Health Program."

Douglas Gilbert, 1981–83. "Buttoned down." University of Iowa Law School. Special effort: *Toward Better Treatment of Jurors by Judges,* 61 Neb. L. Rev. 469 (1982); *Smith, Gettemy, Polk & Baulder v. Sorensen,* Nos. CV81-L-273, 275, 359 (D. Neb. Dec. 17, 1982); and *Smith v. Sorensen,* 748 F. 2d 427 (8th Cir. 1984). Douglas's fifty-word description of his life after the clerkship: "Since 1983, activities have included five years private practice in Phoenix/Denver, 11 years in Switzerland completing an MBA and then with Novartis, and then five years with the University of Phoenix, completing a DBA degree. Cheryl and I have two children, Andre (b. 1993) and Danielle (b. 1995)."

Michael Gibson, 1982–84. "Lover of trains, who prepared for us a straight track and a smooth ride." Law school, Yale University. Special commendation: *KN Energy, Inc. v. Marathon Oil Co.,* No. CV82-L-564 (D. Neb. Mar. 20, 1985) and *Missouri v. Andrews* (ETSI), No. CV82-L-442 and 443 (D. Neb. Mar. 7, 1984). Michael is a professor at Oklahoma City University School of Law.

Ray Walden, 1983–85. "The deliberate one." University of Nebraska College of Law. Special commendation: *Burlington Northern Railroad Company v. Nebraska,* No. CV83-L-423 (D. Neb. May 10, 1985), *aff'd in part, rev'd in part and remanded,* 802 F. 2d 994 (8th Cir. 1986). Describing his professional work after the clerkship, Ray said, "I was an associate with Kennedy Holland Delacy & Svoboda (renamed Lamson Dugan & Murray) from 1985 through 2002 in Omaha. In 2003 I opened my own solo practice focused on serving as co-counsel with other lawyers on civil cases and researching and writing major briefs and arguing appeals. So, still doing pretty much what I did for Judge Urbom, and still behind the scenes."

Tom Ross, 1985–86. "Solid." Law School at University of Iowa. Special thanks for guiding us through our personal computer infancy. Following the clerkship Tom practiced law in Omaha and Des Moines. He opened his own office in Des Moines in 1988. Tom leads an active civic life, including a run for Des Moines City Council in 2001. He enjoys dancing, piloting airplanes, cutting gemstones, and scuba diving.

Kirk Dielman, 1984–86. "Spirited." "Swift of mind, buoyant of nature, warm of manner." Law school at University of Missouri at Kansas City. Special mark: the farmers' cases of the economic letdown of 1985, including *Westcott v. U.S. Department of Agriculture*, 611 F. Supp. 351 (D. Neb. 1984), *aff'd*, 765 F. 2d 121 (8th Cir. 1985). After his clerkship Kirk engaged in private practice in Kansas City. During the savings and loan crisis of the 1980s, he began working for the Office of Thrift Supervision and was assistant regional counsel in Topeka and Chicago. Since 1998 he has been general counsel for First National Bank of Holdrege, Nebraska.

Maureen Lauren Allman, 1985–87. "Exuberant." Law School at Creighton University. Special applause: *Brown v. Board of Regents of the University of Nebraska*, 640 F. Supp. 674 (D. Neb. 1986) and *Medical Devices v. P.I.O.*, No. 86-L-764 (D. Neb. Dec. 11, 1986). Following clerkship Maureen practiced law in Seattle with Karr Tuttle Campbell PC and in Lincoln with Perry Guthery Haase and Gessford PC and Brooks Pansing Brooks PC. She assisted in the founding and operating of Lighthouse for teenagers. Currently she is pursuing a master's degree in holistic nutrition.

C. Ann Olson, 1986–88. "The wood chopper." Law School at Washington University in St. Louis. Special commendation: *Bostwick Irrigation District v. United States*, No. CV84-L-759, (D. Neb. Jul. 6, 1987), *aff'd*, 900 F. 2d 1285 (8th Cir. 1986) and *Rudd v. Laughlin*, No. CV88-L-195 (D. Neb. July 26, 1988), *aff'd*, 866 F. 2d 1040 (8th Cir. 1989). Ann explains her life after the clerkship this way: "Teaching, mediation, coaching, and consulting in areas of negotiation; personality conflict, and communication styles; blending energies; peaceful communication; and effective writing. Occasional solo practice. Prior: Director of Legal Writing, University of Minnesota Law School; private practice, Dorsey & Whitney, LLP, Minneapolis."

Patricia O'Leary Kiscoan, 1987–89. "Calm in the storm, quiet in the noise, orderly in the disarray—Ms. Cool." Creighton University College of Law. Special note: *Trailer Train v. Leuenberger,* No. CV87-L-29 (D. Neb. Dec. 11, 1987), *aff'd,* 885 F. 2d 415 (8th Cir. 1988), and *Murdock v. United States,* No. CV86-L-492 (D. Neb. Nov. 30, 1988), *aff'd,* 917 F. 2d 1065 (8th Cir. 1990), *reh'g en banc aff'd,* 951 F. 2d 907 (8th Cir. 1992). In 1989–97 Patricia worked with Popham, Haik, Schnobrich & Kaufman law firm in Minneapolis. She returned to Nebraska, telecommuted to work for the Minneapolis office of Hinshaw & Culbertson. On my recommendation Patricia became a law clerk for the Honorable Laurie Smith Camp, whom she served from December 2001 to February 2008. She has been a labor relations attorney for Union Pacific Railroad Company in Omaha since March 2008. She married Steve Kiscoan of Omaha, and they are the proud parents of Peter and Mary.

Jillane Hinds, 1988–89. "A scrupulous attention to quality." University of Nebraska College of Law. Special note: *Timm v. Gunter,* No. CV85-L-501 (D. Neb. Sept. 6, 1989), *aff'd in part, rev'd in part,* 917 F. 2d 1093 (1990). After the clerkship Jillane worked in Washington DC as an attorney-advisor for the Department of Defense. She obtained a Master of Arts concurrently with her law degree and subsequently has been trained as a mediator, using her training in law and psychology.

Michelle Tapken, August-September, 1989. Law School at University of South Dakota. Special interest: *United States v. M-KEnterprises, Inc.,* No. 4:89CR06 (D. Neb. Sept. 11, 1989). Michelle writes, "I am currently living in Washington DC and am on detail as Deputy General Counsel to the Executive Office of United States Attorneys. I have been serving in that capacity since March of 2007. Prior to that I served as United States Attorney, Acting United States Attorney and Assistant United States Attorney in the District of South Dakota from 1990 until present. Although my clerkship with Judge Urbom was short I am positive it led to the many wonderful opportunities I have experienced in the Department of Justice and I will forever be grateful for that."

Robin Hadfield, January-August 1990. "Unflappable." University of Nebraska Law School. Special note: *Camp v. Dema,* No. CV88-L-498 (D. Neb. June 13, 1990), *aff'd,* 948 F. 2d 445 (8th Cir. 1991). "Clerking has been my career," she says. "I have clerked for four judges on three courts and am currently career law clerk for John F. Wright on the Nebraska Supreme Court. I also worked as an Appellate and Administrative Attorney for the Nebraska Commission on Public Advocacy."

Alison Lonsdale McGinn, December 1989–August 1990. University of Nebraska Law School. "Luckily between jobs." Memorable work: *Omaha Indian Tribe v. Agricultural Industries Investment Co.,* No. CV75-4067, (N. D. Iowa May 4, 1990) and *Budden v. United States,* No. CV88-L-493 (D. Neb. Feb. 16, 1990), *aff'd,* 8 F. 3d 1278 (8th Cir. 1993) and 15 F. 3d 1444 (8th Cir. 1994). Alison says she "joined Omaha law firm in 1990 until 2004. Now practice school law as in-house legal counsel for Westside Community Schools in Omaha, Nebr."

Jeff Golden, 1990–91. "The Chicago Boy." The John Marshall Law School, Chicago. Special notes: *Giove v. Stanko,* No. CV89-L-236 (D. Neb. Jan. 11, 1991), *aff'd,* 977 F. 2d 413 (8th Cir. 1992) and *Sioux City Foundry v. South Sioux City,* No. CV89-L-470 (D. Neb. Mar. 20, 1991), 968 F. 2d 777 (8th Cir. 1992). Jeff describes his life after clerkship: "Current Exec. Dir., The National Justice Group; former Deputy Platte County Attorney; Dept. Dir., NE Crime Commission; Exec. Dir., Children and Family Coalition of NE; and Govt. Relations Dir., Boys and Girls Home and Family Services. All credited to the Judge." (I don't believe it.)

Krista Kester, 1990–92. "The Wordsmith." University of Nebraska College of Law . Special commendation: *The Heil Co. v. Snyder Industries, Inc.,* 763 F. Supp. 422 (D. Neb. 1991).

Linda Crump, August 1, 1991–February 15, 1993. "Motherly. She keeps dreams alive." University of Nebraska College of Law. Special notice: *Hoover Group,*

Inc. v. Custom Metalcraft, No. 4CV91-3053 (D. Neb. Feb. 1, 1993), *aff'd in part and rev'd in part*, 84 F. 3d 1408 (8th Cir. 1996). When Linda didn't apply for the clerkship, I called her and invited her to apply. She did, and I hired her. Since the clerkship, Linda says the big legal challenge she's faced was being the first person of color to serve as the Nebraska State Bar president. She created a Leadership Academy during her term to encourage a more inclusive slate of potential leaders in the Bar Association. She's continued to work on the Minority and Justice Committee, making some progress addressing racial disparities in the juvenile and adult justice systems, but says, "We still have a long way to go." (She also loves being a grandmother.)

Kristi Bohling Drefke, February 15–November 15, 1993. University of Nebraska College of Law. Aerobics instructor. Transition to a single law clerk. Special touch: *Anderson v. Homedco*, No. 4CV92-3076 (D. Neb. Oct. 1, 1993). Kristi's professional biography speaks of her practicing in the areas of general corporate, transactional, and securities law, with a primary focus on mergers and acquisitions. She has handled a number of acquisitions and dispositions for Bayer Corporation, the Pepsi Bottling Group, and the U.S. subsidiaries of Bongrain, SA, plus recent representative transactions in which she played a key role, including the formation of Bayer Pharmaceuticals Corporation's strategic alliance with Schering-Plough Corporation.

Jeanne A. Burke, August 1, 1992–April 30, 1995. "Endless curiosity plus." Creighton University Law School. Special attention: *Griffin v. Delo*, 33 F. 3d 895 (8th Cir. 1994); *U.S. v. Durenberger*, No. 3-93-65, 1993 WL 738477 (D. Minn. Dec. 3, 1993); and *Vann v. Hopkins*, 829 F. Supp. 293 (D. Neb. 1993). After the clerkship Jeanne worked for the Civil Rights Division of the Douglas County Attorney's Office (1995–97), clerked for two federal judges, Joseph F. Bataillon (1997–2001) and William Jay Riley (2001–5), and currently serves as director and legal education liaison for the Nebraska Innocence Project (2005–present).

Kenneth Kula, June 1994–April 1996. "Gentlemanly." Washburn University Law School of Topeka, Kansas. Special commendation: *ITT Commercial Finance Corp. v. Wal-Mart*, No. Civ.: 93-CV-2297-H, (N.D. Tex. Jan. 2, 1996), *aff'd*, 139 F. 3d 899 (5th Cir. 1998). Ken became a litigator, focusing on intellectual property and technology law. He is heavily involved in providing *pro bono* legal services for juveniles. He obtained the only known punitive damages award in Kansas based on corporate defamation. He aspires to be a judge.

Patrick Ickes, 1995–97. "Crossword Whiz." Ohio Northern University Law School, Ada, Ohio. Special attention: *Nebraska v. Moore*, No. 4:CV96-3255 (D. Neb. Jan. 31, 1997), Nebraska's antifusion election law. After clerkship Patrick was an associate and then partner at Baird Holm, LLP (1997–2004); took a sabbatical from 2004 to 2006; was in-house counsel with First National of Nebraska, Inc. (2006–present); and is currently vice president and assistant general counsel, litigation management, with FNNI.

David McManaman, May–July 1996. University of Nebraska College of Law. "Quiet." "Your quiet confidence pushed us through a difficult period. Thanks." Special attention: *John Doe v. Nebraska*, No. 4:CV95-3381 (D. Neb. May 13, 1996), *aff'd*, 345 F. 3d 593 (8th Cir. 2003). David joined Legal Services in 1996, serving low-income Nebraskans for nearly ten years, eventually becoming senior attorney. In 2006 he joined the State Department of Health and Human Services, where he currently focuses on employment law. David and Zoe, his wife, are the proud parents of daughter Brianna. They live in Lincoln.

Audra Hamilton, 1996–98. "Movie aficionado." Law School at University of Arkansas at Fayetteville. Special touch: *Duggan v. Moore*, No. 4:97CV3074 (D. Neb. Jan. 16, 1988) (term limits in amendment of Nebraska's constitution) and *Tennessee v. Surety Bank*, 84 F. Supp. 2d 803 (N.D. Tex. 1998), *aff'd*, 200 F. 3d 373 (5th Cir. 2000). Since her clerkship, Audra has lived and worked as an attorney in Tulsa, Oklahoma, focusing primarily on employment law. She has also continued her love of film, and is most recently proud that Internet Movie Database (IMDb) contains an entry on her, thanks to her involvement in a documentary film in Tulsa.

James Morgan, August 1997–February 2000. "Writer unparalleled." Law School at Washburn University, Topeka, Kansas. Special mention: *Hefti v.*

School District No. 008, No. 4:98CV3003 (D. Neb. Aug. 17, 1998) (Loss of an A for a B). James writes of his life after clerkship, "I worked as an associate for several national law firms advocating for the rights and protections of elderly people who reside in nursing homes. In 2009, I formed a partnership with fellow attorney, Anthony Lanzone, and we have a law firm in Long Beach, California, focusing on elder abuse and personal injury cases."

Patrick Evatt, August 1998–August 2000. University of Nebraska College of Law. UW Husky Fan. Special and prolonged effort: *Scranton-Gillette Communications v. Dannhausen*, No. 1:96CV8353, (N.D. Ill. July 22, 1999). He describes his postclerkship this way: "Patrick is a shareholder at Kantor Taylor Nelson Boyd & Evatt PC, a boutique firm that counsels clients in complex real estate development and finance transactions. Patrick specializes in multi-family housing finance transactions and tax credit property financings. Prior to joining firm, he served as in-house counsel to Freddie Mac and practiced at two nationally-ranked public finance firms."

Denise Karst Pearce, August 2000–August 2002. "Simply Super." University of South Dakota Law School. Special credit: *Anderson v. Sefani*, No. 99CV5410 (N.D. Ill. Feb. 5, 2001); *Fleet Business Credit Corp. v. National City Leasing Corp.*, No. 99CV5501 (N.D. Ill. July 5, 2001); and *EEOC v. Dial Corp.*, 156 F. Supp. 2d 926 (N.D. Ill. 2001). After clerkship Denise clerked for Circuit Judge Roger Wollman; was aide to Lincoln's mayor Chris Beutler; and married Marc Pearce (below). She and Marc are the parents of Erica and Keelyn.

Marc Pearce, 2000–infinity. University of Nebraska College of Law. We've made the circle; he's another Rodney Johnson. We talk, he writes, I accept. Special credit: *Windstream Corp. v. Berggren*, No. 4:08CR3173 (D. Neb. Aug. 14, 2008). My only career law clerk, Marc wrote, while clerking, his doctoral dissertation in psychology and received the Director's Award for Excellence in Court Operations. He married Denise Karst (above) in a ceremony I presided over.

Notes

PROLOGUE

1. Treaty Defense Hearing Transcript at vol. II, 1782:23–1786:5, United States of America v. Consolidated Cases, CR 73–5019 (D. Neb. Dec. 31, 1974); italics added. Duane L. Nelson and Kenneth Fields for the plaintiff and John Thorne and Larry Leventhal for the defendants.

1. THE ROCKY ROAD TO A JUDGESHIP

1. Robert Van Pelt had been appointed a U.S. district judge by President Dwight D. Eisenhower in May 1947, succeeding Judge John W. Delehant. Judge Van Pelt announced at the time of his reaching age seventy-two that he would take senior status (semiretirement) when his successor took office. He was a much admired and able judge, who had been a renowned trial lawyer, practicing law in Lincoln before his appointment. In introducing him at speaking engagements I have said, "He *is* what the rest of us *want* to be."

2. I had read that stately, brilliant Richard "Dick" Smith was Senator Curtis's campaign manager for reelection in 1966. I didn't think of it at the time of my conversation with him.

3. The organization limits its membership to lawyers "actively engaged in trial work as their principal activity," who "have high ethical and moral standards" and "excellent character" and are "outstanding and considered the best in a state." "American College of Trial Lawyers: Roster, Bylaws, Codes of Pretrial Conduct, Codes of Trial Conduct." 451. 2009.

4. See In Memoriam, 185 Neb. at xxiii (1970).

5. Dr. Darrel Berg was Joyce's and my pastor for thirteen years; before that, he and his wife, Ruth, had been our close friends since college days.

6. Perhaps "near antique" is more accurate. In the 1990s, when Southside Repair in Lincoln reconditioned the furniture, I bought from antique dealers some small tables for an office in the new courthouse (built in 1975) at 100 Centennial Mall North. The dealers told me that furniture one hundred years old or older was considered "antique." By the time of my possession of the furniture in about 1994–95 it probably had not reached the age of one hundred; by now it certainly has.

7. Mark Anderson, "Courtroom No. 1," *Lincoln Journal Star,* May 5, 2000.

8. "During good behavior" is the wording of Article III of the U.S. Constitution. Forced removal from office is by impeachment and conviction only. The House of Representatives impeaches, which is the equivalent of an indictment or set of charges. The Senate then hears evidence and decides guilt or innocence. Charges are limited to what the Constitution calls "high crimes and misdemeanors."

9. Regis Courtemanche and Carl T. Curtis, *Forty Years against the Tide* (Washington DC: Regnery, 1986).

10. Dr. Vance Rogers first learned of my movement toward the judgeship on or about October 10, 1969, two days after I returned from Washington at the invitation of Senator Curtis. Vance had been central in several of my activities: joining the church where he was the new pastor; joining and serving in the YMCA; becoming a member and later president of Nebraska Wesleyan University's governing board; receiving recognition by the university with a Young Alumni Award and an honorary degree. But he had no initiating role, at least, on my road to the bench.

2. GROWING UP

1. Marlene Harvey Wilmot, *Bluff-to-Bluff: The 1935 Republication Valley Flood* (Greeley CO: Wilmot, 1995), 256.

2. Regis Courtemanche and Carl T. Curtis, *Forty Years against the Tide* (Washington DC: Regnery, 1986), 75–77.

3. Courtemanche and Curtis, *Forty Years against the Tide,* 75–77.

4. Paul Riley, "Massacre Canyon Monument,"

http://www.usgennet.org/usa/ne/county/hitchcock/history/canyon .html (accessed January 4, 2011).

5. Roxanne Dunbar Ortiz, *The Great Sioux Nation: Sitting in Judgment on*

America. An Oral History of the Sioux Nation and Its Struggle for Sovereignty (New York: Moon Books, 1977).

6. Luke 12:48.

7. The account of Ward's military service is based on his 1990 unpublished writing, "How I Won the War."

8. Robert F. Famighetti, *World Almanac and Book of Facts 2000* (Mahwah NJ: World Almanac, 1999), 527.

9. *The New Encyclopaedia Britannica*, 15th ed., 351.

10. Stanley P. Hirshson, *General Patton: A Soldier's Life* (New York: HarperCollins, 2002), 490.

11. A sergeant concocted an arrangement of fastening two iron prongs on the front of a tank so they would stick in the dirt and prevent the tank from bellying up. The tank would then push the terrace dirt, trees, and hedges out of the way, allowing tanks and troops to go through. Hirshson, *General Patton*, 494.

12. The 446th Bomb Group, "Missions of the 446th," *www.446bg.com/index*, August 1944 (accessed January 4, 2011).

3. LOOKING FOR ANSWERS AND FINDING THEM

1. My other major was history; my other minor was English.

2. Dr. Enid Miller Hoffman, known by all her students affectionately as "Doc Miller," tagged many students with nicknames of their own. Mine was "Bommy."

3. *Chicago Herald-American*, May 4, 1950.

4. The U.S. Department of Labor Consumer Price Index calculates that amount would be about $2,766 in 2010.

5. My contributions were notes: *Banks and Banking—Deposits—Resulting Trusts under the Contract Theory of Joint Bank Accounts*, 51 MICH. L. REV. 100 (1952); *Personal Property—Liens—Artisan's Liens on Unimproved Goods for Improved Goods Delivered under a Single Contract*, 51 MICH. L. REV. 315 (1952); *Civil Procedure—Parties—Real Party in Interest When Insurer Has Equitable Interest in Class*, 51 MICH. L. REV. 587 (1953); *Equity—Criminal Contempt—Violation of Court Order or Decree—Attorney's Responsibility*, 51 MICH. L. REV. 1084 (1953); *Civil Procedure—Service of Process under Non-*

resident Motorist Statute—Effect of Death of Nonresident Defendant, 52 MICH. L. REV. 144 (1953).

6. Al and Ellie Feldman of Omaha; Don and Diane Johnson of Burbank, California; John and Barbara Wolfe of Cuyahoga Falls, Ohio; Bill and Dottie Ahonen of Akron, Ohio; and Cal and Ann Hudson of Royal Oak, Michigan. There were women in our class, but only three, a marked difference from the present time, when a majority of women in law school classes is often the case.

4. PRACTICING LAW

1. In 2010 that amount would be about $234,572.34.

2. Letter from Walt Hughes to Si Parks of Hawkeye Casualty Company, March 24, 1958.

3. District Court of Lancaster County, Nebraska, Docket 253, page 157. Tried before Judge William C. Hastings November 4–6, 1969.

4. Affidavit of Mary Ann Norval, September 24, 1964, filed in the District Court of York County, Nebraska, Case No. 10215. I understand that Judge Ach referred the matter to the Supreme Court of Nebraska, but Chief Justice Paul White refused to excuse him from the case.

5. Tried in District Court for Lancaster County, Nebraska, before Judge Elmer Scheele, October 23–25, 1963. Affirmed on appeal, Baylor v. Tyrrell, 177 Neb. 813, 131 N. W. 2d 393 (1964).

6. District Court of Lancaster County, Nebraska, Docket 229, page 299.

5. CHURCH AND FAMILY

1. I've heard my father sometimes pronounce our family name with a short "u" after the "b." That may account for the spelling on the certificate, though I never saw my father write the name that way.

2. In 1968 the Methodist Episcopal Church (which had been formed by a merger in 1938 of the Methodist Episcopal Church North and the Methodist Episcopal Church South, and was often referred to as the Methodist Church) merged with the Evangelical United Brethren Church to form the United Methodist Church.

3. What our family knows of its genealogy is not extensive. My father's parents, Andrew and Anna Young Urbom, emigrated from Sweden, probably from the village of Vitsand in Varmland, in the 1880s. Andrew did some farming in Phelps County, Nebraska, and I have heard it said that he had been a tailor, but that has no documentary support that our family knows. He was preceded in ancestry by nail makers and hammer makers who moved about Sweden freely to learn their trades by apprenticeships. The earlier family name was apparently Ersson. The name Urbom seems to have referred to "the outskirts of town" and was first used as a surname by Heinrich Ersson Urbom, born in Kinstcorsbro, Sweden, in 1719. His son is listed as Hinrick Uhrbum, born in 1758. The spelling "Uhrbum" or anything like it does not reappear. Andrew Urbom, my grandfather, in addition to farming, served for a time as a county supervisor of Phelps County, was instrumental in the constructing of his Swedish Lutheran church in Holdrege, was active generally in church work and a cooperative, and raised a family of six children, three boys and three girls: Walter, Clarence (my father), Alvin, Edna, Dora, and Elsie. He died at age seventy-nine in Holdrege on August 19, 1928. His wife, my father's mother, was Anna Bertha Young Urbom, who died on May 5, 1948, at the age of eighty-five. They had been married forty-five years when Andrew died.

4. Matthew 5:23.

6. A FEDERAL TRIAL JUDGE GIVES ANSWERS

1. Carl Sandburg, *Complete Poems* (New York: Harcourt, Brace & World, 1950), 558–59.

2. Warren K. Urbom, *Toward Better Treatment of Jurors by Judges,* 61 NEB. L. REV. 409, 417 (1982).

3. Black v. Cothren, 316 F. Supp. 468, 470 (D. Neb. 1970).

4. Reichenberg v. Nelson, No. Civ. 1620 L (D. Neb. 1970); 419 F. 2d 1034 (7th Cir. 1969).

5. Black, 316 F. Supp. at 469.

6. No. 4:91CV3034 (D. Neb. 1991).

7. 341 F. Supp. 258 (D. Neb. 1972).

8. Article I-A, § 16(d) of the Association's by-laws said, "Girls and boys

may not compete on the same athletic team, and girls and boys may not compete against each other."

9. 327 F. Supp. 1391 (D. Neb. 1971).

10. 443 F. 2d 353 (8th Cir. 1971), *cert. denied,* 404 U.S. 859 (1971).

11. Rozman v. Elliott, 335 F. Supp. 1086 at 1088 (D. Neb. 1971).

12. Rozman, 1095.

13. Rozman, 1097.

14. 347 U.S. 483, 74 S. Ct. 686, 98 L. Ed. 873 (1954).

15. 327 F. Supp. 829 (D. Neb. 1971), *aff'd,* 456 F. 2d 1266 (1972).

16. No. Civ 879L (D. Neb. 1967).

17. 377 F. 2d 228 (8th Cir. 1967).

18. McClelland, 327 F. Supp. at 834.

19. Minden Beef Co. v. The Cost of Living Council, 362 F. Supp. 298 (D. Neb. 1973).

20. "Injunction Is Denied in Beef Price Freeze Case," *Lincoln Journal,* August 13, 1973.

21. 333 F. Supp. 173 (D. Neb. 1971).

22. Potato Chip Institute v. General Mills, Inc., 461 F. 2d 1088 (8th Cir. 1972).

23. State v. Rice, 188 Neb. 728, 737, 199 N. W. 2d 480 (1972). The concurrence by Judge Hale McCown was on the ground that, although the affidavit in support of the search warrant omitted much of the information the police had, the fact that the police had the information at the time the affidavit was made was sufficient to validate the warrant.

24. 232 U.S. 383, 34 S. Ct. 341, 58 L. Ed. 652 (1914).

25. Rice v. Wolff, 513 F. 2d 1280, 1295 (8th Cir. 1975). The draft of my opinion was written by my law clerk, David Pedersen. It is a beautiful piece of work, clear, analytical, and spotlessly supported by case law.

26. Wolff v. Rice, 422 U.S. 1055, 95 S. Ct. 2677, 45 L. Ed. 2d 707 (1975).

27. Stone v. Powell, 428 U.S. 465, 96 S. Ct. 3037, 49 L. Ed. 2d 1067 (1976).

28. See Wopashitwe Mondo Eyen We Langa, *also known as* David Rice v. Robert P. Houston, Docket 8:10CV00229 (D. Neb. 2010). Rice has made other attempts to find error in his trial, mostly aimed at the credibility of Duane Peak. None has been successful. They are summarized in Circuit

Judge Donald Lay's opinion for a three-judge panel in *Rice v. Clarke,* 923 F. 2d. 117 (8th Cir. 1991).

29. 370 U.S. 421, 82 S. Ct. 1261, 8 L. Ed. 2d 601 (1962).

30. Rowland v. Jones, 452 F. 2d 1005 (8th Cir. 1971).

31. 504 F. Supp. 585 (D. Neb. 1980).

32. Chambers v. Marsh, 675 F. 2d 228 (8th Cir. 1982).

33. Marsh v. Chambers, 463 U.S. 783 (1983).

34. Lemon v. Kurtzman, 403 U.S. 602, 91 S. Ct. 2105 (1971); Committee for Public Education and Religious Liberty v. Nyquist, 413 U.S. 756, 93 S. Ct. 2955, 37 L. Ed. 2d 948 (1973).

35. Marsh v. Chambers, 463 U.S. 783 at 786, 792, 103 S. Ct. 3330, 77 L. Ed. 2d 1019 (1983).

36. Marsh, 793–94.

37. Marsh, 795, 796, 797, 798.

38. Marsh, 823.

39. My opinion was unpublished. At the circuit court level the citation is Quaring v. Peterson, 728 F. 2d 1121 (8th Cir. 1984); at the Supreme Court level it is *Jensen v. Quaring,* 472 U.S. 478 1984)(per curium).

40. Quaring v. Peterson, 728 F. 2d 1121 (8th Cir. 1984).

41. Jensen v. Quaring, 472 U.S. 478 (1985).

42. 640 F. Supp. 674 (D. Neb. 1986).

43. Brown, 676 (quoting Plaintiff's Exhibit 2, 29:25–30:13).

44. Brown, 682.

45. State v. Faith Baptist Church of Louisville, 207 Neb. 802, 301 N. W. 2d 571 (1981), *appeal dismissed for want of a substantial federal question,* 454 U.S. 803, 102 S. Ct. 75, 70 L. Ed. 2d 72 (1981).

46. See *McCurry v. Tesch,* 738 F. 2d 271 (8th Cir. 1984) and *McCurry v. Tesch,* 824 F. 2d 638 (8th Cir. 1987), regarding the facts.

47. *Temple Times: The Weekly Voice of Calvary Temple* (East Point, Georgia), September 4, 1983.

48. McCurry v. Tesch, No. CV 82-L-659 (D. Neb. April 21, 1986).

49. McCurry v. Tesch, 824 F. 2d 638, 641 (8th Cir. 1987).

50. McCurry, 642.

7. WOUNDED KNEE AND THE FORT LARAMIE TREATY OF 1868

1. 490 F. 2d 345 (8th Cir. 1974), *cert. denied*, 421 U.S. 1002 (1975).

2. Rolland Dewing, *Wounded Knee II*, 2nd ed. (Chadron NE: Great Plains Network 2000).

3. This description of the events is more fully developed in my Memorandum of Decision on the Merits in *United States v. Jaramillo*, 380 F. Supp. 1375 (D. Neb. 1974). It is based on evidence received at that trial as well as other hearings in 1974.

4. Frank Clearwater was shot on April 17, 1973, and died a week later; Lawrence Lamont, thirty-one, was shot and killed on April 27, 1973. Clearwater may have been a Caucasian named Frank Clear, who had been discharged from the army with an other-than-honorable discharge, according to FBI records, whereas AIM contended he was Frank Clearwater, an Apache from North Carolina. He was buried on the Rosebud Reservation. See Dewing, *Wounded Knee II*, 179. Lloyd Grimm, appointed by President Richard Nixon in 1969 U.S. marshal for the District of Nebraska, was shot while on duty at a roadblock just outside Wounded Knee on March 26, 1973. He remained paralyzed from the waist down until his death. He resigned his office in 1974, as reported in "L. Grimm Will Retire as Marshal," *Lincoln Journal*, October 28, 1974.

5. That wasn't quite true, of course. I'm glad I didn't see them not standing, because it meant I didn't make a decision on the spur of the moment.

6. That proved to be not quite true. All cases were assigned to Judge Andrew Bogue of the Western Division of the District of South Dakota, where they originated. While probably about 130 defendants were indicted, most of them separately, about 120 were actually assigned to me. I never knew the exact number pending at any time because the number was fluid. Some cases were assigned to other judges and then reassigned to me; some indictments came down after I had begun hearings.

7. He testified several times that he was not an Indian. Transcript of hearing January 24 and 25, 1975, at 139, 150, and 194. The Eighth Circuit's opinion affirming his sentence characterizes him as an Indian and, when justifying jurisdiction, cites only law applicable to "Indians on Indian reservations." *United States v. Dodge*, 538 F. 2d 770, 774 (8th Cir. 1976).

8. My holding that the informant did not prejudicially violate the attorney-client privilege or the right to counsel was affirmed in *United States v. Dodge*, 538 F. 2d 770 (8th Cir. 1976).

9. Joe Pasquale, my regular court reporter, who recorded entirely in shorthand, was in charge of daily copy and worked with Dick Thiewes of Sioux City to bring it about.

10. Jim DeCamp, "Indians Say of Reception Here: Pretty Damned Bad," *Lincoln Star*, January 2, 1975.

11. See Albert J. Krieger, *Wounded Knee Revisited: The Personal Reflections of a Defense Attorney upon a Water-shed Life Experience*, 10 ST. THOMAS L. REV. 45 (1997).

12. Hearing Transcript at 126–29, 130, United States v. Cooper, No. 73–5102 (D.S.D. Jan. 24–25, 1975).

13. The attorneys usually scheduled the trials in groups according to the primary issues involved. For example, if a case involved the issue of interfering with a federal officer during a civil commotion, the understanding was that the ruling I made on the issue of the existence of a civil commotion would usually be the same as the previous ruling without hearing any more evidence on the subject. Many were handled in that fashion. Also the government lawyers voluntarily moved for dismissal of some cases, so by the time I ended my service on the Wounded Knee cases, there were not more than about forty-nine remaining. Those remaining cases were transferred back to Judge Andrew Bogue of South Dakota for possible trial in Council Bluffs, Iowa. Most of those were dismissed by the government. One or two trials were in fact held by Judge Edward McManus in the Northern District of Iowa.

14. 380 F. Supp. 1375 (D. Neb. 1974).

15. 18 U.S.C. Sec. 232.

16. Nonjury trial of four defendants in Lincoln, October 1 to 17, 1974. Counsel: Duane Nelson and Alan Kirshen for the government and Anthony C. Muller, Denver, for Def. Dodge; Elliott A. Taikeff, New York City, for Def. Fleury; Terry Gilbert, Cleveland, for Def. Wesaw; Forest S. Mosten, Los Angeles, for Def. Johns. Dodge: sentenced March 7, 1975, to Federal Reformatory, El Reno OK, under Federal Youth Corrections Act for conspiracy, conviction overturned on appeal, insufficient evidence. Fleury:

sentenced June 30, 1975, for conspiracy, three years imprisonment, but on condition he spent ninety days in jail on weekends, remainder suspended; breaking and entering ninety days, simple assault, ninety days, all concurrent, conviction for conspiracy overturned on appeal, insufficient evidence; rest of charges overturned for lack of jurisdiction over him. Wesaw: sentenced June 30, 1975, for conspiracy, two years imprisonment suspended, two years probation; conviction overturned on appeal, insufficient evidence. Johns: sentenced June 30, 1975, for conspiracy, two years imprisonment suspended, two years probation; conviction overturned on appeal, insufficient evidence.

17. This was because, as I understood it, the National Association of Criminal Defense Lawyers and perhaps the National Lawyers Guild had offered to provide counsel as volunteers. My information was that Judge Bogue found no South Dakota lawyers available or willing to defend the Wounded Knee cases. When I inquired about appointment, I was told that the defendants wanted to select their own lawyers. I set the policy, then, of saying that if I were not to select them, I would not use government money to pay them, except for twenty-five dollars a day for subsistence and airfare for one round-trip home and back to a place of trial. The only exception to this, I believe, was that I awarded Joe Beeler a slight fee at one time and John Thorne a fee of $2,000 for the extraordinary time and effort they gave to the trials and the treaty defense, respectively.

18. No. CR 74-L-12 (D. Neb. 1974), tried August 26 to September 11, 1974, in Lincoln. Counsel for the United States were Duane Nelson and Michael Schleich; for the defendants were Roger A. Finzel, Bruce Hartigan, Bruce Hiller, Ray Twohig, and Jerry Worksman.

19. Harvey Pirofsky, psychiatrist, Palo Alto CA; Bruce Dennis Sales, assistant professor of psychology, University of Nebraska–Lincoln; Fred Ware Jr., clinical psychologist, University of Minnesota–Minneapolis; and J. Y. Schulman, sociologist, Department of Psychiatry, Columbia University. Hearing Transcript at vol. I, 3–126, U.S. v. Baker, No. CR 73–5021 (D.S.D. 1974).

20. Hearing Transcript at vol. I, 712–780, United States v. Iron Cloud, CR 74-L-12, 13 (D. Neb. 1974).

21. Hearing Transcript at vol. III, 1833, (1974), 1839–40, 1867–69.

22. Hearing Transcript at vol. III, 1861–62 (1974). Briefly, the Witness Protection Program, as explained to Cut Grass by Prosecutor Alan Kirshen,

is a voluntary program that isolates a witness and his or her family and gives them twenty-four-hour protection in an undisclosed place until the program is terminated.

23. The statistician was Dr. John Joseph Berman, assistant professor in the Psychology Department of the University of Nebraska. Hearing Transcript at vol. II, 445ff, United States v. Iron Cloud, No. CR 74-L-12, 13 (D. Neb. 1974).

24. United States v. Banks and United States v. Means, Nos. CR 73–5034, CR 73–5062, CR 73–5035, and CR 73–5063 (D.S.D. 1974), 383 F. Supp. 389 (1974).

25. *Hamlet,* Act 1, sc. 3, l. 78.

26. Treaty Defense Hearing Transcript at 4, United States v. Consolidated Cases, No. CR 73–5019 (D.S.D. 1974).

27. Treaty Defense Hearing Transcript at 4.

28. Treaty Defense Hearing Transcript at 5; 163 U.S. 537, 16 S. Ct. 1138, 41 L. Ed. 256 (1896).

28. Johnson v. McIntosh, 21 U.S. 543, 587 (1823).

29. Johnson at 573, 587, 590.

30. Johnson at 591.

31. Treaty Defense Hearing Transcript at vol. I, 51, United States v. Consolidated Cases, No. CR 73–5019 (D.S.D. 1974), (testimony of Father Peter John Powell).

32. United States v. Consolidated Cases, 389 F. Supp. 235, 236 (D. Neb. 1975).

33. Consolidated Cases, at 238.

34. 21 U.S. 543 (1823).

35. 18 U.S.C. § 1153.

36. United States v. Consolidated Cases, 389 F. Supp. 235, 238–239 (D. Neb. 1975).

37. Plessy v. Ferguson, 163 U.S. 537, 551, 16 S. Ct. 1138, 41 L. Ed. 256 (1896).

38. Brown v. Board of Education of Topeka, 347 U.S. 483, 494, 74 S. Ct. 686, 98 L. Ed. 873 (1954) (citing Brown v. Board of Education of Topeka, 98 F. Supp. 797 (D. Kan. 1951)).

39. Brown v. Board of Education of Topeka, 98 F. Supp. 797, 798 (D. Kan. 1951).

40. William S. Laughlin, quoted in Ortiz, *The Great Sioux Nation,* 58.

41. Laughlin, quoted in Ortiz, *The Great Sioux Nation,* 174–75.

42. United States v. Dodge, 538 F. 2d 770, 775 (8th Cir. 1976), *cert. denied*, 429 U.S. 1099, 97 S. Ct. 1118, 51 L. Ed. 2d. 547 (1977).

43. United States v. Crow Dog, Nos. CR 75–18, 19, 20 (N.D. Iowa 1995).

44. *Bartlett's Familiar Quotations* (13th ed. 1955), 860a.

8. THE PROGRESSIVE FARMERS ASSOCIATION TRIAL

1. There were six, until one was severed late in the trial: Carl L. Bledsoe Jr., represented by Brooks Wood; Donald E. Burks, represented by Richard L. Anderson; Quentin Darence Cloninger, represented by James L. Crabtree; Thomas B. Moffitt, represented by Mark Slatkin; Russell Phillips, represented by Thomas M. Bradshaw, and Ronald Stafford, represented by James H. Bernard Jr.

2. My staff were secretary Marlene McGuire and law clerks Brian Riepen and Kerry Kester. The law clerks alternated between Lincoln and Kansas City, one at each city.

3. Scott and Patsy Moore were attending medical school and seminary, respectively, in Kansas City and living in Lee's Summit, perhaps twenty-five miles east and south of Kansas City. I stayed with them for about six months, until the trial was nearing its end. The Moores refused compensation, so I bought tickets to entertainments, and we became acquainted with the Kansas City Royals baseball team, the Kansas City Kings basketball team, and some dinner theaters and restaurants. The Royals won the American League championship, and in a first-ever all-Missouri World Series in October 1980 lost to the National League's St. Louis Cardinals just a few weeks after the trial ended. I had put my name in the pot for World Series tickets, but got none.

4. After teaching at the law school in 1979–80, I continued for ten more years, quitting when I took senior status on January 1, 1991, to be free to travel about the country trying cases in other states. More about that later.

5. The four were Ronald Elia, represented by Dennis J. C. Owens; Thomas Thrower, represented by David Rhodes; Gerald Nance, represented by Timothy Shea III; and Charles Thrower, represented by Judith Sharp. Months later Donald E. Burks, represented by Richard Anderson, was severed.

6. Joe Pasquale, my regular court shorthand reporter from Lincoln,

thereafter divided the reporting duties during the PFA trial with John M. Bowen & Associates of Kansas City, namely, I think, Katherine Arel and Richard Grigg.

7. This number reflects my acceptance of the prediction of three months, but also my total unbelief that it could go on for ten and a half months. We were very lucky that the trial survived by actually needing and using only two alternates.

8. 28 U.S.C. § 455.

9. Transcript of Proceedings, 24:8–24, held in chambers, March 31, 1980.

10. Transcript at 24:25–26:19.

11. United States v. Anderson, 626 F. 2d 1358 (8th Cir. 1980), *cert. denied,* 450 U.S. 912, 101 S. Ct. 1351, 67 L. Ed. 2d 336 (1981).

12. Transcript at vol. 175, 209:16–210:11, July 16, 2008.

13. Transcript at vol. 5, 54:11–12, October 8, 1979.

14. Transcript at vol. 120, 195:16–24.

15. United States v. Bledsoe, 674 F. 2d 647 (8th Cir. 1984).

16. United States v. Phillips, 726 F. 2d 417 (8th Cir. 1984).

17. Phillips at 418–19.

9. BACK TO NORMAL

1. 410 U.S. 113, 93 S. Ct. 705, 35 L. Ed. 2d. 147 (1973).

2. 483 F. Supp. 1022 (D. Neb. 1979). The lawyers were Lawrence Batt, Omaha, for plaintiffs Women's Services, PC and G. William Orr, MD; Michael Levy, Omaha, for plaintiffs Ladies Center, Nebraska, Inc. and M. John Epp, MD; Judith Levin, New York City, for plaintiff Betty Roe and plaintiff-intervenor Elizabeth F.; Jerold V. Fennell, assistant attorney general, Lincoln, for defendants Charles Thone and Paul L. Douglas; Henry Wendt, deputy Douglas County attorney, Omaha, for defendant Donald L. Knowles; James E. Schneider, North Platte, Nebraska, for defendant-intervenor Marilyn A. Schneider.

3. NEB. REV. STAT. ANN. § 28-325 (LexisNexis 2009).

4. Women's Services, PC v. Thone, 636 F. 2d 206 (8th Cir. 1980).

5. 452 U.S. 911, 101 S. Ct. 3043, 69 L. Ed. 2d 414 (1981).

6. 690 F. 2d 667 (8th Cir. 1982).

7. 567 F. Supp. 522 (D. Neb. 1981).

8. 439 U.S. 379, 387, 99 S. Ct. 675, 681 (1979).

9. 655 F. 2d 848 (8th Cir. 1981).

10. Women's Services, PC v. Thone v. Douglas, 710 F. 2d 465 (8th Cir. 1983).

11. Thornburn v. Roper, 39 F. Supp. 2d 1199 (D. Neb. 1999), *aff'd sub nom.;* Thornburn v. Austin, 231 F. 3d 1114 (8th Cir. 2000).

12. Thornburn v. Austin, 231 F. 3d 1114 (8th Cir. 2000).

13. The statute defined "partial birth abortion" as "an abortion procedure in which the person performing the abortion partially delivers vaginally a living unborn child before killing the unborn child and completing the delivery." NEB. REV. STAT. ANN. § 28-326(9) (Supp. 1999). The statute was unconstitutional, said the Supreme Court, for "at least" two independent reasons: it lacked any exception "for the preservation of the . . . health of the mother," and it "impose[d] an undue burden on a woman's ability" to choose an abortion. *Stenberg v. Carhart,* 530 U.S. 914, 930 (2000).

14. Carhart v. Stenberg, 11 F. Supp. 2d 1099 (D. Neb. 1998); Carhart v. Stenberg, 192 F. 3d 1142 (8th Cir. 1999); Stenberg v. Carhart, 530 U.S. 914, 930 (2000).

15. 530 U.S. 980 (2000).

16. 408 U.S. 238, 239–40 (1972).

17. 428 U.S. 153, 187–88 (1976).

18. Gregg, 179.

19. Gregg, 181.

20. Harold "Wili" Otey, convicted June 20, 1978, executed by electrocution September 2, 1994; Robert Williams, convicted June 30, 1978, executed by electrocution December 2, 1997; and John W. Joubert, convicted October 9, 1984, executed by electrocution July 17, 1996. Nebraska's Supreme Court in *State v. Mata,* 275 Neb. 1, 745 N. W. 2d 229 (2008), held that Nebraska's use of electrocution is unconstitutional as cruel and unusual punishment under the Nebraska Constitution.

21. Legislation in Nebraska in 1973 and 2002, especially in response to the *Furman* case and *Ring v. Arizona,* 536 U.S. 584, 122 S. Ct. 2428, 153 L. Ed. 2d 556 (2002), requires the death penalty to be pronounced by a judge after a jury has determined beyond a reasonable doubt involvement of any aggravating circumstances specified in the legislation. *State v. Gales,* 265 Neb. 598, 658 N. W. 2d 604 (2003).

22. This is not to say no progress has been made. Congress passed the Prison Litigation Reform Act of 1996, which has necessarily reduced the time spent in prison litigation and has been stricter in requiring the inmate to pay the cost of filing cases in accordance with the inmate's ability to pay over time.

23. Gregg v. Georgia, 428 U.S. 153 (1976); Godfrey v. Georgia, 446 U.S. 420 (1980).

24. No. CV 84-L-393 (D. Neb. Nov. 5, 1986); 654 F. Supp. 515 (D. Neb. 1987).

25. The defendant died before his sentence of death was carried out.

26. Harper v. Grammer, 895 F. 2d 473 (1990).

27. 197 Neb. 544, 250 N. W. 2d 876 (1977).

28. Harper v. Grammar, 654 F. Supp. 515, 540 (D. Neb. 1987).

29. An examination of aggravating circumstance 1(d) as of 1991 appears in Jeanne A. Burke, Casenote, *Nebraska's "Exceptional Depravity" Language at Death's Door:* Moore v. Clarke, 24 CREIGHTON L. REV. 1019 (1991).

30. Otey v. Stenberg, 34 F. 3d 635, 640 (1994).

31. United States v. Sheets, 443 F. 2d 353 (8th Cir. 1971).

32. Missouri Valley Construction Company/Joseph Thoendal, Docket No. CR 82-L-01; Wm. Anderson Company, Inc.,/John A. Anderson, Docket No. CR 82-L-06; W. A. Biba Engineering Company/ James A. Biba, Docket No. CR 82-L-07; Constructors, Inc./William H. Bowen, Docket No. CR 82-L-08; Dobson Brothers Construction/Arthur Dobson, Docket No. CR 82-L-09; Paulsen Building & Supply, Inc./Ivan Paulsen, Docket No. CR 82-L-10; Metro Pavers, Inc./Samuel P. Olson, Docket No. CR 82-L-11; Werner Construction, Inc./Phillip F. Werner, Docket No. CR 82-L-15; Nider-Jergensen Construction Company/Bernard W. Nider, Docket No. CR 82-L-16; James E. Simon Company, Inc./Gary Meyer, Docket No. CR 82-L-18; Central Sand & Gravel Company/Robert Harrington, Docket No. CR 82-L-23.

33. U.S. v. Land Paving Company, No. CR 83-L-23 (D. Neb. 1984).

34. U.S. v. Irving F. Jensen Company, Inc., No. CR 82-L-20 (D. Neb. 1982); U.S. v. Stannard Construction Co., Inc., No. CR 82-L-19 (D. Neb. 1982).

35. U.S. v. Bennett, No. CR 82-L-15 (D. Neb. 1982).

36. "A $2 Million Message," editorial, *Lincoln Journal & Star*, February 21, 1982.

37. A fairly regular practice of the appellate courts is to invite senior district judges (semiretired) to sit on a panel.

38. United States v. William Anderson Company, Inc., 698 F. 2d 911, 914, 913 (8th Cir. 1982).

39. 741 F. 2d 1542, 1544, 1547, 1548, 1550, 1554 (8th Cir. 1984).

40. Pub. L. No. 98-473, § 217(a), 98 Stat. 1837, 1976–2026 (codified as amended at 28 U.S.C. §§ 991–98 (2006)).

41. As of June 30, 1985, the District of Nebraska had 1,427 cases pending. Even if 100 of those were handled by each of the two *senior* judges, each *active* judge would have 647. Computed on the basis of *three* active judges, the load was 476, placing Nebraska the second highest number of pending cases in any district in the Eighth Circuit. If computed on the basis of two active judges only, which is all we had after the death of Judge Schatz and until the appointment of Judge Strom six months later, each of the two would carry 713. Administrative Office of United States Courts, *1985 Federal Court Management Statistics,* 118.

42. United States Sentencing Commission Alternatives to Imprisonment Project Report, *The Federal Offender: A Program of Intermediate Punishment,* December 28, 1990.

43. United States Sentencing Commission, *Guidelines Manual,* ch. 1, pt. A, subpt. 3, policy statement (2008).

44. United States Sentencing Commission, *2006 annual report,* 1 (2006).

45. United States Sentencing Commission, *Guidelines Manual,* ch. 1, pt. A, subpt. 3, policy statement (2008).

46. Sentencing Transcript at 26, United States v. Dana G. Stephenson, No. CR 84-L-18 (D. Neb. March 26, 1985).

47. United States Sentencing Commission, *Guidelines Manual,* ch. 1, pt. A, subpt. 3, policy statement (2008).

48. United States Sentencing Commission, *Fifteen Years of Guidelines Sentencing: An Assessment of How Well the Federal Criminal System Is Achieving the Goals of Sentencing Reform,* vi, 139 (2004).

49. United States Sentencing Commission, *Sentencing Guidelines and Policy Statements,* 1.12 (1987).

50. United States Sentencing Commission, *2008 Sourcebook of Federal Sentencing Statistics,* 51.

51. United States Sentencing Commission, *2008 Sourcebook,* 11, 114, 29.

52. United States Sentencing Commission, *2008 Sourcebook,* 110.

53. United States Sentencing Commission, *2008 Sourcebook*, 111.

54. United States Sentencing Commission, *Changing Face of Federal Criminal Sentencing*, p. 1 (2008).

55. United States General Accounting Office, *Federal and State Prisons: Inmate Populations, Costs, and Projection Models*, GAO/GGD-97-15, Tbl.II.1, p. 23 (1996).

56. United States Bureau of Prisons, *Weekly Population Report, Total Federal Inmates*, available at *http://www.bop.gov/locations/weekly_report.jsp* (accessed January 7, 2010).

57. 18 U.S.C. § 994 (k).

58. United States Sentencing Commission, *Measuring Recidivism: The Criminal History Computation of the Federal Sentencing Guidelines*, (2004).

59. United States Sentencing Commission, *Measuring Recidivism*, 11.

60. United States Sentencing Commission, *Measuring Recidivism*, 11–15.

61. United States Sentencing Commission, *Measuring Recidivism*, 16.

62. 773 F. 2d 960 (8th Cir. 1985).

63. Nebraska Public Power District v. Austin Power, 773 F. 2d 960, 8th Cir. 1985).

10. JUDGING THROUGHOUT THE NATION

1. U.S.C. § 371 (b)(1).

2. Title 28, § 294 of the United States Code sets the procedure for assignment of senior judges. A senior district judge may be assigned to perform such duties as "he is willing and able to undertake." The assignment is by the chief judge of the senior judge's circuit if the assignment is to a district within that circuit; by the chief justice of the United States if it is to another circuit and if a "certificate of necessity" has been provided by the chief judge or circuit justice of the "circuit wherein the need arises."

3. United States v. Chang, 67 F. 3d 313 (11th Cir. 1995) (Table).

4. United States v. Feinberg, 89 F. 3d. 333 (7th Cir. 1996).

5. 89 F. 3d. 333 (7th Cir. 1996).

6. 47 F. 3d 511, 516 (2d Cir. 1995).

7. United States v. Viscome, 144 F. 3d 1365 (11th Cir. 1998).

8. Gentile v. United States, Nos. 99-01-1386-CIV-T-25E (M.D. Fla. 1999), 96-00004-CR-T-2 (M.D. Fla. 1996). As recently as June 1, 2009, Gentile

filed a petition for writ of error *audita querela*. Denied July 8, 2009. Notice of appeal; motion to appeal in forma pauperis denied September 16, 2009.

9. No. 4:98 CV 3209 (D. Neb. 1998).

10. No. 90-1588-CIV-T-99C (M.D. Fla. 1993) (tried in Tampa, May 24 to June 2, 1993).

11. I submitted the issue to the jury so its recommendation could be considered in the event the circuit court would hold the act retroactive before the culmination of this suit. It did not do so.

12. No. 4:93 CV 00519 (D. Ark. 1994).

13. Bolden v. Jacksonville, No. LR-C-93-519 (E.D. Ark. Oct. 25, 1994).

14. Bolden v. Jacksonville, No. 94-3825, 1995 WL 507356 (8th Cir. 1995).

15. No. 3:94-CV-02545-WKU (N.D. Tex. 1994).

16. My recollection of Sheryl Leach's testimony is that her original idea of *something* to appeal to two-year-olds or older developed from the video character into a friendly dinosaur-like plush toy.

17. This material is taken from my Memorandum and Order on Lyons' Motions for Judgment as a Matter of Law, New Trial, or Remittur [*sic*], Alternatively, dated April 8, 1997, when a full transcript of the testimony before me was available. The draft of this memorandum and order was written by my law clerk Patrick Ickes, done beautifully and admirably explanatory.

18. Nelson v. Production Credit Association of the Midlands, 930 F. 2d 599 (8th Cir. 1991).

19. No. 93 C 2460 (N.D. Ill. 1993).

20. Count I for breach of contract by TSI; Count II for breach of fiduciary duty by Michael Childers, John Childers, Frank Schuette, and TSI; Count III for fraud by John Childers, Michael Childers, Frank Schuette, and TSI; Count IV for fraud by the Bercoon firm and Elwood Kreger; Count V for civil conspiracy to commit fraud by all the defendants; Count VI for negligent misrepresentation by John Childers, Michael Childers, Frank Schuette, and TSI; Count VII for negligent misrepresentation by Elwood Kreger and the Bercoon firm; Count VIII, seeking a declaratory judgment to be decided by me, not by the jury, regarding the Pine Street property investment; Count IX for accounting malpractice by Elwood Kreger and the Bercoon firm; Count X for consumer fraud by Elwood Kreger and the Bercoon firm; and

Count XI for operating by John Childers, Michael Childers, and Frank Schuette an enterprise through a pattern of racketeering activity.

21. Trial Transcript at 38:14–15, Terrell v. Childers, No. 93 C 2460 (N.D. Ill. Sept. 4, 1996).

22. Trial Transcript at 17:10–29:16, Terrell v. Childers, No. 93 C 2460 (N.D. Ill. Sept. 20, 1996).

23. Freemon v. Foley, 95 C 0209 (N.D. Ill. 1995).

24. United States v. Durenberger, No. 3:93-CR-00065-WKU, 1993 WL 738477 (D. Minn. Dec. 3, 1993).

25. U.S. CONST. Art. I, § 6: "[F]or any Speech or Debate in either House, [the Senators and Representatives] shall not be questioned in any other Place."

26. 408 U.S. 606, 616 (1972).

27. United States v. Durenberger, No. 3:93-CR-00065-WKU, 1993 WL 738477, at *4 (D. Minn. Dec. 3, 1993).

28. 442 U.S. 477, 491 (1979) (emphasis added).

29. Editorial, *Roll Call*, December 9, 1993.

30. "Don't Let the Case End with This Whimper," editorial, *Star-Tribune (Minneapolis)*, December 9, 1993.

31. United States v. Durenberger, No. 94-CR-0066 (D.D.C. 1995).

32. Richard Hantula, "The Year 2000 Problem," in *World Almanac and Book of Facts* (Mahwah NJ: World Almanac Books, 2000), 37–38.

33. United States v. Wright, 4:01-CR-3040 (D. Neb. 2001). Federal Public Defender David R. Stickman and Alan G. Stoler for the defendant; Assistant U.S. Attorneys Alan L. Everett and Michael P. Norris for the United States of America.

34. Transcript of Sentencing Proceedings at vol. XIII, 28–30, United States v. Wright, 4:01-CR-3040 (D. Neb. Sept. 16, 2002).

35. United States v. Wright, 340 F. 3d 724 (8th Cir. 2003).

36. Jennings v. King, No. 95 CIV 2523 PHX (WKU), (D. Ariz. 1995).

37. 517 U.S. 559 (1996); 538 U.S. 408 (2003).

38. Campbell, 538 U.S. at 425.

39. United States v. Koch, 8:03-CV-406 (D. Neb. 2003).

40. 42 U.S.C. § 3604, *et seq.*

41. See Chicago Rock Island and Pacific R.R. Co. v. Speth, 404 F. 2d.

291, 295 (8th Cir. 1968); Solomon Dehydrating Co. v. Guyton, 294 F. 2d 439, 447–48 (8th Cir. 1961); School District No. 11 v. Sverdrup & Parcel and Associates, Inc., 797 F. 2d 651 (8th Cir. 1986). None of these cases deals with damages claimed to be too small, however.

42. 259 F. Supp. 2d 710 (N.D. Ill. 2003).

43. Equal Employment Opportunity Commission v. Dial Corporation, 259 F. Supp. 2d 710 (N.D. Ill. 2003); 538 U.S. 408, 123 S. Ct. 1513, L. Ed. 2d 585 (2003); 517 U.S. 559, 116 S. Ct. 1589, 134 L. Ed. 2d 809 (1996).

44. Cooper Industries, Inc. v. Leatherman Tool Group, Inc., 532 U.S. 424, 436, 121 S. Ct. 1678, 149 L. Ed. 2d 674 (2001).

45. No. CIV 97-1899 PHX-RCM (WKU) (D. Ariz. 1997).

46. California Public Employees Retirement System v. Arthur Andersen LLP, No. CIV 97-1889 PHX-RCM (WKU) at 7 (D. Ariz. Mar. 19, 1999). "Bates-labeled" is numbering by a machine manufactured by Bates Manufacturing Company.

DIMINUENDO

1. *Webster's New World College Dictionary*, 4th ed.

2. No. 95-1524-CIV-T-23A (M.D. Fla. 1995).

3. U.S. District Judge Richard P. Matsch, a law school classmate of mine, had accepted my offer to help with his other cases while he presided over the Timothy McVeigh trial in Denver, arising from the Oklahoma City bombing of the Alfred P. Murrah Federal Building in 1995.

4. That decision was not made because of this accident only. A year or so before that, I had fallen asleep while driving and had run off the highway, causing damage only to our 2003 Lincoln, but luckily no personal injury. Given both events and the blurriness of my seeing eye, it was time to quit driving.

5. *Almanac of the Federal Judiciary*, vol. 1 (2006).

6. *Almanac of the Federal Judiciary*, vol. 1 (2010).

IN THE LAW IN THE AMERICAN WEST SERIES

Federal Justice in California: The Court of Ogden Hoffman, 1851–1891
Christian G. Fritz

Practicing Law in Frontier California
Gordon Morris Bakken

A Germ of Goodness: The California State Prison System, 1851–1944
Shelley Bookspan

Flooding the Courtrooms: Law and Water in the Far West
M. Catherine Miller

Lone Wolf v. Hitchcock: Treaty Rights and Indian Law at the End of the Nineteenth Century
Blue Clark

Imperfect Victories: The Legal Tenacity of the Omaha Tribe, 1945–1995
Mark R. Scherer

The Trial of "Indian Joe": Race and Justice in the Nineteenth-Century West
Clare V. McKanna Jr.

Slipping Backward: A History of the Nebraska Supreme Court
James W. Hewitt

Law and Order in Buffalo Bill's Country: Legal Culture and Community on the Great Plains, 1867–1910
Mark R. Ellis

The Nebraska-Kansas Act of 1854
John R. Wunder and Joann M. Ross

Women Who Kill Men: California Courts, Gender, and the Press
Gordon Morris Bakken and Brenda Farrington

Called to Justice: The Life of a Federal Trial Judge
Warren K. Urbom

To order or obtain more information on these or other University of Nebraska Press titles, visit www.nebraskapress.unl.edu.